THE COMPLETE IDIOT GUIDE

The Life of Buddha

by Victoria Kennick Urubshurow

ALPHA

A member of Penguin Group (USA) Inc.

This work is dedicated to my teacher, the Venerable Geshe Ngawang Wangyal.

ALPHA BOOKS

Published by the Penguin Group

Penguin Group (USA) Inc., 375 Hudson Street, New York, New York 10014, U.S.A.

Penguin Group (Canada), 10 Alcorn Avenue, Toronto, Ontario, Canada M4V 3B2 (a division of Pearson Penguin Canada Inc.)

Penguin Books Ltd, 80 Strand, London WC2R 0RL, England

Penguin Ireland, 25 St Stephen's Green, Dublin 2, Ireland (a division of Penguin Books Ltd)

Penguin Group (Australia), 250 Camberwell Road, Camberwell, Victoria 3124, Australia (a division of Pearson Australia Group Pty Ltd)

Penguin Books India Pvt Ltd, 11 Community Centre, Panchsheel Park, New Delhi—110 017, India

Penguin Group (NZ), cnr Airborne and Rosedale Roads, Albany, Auckland 1310, New Zealand (a division of Pearson New Zealand Ltd)

Penguin Books (South Africa) (Pty) Ltd, 24 Sturdee Avenue, Rosebank, Johannesburg 2196, South Africa

Penguin Books Ltd, Registered Offices: 80 Strand, London WC2R 0RL, England

International Standard Book Number: 1-59257-532-3
Library of Congress Catalog Card Number: 2006927520

08 07 06   8 7 6 5 4 3 2 1

Interpretation of the printing code: The rightmost number of the first series of numbers is the year of the book's printing; the rightmost number of the second series of numbers is the number of the book's printing. For example, a printing code of 06-1 shows that the first printing occurred in 2006.

Printed in the United States of America

Note: This publication contains the opinions and ideas of its author. It is intended to provide helpful and informative material on the subject matter covered. It is sold with the understanding that the author and publisher are not engaged in rendering professional services in the book. If the reader requires personal assistance or advice, a competent professional should be consulted.

The author and publisher specifically disclaim any responsibility for any liability, loss, or risk, personal or otherwise, which is incurred as a consequence, directly or indirectly, of the use and application of any of the contents of this book.

Most Alpha books are available at special quantity discounts for bulk purchases for sales promotions, premiums, fund-raising, or educational use. Special books, or book excerpts, can also be created to fit specific needs.

For details, write: Special Markets, Alpha Books, 375 Hudson Street, New York, NY 10014.

Publisher: *Marie Butler-Knight*
Editorial Director: *Mike Sanders*
Managing Editor: *Billy Fields*
Executive Editor: *Randy Ladenheim-Gil*
Senior Development Editor: *Phil Kitchel*
Senior Production Editor: *Janette Lynn*
Copy Editor: *Keith Cline*

Cartoonist: *Richard King*
Cover Designer: *Bill Thomas*
Book Designers: *Trina Wurst/Kurt Owens*
Indexer: *Tonya Heard*
Layout: *Brian Massey*
Proofreader: *Aaron Black*

Contents at a Glance

Appendixes

Contents

Appendixes

Introduction

Welcome to the world of ancient India! Before you begin the journey into Buddha's life and times, let's look at a few names that traditionally have been applied to the man who woke up. You'll see them plenty of times in the pages ahead, and it's nice to be aware of what means what.

The word Buddha is actually a title coming from the Sanskrit root "budh," to awaken or enlighten. Hence, Buddha is the Awakened or Enlightened One. Up to the time of his awakening, he's called Siddhartha (One Whose Aim is Accomplished) or the Bodhisattva (Buddha-to-be). He was dubbed Maha Sramana (Great Striver) after taking up the homeless life. He's called Gautama any time, for that's his family name. After his enlightenment, people called him Sakyamuni (Sage of the Sakyans) because he was born into the Sakya clan. But above all … after waking up he liked to call himself a Tathagata (Thus-gone One).

Tathata is the Sanskrit word for reality as it is. It means "thusness," "just so," or "just like that." And that's what waking up is all about: seeing what is just so, and being just like that. After reading this book, you'll have a much better idea why Buddha best liked to call himself Tathagata, meaning one who went (gata) according to tathata. A person who lines up with tathata remains clear, insightful, and compassionate through thick and thin.

Wow! Well, for such a remarkable person, it's natural that various names would be used to capture different aspects of Buddha's character. Just look at Appendix B, "People and Places," to see a list of Buddha's names. In fact, make use of the glossary in Appendix A, too.

In books about Buddha's life taken off a shelf almost anywhere, you'll find that names and concepts are given according to either their Sanskrit or Pali form. I've chosen to go with the Sanskrit language versions of most words, given a choice. But the Sanskrit and Pali are so close as to be basically interchangeable. Again, just hit Appendixes A and B anytime for clarification. Before you know it, you'll have this all down pat!

Your *Complete Idiot's Guide* presents Buddha's biography in a rich format that allows you to find out about his culture, personal life, community, and teachings. Feel free to skip to your favorite parts—and build up from there. No matter which way you approach this book, it should lead you to a deeper understanding of Buddha and what it means to wake up.

What You'll Find in This Book

Part 1, "The Buddha in Historical Context," discusses the life of Buddha, a sacred biography about a man who woke up from the sleep of ignorance. Traditional biographers wove extraordinary events into his story, and you'll see how their symbolic language reflects Buddhist ideas about reality. To bring this great historical figure squarely into focus, you'll see Buddha's spiritual journey in terms of a worldwide quest for understanding. This involves a look at Buddha's near contemporaries in Greece, the Middle East, India, and China—such as Pythagoras, Socrates, Jeremiah, Zoroaster, Confucius, and others. Finally, you'll take a good, long look at northern India in Buddha's day.

Part 2, "The Making and Breaking of a Prince," is the story of Buddha's early years, chock-full of mythic details. Culture abhors a vacuum, so gods, elephants, and flowers rush to fill the gap left by historical records. Yet you'll see that within the sacred story lies a psychologically compelling tale of personal indulgence, disillusionment, and determination. The daily life of Prince Siddhartha (Buddha's youthful name) becomes even more interesting in light of his culture, set in the Himalayan foothills.

Part 3, "Waking Up: Siddhartha Becomes a Buddha," is an account of Siddhartha's spiritual journey from the moment he gave up his privileged life as a prince of the northern Indian Sakya clan through his return to the world after enlightenment. You'll see how Buddha went on an intensive six-year quest, woke up to the nature of reality, set up a spiritual community, and convinced his family that he wasn't a failure.

Part 4, "Nobody Teaching Nothing," discusses how the Four Noble Truths encompass all Buddha's teachings, as an elephant's footprint holds all other footprints on the forest floor. You'll ponder the great facts Buddha taught about suffering, its causes, its cessation, and the path to end suffering. You'll also find out how mindfulness of one's body and mind can lead to a profound understanding of the Buddhist concept of nonself.

Part 5, "Buddha's Disciples," recounts how after Buddha's enlightenment, a diverse spiritual community gathered around him. You'll meet the men and women of his mendicant community and the lay disciples from many walks of life. You'll also get wind of extraordinary feats that some disciples accomplished through meditation. Last but not least, you'll hear the inside scoop on political intrigue and jealous detractors who sometimes made life tough for the Tathagata.

Part 6, "Buddha's Great Decease and Legacy," details how Buddha traveled extensively in the final year of his life and left a powerful legacy. You'll follow Gautama's last journey as he kept teaching—even while smitten with a grave illness. Then you'll find out how the Tathagata's words inspired a new spiritual practice that spread throughout Asia and manifested in the art of awakening. Finally, you'll explore ways that Buddha's life experience continues to enrich our lives today.

Bonus Bulletins

In addition to maps, diagrams, and line drawings, you'll find four bonus bulletins to guide you through the narrative on Buddha's life:

Be Mindful!	Buddha Basics
Avoid misunderstandings about events in Buddha's life. Ponder stuff such as this: did Buddha really see into other worlds? Does the teaching of "nonself" mean we don't exist?	Meet people. Go places. Learn extra Buddhist facts. Here you'll find asides about Buddhist characters, cities, history, and ideas. Many of these items appear again at the back of the book in Appendix B.

Enlightening Extras	Dharma Dictionary
Enlighten yourself with tidbits that provide cool facts and new ways of thinking about Buddha's life and times. Lots of these range around the world from many times and places.	Get clear on the meaning of key concepts from Buddha's life story. These terms appear again at the back of the book in Appendix A.

Acknowledgements

First off, my thanks go to Joshua and Diana Cutler, co-directors of the Tibetan Buddhist Learning Center in Washington, New Jersey. I thank them for "holding down the fort" where I studied with the Venerable Geshe Ngawang Wangyal, and for recommending that I submit a proposal to Jacky Sach, the woman who'd become my most capable and positive thinking agent.

Beyond the steady encouragement that Jacky provided, I became ever more intrigued with the process of bringing this book to completion. As if layer by layer, I was introduced to one wonderful Alpha Books person after another. They all pleasantly surprised me in the richness of their communication, and the subtle twists they contributed to my writing process. Executive editor Randy Ladenheim-Gil somehow knew when to push and when to be patient. Senior development editor Phil Kitchel has a sense of humor that would lighten anyone's load. (He also has a knack for phrasing things just right.) Copy editor Keith Cline's voice I heard between the lines through insightful comments and suggestions that I appreciated. And senior production editor Janette Lynn stood as a woman of wisdom overseeing the project and moving it forward with alacrity.

Other talented folks contributed in complementary ways to bring my thoughts into the form you see printed here today, including foremost the publisher Marie Butler-Knight, editorial director Mike Sanders, managing editor Billy Fields, cover designer Bill Thomas, book designers Trina Wurst and Kurt Owens, indexer Tonya Heard, layout artist Brian Massey, and proofreader Aaron Black. Of course, where would we be without cartoonist Richard King to make everything more fun? Thanks to all! (Needless to say, any faults of commission or omission entirely rest with me.)

Part 1

The Buddha in Historical Context

The life of Buddha is a sacred biography that often uses symbolic statements to go beyond literal truth. This fascinating story comes from a culture that placed great stock in the power of meditation and held a mystical view of the relationship between human beings and their world. It's important to see how modern readers can approach it.

Buddha lived in what's called the Axial Age. This was a time in world history when many prominent figures from Greece all the way to China sought deeper knowledge of the cosmos, society, and human potential. Buddha was a man of his time, wandering around the Middle Ganges Basin when India was on the brink of cultural transformation. Thriving in the atmosphere of curiosity, exchange, and innovation, Buddha took what opportunities were at hand and fashioned something old, yet new.

Chapter 1

The Man Who Woke Up

In This Chapter

- On sacred biography
- Historical truths about Buddha and the scriptures
- Psychological truth in sacred biography
- The role of the extraordinary in ancient India
- The meaning of wisdom and compassion

What can you expect from a book on the life of Buddha? In this book, you'll learn facts about Gautama's habits, travels, and social environment.

But Buddha's life story is a sacred biography—which means it's an account of a spiritual journey with meaning on many levels. So one would not expect the story of a man who woke up from the sleep of ignorance to read like straight history. Traditional Buddhist biographers present the life of their founder with psychological turning points and extraordinary events right along with the historical details. Therefore, in this book, you'll hear not only about where Buddha went but also about what moved him and what he experienced in the depths of meditation to cause an awakening that shook the world.

This chapter samples parts of Gautama's life story to show the fascinating blend of historical, psychological, and mystical material usually contained in Buddha's biographies. We consider what sounds like the literal truth and then reflect on the psychological meaning. Finally, we mull over the strange talk of supernormal powers and extraordinary acts of nature.

What's a Sacred Biography?

A *sacred biography* is an account of a person's spiritual journey with three levels of meaning: literal, mental, and symbolic.

- ◆ The literal meaning is based on events that are historically "true." They happen in the physical world of ordinary time and space where a person lives daily life.

> **Dharma Dictionary**
>
> A **sacred biography** is an account of a person's spiritual journey with three dimensions: literal, mental, and symbolic. These involve historical, psychological, and mystical events. **Religious symbols** are objects representing extraordinary things that cannot be expressed literally.

- ◆ The mental meaning is based on events that are psychologically "true." They happen in the thoughts of a person and include pivotal moments that move a person forward on the spiritual path.

- ◆ The symbolic meaning is based on events that are mystically "true." There's often disagreement about where they happen or whether they actually *did* happen. But we can say, mystical events "happen" through *religious symbols*, which represent extraordinary things that cannot be expressed literally.

Viewing One's Own Spiritual Journey ... a Suggestion

A great way to learn about sacred biography is by examining your own spiritual journey. You can start by identifying in your own experience the three kinds of events that sacred biographies contain. Here's a suggestion:

- ◆ Historical events identify plain physical facts, such as where one was born, who is in one's family, and so on. These events are literally true—or as close to historically accurate as possible. A sacred biography or autobiography usually includes only the historical events that are most useful in framing psychological and mystical events.

◆ Psychological events identify pivotal moments in one's life that brought on a new way of looking at the world, and possibly a new vocation. Mental turning points can include poignant reactions to the death of a loved one, falling in love, getting sick, winning a million dollars, and so on. These events often are well described in poetic terms. They are based in history but need not be literally true.

◆ Mystical events identify extraordinary occurrences in one's life, such as might happen hiking on a mountainside or kneeling in prayer. These may include meaningful coincidences, seeing light fill the room when a baby is born, sacred visions, and so on. To describe mystical events, it helps to see what special objects helped shape the experience. Describing the event in terms of those objects conveys a symbolic truth.

> **Be Mindful!**
>
> Traditional biographers call Gautama Buddha by many names. Some names are used for Gautama only before his enlightenment, others only afterward, whereas a few apply throughout his life. Look in Appendix B under Buddha's names for a detailed list.

Historical, psychological, and mystical events are all meaningful. But each is meaningful in its own way. When reading sacred biographies, we can separate the literal, mental, and symbolic meanings and take each for what it's worth. Let's now turn to samples of the three kinds of events in Buddha's life story.

What We Know ... Almost: The Literal Meaning

What happened more than 2,500 years ago is hard to pin down exactly. But there are things we know ... almost. Here are a couple of facts from the basic history of Buddha's life.

Say When? Say What?

The year Buddha passed into final nirvana is the first year of the Buddhist calendar. But Buddhists don't all agree on the actual date of Gautama's death. People in Southeast Asia put the great decease in the year 533 B.C.E. (Before the Common Era). Some others believe he died 50 years later, in 483 B.C.E. But despite this uncertainty, Buddhists all agree that the founder lived for 80 years. Thus two of the most commonly used dates for the duration of Buddha's life are 623 through 543 or 563 through 483. Based on the 20-year overlap, we can say Gautama was alive and well in the mid-sixth century B.C.E.

Buddha taught in a language we call Ardhamagadhi. It's a dialect from the Middle Ganges Basin. You'll notice the word *Magadha* in there, which is the name of a large territory that Buddha frequented in his years roaming around northern India. And though Buddha taught in a dialect understandable to the common people, apparently he chose not to write those teachings down. It's a good thing Indians of his day had a very strong oral culture. Thanks to the extraordinary memories of Buddhist meditators, a good portion of Buddha's 45 years' worth of teachings survived.

Buddha Basics

It's presumed that neither Gautama nor his disciples wrote anything—though later biographies say Buddha learned various alphabets, and artwork shows the young Siddhartha with pen in hand. The earliest written Buddhist texts found so far are from eastern Afghanistan/northern Pakistan—including 20 texts from the first century C.E. These are written using the Kharosthi script in the Gandhari language.

The Three Baskets

Roughly 300 years after the Master passed away, somebody wrote down Buddha's oral teachings. And that's fortunate because the written scriptures provide people today not only with a record of what Gautama taught but also with lots of detail about life in the Ganges valley of Buddha's day. Some even say that "true" history begins in India at the time of Buddha, because the Buddhist and Jain scriptures are the earliest documents that make reference to cities and rulers of the sixth century B.C.E.

Dharma Dictionary

Tripitaka means three baskets. It refers to the three sections of the Buddhist canon: **sutra**, **vinaya**, and **abhidharma**. The sutras are Buddha's discourses. The vinaya is a collection of writings on the Buddhist lifestyle, including the pratimoksha or training precepts. The abhidharma is the systematic presentation of major concepts set forth in the sutras.

Buddhist scriptures don't focus specifically on politics. But Gautama was so involved in his society that the texts provide fascinating details on the activity of leading political figures, people with commercial interests, renunciate communities, villagers, and townsfolk. These rich scriptures give modern researchers their earliest accounts of India's history. They are comprised of three portions, known as the *tripitaka*:

◆ Buddha's discourses (*sutras*). This includes what remains of the teachings the Tathagata gave in the 45 years between his enlightenment and final nirvana.

◆ Writings on the Buddhist lifestyle (*vinaya*), including training precepts (*pratimoksha*). The vinaya reports the circumstances under which various monastic rules were adopted, because Buddha only made rules in response to particular situations as behavioral issues arose.

◆ Buddhist philosophical psychology (*abhidharma*). The abhidharma teachings systematically present ideas discussed in the sutras, and include many lists and definitions.

Poignant Turning Points: The Mental Meaning

We gain confidence that Gautama was an influential historical figure by knowing when he lived and learning of works that document his teachings. But Buddha's biography becomes more meaningful when read as a psychological document that reveals stages of a spiritual journey. Let's look at a few mental moments from Buddha's life story. Later chapters go into more detail.

What's True About the Four Sights?

A famous scene in Buddha's biography states that at the age of 29, the Sakyan prince took a ride into his town of Kapilavastu and saw Four Sights: an old man, a sick man, a corpse, and a religious seeker. Who's to say whether that event was historically true? Did Siddhartha really see these four people? All in a row? Why have Buddha's biographers made a big deal out of it?

It is historically true that Siddhartha left his home in Kapilavastu to pursue an ascetic life. Now, something must have psychologically motivated the Sakyan prince to renounce his family and worldly life and devote himself to awakening. So Buddha's biographers packaged his experience and stated that prince Siddhartha saw an old man, a sick man, and a corpse carried in a funeral procession. They went on to find meaning in this event and suggested that by seeing these three people, Siddhartha thought deeply for the first time about suffering.

Be Mindful!
Duhkha means suffering. But its meaning is much broader than you might think. It means everything from the physical trials of illness or abuse to the most subtle alienation between one person and another. Because suffering plays such a key role in the Buddha-dharma, some people mistakenly think Buddhism is pessimistic. But the outcome of Buddha's enlightenment was hope and the knowledge that suffering could be overcome. That's why in statues you see Buddha smiling, not frowning.

Furthermore, they declared that the sight of a religious seeker gave Siddhartha hope that his goal could be accomplished and transformed his thinking about what to do with his life.

The incident of the Four Sights helps us understand Buddha's motivation to leave home, whether or not the account is literally true. It doesn't matter whether Siddhartha literally "saw" the old man, sick man, corpse, and religious seeker—or whether the Four Sights occurred on one day, four days, over the course of several weeks, or whatever. The Four Sights don't have to be considered part of the literal dimension of Buddha's life. The incident is part of the biography's mental dimension, which gives meaning to Buddha's life as a spiritual journey.

The Universal Human Struggle to Awaken

Buddha's sacred biography is just one among many stories in world literature that give us insight into the spiritual journey. It's fun to look for turning points in the lives of characters from world myths. If one stays alert, one finds poignant meaning in mental moments when heroes come face to face with themselves. Consider these examples from famous myths to get a feel for the universal human struggle to awaken:

- The Babylonian King Gilgamesh is stricken with grief over the death of his companion Enkidu and asks, "Must I die, too?"

- The Trojan Prince Aeneas is pried away from the loving Dido because his commitment to duty overrides all personal ambition and sentiment.

- The Arthurian knight Parzival is crushed by the realization that he neglected to speak from the heart and ask the Fisher King, "What ails thee, Father?"

> **Enlightening Extras**
>
> In his book *Hero with a Thousand Faces*, Joseph Campbell explored how world hero myths follow a similar pattern, which he called the monomyth. He posits three stages of the hero's journey: departure, initiation, and return. He noted that obstacles occur in each stage of this universal monomyth. Phases in which the most intense obstacles appear include refusal of the call, road of trials, and refusal of the return.

Buddha's life story includes mental moments comparable to those portrayed in the myths of Gilgamesh, Aeneas, and Parzival. Gautama's realization of suffering on seeing the Four Sights parallels Gilgamesh's grief. His leaving home and family for a greater calling reminds us of Aeneas's tragic departure from Carthage. And his determination to find, against all odds, the pure heart that spontaneously responds to the needs of other beings is none other than Parzival's quest for the Holy Grail.

Even without knowing details about the Babylonian Gilgamesh who reigned in Uruk around 2700 B.C.E., his story still offers poignant lessons. The same goes for Aeneas, the Trojan prince who presumably escaped to Italy after the Trojan War. Even without knowing when Troy fell, or whether Aeneas was truly the father of the Italian people, we still are moved by his struggle to remain dutiful. And so it is with Parzival, the famous knight of King Arthur's British court. The mental dimension of his quest for the Holy Grail is psychologically meaningful, even when considered apart from history.

Now That's a Stretch: The Symbolic Meaning

Moving beyond history to look for psychological meaning makes sense, and one expects lots of wiggle room while interpreting mental attitudes. But there's still one more kind of event in the Buddha's biography whose meaning we have to probe: mystical events. Buddha's life story is full of extraordinary occurrences where something from the normally invisible world (some call it the sacred) bursts through the cracks in our everyday profane life. What kind of meaning is in the extraordinary symbolic events that run throughout Buddha's life story?

India's Panoply of Godlings

The Four Sights that Buddha's biographers put in front of him had psychological meaning. And it's easy enough to forgive them for taking the liberty to shape the literal truth—which they seem to have done. But how about more fantastic claims that appear in the traditional accounts of Buddha's life story? How about the fact that a

deva, a godling, was supposed to have arranged for Siddhartha to see the old man, sick man, corpse, and ascetic? Some versions of the story even have a deva manifesting as the old man and so on. These and many other hierophanies are woven into the Buddha's life story. What meaning do they bring to the biography?

Devas often appear in traditional accounts of Buddha's life. These Vedic godlings had already been part of India's worldview before Buddha came along. And biographers as well as Buddha himself gave them a place alongside regular human characters. According to Buddhist

> **Dharma Dictionary**
>
> A **deva** is a male godling, while a **devi** is a female godling. The cosmology of India includes numerous Vedic godlings. Buddhists say they are not enlightened and therefore don't appeal to them for help on the spiritual path. Thirty-two devas plus their leader Indra abide in the Heaven of the Thirty-Three, which is still part of samsara (the cycle of rebirth and death).

scriptures, Buddha spoke of eight assemblies that tathagatas are able to teach: warriors, brahmins, householders, ascetics, devas from the Realm of Four Great Kings, devas from the Heaven of the Thirty-Three, maras, and brahmas. Notice that human beings only comprise half of these groups; subtle beings comprise the other half. Buddhist scriptures are not alone in the world's religious literature in speaking of normally invisible beings. Think, for example, of the angels who appear in the Judeo-Christian scriptures. What are we to make of the symbolic appearance of characters popping into Buddha's life from the unseen world?

No Easy Answer to This One

The appearance of devas, and other subtle beings seems to correlate with certain important moments on Buddha's spiritual journey. And Buddha's interaction with them indicates a certain level of achievement in his meditation. The lesser godlings, as well as more powerful characters such as Brahma and Mara, are portrayed as taking a great interest in the Bodhisattva's spiritual progress. And all but Mara, Lord of Illusion, seem to want to help Siddhartha wake up. So what's one to think about these extraordinary figures? Are they just thrown into Buddha's biography because people of ancient India expected to hear about them? Are they figures that somehow symbolize Buddha's mental states? Or do they "really" exist?

Unfortunately, there's no easy answer to the question of the reality of the various subtle beings that appear in Buddha's life story. It may come down to a matter of faith. Yet regardless of whether or not such nonhuman beings exist, it's important for modern readers to note that they were part of the ancient Indian worldview. There is something to be gained by not simply discounting the symbolic events woven through Buddha's sacred biography: we gain an appreciation of the rich imaginative life of Gautama—or at least Buddhists who wrote down the scriptures and biographies. This religious imagination need not be dismissed as pure naiveté. It can be seen as part of India's contemplative tradition, which believed the world was vast and human potential was great.

Be Mindful!
The Buddhist scriptures were first composed around 300 years after Buddha passed away, and the first biographies were composed some 300 years after that. Some biographies were more flowery than others, depending on the social circumstances under which they were written. But even the very conservative scriptural presentations of Buddha's life make room for devas, supernormal powers, and extraordinary manifestations of nature. So the modern reader—tempted to dismiss all unusual claims—must be cautioned: "Don't throw the baby out with the bathwater." Remember: there's more to a spiritual biography than history!

India Extraordinaire!

People of ancient India accepted the possibility that human beings could exercise supernormal powers. They also accepted the possibility that the universe could respond to human beings in extraordinary ways. Some of Buddha's biographers claim that flowers rained down from the sky, the smell of sandalwood wafted through the atmosphere, and the music of the spheres was heard when the Tathagata passed away. These unusual manifestations are supposedly part of the workings of our world. Just as an acorn produces an oak tree under the proper conditions, so flowers bloom out of season, the earth quakes, or rainbows spontaneously appear when a person does something truly extraordinary—such as attain enlightenment, manifest great compassion, or pass to final nirvana.

Clearly the people of ancient India saw nature as both powerful and responsive to sentient beings. And these work in response to each other. Even mountains and rivers were—and still are—considered sacred in India. So it's no wonder that biographers included many supernatural beings and extraordinary events in Buddha's life story. Modern readers generally don't regard supernormal events scientifically plausible, but it's still possible to empathize with the worldview of ancient India, which was characterized by openness to the sacred. This openness actually can give modern readers a sense of the early environmentalism of the Buddhist tradition. In fact, modern engaged Buddhists see great meaning in Gautama's teaching on interdependence. All living beings are dependent upon nature and upon each other.

Buddha Basics

According to Buddhist scriptures, eight events cause earthquakes: a mighty wind blows and stirs up water; a brahmin develops psychic powers; a bodhisattva descends from Tushita Heaven into the mother's womb; a bodhisattva emerges from the mother's womb to begin the final lifetime; a tathagata attains enlightenment; a tathagata begins turning the Wheel of the Law; a tathagata renounces the life principle; a tathagata attains final nirvana. Only the first sounds mildly scientific. And until scientific research on paranormal events confirms these, it'll be hard for modern readers to take them seriously.

Buddha's Daily Routine

We've just sorted through some examples of historical, psychological, and mystical events in Buddha's life story. Now let's see how the literal, mental, and symbolic levels of meaning are woven together. To do this, we look at a traditional presentation of

Buddha's daily routine. Buddha divided his day into five watches or portions. These included two six-hour sessions during the day and three four-hour sessions overnight.

Morning Session: 6 A.M. to Noon

Buddha started his day by setting a morning itinerary. He wished to help all kinds of people, so he surveyed the world with his *divine eye* to figure out what individuals most needed his help that morning. They appeared vividly in his mind's eye, even if they lived far away. With this knowledge, Buddha went uninvited by foot, or by air using psychic powers, to visit vicious or troubled individuals. He would also visit people on the brink of awakening, to provide a very simple instruction to help them see reality as it is. Generally, virtuous beings tended to seek out Buddha. The others *he* had to seek out.

> **Dharma Dictionary**
>
> **Divine eye** is a supernormal power acquired through meditation that allows a person to see things that are far away in this world, or in other realms of time and space. Things appear vividly in the mind's eye. During Buddha's morning meditation, the virtuous and nonvirtuous who needed his help appeared vividly, even if they lived far away when he opened the divine eye (divya-cakshu in Sanskrit).

Before noon, Buddha ate his single meal of the day. If any lay supporters had extended an invitation, he and the disciples went to partake of alms in the agreed upon place. If he didn't have any appointments, the Teacher went alms begging from hut to hut, either with disciples or alone through the alleys and streets. Even as an old man of 80 years, Buddha would stand silently at the door of each dwelling, bowl in hand, to receive alms. Taking only what was given, and never frequenting the same homes repeatedly, Sakyamuni, like any other monk, returned to where he was staying with whatever food was placed into his bowl.

Afternoon Session: Noon to 6 P.M.

After eating, Buddha gave a short discourse to people who may have assembled to hear the dharma or pay their respects. Depending on the wishes and needs of each person, he gave teachings, including establishing people in the Three Refuges and Five Precepts, ordaining men as monks and women as nuns, and assigning suitable objects of meditation according to their temperaments. Following these dharma activities, Buddha rested. Sometimes he would lie on his right side to sleep for a while with mindfulness.

After resting, Buddha generated a mind of great compassion and again opened his divine eye to find people who needed his help. And though his morning survey with the divine eye was directed toward the general public, the afternoon session was geared toward his monks and nuns, including those in solitary meditation. As in the morning, the Tathagata often used his supernormal powers to appear before disciples who were having problems. Or else he went in person to offer spiritual advice. After these remarkable activities, Buddha again retired to his quarters.

Toward evening, lay followers would come to hear Buddha teach for about one hour. To some, he preached about morality and attaining the bliss of the Abodes of Brahma (a high-level meditation). He encouraged more advanced disciples to practice renunciation. The Teacher expounded more subtle points of realization and practice to the most-experienced practitioners.

> ### Enlightening Extras
>
> Siddhis or supernormal powers are not exclusive to Buddhist meditation. Meditators from Hinduism, Taoism, and other traditions seriously discuss the development of supernormal powers—along with injunctions not to use them for immoral ends. Systematic treatments of the siddhis are found in Patanjali's Hindu *Yoga Sutras*, and Buddhaghosa's Buddhist *Path of Purification*. These texts present skills such as remembering past lives, walking on water, and becoming invisible as normal fruits of deep states of samadhi.

The Overnight Sessions

Buddha's night was divided into three four-hour watches. The third of these he preferred to divide up into one-hour slots. As during the daytime sessions, the Teacher did not hesitate to make use of supernormal powers. But it is evident that he paid more attention to the worldly spiritual beings late at night between 10 P.M. and 2 A.M. … while his human disciples were busy sleeping.

- ◆ **First watch of the night: 6 P.M. until 10 P.M.** Buddha reserved the first watch of the night to instruct his mendicant disciples. They could approach the Teacher to question him on points of dharma, hear him talk, or ask for a suitable object of meditation for the evening and beyond.

> ### Dharma Dictionary
>
> **Samsara** is the cycle of becoming. There are three realms of samsara: the sense desire realm that has devas, titans, humans, animals, hungry ghosts, and hell beings; the realm of pure form that has brahmas; and the realm of no form that has four levels of abstract consciousness. **Nirvana** means blown out. To attain nirvana means to be free from suffering and compulsory rebirth in samsara.

- **Second watch of the night: 10 P.M. until 2 A.M.** In the second watch of the night, Buddha made himself available to invisible beings, such as worldly devas from the desire realm, and brahmas who abide in the realm of pure form. While he meditated at their level—synchronizing his consciousness with theirs—these beings could approach the Teacher to ask about the nature of *samsara* and the means to attain *nirvana*.

- **Third watch of night: 2 A.M. until 6 A.M.** In the third watch of the night, Buddha varied his activity depending upon the hour: from 2 to 3 o'clock, he did mild physical exercise, pacing to and fro. From 3 to 4 o'clock, he slept mindfully, lying on his right side. From 4 to 5 o'clock, he entered the bliss of nirvana. From 5 to 6 o'clock, he generated great compassion and radiated loving kindness to all beings.

What to Make of It

What can we make of the straight-faced account Buddhists give about their Teacher? Plenty of details fit into the mold of a historically serious biography. Buddha regularly slept on his right side, paced to and fro, sat cross-legged, wandered about on alms rounds carrying a simple bowl, and taught people who'd assembled to hear him. Some of those assembled wore the renunciate robes; others wore the clothes of aristocrats, merchants, or simple villagers. These things literally happened.

But what do we make of the mystical events scattered through the account of Buddha's daily routine? What was the Tathagata doing as he sat cross-legged? As he paced to and fro? How did he use the divine eye? How did he perform psychic travel to contact people in need? How did he synchronize his consciousness with beings in various realms of samsara to communicate with them? The rest of this book will help fill out answers to puzzling questions such as these. But for the moment, it'll be enough to say that Sakyamuni spent years researching the mind, using introspective methods.

Enlightening Extras

In his book *The Universe in a Single Atom,* the Dalai Lama says that established contemplative traditions such as Buddhism can contribute to the science of consciousness in our day. For example, modern psychologists or physicists might be stimulated by traditional discussions that have been "major areas of interest for Indian and Tibetan philosophers" such as "what the relationship is between a perceptual event and its objects." For his part, the Dalai Lama is willing to abandon anything in Buddhist thought that's proven to be false.

Given Gautama's intense interest in mental development, even a modern reader should at least recognize the seriousness with which Buddha's biographers treated his accomplishments in meditation. So accounts of the Tathagata visiting people without physically walking to see them or communicating with beings from normally invisible realms have what we've called symbolic meaning. Whether or not devas, brahmas, or maras really "exist," we can simply keep this in mind while reading about Buddha's life: the mystical events reported in the sacred biography are a meaningful way to speak of Buddha's contemplative training.

Meditation was really Buddha's expertise. Before enlightenment he perfected a type of meditation that quiets the mind and brings supernormal powers. Serenity meditation is the actual foundation of Buddha's mystical experiences. But that type of meditation was not enough for Gautama, because it did not cut the bonds of rebirth. So he went on to develop a second type of meditation, which brought wisdom. Insight meditation led to his realization of *tathata*—which is the Buddhist way of saying reality as it is. And from this realization sprung spontaneous, unbounded, and incorruptible compassion.

> **Dharma Dictionary**
>
> **Tathata** is thusness or reality as it is with no preconceptions. It's the "just so" perspective on existence that the awakened have when they perceive reality as no more and no less than it is in the moment. Realizing thusness means penetrating the surface appearance of things to notice that everything is in motion.

The Meaning of Hope

It's pretty easy to relate to the literal truth of what Buddha did every day, such as walk around, teach people, and so on. And it's possible to isolate (and dismiss or not) the symbolic truth of events such as his teaching beings normally invisible to others. But what about the psychological truth embedded in Buddha's sacred biography? It turns out that events dealing with Buddha's wisdom and compassion have meant the most for Buddhists through the ages.

Two major turning points really define Gautama's spiritual journey from the psychological point of view: seeing the Four Sights and attaining enlightenment. The first made him realize the problem of suffering. And the second resolved that problem. Compassion flowed from both these insights. With the Four Sights came a mental moment that motivated the Sakyan prince to seek help for suffering beings. And with enlightenment came Buddha's unfettered ability to actually help them. And here we come down to the hope that Buddha's life story inspires in people.

Gautama said, "Whoever knows Buddha, knows dharma." This means that the story of the man who woke up is part of the Buddha-dharma. Hearing about Buddha's life is sort of like seeing the Four Sights. Contemplating Gautama's concern over suffering opens the way to personal experience of the first three sights: the old man, sick man, and corpse. And contemplating Siddhartha's struggle to awaken opens the way to personal experience of the fourth sight: the religious seeker. Thus one becomes sensitive to the sufferings of old age, sickness, and death. And one gains hope that he or she, too, can wake up. And perhaps, one also becomes inspired to try doing as Buddha did: from 5 to 6 o'clock in the morning, generate compassion and radiate loving kindness to all beings.

The Least You Need to Know

- ◆ Sacred biographies have historical, psychological, and mystical events that convey literal, mental, and symbolic meaning.

- ◆ Key turning points in Buddha's spiritual journey are comparable to poignant moments in the sacred stories of other hero figures in world literature.

- ◆ Ancient India accepted the possibility of extraordinary mental perceptions based on meditation in the midst of a responsive universe.

- ◆ Buddha was an expert in mental development who perfected both serenity and insight types of meditation. The first led to mystical experience; the second led to wisdom and incorruptible compassion.

- ◆ The sacred biography of Buddha—the man who woke up—has inspired generations of Buddhists around the globe.

2

Twilight of the Gods

In This Chapter

- Prophets of the Babylonian exile: Jeremiah and Ezekiel
- Perfection of humanity: Confucius and Mahavira
- An orderly universe: Pythagoras and Thales
- A question of becoming or being: Heraclitus and Parmenides
- A Persian prophet: Zoroaster
- Moral argumentation: Socrates

The period between around 800 and 200 B.C.E. (Before the Common Era) is sometimes called the Axial Age. It includes an amazing array of thinkers along a geographical belt from the Mediterranean to the Yellow seas. Even narrowing the historical period down to around 600 to 400 B.C.E., we find Buddha along with numerous prophets, philosophers, and teachers who contributed immensely to the store of human knowledge and thought.

The Axial Age seemed to be a twilight period for the gods. Confidence in the worldly deities was waning. What began to stand in place of the gods varied from one culture to the next, of course, but what seemed to be common among prominent thinkers was an emphasis on human responsibility. This could be human responsibility directed at improving the culture or one's personal character.

Let's now get into our time machine, and set it for Buddha's day. When we're in the sixth to fifth century B.C.E, we'll touch down in some Greek city-states to become acquainted with Thales, Pythagoras, Heraclitus, and Parmenides. We'll also make stops in Persia, India, and China—to find out about Zoroaster, Mahavira, and Confucius. But to begin our journey into the past, let's learn of two great Hebrew prophets: Jeremiah and Ezekiel.

Jeremiah's Sour Grapes

Jeremiah was born near Jerusalem as the son of a priest and became a prophet of the Lord while a young man. He prophesied to the people of Israel before and throughout the Babylonian exile. And he warned the people of Jerusalem to take personal responsibility for their future and discontinue all worship of idols.

The Lord told Jeremiah to stand at the gate of Solomon's temple and tell all who entered to change their ways. So he did. Jeremiah called out to his people, predicting a catastrophe. He warned that each person would die for his or her own sins. The prophet warned that people should not blame the coming destruction and hardships on the wrongdoings of their fathers, but should take personal responsibility for their actions. Jeremiah's famous phrase to this effect goes: In those days, they shall not claim anymore that "the fathers eat sour grapes, and the children's teeth are set on edge." Jeremiah prophesied that the people of Jerusalem should not take for granted that the Lord would sustain them, the temple, and the holy land. The best thing would be for the people of Judah to repent before it was too late and take personal responsibility for their actions and devote themselves with faith to the one and only Lord. In fact, thousands of his people were exiled from Jerusalem to Babylon by King Nebuchadnezzar. This catastrophe was followed by the destruction of Solomon's temple.

> **Be Mindful!**
>
> Based on Jeremiah's statements, the number of men deported to Babylon from Jerusalem by King Nebuchadnezzar may have been 3,023 in 597 B.C.E., 832 in 582 B.C.E., and 745 in 582 B.C.E. But this number of 4,600 does not account for everyone. When entire families are figured in, it becomes 14,000 to 18,000 people. Perhaps one eighth to one quarter of the population was exiled.

Ezekiel's New Heart and New Spirit

The catastrophe that Jeremiah prophesied began with the removal of King Jehoiachin from Jerusalem to Babylon in 597 B.C.E. Ezekiel was among the deported leaders. He was a silent recluse for seven years, going out in public only to deliver prophetic messages—because that's what the Lord wished of him. After Solomon's temple was burned, Ezekiel began talking again. Like Jeremiah, he emphasized personal responsibility for every member of the community. The Lord spoke to him about the very same proverb Jeremiah liked to contradict. Ezekiel prophesied:

> The word of the Lord came to me: "What do you people mean by quoting this proverb about the land of Israel: 'The fathers eat sour grapes, and the children's teeth are set on edge?' As surely as I live," declares the Sovereign Lord, "you will no longer quote this proverb in Israel .... The soul that sins is the one who will die."

Ezekiel was very concerned about the development of proper rituals among his people during the exile in Babylon, where there was no temple. He emphasized that rituals in Judaism should be performed properly, along with the development of his people's inner morality. When Ezekiel found out that Solomon's temple had been burned, he encouraged the exiles to have a new heart with a new spirit of hope. The Lord then revealed through Ezekiel the specific dimensions of the sanctuary that was the core of the rebuilt temple in Jerusalem. But even after the temple was rebuilt, the impact of Ezekiel's message continued: perform rituals sincerely and take personal responsibility for your actions.

Many of Ezekiel's concerns were shared by a man who lived (as the crow flies) some 4,500 miles away at about the same time: Confucius. And though the culture of western Asia and eastern Asia differ a lot, perhaps Ezekiel and Confucius would have enjoyed each other's company. They shared concerns about the sincere, authentic performance of traditional ritual, and they both emphasized the development of personal morality in the midst of tight-knit communities.

Enlightening Extras
According to Hebrew tradition, the architecture of the temple in Jerusalem was divinely inspired. Moses was shown a plan for the tabernacle, Solomon was shown a plan for the temple, and Ezekiel was shown a plan for the sanctuary in the restored temple.

A world of thought. Prophets, philosophers, and religious teachers were active in the places marked here at around the time Buddha was living in India.

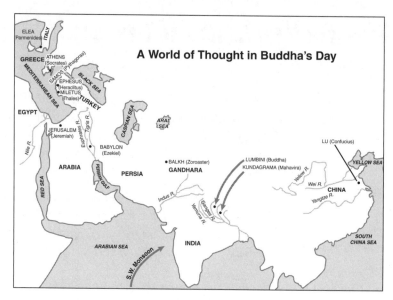

Confucius: Ren and the Art of Benevolence

Kung Fu Tzu is the person you probably know as Confucius. He was born in the state of Lu in what is now China (though at the time there wasn't a "China" as such). Confucius lived in a culture where ancestors were considered divine. But his position was "respect the gods, but keep them at a distance." He preferred to concentrate on what humans knew best and could control—their social propriety, and character development.

Confucius was a trained master of ceremony who emphasized that every ritual act should be done with perfect sincerity, not just for show. He believed that traditional rituals had been corrupted, as society became morally corrupt. Public rituals as well as personal relationships should be conducted properly, with sincerity. Only then would society flourish. Culture should be a work of art, in harmony with nature and the lives of generations gone by. To make this happen, Confucius taught that people should develop *ren*.

Dharma Dictionary

Ren is the Chinese word for humaneness or benevolence. Confucius considered ren as the perfection of human character. It is developed through five social relationships where loyalty and responsibility come into play: ruler-subject, teacher-student, elder-younger, husband-wife, and friend-friend. The Chinese character for ren is composed of symbols for a human being and the number two, signifying mutuality and relationship.

Confucius was a teacher who had about 72 main pupils. In theory, he opened his teaching to any man who truly loved to learn. And he argued that positions of government leadership should go to the most-qualified candidates, not to those who inherited their positions through social standing. In this way, he prepared the way for civil service examinations and public schooling. Confucius wanted people to learn to think and not just follow others by rote. He was convinced that a wholesome society was based on good education.

Would Confucius have been curious about the teachings of Mahavira, the Jain leader in India? Both Confucius and Mahavira wanted people to develop their humanity to the fullest. But how do you think the two men would have gotten along? Mahavira thought that humanity was perfected through restraint from violence and would not kill even a mosquito. On the other hand, Confucius was not against hunting, if done responsibly. So he fished ... but didn't use a net; he shot at birds ... but not if they were at rest.

Mahavira: Kill Not. Cause No Pain.

Mahavira was an important leader of the very old Indian religion known as Jainism. Mahavira was nontheistic. That means, although he didn't deny the existence of devas or godlings within the universe, he was not in favor of worship. Mahavira's goal was to become free from the cycle of rebirth. Because devas themselves were not free from rebirth, they were not relevant to his spiritual practice. The Jain path to salvation involved freeing the soul or *jiva* from the contamination of karma. This was to be accomplished by practicing *ahimsa*, which is restraint from any and all forms of violent conduct. At the time of death, if the jiva were clean of karmic dust, it would rise unobstructed to the top of the universe. Attaining such freedom from the world was Mahavira's ultimate spiritual goal.

Mahavira was exposed to theories of nonaction and materialism—which he rejected. He thought a person could change his or her fate through action, and the most human authentic action was action without violence. Jains emphasized personal responsibility. Mahavira and his disciples tried to become as nonviolent

> **Buddha Basics**
>
> Mahavira and Buddha both taught about karma. But Mahavira called karma a fine, material dust that attached to the eternal jiva when any act of violence was done. Through the practice of ahimsa or nonviolence, karmic dust gradually wore off of the jiva. By contrast, Buddha did not speak of an eternal soul and described karma from a psychological rather than a material point of view.

as humanly possible and would not hurt even a mosquito or a fly if possible. So it follows that Jains were strict vegetarians. The Jain commitment to nonviolence extended to restraint from harming others in thought, words, and deeds.

Mahavira set up Jain communities for monks and nuns in India. He wanted to support people's efforts to develop fully their humanity. In their quest for living a life of nonviolence, Jain monks and nuns normally ate one meal per day—no meat at all—gathered by alms begging and undertook periodic fasts. A Jain who'd refrained from violence for long periods of time (including many former lifetimes) could stop all action, including the act of eating. Through this restraint the last bit of karmic dust would be removed from the jiva and it would pass out of the body untainted at the moment of death.

Mahavira and Confucius might not have seen eye to eye on how to fulfill one's humanity. Besides condoning hunting, Confucius was more political and ritualistic than Mahavira. But Mahavira surely would have found a soul mate in Pythagoras. It seems that Pythagoras actually may have visited India—though people usually emphasize his travel to Egypt and Babylonia. Pythagoras was a strict vegetarian and was head of a community of disciples who (like the Jains) sought inner knowledge and freedom from rebirth. What do you think Pythagoras and Mahavira would have talked about if they met? Or would they have talked at all? As you'll see, Pythagoras really liked silence.

Pythagoras: Music Anyone? Or Math?

Pythagoras was born on the island of Samos in the Aegean Sea close to Turkey. He moved to Croton, a city-state in southern Italy founded by émigrés from Ionia and was instrumental in governing there for two decades. But Pythagoras was involved in much more than politics. He was a mathematician and the leader of a religious cult that lived under strict guidelines. Take a look at some rules observed in his community:

- You had to be a vegetarian, living mostly on milk, honey, and vegetables.

- You could not be buried in woolen clothing, urinate facing the sun, or eat beans.

- You shouldn't get out of bed in the morning without mentally reviewing what you did the day before.

Pythagoras believed in the transmigration of souls and that the aim of life was to get a good future for the soul. To do this, a person should recognize that everything in the universe is based on the number 10. To come to that realization, a person should listen to the music of the spheres and experience the vibrational relationships that govern life. In studying numbers, Pythagoras paid particular attention to three musical relationships:

◆ The octave, which goes from C to C with a proportion of 2:1

◆ The fifth, which goes from C to G with a proportion of 3:2

◆ The fourth, which goes from C to F with a proportion of 4:3

Be Mindful!

In the ancient world, it's helpful to recall that the names used to describe places were not necessarily used back then. For example, "Greece" was just an association of independent city-states around the Mediterranean Sea. So it's more accurate to say Socrates, Thales, and Pythagoras lived in Athens, Miletus, and Croton—rather than say they were from "Greece."

Pythagoras believed that moral conduct was a key to finding the secrets of the universe. Ethics have form, just as music has form. There is balance in conduct as there is symmetry in nature. So whom would Pythagoras most like to speak with among his peers in the sixth to fifth centuries B.C.E.? Perhaps Pythagoras would love to spend time in India (if he wasn't there already) speaking with Mahavira and Buddha on the stages of meditation. But he surely would have wanted to compare notes with Thales about what each had learned in Babylonia—where Ezekiel was prophesying! They could have talked a long time about Babylonian astrology and mathematics.

Enlightening Extras

What's left of the teachings of Pythagoras? Most people aren't taught that Pythagoras wouldn't eat beans or that he remembered his past lives. But the Pythagorean theorem is well known: $a^2 + b^2 = c^2$, where a and b are the sides of a right triangle and c is the hypotenuse. In Euclidean geometry, this theorem helps define the distance between two points.

Thales: The Sun Ain't Gonna Shine.

Thales was born in Miletus (in present-day Turkey). We visit him because both he and Buddha were deeply interested in problems of causality. Thales is often called the first Greek philosopher because he was the first Mediterranean thinker to explore the causes of natural events. At the time, people generally said that natural events were caused by gods and goddesses: Zeus made thunder, Artemis made wind, Poseidon made sea storms, and so on. But Thales looked for the cause of natural events in the material world, and he thought water was the basis of everything.

Some say Thales predicted an eclipse of the sun that happened on May 28, 585 B.C.E. at 6:13 in the evening. Did Thales simply repeat a Babylonian astrological prediction? In any case, he not only went to Babylonia but also to Egypt. With mythic stories of the Olympian deities on one hand and Babylonian mathematics on the other hand, Thales was almost forced to ask: isn't there something more we can know about how our world works? Is it enough to say that this or that was caused by the beneficence or anger of an Olympian god?

Dharma Dictionary

Cosmogonic refers to the creation of a cosmos. It's a term used by historians of religions.

Monism is from the Greek word *monos*, meaning one. It's a doctrine that posits a single entity that pervades the entire universe. The ancient Miletian philosophers were monists. Other monists were the seers of ancient India who wrote in the Upanisads of brahman—the impersonal spiritual force running through all things.

The way Thales practiced science was not completely divorced from mythological thinking. His notion that everything is based on water sounds like something of a *cosmogonic* myth, relating the origins of the world. And his experiments with magnetic rocks and amber (which has magnetic properties when rubbed) referred to the living soul of the substances. Yet the fact that Thales began to consider what a human being can learn about the world through mathematics and experimentation indicates a twilight of the gods in the Mediterranean world. The power the Olympian deities had over the imagination of the "Greek" people was waning, and Thales was the first to try alternative explanations for what's happening around us.

Thales often is grouped with Anaximander and Anaximenes because they're all from Miletus. In fact, the two were students who thought up variations on Thales' theories. Anaximander thought the foundation of all things was a boundless substance; Anaximenes said it was air. Okay! These guys are all called *monists* because they thought of reality in terms of one unified whole. And there were other monists to keep Thales company in the Greek world. But philosophy wasn't his only interest. Thales was also a mathematician, engineer, and politician. He proposed that eligible people from the 12 Ionian cities should have common citizenship. So might Thales have wanted to speak with Heraclitus—a fellow monist whose Ionian city was overtaken by the Persians? When they finished discussing science, they could've turned to politics. Unfortunately, Thales passed away about seven years before Heraclitus was born.

Heraclitus: You Can't Step into the Same River Twice.

Heraclitus was born to an aristocratic family of Ephesus. He was to have taken up a hereditary post of priest-king of the Ionian city-state, but resigned it to his brother. Heraclitus became a sort of prophet-priest with a vision of reality centered on the *logos* (cosmic intelligence that took the form of fire). He believed in salvation through knowledge that makes a person resemble the divine. According to Heraclitus, most people are living in the sleep of ignorance, as if in a private dream world. They don't understand the logos, or intelligent principle of the universe. (He complained that they didn't understand him either! And it may be no wonder, because Heraclitus wrote in short, pithy riddles.)

Heraclitus claimed that everything is in flux. Things that appear to stay the same are also in flux. (It's just that the flux consists of the same kind of new thing appearing in place of the old thing over time.) There's no stability, and everything plays against its opposite. And without the tension of opposites, nothing would happen in our world. But this is not obvious. Here are two examples he used to illustrate the truth of flux and dynamism:

- A strung bow illustrates how "nature loves to hide" the tension between opposites that pervade the universe. The bow pulls one way, and the string pulls the other. This tension is undetected, yet the bow is useless without it.

- Heraclitus said you can't step into the same river twice. But he didn't say there was no river. And here's where things become paradoxical. On one hand, there's unity and things exist: there's the river. On the other hand, unity brings forth diversity: the river is not the same water from moment to moment.

Heraclitus lost enthusiasm for the Olympian deities, even though he brought his book of maxims to the temple of Artemis. And he associated fire with the logos or intelligent principle of the universe. In these two ways, he was probably influenced by the Zoroastrian tradition. You see, Heraclitus lived his life under Persian rule in Ephesus. And the Persian king Darius I Hystaspis (521–485 B.C.E.) promoted the faith of the prophet Zoroaster, who revered fire as a symbol of truth and did not tolerate worship of lesser deities. Although it's not certain that Zoroaster was alive at the same time, we can bet that Heraclitus would have wanted to speak with the Persian prophet

Zoroaster: Truth or Lie?

Zoroaster is included in our tour of the world in Buddha's day because he had tremendous influence on thought throughout western Asia (the Middle East). He was a prophet, but somewhat different from Jeremiah and Ezekiel. Zoroaster was the mouthpiece of a deity known as Ahura Mazda. Zoroaster spoke of our world as a battleground between two powerful forces, who were children of Ahura Mazda: Spenta Mainyu (beneficent spirit) and Angra Mainyu (hostile spirit). And though Ahura Mazda ultimately is the superior force, human life is caught in the struggle between the two spirits.

Be Mindful!

Of all the people on our tour of the "world" in Buddha's day, the dates of the Persian prophet Zoroaster are the least certain. He is often placed in the sixth century B.C.E—as in this chapter. However, some people think he may have been born about 300 years earlier, around 900 B.C.E. In any case, Zoroastrian thought deeply influenced the Persian Empire and life for all who contacted Persia in the Buddha's day.

Spenta Mainyu is the Truth, and Angra Mainyu is the Lie. Human beings always have to contend with the negative influence of the Lie, and must strive for Truth. This puts human beings in the middle of a cosmic battle. But for each and every person, it is an individual ethical battle. At the end of time comes a resurrection of the dead. At that time, human beings will participate in the last judgment, and the content of each person's struggle with the Lie (darkness, evil, negativity, sin) will be exposed.

The prophet Zoroaster used a sacred fire as the centerpiece of worship. This fire is Truth (light, goodness) and a manifestation of Ahura Mazda. He kept a sacred fire burning continually with a special wood, prayers, and gestures. Perhaps he could have agreed with Parmenides that fire is being itself. In fact, Zoroaster and Heraclitus would both have much to talk about with Parmenides.

Parmenides: That It Is, and It Cannot Not Be!

Heraclitus taught that everything was in flux. And just the opposite, Parmenides taught that motion does not exist. Parmenides would object to Heraclitus' claim that "you can't step into the same river twice." Why? Because there is no stepping. There is no movement. All is being, not becoming! How did he figure this out? Well … Parmenides received a strange sort of revelation. He heard a goddess tell him, "That it is, and it cannot not be." He was then given teachings of two types: one true and one false. He should know the way of truth, but he should also know the way of appearance (so he competently could defend truth against the arguments brought by mortals).

Parmenides taught that what "is" is unborn, imperishable, unique, entire, and indivisible. To him, this meant that all not being was eliminated. And if there was no becoming (as Heraclitus claimed), then what's left is being. And this being was actually consciousness. With only being there is …

- ◆ No origination or perishing.

- ◆ No past, present, or future.

- ◆ No qualities or intensity.

> **Buddha Basics**
>
> Buddha spoke of flux and transformation. In this he emphasized becoming, as Heraclitus did. However, the philosophy of being taught by Parmenides finds echoes in an early Buddhist philosophical school known as the all-exists school (Sarvastivadins), who claimed that the past, present, and future all "exist."

Parmenides became very famous in the Greek-speaking world because he introduced something new to philosophy: argumentation. And it's said that when Parmenides at age 65 was in Athens, he met a young man by the name of Socrates. Well … if there's anyone who liked to "argue" among the Greek speakers of the day, it would be Socrates! But what Parmenides and Socrates liked to argue about was very different.

Socrates' Annoying Questions

Socrates was the son of a stonemason and a midwife. And he claimed to follow his mother's profession: a philosopher was a midwife who birthed ideas. Socrates insisted that people should examine things relentlessly—including their own lives. So after earning distinction as a young soldier and gaining a small inheritance from his father, Socrates devoted himself to asking questions. Early in his life, he'd been interested in cosmology, but Socrates became convinced that critical reasoning about our own ethical assumptions was more important.

Socrates asked questions such as: What is Justice? What is Love? His questions were often annoying because he kept pressing people about their assumptions. Sometimes he would ask more and more, until they worked themselves in to an embarrassing contradiction. Often his unwitting victims were people of high rank in Athenian society. And it was not pleasant for them when in the course of conversation they realized they didn't know what they were talking about! Socrates called his method *elenchus*. We know it as dialectic.

Dharma Dictionary

Elenchus is the Greek term for cross-examination. Socrates questioned people about what they thought in order to clarify issues central to human well-being. Through cross-examination, contradictions in a person's assumptions were exposed, leading to self-knowledge. Elenchus developed into the dialectic, in which the truth of a matter is reached through back-and-forth questioning that makes its way through contradictions.

With Socrates we come to the end of our tour. We visited 10 figures of the sixth to fifth centuries B.C.E. within a span of some 5,000 miles. There are many more within this range of time and space—and outside the "narrow" geographic band between Italy and China. But at least you've gotten a sampling of the cultural richness of the Axial Age. And as you read about Buddha's life in the chapters ahead, you can consider how his view of the world compares and contrasts with the perspectives of such great figures as Zoroaster, Jeremiah, Ezekiel, Thales, Mahavira, Pythagoras, Confucius, Heraclitus, Parmenides, and Socrates.

The Least You Need to Know

- During the Axial Age (800–200 B.C.E.) thinkers from the Mediterranean to Yellow seas emphasized personal responsibility in ritual, society, and/or individual development.

- Jeremiah and Ezekiel prophesied during the Babylonian exile and warned the Hebrew people to stop all bits of idol worship and take personal responsibility for their actions.

- Thales, Pythagoras, Heraclitus, Parmenides, and Socrates lived in various Greek-speaking city-states in the Mediterranean world.

- The religion of the Persian prophet Zoroaster probably influenced the thought of Heraclitus who took fire to be the basic principle of the universal logos.

- Confucius, Mahavira, and Socrates focused their messages on developing human excellence through the moral gateways of ren (humaneness), ahimsa (nonviolence), and elenchus (knowing oneself through cross-examination).

Buddha's India

In This Chapter

- ◆ The geography of ancient India
- ◆ The mysterious Harappan culture
- ◆ Who were the Aryans?
- ◆ Chiefs and kings in the Ganges Basin
- ◆ The class system of Buddha's day—or not
- ◆ Merchants and money
- ◆ Ascetics with bad hair and no money

Life in the Middle Ganges Basin was in the midst of cultural transformation during Buddha's lifetime. The word *basin* appropriately describes Buddha's part of the Ganges Valley not only because the area is run through with waters, but also because it was a cauldron in which new ideas brewed. If you look at the map in this chapter, you'll see that the Ganges Valley does form a "basin" of waters. Starting 1,360 feet above sea level in Rishikesh—north of the ancient city of Hastinapura—the Ganges flows 1,557 miles (2,510 km) southeast to the Bay of Bengal. Originating in the holy Himalayan "abode of the seers," the river offers itself as a bowl that gives life to numerous villages, towns, and cities before draining into the Bay of Bengal.

Numerous smaller rivers and rivulets join the Ganges as it cascades down from the great Himalayan Mountains that sit majestically to the north. All these running waters—and others such as the great river Indus—have bathed inhabitants of north India for millennia. Some of these waters, looked upon as goddesses, beneficently supported waves of life along their shores. Yet sometimes these goddesses blotted out all signs of that life.

The streaming waters of India were not the only powerful forces to change course from time to time. Like the rivers, the great cultures of India that lay along their banks occasionally took radical turns, too. One period of deep social transformation occurred in the ancient Vedic era around 1200 B.C.E., when a group known as the Aryans took center stage from the most ancient Harappan people. Then, about 600 years later, during Buddha's lifetime, a period of cultural chaos erupted to challenge what the Aryans had established.

Sacred Rivers and Mountains

India is a land of sacred rivers. And four of them are especially important to our story: Indus, Sarasvati, Yamuna, and Ganga. But rivers change, and, given a cataclysmic event, change abruptly. And when rivers radically transform, the inhabitants on their banks either perish or move. Massive flooding of the Indus sent its most ancient inhabitants—the Harappans—away in 1750 B.C.E. Nobody knows for sure where they went. And sometime later, the Sarasvati went dry, sending the Aryans into the Doab, the land between two other rivers—the Ganga and Yamuna. Buddha spent most of his life crisscrossing the Ganga, moving between western places that were entrenched Aryan settlements and the less "civilized" areas to the east.

Now let's look at the mountains. *Himavat*—as the Himalayan Mountain range was known in ancient times—has the highest peaks in the world. And to those living in the mountains and foothills, Himavat is sacred, like the waters that stream down like hair from its peaks. The magnificent Himalayan range runs across the northern frontier of India, separating her from the rest of Asia. But despite the imposing line it draws to mark off the edge of the great peninsula, people have always come and gone through the treacherous mountain passes. They also have walked for miles in the foothills. Buddha was born in these foothills.

The Vindhya Mountains are a low range of central India. They run some 675 miles east-west to form a barrier between the northern plains and the southern plateau. The Ganges Basin occupies a large part of the space between them. And Buddha spent 45 years of his life teaching in the Middle Ganges Basin, which includes some northern plains and Himalayan foothills. The southern plateau of India mostly enters Buddhist history after the Master passed away, whereas the Indus Valley and Punjab were significant in the time well before his birth.

Buddha Basics

India used to be completely separate from Asia. About 90 million years ago, the India tectonic plate split from Africa's east coast and started inching northward at the rate of 6 inches (15 centimeters) a year. It floated faster than any other plate and began pushing into Asia some 50 or 55 million years ago. The Himalayan Mountains were formed as the wandering continent slammed into the standing land mass. India continues to plow under the mountains at a rate of 0.15 inches (4 millimeters) each year!

Harappans on the Indus

Mystery surrounds the people who lived in the Indus Valley during the second millennium B.C.E. Nowadays we call these people the Harappans, after a major archeological site unearthed along the Indus River. They had a script, but no one has been able to figure it out yet. But the Harappans left behind artwork suggesting they had a peaceful, possibly matriarchal culture, including the following:

- Mother goddess figures
- A horned fertility god
- Sacred trees
- Sacred animals
- Ritual ablutions in bathing tanks

The Harappan people left the Indus Valley by about 1750 B.C.E. Why? Aside from a possible invasion of the cities of Harappa and Mohenjo-Daro, a series of disasters occurred that led to the breakdown of their economic system. Possibly, a geological lift near Mohenjo-Daro caused the Indus to flood. The soil turned salty, and vegetation could not survive. The soil eroded. And the ensuing poverty forced a cut in trade with Mesopotamia.

Aryans on the Sarasvati

After the Harappan culture declined, another people made their mark on northern India. They called themselves Aryan or noble, and they called their collection of sacred hymns the Rig Veda. We know the Aryans solidly impacted Indian culture by 1200 B.C.E. But who were they? From where did they come? And what was the relationship between Aryans and Harappans? People are still looking for good answers to these questions. And though there's much to be learned, we do know something about Aryan life along the rivers of western India (including Pakistan) during the late second millennium B.C.E.

Be Mindful!

Today a fierce debate rages over the origins of Aryan culture. Nineteenth-century Europeans—conducting linguistic research—claimed that Aryans (also called Indo-Europeans) entered India, Iran, and Europe from somewhere in central Asia. With growing archeological evidence, proponents of the theory stopped saying that Aryans "invaded" India and now claim that Aryans "immigrated" to India. On the other hand, Indians themselves traditionally assumed that Aryans were indigenous. Their position now has become quite sophisticated and poses a serious challenge to the Aryan invasion/immigration theory.

The Rig Veda contains 1,028 hymns to gods and goddesses revered by the Aryans. If you read these texts, you get the idea that the Aryan people lived along the many rivers of the Punjab, including the Indus and the Sarasvati (of which only a trace is left today). Their worship involved reverence for the spiritual essence of natural objects such as dawn, sky, the earth, fire, and the sun. They also worshipped a plant—a god—who was associated with the moon. The plant—which may have been a hallucinogenic mushroom—was used to prepare a special drink known as soma. Aryan priests would gather the plant, perhaps from a special place in the mountains, press it between stones to extract its liquid, mix the liquid with milk, strain the mixture, and consume the soma on the day it was prepared.

After priests ritually prepared soma, they shared the sacred drink with elite warriors in the Aryan community. Under the influence of soma, the worshippers were said to see the gods. In turn, they sang hymns in praise of soma.

Off to the Ganga-Yamuna Doab

In the early first millennium B.C.E., a cataclysmic geological event caused the Sarasvati River to dry up. For its own survival, the Aryan community abandoned its home in the Punjab. Whether or not the area around the Sarasvati was their original home, it is clear that the Aryans began to migrate into the land between the Ganges and Yamuna rivers—known as the Ganga-Yamuna Doab. On this move, the Aryan priests took with them the god Agni, who was none other than the sacred fire.

The Aryan migration from the Punjab probably occurred around 900 B.C.E.—sometime after the Mahabharata war in which two branches of the Bharata family slaughtered each other on the field of the Kurus. This field, Kurukshetra, is located in the Punjab, about 75 miles (118 km) north of the ancient Indraprastha, modern Delhi. There you will find a tank that—during an eclipse—mystically contains healing water from every other sacred tank in India. It is interesting that this Aryan site should have a sacred tank—because tanks built by Harappans have been unearthed along the Indus River. In fact, Indians still like to build sacred tanks in front of their holy places. So though no one knows just where the Harappans went as the Aryans took over, something of their legacy remains.

After devastating their population through the great Mahabharata war, the Aryans left the Punjab, never to return. Those who migrated to the valley between the Ganga and Yamuna rivers—the Ganga-Yamuna Doab—went through a period of crystallizing their Aryan cultural values. As they advanced materially, this group paid less attention to the places they had lived before. As their lives became more sedentary, they gave more power to the priests. And as their views of life and death changed, they wrote new sacred texts. In fact, this early Aryan culture proved to have a lot of staying power. Even when new texts were composed, the old ones were not abandoned. Thus, you can still find traditional brahmins or priests performing the fire sacrifice in India today.

From Vedic to Brahmanic

Back in the Punjab, the Aryans had a pastoral lifestyle that emphasized horses and cattle. Horse-riding warriors had occupied a privileged place in society, and the Rig Veda was the key scripture in their *Vedic* culture. But the land between the Ganga and Yamuna rivers was very fertile. So after the tribes settled in the Doab, they turned to agriculture and began using the plow. These Aryans called their new home Madhyadesa or Middle Country. Over time, Madhyadesa became the seat of a new *Brahmanic* culture and was called Aryavarta—land of the Aryas.

In the Ganga-Yamuna Doab, the brahmins became the preeminent members of the Aryan community. They performed elaborate ceremonies using milk, ghee, and grains as offerings in the sacred fire. Brahmins trained intensively to recite mantras (sacred syllables) based on the Rig Veda. The priests' strict ritual observance and knowledge of scripture distinguished them from Aryans with other vocations, such as warriors and workers. Thus, the priests established themselves as the purest Aryans. The warriors (later known as kshatriyas) and the upper echelon of workers (later known as vaishyas) gradually fell into rank behind the brahmins in the Aryan ritual hierarchy.

> **Buddha Basics**
>
> The Aryan culture of western India from about 1200 to 900 B.C.E. is called **Vedic**, because worship centered on the gods of the Rig Veda. The second phase of Aryan culture—embedded in the Ganga-Yamuna Doab between 900 and 500 B.C.E.—is called **Brahmanic**. Sacrifice became the key ritual in this period, and both priests and their handbooks were called "brahamanas"—meaning possessors of Brahman (spiritual energy).

The brahmins of Aryavarta called areas outside their territory mlecca-desa, which means non-Aryan (barbarian) country. They looked down on people of the Punjab from whence their ancestors had come and of the Middle Ganges Basin where splinter groups of Aryans, including Buddha's Sakya clan, had settled. Those clan territories were not observing the Aryan rituals purely! They were not perfectly observing the fire rituals in worship of Agni. In other words, the newly distinguished brahmins felt that the people of the mlecca-desa areas were not true Aryans—or no longer were.

Oh, Those Barbarians

The Punjab and Middle Ganges Basin—the two barbarian regions—developed very differently over time. Urban centers in the Middle Ganges Basin grew up more quickly than in either the old or new Vedic territories (Punjab and Doab). And while the brahmins of the Ganga-Yamuna Doab castigated wayward Aryans in the Middle Ganges Basin, this mleccha territory buzzed with ambition. It turned into a vibrant marketplace not only for new commercial ventures, but also for bold new ideas. By contrast, the Punjab waned in power and couldn't revitalize itself as a focal point of Aryan culture.

In the centuries after the Aryan migration into the Doab, new settlements continued to form in the Middle Ganges Basin as families sought open land that promised abundance. For example, the Sakyas (Buddha's clan), Koliyas (Buddha's wife's clan), and Licchavis all migrated northward toward the Himalayas from Varanasi to establish new clan territories where, through the use of iron technology, they were able to clear land and plow the earth. The old-fashioned method of clearing land would have been to bring the sacred fire and burn forested land. But now, the hardworking clans could sustain themselves by the plow, independent of the brahmins and their sacred fires.

Dharma Dictionary

Copper and bronze started going out of style during the **Iron Age.** At the start, primitive metallurgists developed iron mainly for weapons, such as arrowheads, spearheads, and knives—and to a lesser extent for tools used to clear land. In India, iron was used in agricultural technology from about the mid-first millennium B.C.E., though it first appeared much earlier. It is interesting that Buddha received his last (indigestible) meal from a man who may have been an "iron" worker, and that Buddha was cremated in an iron vessel.

Chiefs and Kings

Two political systems undergirded the management of territory in Buddha's day: the republics and the monarchies. We can call them the chiefdoms and kingdoms, according to who ruled. The republics, ruled by a council of chiefs, were a dying political form, while the monarchies, ruled by kings, were infant states. The large republican estates were owned by kshatriya, warrior families. Gradually, the most powerful kshatriya families collected for themselves land that had been kept within the larger social group for generations.

As power was concentrated more and more in the hands of a few, the state—which was the seed of monarchy—evolved as an alternative to the republic. A state was based on territory and ruled by a monarch. On the other hand, counsels of tribal chiefs ruled a republic even-handedly. In Buddha's time, Kausala and Magadha were the two budding monarchies in the Middle Ganges Basin that were vying to swallow up any republic they could get their hands on. You will hear plenty more about the kings of Kausala and Magadha in the coming chapters.

Be Mindful!

Events seem to take on the status of "facts" in history books. With hindsight, political movements often appear as clear-cut. Yet, people immersed in events do not perceive clearly the "signs of their times." So although we speak of monarchy versus republic, the people of Buddha's India would not have perceived the contrast so sharply. They were too close to the action, and no territories had yet coalesced into an empire.

The Varna System

From ancient times, India's Aryan society was based on the varna system of social classes. Because one meaning of the word *varna* is color, some people think social classes in ancient India were based on racial discrimination. Others think that varna related to ritual status, not ethnic status. In fact, the varna system was not applied uniformly everywhere in India, and its practice varied over time. Eventually, there were non-kshatriyas who became rulers, and the role of sudras differed between southern India and the Ganges valley. There was even prejudice within castes, based on the location of one's territory and the lineage to which one belonged. We already know that brahmins from the Ganga-Yamuna Doab looked down on the brahmins of Magadha.

There was an ancient law book called the Laws of Manu that compared the four varnas to the head, arms, torso, and feet of society. The head sustains spiritual and intellectual life, the arms govern and protect, the torso generates sustenance and wealth, and the feet stand in servitude to the upper members. But though the four castes are demarcated strictly, people may not always have been as divided in practice as in theory. There was a practical difference between social status and ritual status. People needed to observe ritual requirements specific to their caste. But social interaction may have been more fluid—at least in certain times and places.

The varna system came to be structured as follows:

- **Brahmin:** Priests and teachers
- **Khsatriya:** Rulers and warriors
- **Vaisya:** Merchants and artisans (possibly peasants)
- **Sudra:** Peasants who labor hard and workers of low profession (including non-Aryan mlecchas)
- **Pancamma:** Untouchable scavengers below the fourth varna

Buddha, Prince, or Pauper?

So, what social status did Buddha—let's more correctly call him Siddhartha here—have according to the varna system? Well, Siddhartha grew up in a clan of rulers and warriors in the Sakyan lineage. His father was a Sakyan raja, or chieftain, which put him among the most prominent members of Sakyan society. People thought Siddhartha would achieve political greatness in a time when military brilliance was linked to amassing territory. Thus, it came as a shock to his father when Siddhartha gave up his noble clothing and donned rags in which a dead body had been wrapped. By doing so, Siddhartha became ritually polluted, lost his caste standing, and in effect became an untouchable.

Eventually Gautama made it clear that he rejected the caste system. In the eyes of people following Vedic-Brahmanical culture, Buddha was technically an outcaste—even though he was highly respected. Technically an Aryan dinner host could not eat with Sakyamuni because he was ritually impure. But regardless of his or their caste standing, people still wanted the Master and his disciples to come for a meal. And once people became Buddhist, they no longer worried about caste standing anymore. Although Buddha was an exceptional person, this example helps to illustrate how a ritual relationship and personal relationship could be very different in the caste system of Buddha's day.

Excitement and Enterprise

Buddha lived through exciting times in the Middle Ganges Basin where busy new commercial centers were sprouting up. Remember that in the eyes of brahmins living in the Ganga-Yamuna Doab, Buddha's stomping ground was considered mlecca-desa—barbarian country where adherence to Vedic ritual was not strict. In this less civilized area you'd find all kinds of artisans freely carting wares from villages to the urban markets for trade. You'd also find people offering new services, some unknown to Aryavarta.

Artisans	Service Professionals
Jewelers	Carpenters
Metal workers	Acrobats
Basket and rope makers	Fortune tellers
Weavers and dyers	Flute players
Potters	Dancers

With the use of iron technology in the first millennium B.C.E., northern India burst into a period of intensive urbanization, after centuries of stagnation. With the iron plow came surplus produce. With that came specialization of crafts and increased production. With that came trade and communication by land and river. And with that came coins and the Brahmi script.

The cities in more purely Aryan territory—such as Hastinapur, Indraprastha, Ahicchatra, and Ayodhya (Saketa)—remained political centers. On the other hand, enthralling economic opportunities opened up in the urban centers of the Middle Ganges Basin. Whereas the older Copper Age cities had palaces and courts, the new cities had marketplaces. Sravasti, Kausambi, Vaisali, and Rajagriha became commercial as well as political centers with external ties established through trade. So after a centuries-long break between India and the Middle East, commercial contact was made with Mesopotamia once again.

Old and new cities in Buddha's day. Buddha spent most of his time in the Middle Ganges Basin where an intensive move toward urbanization was on. New commercial centers grew up where merchants became wealthy, and people exchanged ideas as well as goods.

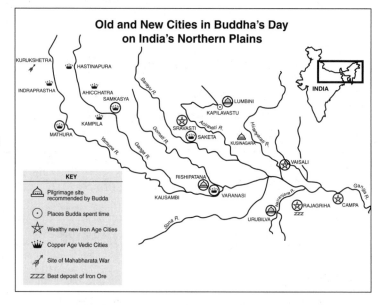

In Buddha's day, members of elite society—priests and rulers—competed not only with each other but also with two new kinds of itinerants: merchants and ascetics. And Gautama seemed to be comfortable with both. He was a religious wanderer who frequented the growing commercial centers and had many disciples who were merchants. He even supported a progressive monetary policy for his lay followers: investment and savings.

Money or Not, Here I Come

Merchants wandered around in the Middle Ganges Basin trading goods, whereas ascetics wandered around trading ideas. Both merchants and ascetics offered a challenge to the status quo. Yet, they were on opposite sides of the coin, so to speak. Merchants accumulated an unprecedented amount of private wealth, whereas ascetics renounced virtually all possessions. The irony is that although the renunciates presumably gave up worldly ties, they were actually dependent on the new urban environment with its surplus wealth. And in general merchants and ascetics got along well together.

You see, merchants were not from the higher two Aryan social classes (brahmin or kshatriya), so they appreciated teachings that did not downgrade their status. Wealthy merchants sometimes made generous donations of land to spiritual communities who tended to stay put during the monsoon rains. In fact, the first people who encountered Buddha after his enlightenment were two merchants. And the Master spent nearly half his rainy seasons at Sravasti in a grove donated by the merchant Anathapindaka.

In an atmosphere of innovation and enterprise, the social identity of people in the Middle Ganges Basin was in flux. Those who migrated to the dynamic urban centers began to trade in their tribal identities to establish a home in the towns. Others opted for the homeless life and shifted their allegiance from a family lineage to a spiritual lineage. Some hankered after wealth; others wandered through villages, towns, and cities seeking to escape the fetters of ownership. Among them was Siddhartha, the wayward son of a raja.

Bad Hair Days in the Ganges Basin

Some 50 groups of ascetics wandered through the Middle Ganges Basin in Buddha's time. (Sakyamuni was the leader of one such group.) They sojourned in forest huts, mango groves, and caves, whereas merchants traded in the cities. When ascetics met each other on the road, they would ask: "Whose dharma (religious teaching) do you follow?" They were religious seekers, interested in each other's views and spiritual practices.

Ascetics of the Middle Ganges Basin not only held a variety of views, they wore a variety of hairstyles. Some had long matted locks because they never cut their hair. Others shaved part of their hair and sported topknots. Others kept their hair short or shaved their heads. And some pulled their hair out by the very roots. These were truly "bad hair days" in India!

Among the wandering ascetics, there were two basic groups: the orthodox and the heterodox. The "orthodox" sustained the Vedic worldview and stayed within the Aryan fold. The "heterodox" undermined the very foundation of the Vedic social and religious system. Three heterodox groups were the Ajivakas, Jains, and Buddhists. Although the particulars of their beliefs and practices differed, they were alike in these respects:

- They rejected the Vedic scriptures, including worship of any gods or goddesses.

- They rejected the authority of the brahmins who were ritual experts on Vedic beliefs and rituals.

- They rejected the varna system of social classes that distinguished the brahmins from other groups of people.

Jump Off the Wheel!

Why did the ascetics renounce worldly life? Why did they reject worldly goods instead of trying to get rich like the merchants? Because they sought liberation from the round of rebirth. They believed in *transmigration*, and were horrified at the prospect of wandering from life to life *ad infinitum*. Whether they accepted the Vedas or not, these wanderers were committed to getting off the wheel of transmigration. But they had different ideas about exactly what a person must do to accomplish this aim. At the same time, however, the traditional brahmins continued to perform their Aryan rituals to favor the gods and ancestors and assure virtue and order in this world.

> **Dharma Dictionary**
>
> **Transmigration** is a theory of the continuation of the spiritual force from one lifetime to the next.

Brahmin Priests

The brahmin priests were the most conservative among the various groups of religious practitioners in sixth-century B.C.E. India. These traditional Aryans carried on their ancient traditions but in a more complex manner than in the old days of the Vedic age (1200–600 B.C.E.). This was the Brahmanical phase of Aryan culture, when the priests had come to the heights of their power and influence. Whereas hymns to the gods and goddesses formerly were recited solo, now there were many priests who together were involved in worship centered on the highly ritualized fire sacrifice. The new liturgy called for specialists trained in preparation of the brick altar, handling of substances offered to the fire, and recitation of mantras.

In Buddha's day, brahmin males were in the Indian mainstream as the highest members of society—especially in the more strictly Aryan areas of the Ganga-Yamuna Doab. A person became a brahmin by being born into a brahmin family and had an automatic obligation to do what was appropriate for a member of that highest caste. For example, brahmins were vegetarian and ate ritually pure food prepared especially for them.

Traditionally, brahmin males became priests after 12 years of training under a spiritual teacher. They would begin serving the teacher around the age that most children start school, and after a dozen years of memorization and ritual instruction they would marry and carry on the vocation of a Vedic priest. They would perform Vedic rituals—such as the fire sacrifice—to worship the ancestors and to attain worldly goals on behalf of their communities, such as success with the harvest, childbearing, warfare, and so on. Buddha's friends, King Prasenajit and King Bimbisara occasionally donated a whole village to one or another prominent brahmin in repayment for Vedic rituals done on their behalf. In fact, many brahmins became quite wealthy by charging large fees for their services.

Sannyasins

The *Sannyasins* were ascetics who "completely cast off" all worldly connections. In theory, they kept ties with the Aryan heritage but did not wear a sacred thread, a tuft of hair on the head, or perform the Vedic rituals. Instead, they internalized the fire sacrifice by generating heat through physical austerities and brightening the heart through mantra recitation. Sannyasins tended to live in the forests and give teachings to disciples who sat at their feet. The conversations between teacher and disciple were preserved in texts known as the Upanishads. They sought to realize the union of their atman (soul) with Brahman, the all-pervasive, formless universal energy.

> **Dharma Dictionary**
>
> **Sannyasin** means one who has completely cast off all worldly things. In the stages-of-life system that developed gradually in India, this represented the last of four stages an upper-caste male would ideally go through in life—following student, householder, and forest-dweller stages. The more radical renunciates moved into homeless life early.

As you can imagine, social tension between the early drop-out Sannyasins and the brahmin priests grew. There was even a term used to highlight the contrast between these two respected but contrasting elements of Aryan society: sramana-brahmana.

The sramanas aimed to unite the atman (true self, experienced as inner light) with Brahman (the pervasive power of the universe), and achieve release from rebirth. On the other hand, the brahmin priests (Brahmanas) performed sacrifice to bring benefits in this world and the next. In Buddha's day, an increasing number of old-style brahmin priests were taking an interest in the teachings of these Vedic Sannyasins and their innovative religious texts, the Upanishads, that had been surfacing in the culture for a century or two already.

Jains

The Jains are a very ancient sect in the Middle Ganges Basin. Their teacher, Nirgrantha Nataputra, was the twenty-fourth Tirthankara (saint) in the spiritual lineage ranging back to mythic times. (He is also called Vardhamana, but is best known as Mahavira, Great Hero.) Jains, like the new-style Vedic Sannyasins, aimed to escape the cycle of rebirth. The Jain method of leaving samsara was through burning off a kind of super-fine dust that stuck to their souls. They labored in the spiritual life to purify and free their souls from imprisonment in the body by avoiding any kind of violence, whether committed by body, speech, or even thought. The most accomplished Jain ascetics gave up food when they were about to free their souls from the dust of mundane action or karma. Jains pulled their hair out by the roots and sometimes wore no clothing at all—so as to completely renounce worldly attachments. Mahavira and Buddha probably lived at the same time and frequented the same villages, towns, and cities in the Middle Ganges Basin. It's known that merchants supported both their renunciate communities.

Buddhists

In Buddha's day, when wandering ascetics encountered each other on the road, they'd ask "Who is your teacher? What dharma do you follow?" So besides the brahmin priests, Sannyasins, and Jains, there were others who held a variety of opinions on what to do about the Wheel of Becoming. You'll read about a few more of these groups in Chapter 11.

Buddha's disciples distinguished themselves from all the other wandering ascetics in the Middle Ganges Basin by rejecting not only the varnas and Vedic authority, but also the notion of an eternal soul. Furthermore, Buddha didn't accept the doctrine of fatalism and the practice of extreme asceticism promoted by the Ajivakas. Nor did he attempt to follow the ideal of complete nonviolence and vegetarianism of the Jains. Overall, Buddha rejected the Aryan caste system and all prevailing views on the nature of reality. He paved a new road for himself and his disciples.

Enlightening Extras

What we've called the bad hair days in the Ganges Basin shaped the religious ethos of India for centuries beyond Buddha's time. The brahmin priests, Sannyasins, and Jains never died out in India. The Ajivakas spread to southern India and flourished there through at least the fourteenth century C.E. Only Buddhism died out in India by around the year 1000 C.E. ... only to return in our own day.

The Least You Need to Know

- Rivers played a large role in the course of northern India's ancient history—especially the Indus, Sarasvati, Yamuna, and Ganga.

- The Harappan-Aryan relationship is still shrouded in mystery, and claims about the original home of the Aryans are hotly debated.

- In the sixth century B.C.E., the Middle Ganges Basin was on a political trajectory from lineage-based societies to monarchic societies, evolving toward the first Indian empire.

- The caste (varna) system of ancient India was not uniformly applied in all times and places, but it was most culturally grounded among Aryans of the Ganga-Yamuna Doab, or Aryavarta.

- Economic disparity in the Middle Ganges Basin led to social upheaval and a new economy—involving merchants with money and ascetics with no money.

- There were many groups of religious seekers in the Middle Ganges Basin, including brahmin priests and a variety of wandering ascetics. In the end, Buddha's views did not match any of these.

Part 2

The Making and Breaking of a Prince

Once upon a time the ascetic Sumedha threw himself down in front of the ancient Buddha Dipamkara and determined to become the next buddha. Over many lifetimes, the Bodhisattva perfected acts such as giving and patience to prepare for his birth as Siddhartha Gautama. After he finally was born in ancient India, Siddhartha's father felt threatened by some uncanny predictions made about the future of his son. The clan chieftain tried (but failed) to mold Siddhartha into an image of himself.

As an aristocratic prince in an age of burgeoning monarchy, Siddhartha was ripe for military greatness. But in his heart something was beckoning him to abandon the life of luxury, privilege, and political ambition. The Sakyan prince decided to leave home on a spiritual quest. The significance of Buddha's story hinges on the deep psychological disconnect he felt between the lap of luxury and the face of suffering.

Chapter 4

The Mythic Past

In This Chapter

- ◆ The importance of Buddha's past lives
- ◆ Jataka Tales (Birth Stories) and Aesop's Fables
- ◆ Overview of the Bodhisattva's Ten Perfections
- ◆ Ten tales illustrating the Perfections

All sentient beings cycle through many, many lifetimes. That's what people of India in Buddha's day thought. And that's what Buddhists think today. So to really get a handle on the life of Buddha—from a traditional Buddhist point of view—we should begin with his past lives!

Buddha told stories about his past lives at about the same time Aesop wandered around Greece telling fables. And both men's tales were remarkably similar. The stories told by Buddha and Aesop weave animal characters into lighthearted plots that suggest a moral. Yet a key difference between their tales is that one character (human and nonhuman) in each of Buddha's stories is presented as having been the Tathagata himself in a former life.

Enlightening Extras

The moral lessons of Aesop's Fables and the Buddhist Jataka Tales often are comparable. Typically Aesop ends with a moral, whereas Buddha emphasizes one of the ten perfections. For example:

Aesop: Greed often overextends itself.

Buddha: Generosity.

Aesop: Revenge will hurt the one who avenges.

Buddha: Virtue.

Aesop: Whatever you do, do with all your might.

Buddha: Determination.

Aesop: A person cannot be a friend if you don't know whether or not to trust him.

Buddha: Friendliness.

Buddhist tradition claims that on the "first watch" of the full moon night of his enlightenment, Siddhartha recalled fine details of his numerous past lifetimes, including name, diet, and manner of death. Thus, after enlightenment Buddha often told stories about his former lives. These ranged back into the mythic past, well beyond any historical record. The stories were of great interest to Buddha's audience, because some of them appeared as characters in the tales. You see, the Bodhisattva had long-long-term relationships with people he encountered later as the Buddha.

Ten Perfections

When Buddha told about his former lives, the stories typically contained a moral lesson. Each tale involved the specific virtue or set of virtues that the Bodhisattva was working to perfect in that particular circumstance. Thus, the Birth Stories, or *Jataka Tales*, were remembered as short lessons on character development. They clarified Buddha's teaching on qualities to be developed by beings seeking enlightenment and qualities to be avoided because they lead to suffering of oneself and others.

The virtues illustrated by the Jataka Tales correspond to what are known as the Ten Perfections. These are 10 positive qualities that Buddha—as various forms of "Sumedha," the Bodhisattva—developed over many lifetimes. In fact, Buddha urged everyone who sought enlightenment to work at perfecting these 10 qualities in their lives, too:

- Giving
- Virtue
- Renunciation
- Wisdom
- Effort
- Patience
- Truthfulness
- Determination
- Friendliness
- Even-mindedness

Dharma Dictionary

The stories Buddha told that referred to his past lives are called **Jataka Tales,** or Birth Stories. They were written down in the fourth century B.C.E. during the Mauryan period of Indian history but contain verses that may date back to Buddha himself, some two centuries earlier. The Jataka Tales were so highly prized that they became part of the Buddhist canon.

The Ten Perfections are qualities developed on the bodhisattva path. These perfections make a lot of sense if you consider the work that a bodhisattva strives to do—namely, working to relieve the suffering of all sentient beings and give them happiness. The bodhisattva vow is supposed to be good over many lifetimes, because all suffering beings cannot be served all at one time. To undertake the huge task of helping numerous sentient beings requires strength of character and lots of practice. That's why the bodhisattva path is called the *practice* of Ten Perfections.

When It All Started

But how far do the Jataka Tales trace back Buddha's life? To a time eons ago. It all started back in the mythic past with a brahmin named Sumedha … who was none other than Gautama Buddha in a past life. The story tells of Sumedha's inspirational encounter with the former Buddha, whose name was Dipankara.

The meeting between Brahmin Sumedha and Buddha Dipankara is the subject of the very first Jataka Tale because it provides the very raison d'etre for every story that follows. Here's the point: when the brahmin saw Buddha Dipankara, he made a firm decision to become a buddha himself. From that critical moment onward, Sumedha was a bodhisattva (Buddha-to-be). All the subsequent Jataka Tales tell us how the Bodhisattva—over many lifetimes—perfected 10 virtues that turned him into the perfectly enlightened being we know today as Gautama Buddha.

> ### Be Mindful!
>
> Jataka Tales often refer to times that are far beyond any markers of historical reckoning—such as a hundred thousand vast cycles and four immeasurable eons ago. Such huge numbers may be considered literary conventions derived from ancient India's oral tradition that were intended to mark specific events, such as when a former Buddha walked the earth, or when Siddhartha met his wife Yasodhara in their early incarnations. We call these times the "mythic past" because they are alive in the traditional imagination, but not grounded in history.

The first Jataka Tale goes like this: Buddha Dipankara was scheduled to arrive in a very ancient and wonderful city. Brahmin Sumedha was among the bystanders preparing for the Tathagata's visit. They were clearing the way and making a beautiful path. However, Buddha arrived in front of Sumedha before he could finish preparations. So Sumedha quickly threw himself down in the mud to allow Dipankara to walk upon him.

When Buddha approached to cross the path, this piercing thought shot through Sumedha's heart: "I want to become a Buddha, too." Thus, at that moment he generated bodhimind, the mind of enlightenment. That instant marked his entrance onto the path of the bodhisattva. Henceforth, Sumedha's heart was aimed toward full enlightenment for the sake of all sentient beings. And, as they say, the rest is history … or should we say sacred story (myth)?

> ### Dharma Dictionary
>
> The **Ten Perfections** are virtues that bodhisattvas cultivate to pave their way to enlightenment. Some Buddhists prefer a list of Six Perfections: generosity, virtue, patience, effort, meditation, and wisdom.

Now let's follow Sumedha's efforts to perfect the 10 key virtues on his bodhisattva path. We'll review one Jataka Tale for each of the *Ten Perfections*. Of course on this journey "Sumedha" becomes many different characters as "he" practices the bodhisattva path en route to becoming Gautama Buddha.

A Tale of Generosity: The Elephant Who Gave His Tusks

The tale of an elephant illustrates the virtue of generosity. Gautama Buddha was this elephant in a past life. And the story makes us consider our own level of generosity.

An elephant with brilliant tusks was enjoying his quiet life in a secluded area of the Himalayan foothills. One day a merchant from Varanasi was searching for valuables to sell. He got lost in the elephant's part of the forest and cried out in fear. Filled with pity, the elephant approached. Petrified of the elephant coming at him, the merchant began to run. Seeing this, the elephant stopped. And so it went. Several times the elephant approached, then stopped whenever the merchant panicked. Gradually they began to trust each other, and finally, the elephant carried the merchant to safety.

But it was not enough that the elephant saved the merchant's life. He soon returned from Varanasi to gather ivory from the grand elephant's tusks—because ivory from a live elephant is most valuable. Pretending to be poor, the merchant asked for a piece of tusk, and out of pity, the bodhisattva elephant complied. The merchant was emboldened by his success, and greed overtook him.

The merchant returned time and again asking for more tusk. And each time, the elephant patiently bowed down to allow the merchant to carve more ivory.

Eventually, the merchant hacked the ivory roots right down to the skull—all without a word of thanks.

With a display of emotion characteristic of ancient Indians, the Jataka Tale tells us that thousands of beings in other worlds who had been born as elephants empathized with the bodhisattva's pain. In retribution, the earth swallowed up the merchant. For his part, the bodhisattva's generosity paved the way for enlightenment. Buddha told this Birth Story to teach his disciples how to practice generosity, and to present the moral: ungrateful people doom themselves.

A Tale of Virtue: The Goat Who Laughed and Cried

Here's a story Buddha used to discourage the ritual killing of animals. In the tale, the Bodhisattva was a tree spirit who claimed that no benefit came from taking life for sacrifice.

One day a brahmin asked his students to prepare a goat for sacrifice. Suddenly the goat laughed and then wept. Asked why he laughed and cried, the animal replied that ages ago he was a brahmin who sacrificed a goat. "For that, I had my head cut off 499 times. I laughed because this is my last birth as a goat, and I can become human once again. I cried for you who will suffer my fate." Well, the brahmin did what you or I might do in his place! He stopped performing animal sacrifices and told his students to care for the goat.

> **Buddha Basics**
>
> Animal sacrifice was practiced in Buddha's day. But the Master strongly objected to taking the life of any being, including those sacrifices performed for religious purposes. Under the influence of Buddhists and Jains, the brahmins gradually eliminated virtually all animal sacrifices.

Yet, as is the case with all sentient beings, the force of what Buddhists call "karma" proved to be great. One day as the goat stuck out its neck to eat from a branch, lightning struck a rock, which in turn sliced its neck. The goat thus died for the five hundredth time in retribution for the goat sacrifice he made as a brahmin in the past.

A tree spirit saw the whole thing, and gave everyone this teaching on the law of cause and effect of karma:

> *People would stop taking the lives of others if they only knew the sorrowful rebirth that it brings upon themselves.*

Buddha (who had been the tree spirit) told this Jataka Tale to illustrate the importance of wholesome action. The moral of the story is this: harming others brings harm to oneself.

A Tale of Renunciation: A Single Strand of Gray

Some Jataka Tales were very personal to Buddha. This one is about his only son Rahula, and his cousin Ananda. It illustrates the virtue of renunciation, the practice of giving up *attachment* to worldly things. If the Bodhisattva hadn't perfected such renunciation, maybe today we'd be talking about King Siddhartha rather than Gautama, the Awakened One.

Makhadeva was a king of Videha who prided himself on his thick black head of hair. One day he ordered the barber, "Let me know the minute you see a gray hair on my head!" Well, the day came when the barber observed, "Sir, you have a gray hair." Hearing this, Makhadeva felt the Lord of Death had come to visit, and ordered his barber to pull the strand and place it in his hand.

> **Dharma Dictionary**
>
> **Attachment** is variously known in Buddhism as clinging, thirst, or craving. It signifies being mentally entrapped by things and ideas—most fundamentally to the idea of an independent self. Buddha taught that clinging leads to suffering.

Pondering the piece of gray, Makhadeva began sweating as if he were trapped in a burning hut. His royal clothes suddenly felt oppressive and the king told his ministers, "A great message has come to me in the form of this gray hair."

On the same day that Makhadeva's one gray hair was spotted, he took up the homeless life. And the moral of this story is this: the heedful recognize signs of impermanence and respond accordingly.

A Tale of Wisdom: The Whatnot Tree

Buddha told a Jataka Tale in which he'd been a caravan leader whose wisdom and leadership saved his group from poison and theft. It happened in northern India like this:

One day a large caravan passed through an unknown village in the midst of a forest. Tired and hungry, the travelers were enticed at the village edge by a tree full of a mango-type fruit. The fruit looked delicious and was easy to reach. But unknown to the famished travelers, this was not a mango tree. It was a "whatnot" tree with deadly fruit.

Well in advance, the caravan leader had warned his charge to first ask his advice before tasting anything they'd never eaten before. And though everyone was hungry, some followed his advice and some did not.

Bandits liked to use the whatnot tree as a trap. They'd stolen from many unwitting travelers who ate the poison fruit and collapsed. But they never got the chance to rob the Bodhisattva's caravan because he suspected that the whatnot tree would be a problem.

People asked the caravan leader how he knew the fruits were not mangos. He gave two reasons: first, the tree was easy to climb; second, the tree stood near a village. Based on these two simple observations, he reasoned that if the fruit were safe to eat, surely villagers would have already picked the tree clean.

Buddha's simple story about the virtue of wisdom shows that insight need not be cultivated only through complex philosophical reasoning about the nature of reality. It can be cultivated in simple acts of common sense. Whatever the circumstances, it's appropriate to think clearly. Hence, the moral: wise people use common sense.

> **Be Mindful!**
>
> The Jatakas contain useful cultural—even medical—information. The story of the poison whatnot tree not only warns of picking fruit from unknown trees, it also recommends vomiting out ingested poison and eating four sweet foods to refresh the taste buds: raisins, cane sugar paste, yogurt, and honey. Folk tales are like mini-encyclopedias. They contain many ideas people want to pass on to the next generation.

A Tale of Effort: Save and Invest!

This tale is interesting for the innovative message Buddha gives: save and invest! He taught people not only how to lead a virtuous life, but also how to conduct their practical affairs. This little story would have encouraged even common people to participate in the great move to a money economy in Gautama's day. You can see the kinds of goods and services Buddha's simple lay disciples might have understood. And beyond that, it contains a deeper religious message about the virtue of effort. In the story the Bodhisattva is a humble young man who became a king's advisor.

The Little Mouse

One day on his way to meet the ruler, a chief advisor saw a dead mouse by the side of the road. He remarked to his colleagues that a person could make a fortune from a dead little mouse like that. A poor young man overheard this remark and took the advisor's words to heart and quickly picked up the mouse. He hadn't gone far when a shopkeeper stopped him, saying, "My cat is quite hungry. I'll give you two copper coins for that mouse." He accepted the deal and decided to buy sweet cakes with the money.

> **Buddha Basics**
>
> Buddha recommended to house-holders a policy of investment and savings. A merchant class was growing rapidly in the Middle Ganges Basin of Buddha's day, and the Master had many lay disciples who were involved in business. He urged them to invest—but wisely—and to save a portion of their income.

Sweet cakes and water in hand, the industrious young man waited by the roadside to sell the cakes. In no time, a group of garland makers came by and gave him flowers in exchange for his goods. That evening he sold the flowers.

The budding entrepreneur made an economic decision to invest some of his money in sweet cakes and save the rest. He returned there day after day to trade with the garland makers—sweet cakes for flowers. And so, the mouse merchant continued his policy of investment and savings—buying sweet cakes with part of his money, while saving another portion.

The Growth of Wealth

One day, a storm blew branches from the king's trees all over the place. The merchant who had found the mouse offered to clean up, if the king's gardener would give him the branches. Getting the go-ahead, he asked some children playing nearby to help pick up branches in exchange for sweet cakes.

Next the king's potter came along and bought the neatly stacked wood to stoke his fires. He paid the merchant in cash along with a couple of pots. Now the young merchant had enough funds to open a little refreshment shop. So he did.

Some grass mowers came into the refreshment shop, and the merchant gave them all sweet cakes for free. Impressed by his generosity, they promised to do something in return. He replied that perhaps later on he might need their help. And sure enough, the following week when a horse dealer came into town, the merchant asked them for grass to feed the horses. (As a good businessman, he also asked the grass mowers not to sell to the horse dealer.) Thus, he got a good price for the grass.

Time passed. And one day the merchant heard that a ship had docked at port. He thought of the opportunities this might present. He bought a gold and ruby ring from a jeweler at a good price and gave the ring to the ship's captain, who greatly prized it. In turn, the captain told the passengers about the merchant's refreshment shop. When people came to the shop, the merchant took them around town to buy what they liked, for which the shopkeepers gave him a commission.

The Wealthiest Man in Town

Acting as a middleman, the merchant gradually accumulated wealth. But he never forgot the words of the king's advisor that he'd overheard many years back: a fortune could be made from a little mouse.

Moved by gratitude, the merchant presented the king's advisor with coins totaling half his wealth and gave humble thanks. The advisor asked how he became so wealthy, and the merchant related the chain of events, beginning with the wise words and a little dead mouse. He told of the cat, copper coins, sweet cakes, flowers, tree branches, potter, refreshment shop, grass, ring, and business contacts.

The advisor was so impressed with the industry of the young merchant (who was single, by the way) that he offered his daughter in marriage. And later when the old advisor passed away, the merchant became the wealthiest man in town. Thus the ruler appointed him a minister of finance.

Never forgetting his humble beginnings, the economic advisor donated his own resources to the needy and advised the ruler on the wise and beneficent use of state funds. A moral to this story highlights the virtue of effort: with ability and perseverance, great results can grow from a modest start.

> **Enlightening Extras**
>
> Gautama Buddha told Jataka Tales in which he played the role of an advisor. In fact, Buddha did advise the kings of Magadha and Kausala. In his lifetime, each monarchy changed hands as the sons of Bimbisara and Prasenajit usurped the thrones. And though Buddha had been close to the fathers, he also advised their ambitious sons on occasion—with mixed results.

A Tale of Patience: Where Does Patience Lie?

Buddha recited this Jataka to teach the benefits of patience. In the tale, the Bodhi-sattva was a brahmin boy from Varanasi whose parents left him a great inheritance. Being intent on the virtue of renunciation, he gave it away and went to live on fruits in the forest of the Himalayan foothills. After a while he went to Varanasi and spent time in the king's grove. (Gautama's audience would have been familiar with this type of activity, for in the Middle Ganges Basin of Buddha's day the sramanas were doing just this type of thing.)

One day the king's courtesans gathered around the sramana to hear some teachings as the king was resting. The king awoke and, angered at being disturbed, asked the sramana what he taught. "Patience" was the answer, so the king decided to test the Bodhisattva's patience.

The king called his executioner to torture the Bodhisattva, and afterwards the king asked again what the Bodhisattva professed. Over and over, "Patience" was the answer. This patience was not in the body, but deep within the heart.

The tale ends sadly with the Bodhisattva's passing away. And when Buddha told the story, he noted that his cousin Devadatta (who tried to kill him in real life) was the king. Patience is considered a most difficult austerity. To practice patience is tremendous spiritual work. So this Buddha story teaches that true patience is a deep-seated practice.

A Tale of Truthfulness: The Caring Fish

Truth has great power to move the hearts of living beings. It builds trust and helps clear the mind of ignorance in preparation for enlightenment—seeing reality as it is. But can a fish be truthful? In this Jataka, the Bodhisattva was a fish who knew the power of truth.

No Rain

Once there was a terrible drought in north India. The rains did not come, and both animals and people began to suffer as rivers, lakes, and especially ponds began to dry up. Everyone was frightened but the crows, for they were feasting on fish and turtles who were hanging on to their lives in the mud.

In one pond lived a large black fish, as shiny as buffed ebony. He was a good-hearted fish who had never taken the life of any being. He did not eat other fish to sustain his life, always resisting the cannibalism of his kind. Actually, he was moved deeply by the suffering of the other fish.

A Bodhisattva's Plea

The ebony fish wanted to do whatever he could to relieve others' suffering from the drought. (We can see here how even a fish can generate bodhicitta, the mind of a bodhisattva!) Moved by pity, he made a sincere plea to the rain deity, asking:

> Oh, friend who brings rain, please heed my call! Keep the rain from me and let me suffer in place of the other fish. I've never killed another fish, or any living being. What I say is true. I never wanted to hurt anyone. And now I appeal to you: please save the fish in this pond.

Rain began to fall in response to the innocent plea of the ebony fish who spoke words of sincerity and truth. He had never killed, and he truly wished to relieve the suffering of others, even at the expense of his own life. The moral of this tale highlights the virtue of truth: even a helpless creature can evoke tremendous results by speaking truth.

A Tale of Determination: The Snake with Attitude

There was once a doctor who knew how to treat snakebites. Buddha was this doctor in a former life, and what he once learned from a snake served him well all the way down to his final rebirth.

When called to the aid of a man bitten by a poisonous snake, the doctor told the relatives about two methods of treatment. One was to give medicine. The other was to have the snake suck out its own poison.

The relatives decided to find the snake and make it suck out the poison, but the snake refused. The doctor threatened to throw the snake into the fire if it did not suck out the poison, but the snake again refused. The snake said it would rather die than suck out the poison—and started slithering toward the fire.

The doctor was amazed at the strength of the snake's determination and took pity. He used medicine on the poisoned man and learned a lesson from the snake. He respected the animal for teaching him the nature of a resolute attitude and applied the snake's teaching to his own spiritual practice. He also released the snake and advised, "Go in peace. Refrain from harm." This story has a moral: determination brings respect.

A Tale of Friendliness: The Dog and the Elephant

In this Jataka Tale, the future Buddha was a minister known for his empathy with animals. The story gives us insight into the nature of friendliness—a quality that Buddhists are taught to cultivate.

The Cycle of Fear and Annoyance

Elephants and dogs do not get along ... at least that's how it is most of the time. They seem to have a naturally difficult relationship, like cats and mice. Dogs annoy elephants with their barking, and elephants scare dogs with their size. It's a vicious cycle: dogs fear the huge elephants and bark. Elephants, uneasy with the racket, chase the dogs. Elephants even attack dogs quietly minding their own business. But this friendship barrier between dogs and elephants proved not to be true in every case.

So there was a scrawny dog living near the shed of a royal elephant. When the elephant was eating, rice fell from its mouth, and the dog realized that it could get this rice while the elephant ate. The skinny dog became very fine looking over time, because he would eat nowhere else. And the elephant gradually got used to having the dog around. Losing fear, the dog did not bark much, and the elephant was not annoyed.

A Slow Friendship

Gradually, the dog and elephant looked forward to their meals together. Over time, they even started playing with each other with true fondness. But one day the elephant keeper sold the dog to a passer-by who was attracted by his healthy appearance and good nature. Having suddenly lost his friend, the elephant became grief stricken. Though he was not ill, the royal animal's sadness greatly affected him.

Be Mindful!

Though the Jataka Tales appear simple and lighthearted, they often contain deep psychological truths—even about animals! This tale of friendship speaks of an elephant's grief when its dog friend was sold. This may seem like an exaggeration, but modern research now confirms that elephants are very social animals. In *The Astonishing Elephant*, Shana Alexander says that elephants appear to grieve and sometimes refuse to leave a dead companion. She goes on to say that people have reported seeing elephants weep.

The king's minister was summoned to see the royal elephant because he empathized deeply with animals. Seeing the royal elephant grieving, he asked the keeper whether the elephant had lost a close friend. Learning that the elephant had spent much time with a stray dog, the minister reported to the king that because friendship is so precious his elephant was grieved at the loss of his companion.

The king ordered the dog to be found and brought back to his sad elephant. Once reunited, both animals were overjoyed. The royal elephant began to eat again, and the minister was rewarded for his insight. The moral of this tale highlights the virtue of friendliness: even natural enemies can become best friends.

A Tale of Even-Mindedness: The Punishing Ascetic Life

This story is about the extremes of ascetic life. Bodhisattva Sumedha wished to experience the life of renunciation under a teacher who was not a buddha. In Gautama's day there were groups of wandering seekers who fit the description in this Jataka, though the action here is set in a time 99 eons ago.

Once upon a time there was a spiritual seeker who joined a band of naked ascetics. He took up the solitary life of a forest dweller, wore only dust for cover, and ate what the forest would provide. Avoiding human company, he chose to spend the coldest, wettest, and hottest times in open air, exposed to the elements without protection of the forest. But when conditions were more severe in the thicket, he would stay there. The renunciate performed all this voluntary hardship for the sake of penance—for he was intent on gaining spiritual progress.

The naked ascetic took upon himself hardships to perfect even-mindedness—not hankering after ease of life. But the four practices of penance brought him to the brink of death, and he saw the signs of hell rise up. Seeing this, the future Buddha judged his extreme asceticism, poverty, rejection of comfort, and solitude to be a mistaken path. He thereby abandoned it. Perhaps these harsh practices contradicted even-mindedness because they were so extreme. A moral this story suggests is to avoid extremes in the search for balance.

The Bodhisattva Path

The Buddhist tradition is rich with teachings on the perfections that mark out the bodhisattva path. And whether they are named as Six or Ten Perfections, these virtues give people a clear idea of what a person should do to become helpful to sentient beings.

The 10 virtues called the Perfections involve complementary spiritual practices. Here's one way to think of how they reinforce each other on the path to enlightenment:

- A bodhisattva deepens his or her willingness to serve other beings through practicing generosity.

- Renunciation of worldly desires lets generosity flourish.

- It takes determination and perseverance to dedicate numerous lifetimes for the sake of sentient beings.

- For this long-term project, the bodhisattva needs patience to keep from getting discouraged.

- Friendliness and truthfulness inspire trust ... and with trust the Buddha-to-be is in a better position to serve.

- To see clearly what others need requires wisdom, and a life of virtue allows wisdom to grow.

- A bodhisattva needs even-mindedness to care about all beings ... without playing favorites.

The hallmark of a Buddha-to-be is not to play favorites. Bodhisattvas have concern for the suffering of all sentient beings, without exception. Thus, even-mindedness circles back up to generosity. The Ten Perfections outline a powerful spiritual path where one virtue beautifies and enhances another.

The Least You Need to Know

- Staying true to Buddhist tradition, an account of Buddha's biography should begin with stories about his past lives as a bodhisattva who was reborn in both human and nonhuman forms in what we can call the mythic past.

- People can appreciate Buddhist Jataka Tales, or Birth Stories, for their cultural and moral value, even when they are not accepted as true stories of Buddha's past lives.

- The Ten Perfections provide the framework for the spiritual path tread by bodhisattvas who strive toward enlightenment for the sake of all sentient beings.

- In the Theravada Buddhist canon, the Jataka Tales are organized according to the 10 key virtues, namely generosity, virtue, renunciation, wisdom, effort, patience, truthfulness, determination, friendliness, and even-mindedness.

5

Birth of a Buddha-to-Be

In This Chapter

- The Bodhisattva's biological lineage as a Sakyan
- Gautama's spiritual lineage as a buddha
- A birth tale that combines myth and history
- Ambiguous predictions about the infant Siddhartha
- Buddha's mother dies and father worries

Eons ago the ascetic Sumedha decided to travel the path to enlightenment because he was inspired upon seeing the former Buddha Dipankara. At the moment he made that wish, Sumedha became a bodhisattva, and began a spiritual path that led through various rebirths until he attained buddhahood. The Bodhisattva experienced many lifetimes as human and nonhuman beings, practicing the Ten Perfections—patience, giving, morality, and so on. Finally, he undertook enough moral and mental training to require only a single additional lifetime to attain the goal of awakening from the dream of cyclic existence.

In what would be his last lifetime, the Bodhisattva was reborn as the son of two northern Indian nobles: Maya Devi and her husband Suddhodana, chieftain of the Sakya clan. The Buddhist scriptures speak of the Bodhisattva's decision to take rebirth in northern India, as many buddhas before him had done. He would become one in a long line of buddhas whose job was to show people how to wake up from the round of rebirths and become free from suffering.

The Bodhisattva was of the Gautama family, within the Sakya clan. He was often called by the name Siddhartha—at least according to later texts. Little is known about the Bodhisattva's birth from the Buddhist scriptures. But the tradition filled in the gaps with some extraordinary stories. These typical creations of the human mythic imagination have great meaning for those who follow a Buddhist spiritual practice.

A Being of Two Lineages: Biological and Spiritual

We have to consider Buddha's background in two ways: biological and spiritual. The biological *lineage* got him a place in history: he is Sakyamuni, sage of the Sakya clan. But the spiritual lineage best describes his contribution to the history of religious ideas: he is an awakened one who showed the way to transcend all history by overcoming rebirth.

> ### Dharma Dictionary
>
> A **lineage** is a group of kin that subscribes to a formal system of authority, headed by a representative male for ritual and political affairs. Families in the group extend back through one parent to an historic or mythic founding ancestor. The basic unit is a three to four generation family. Several family lines can band together to form a clan. Buddha was from Ikshavaku's Solar lineage, Sakya clan, and Gautama family.

Before Siddhartha was enlightened, he described his background to King Bimbisara: "Up in the Himalayan foothills is a territory where the Kausala people live. They are of the Solar lineage, and Sakya clan. It's from them I went forth into homelessness."

After he was enlightened, Gautama told his father he was no longer a Sakyan. When Suddhodana saw his son begging in the streets upon returning to Kapilavastu after awakening, he was angered, saying no one of the Sakya tribe begs. The new Buddha replied, "My lineage is the Buddha lineage ... and all buddhas go for alms."

Awakening to reality as it is—tathata—transformed Siddhartha into the Tathagata—one who goes just so. He was no longer operating under the assumptions about reality that most people harbor. He no longer belonged to any worldly lineage.

The Biological Lineage

Buddha's ancestral line was headed by King Ikshavaku. The Ikshavaku dynasty is one of two major Aryan descended groups of traditional India whose lines fan out to cover northern India. The Ikshavaku line claims descent from the sun; the other line (Aila line) claims descent from the moon. Ancestors of King Ikshavaku settled in Ayodhya, Videha, and Vaisali. The Sakyan capital of Kapilavastu is in the area of ancient Videha.

King Ikshavaku had five sons and he loved them all. But he seemed to care most for the youngest, who was born of his favorite queen. So the king sent the oldest four to find fertile land for settlement and kept the youngest at home to lead the clan. These men became part of a larger migration from Kasi northward and westward toward the Himalayan Mountains. The Koliya and Licchavi clan are said to have come from similar beginnings. You'll be hearing about them, too, later on.

Enlightening Extras

King Ikshavaku was the eldest son of Manu—the primeval man saved from a great flood ... like Noah! All legitimate kshatriyas are traced to King Ikshavaku, including Rama and Buddha. The Ramayana epic tells of Rama, an ancient king of Ayodhya who is the ancestor of the rulers of Kausala. Hindus see Rama as an incarnation of the god Vishnu. Hindus also count Buddha among Vishnu's incarnations.

The "Clever Ones" of Kapilavastu

King Ikshavaku's four sons moved northward to the Himalayan foothills in search of land suitable for settlement. On the way, the princes met a sage named Kapila on the bank of the Bhagirathi River, who advised them to marry their sisters who'd been born from different mothers. Kapila then sprinkled golden sand mixed with water by a pond in a grove of saka trees.

Following the sage Kapila's advice, Ikshavaku's four sons continued the patriarch's family line through their sisters, and founded a new town, which they called Kapila's farm or vastu. When King Ikshavaku heard about the new settlement, he was pleased and exclaimed, "My sons are *sakya* (clever)." Thus, the descendents of the four Ikshavaku princes became known as the Sakyans of Kapilavastu.

Cross-Cousin Marriages

Only one of Ikshavaku's elder sons survived. So to keep their clan going, the Sakyans began to intermarry with their cousins from the neighboring Koliya clan. Sakyas men married Koliyan, and their sisters were offered to Koliyan men. And through the cross-cousin system, down the generations a male named Suddhodana was born into the Gautama family of the Sakya clan. We're going to hear a lot about Suddhodana. He would become Buddha's father.

Suddhodana took two daughters of a Koliyan raja as his brides: Maha Prajapati and Maya Devi. Meanwhile, Suddhodana's sister Pamita married one of the Koliyan chief's sons. Siddhartha was the product of Suddhodana's marriage to Maya Devi. And Yasodhara, Siddhartha's future wife, was born of Pamita and the Koliyan prince.

> ### Dharma Dictionary
>
> The term **raja**, a member of the ruling class, initially meant leader in battle or tribal chieftain. It changes meaning to signify a protector of settlements, or raja in chief. Gradually the term was associated with prosperity and fertility—and even with the gods. The great Asoka Maurya in the third century B.C.E. called himself raja. The term *maharaja*, great king, came into use during the Gupta Empire (c. 320–550 C.E.)—along with *rajatiraga*, king of kings, which imitated Persian royalty.

The Gautama Family

At the time of Siddhartha's birth, his father was the head raja of the Sakya clan. Suddhodana lead the government of their modest territory from Kapilavastu, its capital. The Sakyan country was just one of several republics in the Middle Ganges Basin. And being chieftain of such a republic meant that Suddhodana ruled in conjunction with an assembly of Sakya householders who gathered in assembly halls to discuss political matters.

Aside from the handful of democratically run republics in the Middle Ganges Basin, two neighboring territories were considered "great" countries: Kausala and Magadha. Their leaders were monarchs. So in our story of Buddha's life, we'll call Siddhartha's father a raja, and save the word king for Prasenajit of Kausala, Bimbisara of Magadha, and the sons who succeeded them in Buddha's lifetime—Virudhaka and Ajatasatru.

The Bodhisattva's Spiritual Lineage

Once awakened, Gautama spoke of himself as a tathagata. He'd gone the way of the former buddhas in seeing tathata. After waking up to the nature of reality, he acted in the manner of every previous buddha. These are the samyak-sambuddhas (perfectly fulfilled buddhas) whose sole purpose for living is to reintroduce the age-old Buddha-dharma after it has been lost in the world. Because Sumedha the bodhisattva wanted to become such a samyak-sambuddha like Dipankara, he had to wait to be reborn until beings in our world had forgotten the Buddha-dharma. This means that even after becoming spiritually prepared to come into the world, the Bodhisattva stayed in Tushita Heaven until the time was ripe.

Buddha Basics

Tushita Heaven is the fourth heaven in Indian cosmology—below the Abodes of Brahma and above the Heaven of the Thirty-Three Devas. It's called tushita or "contented" because gods there are not plagued with desire—although it is within the desire realm of samsara. The Bodhisattva was in Tushita Heaven before he was conceived in Maya Devi's womb, and the future Buddha Maitreya is there now. Humans (Maya Devi, for example) sometimes are reborn in Tushita Heaven due to their own virtue.

Buddhas reintroduce the age-old Buddha-dharma through teachings of body, speech, and mind. This means by verbal teaching, by silence and psychic communication, and by gestures and the very example of their life stories. Thus Gautama delivered discourses to assemblies of gods and men; gave personal counsel to people in need of guidance in the beginning, middle, and final phases of their spiritual development; and showed through gestures the proper manner of living.

A buddha's teachings of speech and mind boil down to the Four Great Facts, which in some way encompass the dharma. Physical gestures indicate points of dharma, and biographical details tend to exemplify the path to enlightenment. Thus, for example, all buddhas collect alms, meditate, and pass into final nirvana with a peaceful attitude. Details of the conception and birth are also included in the acts of every tathagata, according to the universal law.

Buddha Basics

The two branches of Buddhism find different significance in the Bodhisattva's life as Gautama. Theravadins suppose that Gautama attained enlightenment in India in the sixth century B.C.E. as the stories portray. Mahayanists suppose that the Bodhisattva was already enlightened in Tushita Heaven but used his life as Gautama to demonstrate for others the path to awakening. Despite these differences, Theravadins and Mahayanists both include miraculous events in the story of Buddha's birth.

The Unusual Birth

Tradition has it that all bodhisattvas wait in Tushita Heaven for the appropriate time to descend for their final rebirths—in which they reintroduce the dharma to the world. According to a universal rule, these events occur as follows:

- When the bodhisattva descends from Tushita Heaven, the earth quakes, and brilliant light shines through the atmosphere.

- The bodhisattva's mother experiences delight, and becomes virtuous—killing nothing, refraining from drink, lies, sensual thoughts toward a man, and so on.

- Both mother and child are protected from harm, and the bodhisattva is carried without sickness or fatigue.

- The bodhisattva's mother can see the fully-formed baby in her womb as a colored thread through a jeweled bead, is pregnant for exactly 10 months, gives birth standing up, dies 7 days after the birth, and is reborn in Tushita Heaven.

- The bodhisattva is born clean from the mother's right side, does not touch the earth, is welcomed first by devas, then humans, and takes seven steps announcing this as the final birth.

- At the birth two streams of water (cold and warm) emerge for the ceremonial purpose of bathing both the bodhisattva and the mother.

The Descent from Tushita Heaven

When the Bodhisattva was waiting to take birth from Tushita Heaven, he was known as a worldly deva named Svetaketu. And before taking birth, Svetaketu made four investigations to find suitable circumstances. Buddhist tradition says that all future buddhas do this. Examining the time, continent, country, and family, he came up with the following conclusions about the birth:

1. It had to be when human life spans were not too long or short. That's our time.

2. It had to be on Jambudvipa; i.e., the continent of the rose apple—that's India.

3. It had to be either a brahmin or kshatriya family. (The future Buddha Maitreya will be of the brahmin class.)

4. It had to be in a suitable territory—and the one in which Maya Devi lived was judged to be the best due to her very presence there.

Before leaving Tushita Heaven, Svetaketu placed his crown on the head of Maitreya, who would take over teaching the dharma there until his time came to descend in a similar manner. Then the contented heavenly beings decided that the Bodhisattva should descend in the form of a white elephant with six tusks. In his culture, the albino elephant was—and is—a royal treasure and symbol of power. Maya Devi dreamed of this elephant at the point of conceiving the child.

Be Mindful!

A number of historical details of Gautama's life are known and have been preserved in the midst of extraordinary claims regarding his birth—such as descending from Tushita Heaven. Yet this event—though extraordinary—does not hold the same connotations of uniqueness that a divine incarnation has in the context of Christianity, for example. The idea of the Bodhisattva's incarnation is very suited to the context of India's culture, which takes rebirth as a matter of course.

Events in Lumbini Garden

Maya Devi was delighted, protected, and energetic in her pregnancy as is every woman who bears a future buddha—according to a universal law in which people of ancient India believed. And when the time came for his delivery, she set off for her home. It was the custom among her people to have a child under the care of her family of origin. On the way there, however, she rested in the Lumbini Garden, and the child was born from her right side as she was standing with her right hand upstretched, holding the branch of a tree. Although Buddhist sources don't agree on whether it was an asoka, plaksa, sala, or pipal tree, all these trees play a key role in Buddha's life.

According to universal law, the child was born clean. Then he and his mother were ceremonially bathed by the warm and cool streams of water that spontaneously appear as nature's way of caring for them. Devas helped wherever needed. The Bodhisattva then took seven steps

Enlightening Extras

The tree is a powerful symbol in world religions. The Hindu god Vishnu was born under a pipal tree ... so the faithful can make offerings to the tree instead of Vishnu's image. African legends speak of the baobab that wanted to be the most beautiful of all trees and so put its head into the ground and reached its roots upward toward heaven. The Norse world tree is Yggdrasil, the giant ash that extends throughout all the worlds.

and announced that this was his last birth. Lotuses cushioned his feet, and trees blossomed throughout Lumbini Garden.

We can't help but notice how the basic fact of Buddha's birth got embellished in Buddhist literature. But the interweaving of history and sacred story makes the portrayal rich and meaningful. For instance, we see the lush and dynamic presence of nature in Lumbini Garden. And this sympathy between the Bodhisattva and nature provides a basis for Buddhist environmentalism in our own day.

The Boy Has Two Fates ... or Not!

Maya Devi's party made their way back to the palace at Kapilavastu after the Bodhisattva's birth. According to ancient rites, brahmins were brought in to predict the child's future. Raja Suddhodana wished to determine the course of life his son would take—and had high hopes that the child would become a kshatriya, even more powerful than himself. These hopes were nourished by the excellent forecast made by the diviners. The child had the marks on his body of a great being ... and all the brahmins agreed that the boy would become a dharmacakrin. But the meaning of that was ambiguous.

> **Buddha Basics**
>
> A dharmacakrin is a great person who turns the Wheel (cakra) of Law (dharma). Such a person can turn the wheel of political law as a universal monarch or spiritual law as a world savior. A great person is recognized by 32 major and 80 minor physical traits. Diviners saw these marks on the infant Bodhisattva's body, and they were later used in Buddhist iconography.

All but one of the brahmin diviners held up two fingers to signify that Suddhodana's son had two possible fates: he could become a great king who masters the law, or he could become a great religious leader. Only Kaundinya, the youngest brahmin, saw clearly that the boy would choose the latter route—so he held up one finger. Moreover, Kaundinya fully expected that if he lived long enough, he could actually become the boy's disciple in the future. Perhaps this brahmin was able to see the future most clearly; he actually did spend years with Suddhodana's son in the future. And, in fact, Kaundinya became the first of Buddha's disciples to attain arhatship.

The other brahmins who predicted the future of Suddhodana's son were too old to expect to become his disciples—should he choose the path of religion. Instead, they urged their sons to keep an eye on Siddhartha and become his disciples if he rejected the kshatriya's life. In fact, Buddhist scriptures identify Gautama's five earliest disciples as Kaundinya, and four sons of these brahmins: Asvajit, Vashpa, Mahanama, and Bhadrika.

Signs of Greatness

According to an ancient Brahmanical tradition, people of superior standing have marks on their bodies. A list of 32 major marks and 80 minor marks was given in the traditional manuals. And the diviners who came to Kapilavastu to view Suddhodana's son were looking for these signs of greatness on the infant's body. And seeing the marks of a great person on him, they predicted that the baby would be a Dharmacakrin. (Later tradition calls the baby Siddhartha, or One Whose Goal Is Attained, because he did become a Dharmacakrin.) The physical traits they found on the Bodhisattva included these features:

- **Feet:** The impression of a wheel with a thousand spokes on the bottom. Pliant and straight with full heels, arched insteps, and webbed toes of uniform length.

- **Arms:** Long, slender, webbed fingers, and long arms reaching past the knees, with hands whose veins don't show. Nails are convex, smooth, and the color of copper.

- **Eyes and nose:** Deep blue eyes with lashes like a royal bull, and right curl of silver hair between eyebrows. Pointed nose.

- **Hair and skin:** Each body hair separate, ascending and curling on soft gold-colored skin that emanates a radiant aura 10 feet around, and a fleshy protuberance on top of the head. Born with black hair.

- **Teeth:** Forty even, close-set teeth with four pure-white canines, and a lionlike bottom jaw.

The brahmin diviners were not the only ones to recognize signs of greatness on the raja's son. An aged sage named Asita, who lived up in the Himalayan Mountains, realized it first. It so happened that one day the thought came to Asita: "An extraordinary person has been born. The child is in Kapilavastu." And in response to this intuition, Asita descended from his mountain retreat to the Sakyan capital by magical means. Then he appeared on foot in front of Suddhodana's palace gates. At the sage's request, Suddhodana delivered the baby to Asita. Upon seeing Siddhartha, the sage sighed deeply and began to shed tears. Asita assured Suddhodana that he had not foreseen anything tragic in the son's future. He was only grieved to realize that he would not live long enough to see this child realize his destiny as a great religious teacher.

> ### Be Mindful!
>
> It's hard to distinguish between history and symbol in Buddha's biography, which contains many extraordinary episodes. But those who appreciate India's sophisticated meditative tradition may take as fact what seems like fantasy. For instance, the sage Asita realized from his place in the mountains that a special infant was staying in Kapilavastu. According to yoga psychology, Asita could have discovered this fact by using the divine eye. That is, if Asita concentrated his mind in a particular way, things would appear to him even from a great distance.

Nature's Balance: Elation and Grief

Raja Suddhodana must have been encouraged by all the predictions that his newborn son was a great person. But the universe seems to maintain a kind of balance, where possession of the exceedingly great calls for some sacrifice. Any elation growing in the heart of the Bodhisattva's father was tempered by a double grief.

Suddhodana grieved because his beloved wife Maya Devi died seven days after giving birth to their son. And having lost Maya Devi, Suddhodana worried that he'd also lose his son, the fruit of their union … not through death but to the religious life.

Suddhodana was married to both Maya Devi and her elder sister Maha Prajapati. Now that Maya Devi had died from complications in childbirth, her elder sister would care for the child. And though Siddhartha was in good hands, the family undoubtedly grieved deeply over the death of Maya Devi. For her part, Maya Devi went the way of every mother who bears a bodhisattva in the final rebirth. One week after giving birth, she ascended to Tushita Heaven. Maya Devi would have to wait about 35 years before her son would come by meditation to Tushita Heaven to tell her about the dharma he discovered. But according to Indian cosmology, the time would have seemed much shorter to her.

> ### Enlightening Extras
>
> Time on Earth does not proceed at the same rate as time in other realms of existence, according to Indian cosmology. This Mahayana Buddhist story about two brother-philosophers illustrates the concept: Vasubandhu died after promising to tell Asanga if he saw Maitreya in Tushita Heaven. He contacted Asanga three Earth years later, but claimed he'd just had time to hear one discourse from Maitreya. This conforms to Einstein's "twins" thought experiment on special relativity: one twin can take a space voyage (moving closer to the speed of light) and return to Earth relatively younger than the twin who stayed put.

Raja Suddhodana began to do everything he could to assure that Siddhartha would have a life of pleasure … and follow in his footsteps. He figured that a life free of difficulty would prevent Siddhartha from souring on the kshatriya's path. Suddhodana was dedicated to having his son become a political Dharmacakrin—with no reason whatsoever to leave home and adopt the life of a religious man. And for a while he did succeed.

The Least You Need to Know

- Buddha's father, Suddhodana, was raja (chieftain) of the small Sakyan republic in the Himalayan foothills, whose capital was Kapilavastu.

- Many extraordinary events are mixed into the historical account of Buddha's birth. But in the context of India's culture, these are not all to be discounted as false elaborations.

- Buddha was the son of the Sakyan chief Suddhodana and Maya Devi. Maya Devi died seven days after giving birth, and her sister Maha Prajapati (Suddhodana's second wife) raised the child.

- Shortly after Siddhartha was born, the sage Asita and several brahmins predicted (on the basis of bodily marks) that Siddhartha would become a Dharmacakrin. But it wasn't clear to everyone which Wheel of Law he would turn—political or spiritual.

Chapter 6

In the Lap of Luxury

In This Chapter

- ◆ The difference between rajas and kings
- ◆ Kshatriyas do more than fight
- ◆ The young Siddhartha's personality
- ◆ The education of a prince
- ◆ Siddhartha marries Yasodhara

Siddhartha grew up in the lap of luxury. As a wealthy young man of nobility in the Middle Ganges Basin, he was raised without material wants. At least, he had the best that could be offered by his father as head chieftain of a noble clan living in the Himalayan foothills. Siddhartha was especially well treated because Suddhodana wanted him to stay content with the kshatriya's lifestyle. The disconcerting prediction that Siddhartha might quit worldly life to become a spiritual leader had bugged the father since Siddhartha was born. But Suddhodana was clever and created many incentives designed to assure that his son would tow the line.

According to cultural standards of the times, Siddhartha was exposed to five standard sources of entertainment to gratify his senses: dancing, singing, instrumental performances, drumming, and women. These were to bind him to the world so that he'd fulfill his promise as a great political

Dharmacakrin. To further satisfy the prince, he was married to a woman of his choice. Her name was Yasodhara, and she bore him one son, Rahula.

The prince was educated in the manner of a kshatriya nobleman in subjects that were academic, practical, and martial. Some kshatriyas figured that Siddhartha was pampered excessively, making him soft, but things seemed to go according to plan for nearly the first three decades of Siddhartha's life.

Be Mindful!

Siddhartha happened to be born into one of the more modest clans in the Middle Ganges Basin. His Sakya clan had a raja (chieftain) whose power was shared among the elite clan members from each family. Probably in the sixth century B.C.E., the position of Sakyan raja was a rotating post. But as accounts of Buddha's life became elaborated, they implied that Siddhartha would inherit his father's role instead of just being elected.

Kshatriyas on the Battlefield ... or Is That on the Field?

Siddhartha can be called a prince. But really, it's best to identify him as a *kshatriya*. What did it mean to be a kshatriya? Well ... in Gautama's day, the term kshatriya referred more and more to members of the most powerful *rajanya* lineages, which in the old days had produced men with skill in battle. In Sanskrit, kshatra means power. So the most excellent rajanya warriors who gradually exercised more power in their territories were called kshatriyas. Eventually, the new rulers of northern Indian society came from the most powerful kshatriya clans.

Dharma Dictionary

A **kshatriya** is a member of the warrior, ruling class of ancient India. In the Middle Ganges Basin of Buddha's day, to be a kshatriya meant to be a nobleman. The most powerful kshatriyas were not simply warriors of the old days. Those ancient Aryan warriors were known as **rajanyas**. By contrast, the kshatriyas were the monarchs and elite rulers of the janapadas, who became deeply involved in the economic life of the territories. Over time, not all Indian monarchs were kshatriyas; but as a rule, they were expected to come from a strong kshatriya line.

As the raja of a relatively small territory, Siddhartha's father Suddhodana knew that only an increase in wealth would preserve the status of the Sakyan republic. So he was involved in promoting agricultural prosperity. Details in Buddha's biography reflect cultural slivers indicating that "warrior" kshatriyas were involved in their rural economy.

◆ Mr. Pure Rice. The names of people tell us a lot about the culture from which they come. Siddhartha's father's name Suddhodana means "pure rice." And indeed, the Sakya clan was involved in rice agriculture.

◆ Ruler plowed first. As the Sakyans' head chieftain, Suddhodana was obliged to initiate the plowing season at the end of summer. He drove a pair of decorated oxen, using a plow embellished with red gold. His ministers followed, driving oxen with plows decorated in silver. These acts had ritual significance: if the ruler plowed first, a good crop of rice was assured.

◆ Kapila's farm. The Sakyan plowing festival was held outside their capital known as Kapilavastu, or Kapila's farm (vastu = farm).

◆ The iron plow. The plow was the fruit of a relatively new iron technology in the Middle Ganges Basin. It spurred the growth of agrarian communities such as the one centered around Kapilavastu.

Buddha Basics

As a child Siddhartha had many nurses. Remember, his mom died when he was only seven days old. But his needs seem to have been met with loving-kindness. His mom's sister Maha Prajapati and a whole cadre of nurses saw to his comfort until the age of seven. As an infant, he probably had several nurses for each basic routine of feeding, bathing, carrying, and amusing him. After age seven, Siddhartha was entrusted into the hands of men for his formal education.

A Kshatriya's Lessons

Siddhartha was under women's care for the first seven years of his life. His aunt suckled him, and a large number of nurses looked to his needs. But at age seven—as was typical of a noble youth's training—his education became the responsibility of male teachers. The Bodhisattva was provided with the best education available for a raja's son. He did intellectual work, learned practical skills, and trained in India's martial arts. The prince's education was designed to prepare him to fulfill the responsibilities of a kshatriya.

Siddhartha was not a brahmin, so his education did not focus on religious studies. Rather, his education was to give him all the martial skills to become an effective warrior chieftain. Yet some people thought that Suddhodana sheltered him excessively exposing him insufficiently to the rigors of martial training.

The prince's academic subjects included grammar, languages, and arithmetic. Four hundred plus years later, Gandhara artists showed the Bodhisattva holding a reed in his right hand for writing, with a slate tablet on his knees. Some carved a few letters in the Aramaic script used by Persian scribes of Cyrus the Great to indicate Siddhartha's wide learning.

The particular training of a kshatriya included wrestling; horse riding; chariot racing; archery; and wielding the sword, lance, elephant goad, and discus. Siddhartha would have to show mastery of these skills in contests designed to prove his worthiness for marriage.

The Bodhisattva also developed practical arts and crafts skills as part of his education. Indeed, after his flight from Kapilavastu some two decades later, Siddhartha knew how to fashion himself an alms bowl made of forest leaves. Making leaf bowls is a craft known to Indian women to the present day. It was this handcrafted begging bowl that Siddhartha carried with him into Rajagriha for gathering alms.

Who Gets the Goose?

The Sakyan community took the education of their youth seriously. So Siddhartha got practical as well as formal training. The story of the royal goose is an example of the practical training in ethics, law, and conflict resolution that Siddhartha received as a youth. This happened when Siddhartha and his cousin Devadatta were about 12 years old.

One day the two princes, Devadatta and Siddhartha, were practicing their archery. Devadatta shot at a royal goose, and it landed near the spot where Siddhartha stood. The tenderhearted Bodhisattva picked up the animal whose wing was injured and wrapped it in a piece of his fine garment. He coddled the bird, wanting to heal it. But Devadatta wished to take possession of the bird, claiming it was rightfully his. Because Siddhartha found the bird, he thought he had the rights to it.

The two boys couldn't settle their argument. Siddhartha wouldn't give up the bird. Devadatta wouldn't stop trying to take it. This dispute between the boys caught the attention of some elders who decided to teach the two princes a lesson in governance and law. Seeing the dispute as a test case to train the little kshatriyas' legal and negotiating skills, they set up a small tribunal. The boys were made to argue their case, and the elders argued it as well. At last a judgment came out in Siddhartha's favor: a life belongs to one who would save it.

The story of the swan shows Siddhartha's love of animals. It also gives a premonition of the troubled relationship he'd have with Devadatta, who was a cousin on his mother's side. You'll hear more about Devadatta later. (See Chapter 12.) But for now, let's see where Siddhartha spent his time.

Pleasures Galore

As Siddhartha moved into adolescence, his father had three pleasure palaces built for the young man—one for each of northern India's seasons. That is … one for the cold season, one for the hot season, and one for the rainy season. They were built using materials most suited to the season—for example, plenty of cool marble for summer. Each had ponds with flowers, such as lotuses and lilies. These were well equipped with materials and personnel to make it comfortable. Especially when Suddhodana felt the threat of his son becoming disenchanted with the noble life, he and his wife Maha Prajapati would encourage the dancing girls to make extra effort to please the prince.

> **Buddha Basics**
>
> As a young man Siddhartha received a residence for each of the three seasons—winter, summer, and monsoon. Later, after renouncing the world, Buddha's communities of monks and nuns would come to have a residence for one of these seasons—the monsoon. Though the renunciates would often sleep under trees, or in caves, the Tathagata accepted the idea of having a temporary residence during the rains. In this, he carried on the rhythms of life he'd known as a kshatriya prince.

Music and Dancing Girls

As Siddhartha was growing up, most women in northern Indian culture were supported by their fathers in youth, husbands through adulthood, and children if widowed. Normally only very poor women worked outside the home. So Siddhartha didn't have much chance to interact with the women who lived regular lives, day in and day out. But he was well known as the son of the Sakyan chieftain. Some say the prince performed his martial skills so impressively that many Sakyan elders sent one woman each from their families to become part of his harem.

Living in the lap of luxury, Prince Siddhartha would have been kept comfortable by his harem women. They played wind, stringed, and percussion instruments. So he was entertained with the sound of cymbals, lutes, flutes, and drums. Along with the music came dancing and singing—probably performed gracefully on large woolen carpets. The job of these women was to make life pleasant for Prince Siddhartha. And Suddhodana was on their side. The raja wanted his son to be enthralled with the kshatriya life so that he could bring greatness and power to the Sakyan lineage.

To a Courtesan's Credit

As a wealthy nobleman, Siddhartha would have had access to courtesans. And in Buddha's day, it was not unusual for wealthy laymen to visit courtesans. But historians don't know the extent of Siddhartha's relationships with women when he was a prince living in Kapilavastu. After his enlightenment, Buddha taught that a man goes against his moral practice by sleeping with courtesans and the women who were normally off limits: girls under the authority of parents, siblings, or relations, married women, marriageable women, and nuns. But how and when Gautama formed that opinion about courtesans is unclear.

> **Enlightening Extras**
>
> Prostitution was one of the service professions that grew up in Buddha's northern India as a consequence of urbanization. Within the profession, a common prostitute (vesi or vesiya) was distinguished from a courtesan (ganika). Ganikas were high-class women who achieved a special status in the culture through their artistic accomplishments. The ganika of ancient Indian was not unlike the Japanese geisha or the ancient Greek haetera.

In ancient India, courtesans made up a special class of women who were supported by wealthy men and upper-class nobles of the court. The Licchavi clan even instituted a special office for the courtesan. And they sometimes were called beautifiers of cities, because a city became more resplendent through a courtesan's loveliness and talent. The foremost example of a courtesan in Buddha's life story is Amrapali who lived in the Licchavi city of Vaisali. She donated a mango grove to the Tathagata for his renunciate sangha. And later in life, she actually joined the community of nuns. (See Chapter 18.)

Those who transmitted Buddha's words underplayed the subject of their Teacher's relationships with women. Perhaps those details seemed irrelevant, or perhaps Buddha spoke little about his personal life as a raja's son in Kapilavastu. Clearly, Buddha had positive interactions with members of the opposite sex after the sanghas of laywomen and nuns were established. But with respect to women in Siddhartha's life as a wealthy kshatriya, much remains a mystery to historians.

Siddhartha, You Need to Marry!

A kshatriya male should have a bride. A king or high chieftain should certainly have a son, and he was entitled to take what measures were necessary to secure his lineage. So for the sake of the family line—and for personal reasons—it was not uncommon for the elite kshatriyas to have more than one wife. Kausala's King Prasenajit and Madagha's King Bimbisara had a number of wives. And even a lesser ruler such as Siddhartha's father married two sisters from the neighboring Koliya clan. But the question of whether Siddhartha had more than one wife is unresolved. Typically, Gautama is presented as having had just one wife, whose name is given as Yasodhara.

When Siddhartha was 16 or 17 years old, Raja Suddhodana thought it was time for his son to marry. So he set to find a bride for the prince. Intermarriage between the Sakyans and Koliyans traced back several generations. So it's not surprising that Suddhodana looked to the family of his own wives to find his son a mate. In fact, his wives' brother had two kids: Devadatta and Yasodhara. Their mother was Suddhodana's sister Pamita. And this Yasodhara would become Siddhartha's wife. But it was not as simple as the raja choosing a wife for his son. The prince had to be consulted.

All in the Family

Siddhartha was asked what qualities he wished his wife to possess. After thinking on it for seven days, he came up with a list: she should be modest, kind, and truthful. She should not be frivolous. She should be pure in body, speech, and mind. She should rise before others and wait until others retire to go to sleep. And so on.

Be Mindful!

Prince Siddhartha listed numerous qualities he would look for in a wife. And the list pretty much sums up what a traditional Indian male would expect of an ideal wife. Yet one must be careful here—as always—to consider the extent to which the texts have been invested with cultural values that Gautama did not necessarily promote. For instance, Siddhartha presumably said that his wife should be young, chaste, and beautiful. At the very least, one should question whether such stereotypes actually dominated Siddhartha's thinking. Also consider that if Siddhartha were alive today, he might express a different cultural opinion.

Suddhodana remarked that his son had unwittingly described his own mother, whom Siddhartha never knew. Then the raja sent out for his chief brahmin advisor to locate a woman who was akin to Maya Devi in her youth. He came up with Yasodhara. But wanting to be assured that a strong match was made, Suddhodana had a number of eligible young women come to a party in which the prince would distribute jewelry to each one. He would see how Siddhartha reacted to them and be convinced that Yasodhara was indeed the right match.

It so happened that Yasodhara was the last to come through the line of young women. Siddhartha had given some gift to everyone who'd been in the receiving line but ran out just before she appeared. Presumably, none of the other girls sparked his interest, but when the prince saw Yasodhara he felt a strong connection. (Later he'd tell her this was from their past lives together.) Feeling this sense of closeness, Siddhartha took a piece of jewelry from his own body and put it on Yasodhara. Some say it was his ring. Others say it was his necklace. In any case, the match was made, and Suddhodana was well pleased.

> **Buddha Basics**
>
> In Siddhartha's family, there were lots of cross cousins … with aunts and uncles who were at the same time mothers-in-law and fathers-in-law. But that doesn't mean everything always ran smoothly between members of the Sakya and Koliya clans. Remember Devadatta's childhood conflict with Siddhartha over the swan? Well, later Devadatta actually tried to kill Siddhartha. Nevertheless, in the immediate family at least six males and three females joined Buddha's renunciate community.

The Pampered Prince Wins a Bride

It was customary for a kshatriya suitor to demonstrate his skills before the family of his hoped-for bride. So the Buddha biographies speak of the contests in which Siddhartha participated to win Yasodhara for his wife. Some thought that Siddhartha had been too pampered and couldn't impress anyone with his martial skills. Yasodhara's father was among them. What, with all that fragrant sandalwood paste from Kasi (Varanasi) and garments of fine cloth—how could the prince be prepared in skills of warfare? Suddhodana was insulted, but Siddhartha assured him that he'd do fine.

If, by chance, Siddhartha had not been as rigorously trained as some less-protected kshatriya youths, he had enough innate talent to overcome that lack. Apparently, Siddhartha was able to defeat a couple of his cousins at their best events in the martial tournament. Devadatta, who was thought to be Siddhartha's match in wrestling, was beat three times. But Siddhartha threw him down without inflicting injury. Furthermore, the prince was able to wield a heavy bow and outdo Nanda, known for his skills in archery. Siddhartha also demonstrated solid abilities in elephant handling and horse riding. By this means, he was given Yasodhara's hand.

The ancient Indian marriage ceremony involved many prayers and ritual acts, including joining of the bride's right hand with the groom's left hand and the two walking several times together around a sacred fire and then taking seven symbolic steps with the right foot leading. The bride is carried on a litter, following her husband who rides on horseback. They proceed to the groom's house.

> **Enlightening Extras**
>
> Gandhara artists presented the Bodhisattva as marrying Yasodhara in typical Indian style, including the joined hands and walking around the sacred fire. The ancient style of Indian marriage is practiced to this very day in India. Gandhi—in Richard Attenborough's movie by that name—is shown walking around the sacred fire with his bride Kasturba in their marriage scene.

A Question of Wives

Siddhartha was married to Yasodhara when they were both in their middle teens. But it was 13 years before Yasodhara bore the prince's child. One can imagine the pressure Yasodhara felt to produce a son. And it's not out of the question that Siddhartha, as the raja's son, was pressured to take another wife. Suddhodana might have thought a male child would help assure continuation of the family line and bind Siddhartha more closely to worldly life. So it was imperative for the Sakyan prince to have a son.

> **Buddha Basics**
>
> Stories of Siddhartha's youth typically present him as having one wife—most commonly called Yasodhara. In any case, no one speaks of Gautama as having more than one child. And the oldest texts refer to his wife as simply Rahulamata, meaning Rahula's mother. Besides Yasodhara, other names found in the texts include Gopa, Bhadra Katyayana, and Bimba or Bimbasundari (beautiful Bimba). Did Buddha have more than one wife, or are these simply different names for the same woman? It's unclear.

The Least You Need to Know

- Siddhartha is often called a prince. But his father was a raja, or head chieftain of the modest Sakyan territory, not a monarch ruling a great country, such as Magadha or Kausala.

- As a raja's son, Siddhartha was an elite kshatriya who lived in luxury, with access to several residences, fine food and clothes, harem women, and a good education.

- Courtesans had a cultural role to play in the Middle Ganges Basin of Buddha's day, but the extent of Siddhartha's involvement with these or other women in his youth is unknown.

- Siddhartha showed early signs of sensitivity to the suffering of animals, though he was supposed to train as a warrior. And despite his son's considerable talent, Suddhodana seemed uneasy about the future, hoping Siddhartha wouldn't reject worldly life.

- Yasodhara, daughter of Suddhodana's sister, became Siddhartha's wife when both were in their midteens and bore him a son after about 13 years.

Siddhartha's Disillusionment and Escape

In This Chapter

- ◆ The question of Siddhartha's destiny
- ◆ Siddhartha sees the Four Sights
- ◆ Disillusioned by the dancing girls
- ◆ Farewell to Kapilavastu
- ◆ The Great Renunciation
- ◆ Chandaka returns to Kapilavastu

The episode of Siddhartha's disillusionment with worldly life and escape from Kapilavastu is peppered with symbolism. At the age of 29, he had a conversion experience that pushed him to reject the kshatriya lifestyle. Siddhartha saw Four Sights that turned him against the life of privilege and power he'd been leading as a Sakyan noble. An encounter with three people made the suffering in this world real to him. Then he saw another person. This one stirred the Bodhisattva's hope that suffering could end.

After seeing an old man, a sick man, a funeral procession, and an ascetic, Siddhartha felt revolted by his life in the palace. He developed a burning wish to solve the problem of suffering. He felt compelled by some inner calling to renounce worldly life. And as much as he loved them, Siddhartha was moved to leave his family. His father, aunt, wife, and newborn son would have to do without him, at least for the time being. Eventually all four attained the highest level on the spiritual path. But that was later. When Siddhartha left Kapilavastu, no one knew what would happen next—their beloved son, husband, and father leaving them, to attain enlightenment or die trying.

No matter how much symbolism runs through Gautama's life story, political realities are never far from the action. When Siddhartha escaped from Kapilavastu to make his Great Renunciation, a tension had been growing both within his heart, his family, and his clan. The Sakyan warrior gave up his commitments to family and clan to pursue a universal good that ranged beyond his particular relationships. He abandoned his roles. He renounced his rank as an elite son of the Sakyan raja. At the height of both physical and mental strength, he turned his attention inward and left others to fend for themselves. Why?

A Father's Anxiety

For years, Raja Suddhodana must have wondered, "When will my son come to greatness?" And behind that, "Will my son become disaffected with the kshatriya's life?" The image of a group of brahmins holding up two fingers at the time of the infant Siddhartha's birth must have nagged at Suddhodana. All but one of the brahmins brought in to predict his son's destiny had held up two fingers indicating an ambiguity: the child will become either a political or a religious Dharmacakrin. Suddhodana hoped for the first option. Yet the aged sage Asita and the young Brahmin Kaundinya were both sure that the infant would turn into the second.

The Sakyan raja tried to make Siddhartha happy with his lot in life, because he wanted Siddhartha to become a great ruler—even a "universal monarch." And Suddhodana was not harboring an empty fantasy. Prospects for increased Sakyan power in northern India were not out of the question in a landscape filled with economic opportunity. A talented leader had real chances for exerting political influence over the small republics in the Middle Ganges Basin, no matter that the Sakyans had only a small territory. Things were changing fast with the increase of trade, use of coins, emergence of a wealthy merchant class, urban development, and the amassing of armies.

The prospect of Suddhodana's son becoming an extraordinary and powerful turner of the Wheel of the Law must have produced a fascinating dream in the mind of the raja.

Siddhartha's lack of a son for his dozen years of marriage must have weighed on Suddhodana. But at last, Yasodhara was pregnant. And things must have been looking up as far as the raja was concerned. But then a kind of restlessness seemed to begin plaguing his son. Siddhartha was asking to travel about. The confines of his palace life were beginning to bind him. But even Siddhartha didn't yet know he was feeling bound.

> **Buddha Basics**
>
> Coins were used regularly in India at least a century before Buddha lived. As trade increased, the states of Kausala and Magadha began to mint their own coins. Silver coins found by archeologists were made by King Prasenajit of Kausala and King Ajatasatru of Magadha.

The Collapse of a Fantasy

So when would the moment of truth come? When would Siddhartha's fate be decided? When would the child's ambiguous fate resolve itself? When would it become clear what kind of Dharmacakrin this talented Sakyan noble would become? In the midst of this anxiety, Raja Suddhodana had seven dreams. With a brahmin's interpretation, Siddhartha's father intensified his efforts to keep the prince satisfied with his current life.

- ◆ Suddhodana had four dreams of various people or objects leaving Kapilavastu from each of its four gates—meaning Siddhartha would soon leave home, accomplish great things, and wake up.

- ◆ Suddhodana had two dreams about Siddhartha beating a drum at the crossroads of Kapilavastu's four highways and casting jewels from Kapilavastu's central tower—meaning his son would teach dharma far and wide.

- ◆ Suddhodana dreamed that not far from Kapilavastu, six men were wailing, weeping, and tearing out their hair—meaning his son would expose weaknesses in the views of six prominent teachers.

After his seven dreams, Raja Suddhodana kept closer tabs on his son. He tried harder to please Siddhartha, providing the prince with more women for entertainment and sending him on pleasure tours. And his son's destiny gradually began to clear up—but not according to Suddhodana's wishes.

It's No Pleasure Trip

So how did destiny finally begin to mold Siddhartha to fit the picture his father's unconscious had drawn in seven dreams? The change began with a number of outings with Chandaka, his charioteer. With Suddhodana's cooperation, the prince was

Dharma Dictionary

Samvega is an inspirational encounter that shocks a person into a new perspective on life and reality. Both art and religion in ancient India deal with these sudden, radical psychological encounters. Even catching a glimpse of a holy person can have a spiritually transformative effect on someone who is ripe for it. Samvega describes such a transformative encounter.

to go beyond the palace compound in Kapilavastu to experience what lay beyond its walls. The raja had arranged everything to be spectacular. In fact, he'd always discouraged his son from seeing anything distressing outside the four luxurious residences. The Sakyan prince may have been naive about the lives of common people and their problems. Perhaps Siddhartha's isolation actually set the stage for the *samvega* (aesthetic shock) he experienced when he saw suffering for the first time.

The raja's son went on several outings beyond the palace compound. Driven by Chandaka, his longtime companion, in a decorated chariot, the prince was supposed to be relaxing. Instead, what Siddhartha saw sent him into a spiritual crisis. Though the streets had been swept, and the houses cheerfully festooned, the prince got a glimpse behind the façade. And though festive music streamed out for the Sakyan prince's pleasure, Siddhartha began to detect the sour notes. He began to realize the suffering of living beings, beneath the surface of their lives.

From a very traditional Indian viewpoint, some say the gods arranged for Siddhartha to see an old man, a sick man, a funeral procession, and a sramana as he went sightseeing with Chandaka. From a modern viewpoint, people may see these four encounters as literary metaphors for something that occurred in Siddhartha's mind. But however it happened—or didn't happen—Siddhartha seems to have undergone a powerful shift in his outlook. After Chandaka explained the nature of old age, sickness, death, and spiritual striving, the prince was greatly disturbed. From then on, the prince was obsessed with and disturbed by the problem of suffering.

The Four Sights

Buddhist tradition uses the term *Four Sights* to describe Siddhartha's encounters with an old man, a sick man, a corpse, and an ascetic. Each had great meaning for the Sakyan prince and led to his Great Renunciation. He had not realized what Chandaka seemed to know as a matter of course. But when he finally heard an account of the human condition, Siddhartha could not gloss over it, as many people seem able to do.

Enlightening Extras

In the early stages of Vedism, the domestic priest of the royal household rode in the raja's chariot and recited mantras of protection. And though Chandaka was not a priest, his role as charioteer was also to help protect the raja's son. In an odd way, Chandaka can be compared to Krishna (an incarnation of the deity Vishnu) in the *Bhagavad Gita*, a Hindu sacred text. There Krishna is the warrior Arjuna's charioteer. And though Krishna is a deity, and Chandaka is an underling, both say things that radically transform the minds of the warriors in their charge.

♦ **Old man:** The sight of an old man shocked Siddhartha and made him lose pride in his youthfulness. For the first time, the prince realized how the beauty of soft skin, black hair, shining teeth, and firm legs all deteriorate with age. Chandaka told him everyone who lives becomes old. Even memory fades. No exceptions.

♦ **Sick man:** The sight of a sick man shocked Siddhartha and made him lose pride in his health. For the first time, he realized how vitality, prowess, and happiness are cut to the quick when ravaged by illness. Chandaka told him that everyone who lives becomes sick at least once (even the strongest). No exceptions.

♦ **Corpse:** The sight of a corpse being carried on a bier shocked Siddhartha and made him realize the attachment to life. As the dead man's family wailed, the prince sensed their profound grief and confusion. Dutifully, Chandaka informed him that everyone who is born will die. Kings, princes, and newborns. No exceptions.

♦ **Sramana:** The sight of a *sramana* shocked Siddhartha. The ascetic looked serene in the midst of the world's drama. Chandaka admitted that occasionally a person would renounce the world and labor in the holy life, seeking a solution to the problem of suffering and rebirth. Seeing the sramana gave Siddhartha hope that he could find an answer to suffering.

Dharma Dictionary

A **sramana** is a laborer in the spiritual life. The word is related to terms meaning to exert, make effort, and strive. Well-respected renunciates of the Ganges Basin were called sramanas because they make tremendous effort to attain their spiritual goal. Soon after he leaves Kapilavastu, Siddhartha would be called Maha-sramana by the ascetics in Rajagriha because he showed unusually "great" (maha) zeal in his spiritual exertions (sramana).

Father, Why Do You Deceive Me?

What should have been a commonplace set of encounters hit Siddhartha suddenly, deeply, and ferociously. After being hit with knowledge of the suffering of old age, sickness, and death, Siddhartha would never be the same. He could not stay in the palace. He could not lead the life of a kshatriya. He had to give it up and become one who labors in the religious life. His whole world was crumbling down. The problem of suffering screamed out in his mind for a solution. And the hope for a solution embedded in the sramana's quest pushed him over the edge.

After the samvega of the Four Sights, Siddhartha confronted his father: "Oh, Father, why did you deceive me?" He asked why Suddhodana had sheltered him for so many years. The raja defended his efforts to keep his son away from suffering, "You didn't want to know such things." Then Siddhartha declared his wish to leave home to find the end to suffering. Suddhodana rejected his son's request. The raja offered to step down from his post and install Siddhartha into a position of influence. But in any case, he was forbidden to leave.

It might have been at this time that Suddhodana sent Siddhartha to watch the plowing at a nearby village (though some biographers place this scene very early in Siddhartha's youth). This was to be a diversion, perhaps to acquaint the prince with the land, laborers, and beasts of burden he would oversee as a raja. Certainly he should be pleased at the spectacle and empowered by the thought of ruling the Sakyan territory with its fast-growing capacity for producing wealth.

But instead of being pleased, Siddhartha was scandalized. He saw the sweat, the sores, the panting, and the exhaustion of men and oxen as they plowed the fields. To make matters worse, he learned that they were his father's property. "From this day forward you are free to go," Siddhartha told the laborers. "Live where you wish." He also freed the oxen. The suffering of man and beast in contrast to the lush palace life impressed itself upon Siddhartha's conscience.

Harem Scare 'im

Nothing was working for Suddhodana, as Siddhartha became increasingly disillusioned with life in the palace. The raja's wife, Prajapati, scolded the harem women for not keeping the prince sufficiently occupied. But things were not the same for Siddhartha after seeing the Four Sights. They had turned the prince's mind away from the pleasing rhythms of daily life to a universal call for the happiness of all beings. Life in the palace soured for Suddhodana's overly protected son after he saw the physical suffering and emotional grieving outside the palace compound. Perhaps Siddhartha could have tried to endure his kshatriya's life with the thought of reducing suffering through political action, but it seemed that no matter which way he turned, the prince was being pushed to renounce life as he'd known it.

One evening Siddhartha's troupe of dancers and musicians were performing. Apparently, the prince got bored and dozed off. Seeing this, the harem women took a break and dozed off, too. When the prince awoke, he was struck by the revolting scene before him. His beautiful women were sprawled out in disarray, spittle dripping from the mouths of some; others were grinding their teeth. Their carefully crafted makeup was smeared, and the lovely garments were undone. How far were these women from the old, sick, and dead men of the Four Sights? Anyhow, what is beauty? Beauty, like youth, fades.

Maybe Siddhartha's mind was ripe for another aesthetic shock, even after seeing the Four Sights. Could it be that the gods took their chance to crush Siddhartha's world, so he'd finally make the break with worldly life? Was it his own deeper human thirst for meaning? Whatever the cause, waking up and seeing the harem women strewn about in the courtyard that evening sent Siddhartha fleeing from these and all women in his life. This display spurred him to leave Kapilavastu—that very night, they say. On that fateful evening, the prince was pushed over the edge. He could tolerate the kshatriya's life no more.

> **Be Mindful!**
>
> It was not the harem women that Siddhartha disliked when he saw them sprawled about in the courtyard. Rather, he experienced samvega, a chilling insight: earthly beauty flees. The Hindu Patanjali in his *Yoga Sutras* denotes three levels of samvega: soft, middling, and burning. An intense samvega can be devastating to the personality.

Yasodhara's Frightful Visions

A number of vivid images appeared to Yasodhara's mind on the eve of Siddhartha's escape from Kapilavastu. Right away, she told him everything. Yasodhara wanted reassurance before going back to sleep, because the images were alarming. They meant he'd be leaving. Yasodhara asked, "Wherever you go, let me go, too." The prince then reassured his wife—the mother of their newborn son—that she shouldn't be alarmed. And he promised Yasodhara, "So it shall be. Wherever I go, you, too, will go."

Well … the prince was thinking of going to where sorrow ends, and he promised to lead his wife there, too. But before he would find that place, he had to leave Kapila-vastu and labor in the spiritual life. Even if Yasodhara did not understand right away, eventually she did. And eventually she became free of sorrow just as Siddhartha did. She became an arhat. But that was later on.

What were the frightful images that appeared to Yasodhara's mind? Many were related to her bodily experience:

- A beautiful umbrella shaded her, then Chandaka took it away.

- Jewels from her headdress and all her ornaments were pulled off and scattered.

- Her body suddenly became ugly; and her hands, feet, and clothing fell off.

- The chair on which she sat turned over, and the four legs of her couch fell off.

These images depict the great loss she was to experience. Siddhartha was going away. Beyond images that dealt with her body, Yasodhara saw visions of cosmic devastation: the deva Indra's banner cracked in two; a jeweled mountain caught fire and collapsed; the great palace tree was blown over by wind; the Earth quaked; armed men ran to the four directions as trees and flowers scattered their leaves; and the sun, moon, and stars plummeted down—leaving a pall of darkness over the world.

Siddhartha spoke of the meaning of the apocalyptic scene of devastation that Yas-odhara had envisioned. He gave what seems to be an early version of the truth of emptiness, sunyata, that he would fully discern in his moment of awakening, gently telling his wife, "Don't let these things alarm you. Go back to sleep. Dreams are empty products of a universal law." Later in life, he would teach that all life resembles a dream. Surely, life has meaning, and dreams have meaning. But beneath the surface of all things one finds a truth that sets one free: one realizes sunyata (emptiness).

My Son, "Fetter"

The prince went for the last time to his wife's bedchamber—not long after Yasod-hara had her frightful visions. Already devastated by the sight of the harem women lying in disarray, Siddhartha saw—by contrast—the beauty of Yasodhara asleep with their newborn child. Yet, the problem of universal suffering already was imprinted on Siddhartha's mind. He had to find a solution. So without waking them up, the prince cast a farewell glance upon his lovely wife and child and left the premises. He found Chandaka; called for his horse, Kanthaka; and together the three left the palace and Kapilavastu. Siddhartha didn't return for seven years.

Buddhist texts don't dwell on the emotional connections between Gautama and his child, so their relationship can be misunderstood easily. For instance, the boy's name was Rahula, which means "fetter." And some take this to mean that Gautama thought having a child was a burden to the spiritual life. But this interpretation seems unfair to Sakyamuni's love for Rahula. The boy was born under the astrological sign of Rahu, and so was called Rahula. If he was a fetter, then Buddha was fettered willingly to his son for practically his whole life. When Buddha returned to Kapilavastu after enlightenment, the young Rahula joined the renunciate community and was tutored by Buddha's two most accomplished disciples.

One could say that the prince abandoned Yasodhara and their son when he paid them a silent farewell on the eve of his Great Renunciation. But later, both mother and child joined the spiritual community of renunciates, and Buddha called Rahula foremost among disciples for his wish to learn. Theirs was a close relationship forged over many previous lifetimes. What kind of karma does it take to be reborn as a tathagata's son? Or a tathagata's former wife? How unfortunate was it for Rahula to spend the first seven years of his life with no father in the house? Or for Yasodhara to live without Siddhartha as a husband? In this case, Rahula and his mother had to take the good with the bad.

Escape into the Night

Siddhartha and Chandaka left Kapilavastu by nightfall. They were both riding the prince's white horse, Kanthaka. This time they didn't leave the palace ceremoniously by chariot. This time the Sakyan prince and his charioteer headed out secretly. One version of the story claims that Siddhartha's cousin Mahanama was patrolling Kapilavastu that night and accosted the prince. In any case, Siddhartha was determined to leave. It's also possible that a guard or spy from Suddhodana's cabinet was trailing the prince. But no one physically detained him.

Chandaka traveled on the horse with Siddhartha for 10 days. That was enough to clear out of Kapilavastu to the borders of Sakyan territory. And though they seemed to be riding unnoticed, someone was taking a keen interest in Siddhartha's flight from the world. This was Mara, Lord of Illusion. It's also said that many godlings were watching Siddhartha as he left Suddhodana's city. Their presence was felt in the form of rain. That is, their tears were falling down upon the prince.

Buddha Basics

Mara is Lord of Illusion, a cosmic counterpart to Brahma. According to the cosmology of ancient India, there's a "place" for both types of beings in samsara. They each have an "office"—like the office of prime minister. And though individual maras and brahmas expire, their offices are always occupied in fulfillment of two cosmic functions: brahmas promote states of consciousness infused with love, compassion, and joyful sympathy; maras promote the illusion of worldly pleasures.

Look Who's Watching

Suddenly, Mara accosted the prince as he was leaving Kapilavastu, though it's unclear what Mara looked like when he appeared. Did he appear in a vision, as a voice, as a humanlike being, or in some other form? In any case, Mara showed up and tried to persuade the Sakyan noble to turn back to Kapilavastu. This cosmic being—or perhaps a reflection of Siddhartha's own mind—informed the prince that he was just seven days away from owning the wheel of a Dharmacakrin. Soon he could rule. Mara thus tried to entice Siddhartha to remain as a kshatriya, tempting him with worldly power.

But Siddhartha rebuffed Mara immediately. At that moment, the Lord of Illusion's psychological grip on the prince broke. And although Mara disappeared, the Lord of Illusion continued to silently stalk the prince for years (like a shadow waiting for the next vulnerable moment when Siddhartha would arrive at a mental crossroads). And every time the Bodhisattva made a decisive step to break the bonds of worldly life, Mara appeared to try to dissuade him.

By rejecting the Lord of Illusion, Siddhartha reaffirmed his resolve to leave Kapilavastu. Yet he wanted to look back upon the city. It's said that at that moment, the earth turned around like a potter's wheel, allowing the prince to cast a glance back at all he was leaving behind. Forthwith, he spurred his horse away from the Sakyan capital. With Chandaka riding behind the prince, Kanthaka carried the two friends on their last trip together. And what happened next is among the great moments of Buddha's life story.

A Kshatriya No More

The three—Siddhartha, Chandaka, and Kanthaka—rode 100 miles or more. Finally, the prince stopped and ordered Chandaka to return with Kanthaka to Kapilavastu. The charioteer begged to remain with the prince, but Siddhartha was determined to renounce the world. He first would remove all the external signs of being a kshatriya. After that he'd have to work on removing all remaining mental attachments to the noble life.

To remove the external signs of his life of privilege and power, the prince cut his hair and beard to a length of 2 inches. Siddhartha did this with his sword. It was his last act with such a weapon. Then he threw the severed locks into the air. Siddhartha also removed his jewelry—which marked him as a nobleman—and gave it to Chandaka to take home.

Be Mindful!

Siddhartha changed his clothes as the final transformation of his outer looks, after giving his jewelry to Chandaka. The basic story says that Siddhartha met a poor hunter and exchanged his noble clothes for the man's simple garment. Some versions of Buddha's biography weave a miraculous tale around this episode: the hunter was a deva in disguise, wearing a simple garment intended for the Bodhisattva. On getting Siddhartha's clothes, the deva carried them off to the Heaven of the Thirty-Three.

To remove the mental conditioning of his kshatriya upbringing, Siddhartha began traveling on foot, by himself, with only the forest or alms to sustain him. He had to get his bearings and deal with a radical change in diet and lack of physical comforts. At first he found the food he ate revolting. And a life out of doors was challenging to one reared in comfort.

This was Prince Siddhartha's Great Renunciation.

The White Horse Dies

Chandaka had no good options. Siddhartha refused to take any companions. So Siddhartha's charioteer was obliged to return to Kapilavastu and report to Raja Suddhodana that the prince had run away. Would Chandaka be blamed for allowing Siddhartha to leave without reporting his departure? Would he be disciplined? Perhaps Chandaka told Siddhartha's father that he rode with the prince to persuade him not to leave Kapilavastu. In any case, Chandaka returned without his charge. Siddhartha was gone, and he had only the jewels and Kanthaka to show. The charioteer must have been extremely uneasy when he returned to Kapilavastu with Siddhartha's valuables and had to explain to the raja that his son was gone.

Siddhartha tenderly bid Kanthaka farewell. And the white horse wept when the prince left him to walk alone as a renunciate. Kanthaka died of heartbreak upon returning with Chandaka to Kapilavastu without his master. Some say he died of grief on the spot where Siddhartha left him. Surely the thought of Siddhartha saying goodbye to his horse provides a rare glimpse into the warrior's heart lodged in the breast of the Sakyan prince.

The Least You Need to Know

- Raja Suddhodana tried to mold Siddhartha in his image. But the prince followed his own path and rejected the kshatriya life of power and privilege.

- Siddhartha saw Four Sights that turned his mind to the problem of suffering and its solution: an old man, a sick man, a corpse, and a sramana.

- The prince became disillusioned with the kshatriya's life upon seeing men and oxen laboring in contrast to his life of luxury, whose impermanence was made plain by the sleeping harem women.

- Siddhartha left his wife and newborn son, Rahula in Kapilavastu to labor in the spiritual life. But after seven years or so, they both joined his new spiritual community.

- The occasion when Siddhartha left Kapilavastu to lead a sramana's life is called the Great Renunciation. It is marked by certain acts: the prince cut his hair and beard, gave up his jewelry and fine clothes, and traveled out of Sakyan territory alone on foot.

Part

Waking Up: Siddhartha Becomes a Buddha

Siddhartha meditated with two accomplished teachers, and then practiced severe mortifications, after leaving his home in Kapilavastu. The way was cleared for enlightenment only after the Bodhisattva resisted the fear of death and the lure of procreation—evoked in his mind by a visionary being called Mara, Lord of Illusion. Upon knowing himself as nonself, Siddhartha became a buddha or awakened one.

After enlightenment, the new Buddha hesitated to teach. But when asked (by the god Brahma) to share his path to awakening, Gautama began his 45-year career as a spiritual advisor. He offered Buddha-dharma to a community of four quarters that was not limited by gender or social class. In the first year after Siddhartha became a buddha, many of his clansmen and clanswomen joined the mendicant communities he established. Others became lay disciples. But everything did not always go smoothly.

The Struggle to Wake Up

In This Chapter

- ◆ The great renunciation
- ◆ Meeting with King Bimbisara
- ◆ Joining Alara Kalama's hermitage
- ◆ Joining Rudraka Ramaputra's hermitage
- ◆ Intensifying the practice of penance
- ◆ On the point of starvation

Remember lifetimes back when Siddhartha was the Brahmin Sumedha? Eons ago, Sumedha experienced samvega—an inspirational, shock—when he saw Buddha Dipankara approach him. That encounter sparked a deep aspiration to become a Buddha himself. So, from that moment, Sumedha was a bodhisattva on the path to buddhahood.

After wandering through samsara as a tree spirit, prince, merchant, elephant, and other beings—the bodhisattva finally took rebirth in the Himalayan foothills, in the womb of Maya Devi. In this (his final) birth, he was the son of a Sakyan ruler named Suddhodana. And at birth, brahmins predicted two possible fates for the infant bodhisattva. Surely, he'd be a Dharmacakrin, but of what sort? A royal turner of the political Wheel of Law? Or the turner of a spiritual Wheel of Law?

It took 29 years for the Sakyan noble Siddhartha to cast the die determining what sort of Dharmacakrin he would become. The prince's escape from Kapilavastu in the dead of night seemed to indicate a decisive moment of renunciation. Siddhartha had seen four shocking sights and decided he would never become a raja. He would become a tathagata—one who goes (*ga*) just like that (*tathata*). One who awakens to end suffering. One who turns the spiritual Wheel of Law.

Let's follow the ascetic Siddhartha through his first six years of renunciation to see how he got to the point of awakening—that long-sought goal of the bodhisattva once named Sumedha.

The Great Renunciation

The 29-year-old father of a newborn son left his home and family in Kapilavastu. He was seeking their greater good. And though his leaving may seem harsh to us, we should never forget that Siddhartha was a man with a mission. Following in the footsteps of the great heroes of humanity, he had been struck by the age-old clarion call to a true vocation. The seed of this vocation had been planted numerous lifetimes in the past and now it was coming to fruition. Now he was driven by a mysterious, deep-seated ambition to save the world.

After sending Chandaka back home, Siddhartha was alone. Owning nothing but a hunter's garment, he headed into territory of the Malla princes and spent seven days alone in a forest of mango trees. Getting his bearings, the Sakyan prince—or should we say ex-prince—stopped at a hermitage and inquired how far he was from Kapilavastu. Hearing he had come only 12 *yojanas* (96 miles/155 km), Siddhartha decided he was still too close to home.

Dharma Dictionary

A **yojana** is a measure of distance used in ancient India. Around 1980 the Burmese teacher Mahasi Sayadaw went on a pilgrimage to India and measured distances between Buddhist sites, comparing them to traditional commentaries. He concluded that a *yojana* equals 8 miles. The *Mahavamsa*, a Sri Lankan chronicle (sixth century C.E.) states that Buddhist *viharas* (temples) were built at a distance of 1 *yojana* from each other.

Wishing not to be disturbed by the Sakyans, Siddhartha traveled on foot some 30 yojanas (240 miles/386 km) to Rajagriha, capital of the ablest ruler of the Middle Ganges Basin. After crossing the Ganges River, he fashioned an alms bowl of leaves before completing the last leg of his journey. The Sakyan ascetic then entered the walled city to beg alms from the king's people.

A Regal Ascetic Comes to the King's City

We should remember that Siddhartha had a privileged existence before he cast off his princely garments. He had been groomed to be a Sakyan ruler, with a superior education and practical training in the martial arts. He had won Yasodhara by competition—the warrior's way according to Sakyan tradition. And he was a person of exceptional intelligence. Even if the texts did not tell us that Siddhartha was good at his studies, would we conclude anything different about a person who used his mind to uncover the nature of reality?

So when Siddhartha—with the regal bearing of a prince—entered Rajagriha and started begging alms, King Bimbisara took note. The king detected something more under the ascetic's ragged, unornamented guise: a beautiful looking man who walked nobly with eyes cast down not looking further than the distance of a yoke. The king inquired about the new arrival in his capital. Learning where Siddhartha went to eat his meal outside the city, Bimbisara set out to meet him and find out his identity. Upon learning that Siddhartha was the son Raja Suddhodana, the king made the Sakyan noble an offer he couldn't refuse … or so he thought. The king proposed to turn over a regiment of his army to Siddhartha. He wanted the Sakyan to affiliate with Magadha. Siddhartha, however, had other ambitions.

> ### Enlightening Extras
>
> In ancient India, a king was duty-bound to keep track of who was in his territory. The famous vetala (vampire) tales in Indian Sanskrit literature illustrate a ruler's obligations through a set of riddles posed to King Trivikramasena by a corpse. One story involves a chancellor's son disguised as a beggar ascetic. After some mishap, the king is found responsible because he hadn't been aware that two strangers had entered the capital. The king had failed in his royal duty to be the all-seeing eye of the realm, and the protector of his people.

Siddhartha's Refusal

Bimbisara's generous offer easily could have given Siddhartha second thoughts about the sramana's life. Here in Rajagriha he could have power and influence. He could have risen to high position and formed alliances between Magadha—the up-and-coming state—and his own people, the Sakyans. He could have enhanced the work of his father and eventually secured his own illustrious future. He could reunite with his wife and child—or have all the women he wanted—and garner new prestige in his association with the king of Magadha.

After all, now Siddhartha had tasted the food of ascetics. The food he'd gotten from begging in Rajagriha made his intestines feel as if they were coming out through his mouth. The ex-prince was repulsed by the scraps—all mixed up in his leaf alms bowl—not even fit to eat for the lowest members of the social order. Siddhartha had just quit the noble life and cast himself out of society. King Bimbisara's proposal tested the strength of Siddhartha's renunciation. He was being given a second chance to lead the worldly life, which was still psychologically in reach. He could easily give up the search for enlightenment and fall back into the first fate predicted for him: become a Dharmacakrin … a wordly Dharmacakrin. After all, he left home against the wishes of his father, who since the time of Siddhartha's birth was planning for his talented son to follow his footsteps.

Promise to King Bimbisara

Siddhartha may or may not have had second thoughts about the lifestyle he'd just chosen for himself, but he did not give in. And seeing this firm sense of purpose, Bimbisara became a kind of early devotee of the ascetic. The king now wanted Siddhartha to succeed in his goal of attaining enlightenment. And Bimbisara requested that Siddhartha return to Rajagriha once he had awakened.

So you see, Siddhartha's renunciation truly seemed to fit the name that later Buddhists would give to his repudiation of politics, privilege, and nobility. Siddhartha discarded his future as a worldly Dharmacakrin. He'd made a decision and was sure of it. Thus it's called the Great Renunciation.

Be Mindful!

In thinking about the geography of Buddha's life story, one must be cautious regarding both the location of certain events and distances between points. Basic terms of measurement from ancient India are inconsistently defined. And even the authenticity of hallowed sites where Gautama presumably was born and passed away still comes under challenge. Take a look at three different maps of ancient India and you're likely to find three different placements of Kapilavastu and Lumbini, for example. Also keep in mind the fact that rivers have not only changed names, but also have changed course over the years.

Before Siddhartha returned to Rajagriha—as a buddha—he went to the brink of this own grave and back. When he eventually returned to Bimbisara's city as the Awakened One, his body was brilliant with the aura of realization. But between the time he declined the king's offer to lead an army and the time he returned as the Tathagata, Siddhartha's body lost all outward traces of his noble upbringing. The martial strength detected by Bimbisara that could have devastated enemies withered away over the next six years. Siddhartha set off to conquer his inner enemies—the Three Poisons of delusion, repulsion, and desire. He pared himself down to skin and bone and was among the strictest ascetics to be found wandering through the Middle Ganges Basin. This warrior was not to be outdone.

Going Beyond This World

Siddhartha remained with some ascetics on Vulture Peak near Rajagriha for a while. This group of sramanas—along with many others around the Middle Ganges Basin—sought rebirth into higher realms of existence. They practiced *samatha* (serenity) meditation, which involved keeping their attention stable for longer and longer periods of time so they could enter higher and higher states of consciousness. These ascetics were especially interested in passing away while abiding in the serene states of awareness produced by their meditation practice. They believed that by doing so they would actually be reborn into the subtle realm of existence that corresponded to their level of *samadhi* (higher consciousness).

Dharma Dictionary

Samadhi is the Sanskrit term for subtle states of consciousness attained by keeping one's attention unwavering for long periods of time. **Samatha** meditation—meaning serenity or calm abiding—is the method that leads initially to samadhi with form and then to samadhi without form. These attainments correspond to experience of the realm of pure form and the realm of no form. The deva Brahma abides in the realm of pure form, while there are no objects in the realm of no form.

Siddhartha practiced samatha meditation and austerities for a while with the sramanas on Vulture Peak. He had such zeal for self-mortification that they called him a maha sramana (great ascetic). Thereafter, many called Gautama "Maha Sramana." But when the Sakyan realized that many of his associates practiced mental stabilization with the goal of becoming a brahma, he left their company. He was looking for a higher attainment of samadhi, and had no interest in becoming a divine being.

The Maha Sramana left the ascetics at Vulture Peak and went away from Rajagriha in search of a teacher who could guide him into higher meditations. He learned of a prominent guru named Alara Kalama, whose hermitage was near the lovely city of Vaisali, some 100 miles (160 km) to the north across the Ganges River. This teacher had some 300 disciples, and Siddhartha set out to live with them. On the way, he stopped at four or five smaller hermitages, including two headed by female brahmin ascetics named Sakya and Panna.

Alara Kalama and Nothing Whatsoever

Alara Kalama had heard about the Sakyan prince by the time Siddhartha arrived at his hermitage. He accepted the new sramana as a student and instructed him in both theory and practice. After some time, Siddhartha mastered what Alara Kalama had to teach. He went beyond the absorptions practiced by the sramanas at Vulture Peak who wanted to identify with Brahma in the realm of pure form. Ranging into a state of consciousness where all concepts have been erased, Siddhartha reached the third level of the realm of no form. He reached the state called "nothing whatsoever."

Buddhist cosmos. This is a simplified version of the cosmos according to Buddha's teachings.

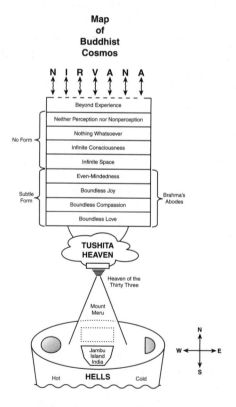

King Bimbisara as well as the ascetics on Vulture Peak had noticed that Siddhartha was highly talented. Now, too, Alara Kalama saw the exceptional quality of the Maha Sramana's performance. The teacher had shared all his knowledge and judged that Siddhartha's realization was equivalent to his own. Thus Alara Kalama formally asked Siddhartha to become his partner at the hermitage to help guide his many disciples.

> ### Buddha Basics
>
> Alara Kalama was the ascetic Siddhartha's first spiritual teacher after he renounced the world at age 29. The name of this guru indicates his affiliation with the Kalamas, a clan whose capital was a market town called Kesaputta in Kausala north of the Ganges. After Siddhartha became enlightened, he gave advice to the Kalamas, who wondered how to decide what is actually true as they hear people praising their own views and putting down others' beliefs.

In spite of the Kalaman teacher's generous offer to share his establishment, the Sakyan Maha Sramana declined. Although the state of concentration he had attained surpassed that practiced by the ascetics of Vulture Peak, Siddhartha was dissatisfied. He did not feel that this formless samadhi was powerful enough to cut the roots of rebirth. But this was not to be Siddhartha's final disappointment with altered states of consciousness (samadhis). He still had high hopes for the samatha method of mental stabilization when he found a second guru to guide him on the samadhi path.

On the Road Again

Ascetic Siddhartha left Alara Kalama, with a polite refusal to stay and join ranks. Both the monarch and the guru saw great capacity in the former Sakyan prince and wanted to tap into his unusual charisma, talent, and vigor. But apparently, the Sakyan was a born leader—as so many brahmins in the birth ceremony recognized by his bodily signs. The baby had the marks of a Dharmacakrin. And apparently, he wasn't going to "turn the Wheel of the Law" for anyone else—be it king of Magadha or a famous Indian guru.

We know by now that Siddhartha had extraordinary ability in meditation, for he had mastered Alara Kalama's teaching relatively quickly. And we know that Siddhartha had unusual zeal. He was a bodhisattva, after all, determined to solve the problem of suffering. Striving for full buddhahood, the ascetic Siddhartha's particular mission was to find and demonstrate the ultimate triumph over suffering. Siddhartha's mission was to cut completely the roots of rebirth.

But Siddhartha was not setting off to turn the Wheel of the Law on his own just yet. Though he may have had some inkling of a future in which he blazed his own trail, the Sakyan renunciate was not finished exploring what his ancient Indian tradition had to offer. Siddhartha was zealous and willing to try any method that held the promise of salvation from suffering. So when he heard of a deceased teacher—called Rama—who had attained a state higher than he'd mastered, he went to find out what he could from Rama's main disciple.

Rudraka Ramaputra and ... What's That Again?

The Sakyan Maha Sramana made his way from Vaisali back to Rajagriha to the hermitage of Rama's disciple, Rudraka Ramaputra. Rama was the deceased ascetic who was said to have ascended to a level of the cosmos higher than nothing whatsoever in the realm of pure form. And in search of yet higher states of consciousness, Siddhartha moved back to Magadha—close once more to King Bimbisara. There he joined Rudraka Ramaputra, head of a hermitage where some 700 disciples dwelled.

Rudraka Ramaputra was older than Alara Kalama. And he had more than twice the number of students. He also reportedly had knowledge of a state of consciousness higher than the one mastered by Alara Kalama. So Siddhartha felt fortunate to become another of his disciples. Soon Rudraka Ramaputra began to share what he could about his guru Rama's samadhi practice—a serenity meditation that led to the level of neither perception nor nonperception in the realm of no form.

And sure enough ... in time, Siddhartha developed the ability to surpass the level of nothing whatsoever and attain the experience of neither perception nor nonperception. It is said that Siddhartha knew he'd attained Rama's level in the realm of no form because he actually encountered Rama in his meditation. While "there," tradition says that Siddhartha also met Asita. Recall that Asita had cried at the time of prince Siddhartha's birth, knowing he'd never live long enough to become the child's future disciple.

Enlightening Extras

The phenomenon of devotees, saints, prophets, and sages "meeting" members of their spiritual heritage is reported in more than one religious tradition—although each case does not necessarily represent the same state of consciousness and being. Buddhist texts say that Siddhartha met the sages Rama and Asita in the realm of no form at the level of neither perception nor nonperception when he himself attained that state of consciousness. A perhaps more spiritually satisfying example would be the transcendent encounters between Hindu devotees and the divine Krishna in a heavenly Vrindavana.

All That for Nothing?

After all his meditation under Alara Kalama and Rudraka Ramaputra, Siddhartha had a nagging feeling that his accomplishments did not get to the heart of his goal. He had gotten to the peak of samsara achieving the state of consciousness known as neither perception nor nonperception. But this was still an *experience*. What remained was to give up experience entirely. The problem was that once a person came out of the altered states of consciousness, he or she still was subject to the three poisons—craving and revulsion based in ignorance about reality. Siddhartha sought to cut the roots of rebirth and transcend the Wheel of Becoming all together. It appeared as though altered states of consciousness alone—no matter how refined—did not hold the promise he sought.

The spiritual poverty of even the highest states of *samadhi* was neither the first nor the last disappointment Siddhartha would endure on the spiritual path. He had begun the renunciate life with mortification and meditation among the ascetics of Vulture Peak. But many of them aimed for rebirth in the realm of pure form, so he left them in search of a means to cut off rebirth completely. Next, under Alara Kalama, he mastered the third level in the realm of no form. But he noticed that nothing whatsoever also was linked to rebirth. Then, under Rudraka Ramaputra, he mastered the highest level in the realm of no form—neither perception nor nonperception. But he noticed that even attaining this level was powerless against the three poisons.

Ratchet It Up!

Rudraka Ramaputra had recognized that Siddhartha reached the highest level of the realm of no form and asked to be the Sakyan's disciple. Siddhartha could have stayed to lead the large body of disciples at Rajagriha but instead he left his teacher's hermitage. The Maha Sramana would never abandon his search for enlightenment. In response to the insufficiency of his spiritual endeavors since leaving his family in Kapilavastu, Siddhartha was determined to intensify his efforts. He thought that perhaps more severe bodily mortification was the key to success. So bidding his second teacher farewell, Siddhartha walked westward through Magadha to the province of Urubilva. He stopped in a village called Senani where there were streams, groves, and shady fords. The hermitage headed by Urubilva Kasyapa was nearby.

At the foot of a tree near the Nairanjana River, Siddhartha began what would be a ferocious campaign against inner enemies such as fear. Gradually he made the mortifications more and more stringent. The Maha Sramana fasted, eating less and less, until he reduced food consumption to a single *masha* (pea) per day. It is said that some devas offered to sustain him with divine food, but Siddhartha refused. Under this punishing regimen, the Sakyan's skin color and texture began to change. He was turning blackish-red, and his body hair was falling out. These are some of the techniques Siddhartha used in an attempt to break ties with the cycle of rebirth.

- To overpower negative thoughts, the Maha Sramana clenched his teeth and sweat began to pour from his armpits.

- Siddhartha held his breath until pain pierced his head, his stomach felt as though a knife was cutting it, and his eardrums felt like they would pop.

- Siddhartha continued holding his breath until he experienced severe burning, as though being pressed and rolled in a pit of lighted charcoal.

Through all these horrors, the Sramana managed to keep his equanimity. He did not allow his mind to become oppressed as the pains tortured his body.

Buddha Basics

In the post-enlightenment period, Buddha used to think back and tell disciples about his austerities in Urubilva after leaving Rudraka Ramaputra's hermitage.

At first his life in the forest was frightening. Some nights he meditated on his fears. If a deer passed by or a peacock dropped a twig, horror arose in his mind. When that happened, he would not stand, or sit, or walk until he could allay his fear by lying down.

Father to the Rescue

Raja Suddhodana, it seems, never lost sight of his son. And Siddhartha's wife—or should we say former wife—Yasodhara kept up with every bit of news. But the news became ever more alarming to the family back in Kapilavastu. After Siddhartha left Rudraka Ramaputra's hermitage in Rajagriha, his father panicked at the regimen his son was keeping in Urubilva. He sent emissaries every day to report back news of his son's condition. He also sent Siddhartha's former close friend Minister Kaludayi to assess the Maha Sramana's condition. And what did these emissaries find? A man almost dead.

Siddhartha's body became tragically emaciated. His limbs were withered up, and his buttocks resembled camel's feet. His ribs stuck out, and his eyes were dark and sunken.

His spine was visible from the front through the abdomen, and his stomach could be felt from the back around his vertebrae.

As Siddhartha's penance intensified, Raja Suddhodana stopped the news from reaching Yasodhara. He was afraid for her and the child Rahula, because Yasodhara had cast off her jewelry and was making effort to follow her (former) husband's spiritual discipline. She too was fasting as much as she could.

Finally, one day Siddhartha's condition deteriorated to the point of death. What would this battered up former Sakyan prince do?

The Least You Need to Know

- Siddhartha refused an offer to affiliate politically with King Bimbisara, but promised to return and spiritually guide the king once he awakened.

- Siddhartha was called Maha Sramana, or great ascetic, by a group of renunciates on Vulture Peak because of his enthusiasm for spiritual practice.

- Under the guidance of Alara Kalama and Rudraka Ramaputra, Siddhartha experienced the two highest levels in the realm of no form: nothing whatsoever, and neither perception nor nonperception—but was unsatisfied and left both teachers.

- Siddhartha was disappointed by all his advances in samatha meditation because they only led to higher and higher levels of samsara instead of to freedom from rebirth.

- The Maha Sramana intensified his effort to find freedom from rebirth by embarking on a campaign of severe mortification that brought him to the point of death—and panicked his father.

The Awakening

In This Chapter

We left Siddhartha on the point of death. He'd done severe mortifications in search of the deathless state—where there would be no more rebirth. Paradoxically, the search for deathlessness brought him to the verge of death. Death would not have been bad if, and only if, Siddhartha had cut the roots of rebirth. Dying was not the problem. Being compelled by karma to take rebirth was the problem. But now—almost dead—the Maha Sramana was convinced that he had not cut the roots of rebirth.

Some six years earlier, Siddhartha cut his hair and beard. He removed his fine clothes and placed the princely royal jewels for safekeeping with Chandaka, who returned them to Kapilavastu. Thus, giving up all markers of rank, Siddhartha signaled his rejection of caste. He was not going to be a warrior—a kshatriya—again. He was going to seek answers to spiritual questions among the sramanas who were beyond caste.

Some sramanas had followed through the traditional stages of life. These were the brahmin renunciates who had already passed through their student, householder, and forest-dwelling days, possibly still with their wives on third stage. They were beyond caste because they fulfilled all the stages of caste. But that course of life was only open to brahmin men, and Siddhartha was not a brahmin. He was born as a kshatriya, and no man could move up the social ladder within a single lifetime. So he could never be a brahmin. (We don't even know whether he ever secretly longed to be a brahmin.)

With the priestly option closed to him, Siddhartha had gone the route of the revolutionary sramanas who skipped life stages and wreaked havoc with the caste system. According to tradition, Siddhartha had studied and followed through to the householder stage. But he dropped out of householding early—before having a grandson. He thought it was more important to find answers to his burning questions that would help his family and all families. He thought that joining the sramana movement would let him crack the code of endless rebirth. But now this course of action appeared to be hollow. Attaining a formless state of consciousness did not take one out of samsara, and penance only confounded ignorance with death. What should he do next?

The Impasse

Siddhartha was gravely disappointed to discover that the sramanas—in whom he'd placed so much hope—did not have what he sought. Sure, he'd attained extraordinary, highly prized meditative states of consciousness. But they did not defeat the enemies that caused rebirth: delusion, revulsion, and desire. Siddhartha had come a long way in minimizing the mental poisons of revulsion and desire. But he had not yet penetrated far enough into the stuff of this dreamlike existence. He was still deluded. But the good news was, he knew it.

The Maha Sramana was neither satisfied nor discouraged, and this is a great recipe for success. He wanted to persist in the spiritual quest. And perhaps this is why, just at the point when Siddhartha hit an impasse—not knowing where to turn to wake up—his unconscious spoke through a dream, or perhaps it was the gods who spoke. Siddhartha dreamed about accepting a food offering. And soon enough, a young woman named Sujata offered him food.

The Maha Sramana had reached a turning point, and perhaps the time for the prince-ascetic to do something new had truly come. Going as far as possible along the path of mortification, he was sleeping among corpses and was mistaken for a ghost by village girls who threw stones and dirt at him. The cloth he'd been wearing was just shreds and now dropped off. Turning over a new leaf, he came upon a shroud from the corpse of a young servant girl who was cremated and decided it would be a proper garment once washed. After washing the linen, he bathed. In his weakened condition, Siddhartha could not get out of the water without the help of a tree, which offered its limb. Now with a fresh perspective, the Bodhisattva made a new cloak for himself.

Milk from a Thousand Cows

Sujata encountered the Sakyan sramana under a banyan tree. But she was unsure whether he was a human or a tree spirit. He looked so strange, with almost no flesh left on his bones, stretched with skin that must have resembled tree bark. She prepared a ceremonial meal of rice-milk as an offering to Siddhartha, for surely he was someone special. Sujata used a highly concentrated milk derived from a thousand cows. Over time, a precious cow was milked, and that milk was fed to another precious cow who would be milked, and so on down the line. The result was a very potent liquid that made a beautiful offering when cooked with rice.

> ### Be Mindful!
> Bear in mind that stories written down after decades of oral transmission normally vary on things such as character descriptions and sequences. For instance: After his fast, Siddhartha might have eaten food donated by two sisters, a girl and her maid, a single village girl, or a goat-herding boy. It might have been milk from a thousand cows, eight cows, or one cow (taken by the Maha Sramana himself). Some versions omit Sujata, stating that Siddhartha ate some unpalatable food.

The Maha Sramana accepted Sujata's offering of milk-rice. Observing propriety, he did not consume the meal in her presence. Instead, he carried the food to the bank of the Nairanjana River, where he ate the wonderful meal, which would last him 50 days. Thus, Siddhartha's energy was restored. His body began to display again the marks of greatness that had characterized him from birth. And now he asked for a sign: sending Sujata's offering tray out onto the water, the prince-ascetic asked that the vessel should float upstream if he could attain enlightenment. It did float against the current. And he was encouraged.

Buddha Basics

Buddhists highlight the occasion when Sujata, a village girl, offers Siddhartha milk-rice as he sat starving under a tree at Urubilva for its teaching value: the Bodhisattva's acceptance of food marks his turn to a moderate attitude towards spiritual practice. So the story explains the origin of the Middle Way approach that came to characterize Buddhism. Tradition also holds that Sujata's offering was among the most auspicious and virtuous meals ever served in the course of history—because great benefit comes to one who donates the last meal before a bodhisattva's nirvana or a buddha's parinirvana. By extension, the story encourages laypersons to practice generosity toward the mendicant sangha.

The Long Arm of Raja Suddhodana

Now the fact that the Maha Sramana nourished himself upset five ascetics who'd been attending him since he left Rudraka Ramaputra's hermitage in Rajagriha. They were disgusted that Siddhartha broke his fast. The Sakyan's will to awaken seemed to have weakened, as he apparently backtracked on the path of penance. The five sramanas were relying on Siddhartha to guide them to enlightenment, but they lost confidence in his commitment to the goal. So they left Siddhartha to his own devices and made their way to a deer park known as Rishipatana some 155 miles (250 km) from where the group of six had been living in Urubilva.

Who were the five ascetics following Siddhartha? One needn't look far to find out. We know that Suddhodana was alarmed at his son's extreme mortifications. And when Siddhartha left Rudraka Ramaputra's hermitage, his father kept a close eye on him. He would send agents to gather intelligence and report back, and the five ascetics were in a perfect position to assist Suddhodana, for two reasons: first, they seemed to have a true interest in learning from the Maha Sramana; second, as his attendants, they had access to Siddhartha.

The five ascetics actually had close ties to Siddhartha that ranged generations. Three were from the Sakyan's father's tribe, and two from his mother's tribe:

♦ Kaundinya was the eldest. He'd been among the brahmins who predicted the newborn Siddhartha's fate. Recall that the priests—skilled in reading body markings—had predicted that the child would become a Dharmacakrin. He would turn the Wheel of the Law—either political or spiritual. Only one of these brahmins predicted without ambiguity that the child would become a great spiritual leader. This was Kaundinya. He had been the youngest of the priests. (See Chapter 5.)

♦ Asvajit, Vashpa, Mahanama, and Bhadrika were the other four sramanas. They were sons of the older brahmins who predicted Siddhartha's fate. The fathers had noted the marks of a great man on Siddhartha's body and told their sons to keep track of Siddhartha as he grew up. They were instructed to become the Sakyan prince's disciples if and when his fate turned in the direction of spiritual greatness.

Indeed, all five ascetics became Siddhartha's disciples and thought they would witness something truly great. But after he broke his fast and ate Sujata's milk-rice, they left him. They did not yet understand that Siddhartha had just turned himself to the *Middle Way.*

Dharma Dictionary

The term **Middle Way** is a way to describe Buddha's teachings. It refers to the practical course of moderation between harsh asceticism and lush indulgence, and the philosophical rejection of extreme views, namely idealism (which posits the independent existence of a self) and nihilism (which radically denies any existent self). A second-century C. E. philosopher named Nagarjuna developed a dialectical philosophy known as the Middle Way based on Buddha's teachings.

Five Great Dreams

Five dreams came to the Maha Sramana after he decided to reject the extreme course of mortification. These were favorable signs of his awakening to come:

♦ The earth stretched out for use as a bed, with Mount Meru as Siddhartha's pillow to the north and oceans in the other cardinal directions to support his limbs. This meant Siddhartha would become enlightened.

♦ A tree grew out of Siddhartha's navel, and the treetop reached high into the sky. This meant that he would master the Eightfold Path and teach it to the world.

♦ White ants with black heads crawled up to Siddhartha's knees, covering his feet and calves. Or according to another version: four white cattle, black from their feet to their knees, licked Siddhartha's feet. This meant that many laypeople dressed in white garments would take refuge in him as Buddha.

♦ Four birds of different colors flew from the cardinal directions toward Siddhartha. When they landed at his feet, they became white. This meant that people from the four varnas would become enlightened in the Buddhist community.

◆ There was a huge pile or mountain of refuse on which Siddhartha walked without getting dirty. This meant that Buddha would not become attached to all the worldly praise and offerings that would be offered to him.

Pondering the five great dreams, Siddhartha took heart. He felt confident in the possibility of awakening. Finally, after years—indeed, eons—of working to perfect generosity, morality, effort, patience, and so forth, Siddhartha's world would open up in ways he had never before imagined.

The Great Resolve

The Maha Sramana gained new confidence from the symbols in his dreams. But still, how would he break through to enlightenment. How could he *wake up?*

Enlightening Extras

Buddha used the metaphor of a dream, saying that to stop suffering we need to awaken. The whole idea of waking up is fascinating to ponder. We do it every day of our lives (unless we don't sleep), yet we may rarely consider how! The metaphor of sleep and awakening are closely related. Staying awake is presented as a kind of initiatory trial in sacred texts throughout the world. Think of Gilgamesh who wished to learn the secret of immortality from Utnapishtim. The Sumerian "Noah" asked Gilgamesh to keep himself awake for a week. Needless to say, our hero falls asleep instantly and fails the test. Or consider Jesus of Nazareth, who asks Peter, James, and John to keep watch with him all night in Gethsemane. Three times they fall asleep because their "eyes were very heavy, " whereupon Jesus asks, "Could you not watch with me one hour?" (Mark 14: 32–42)

Encountering Mara, Lord of Illusion

Siddhartha had renewed energy from the milk-rice and renewed confidence from the positive indications in his dreams and the offering tray that floated upstream. Thus the Maha Sramana proceeded to locate a tree that he favored one evening. It was dusk on a full moon in the month of Vaisaka. This was the same month on which Siddhartha had been born, also at the time of a full moon. Would this be the day he attained a spiritual birth to end all births?

On the way to what has since been called the bodhi (enlightenment) tree, Siddhartha met a grass-cutter who offered eight bundles of kusa grass. Coming to the tree, the

Maha Sramana prepared a seat with the grass. He faced east, where the sun would rise after his long night of struggle.

The Bodhisattva—who had been the Brahmin Sumedha, an elephant, a caravan leader, and most recently Prince Siddhartha—was now ready to cut the ties to any more births. He sat down determined to break out of samsara. He resolved to sit unmoving until he awakened—even if it meant sitting until he turned into a skeleton.

An Easier Path

Sitting under the tree in Urubilva facing east, the Maha Sramana had a strange encounter. As he sat in meditation, he heard kind words spoken to him. Was this an inner voice? Was it a vision? The texts say that a manifestation of Mara, Lord of Illusion, somehow appeared to Gautama as he sat on his cushion of kusa grass. He heard something like this:

> *Oh, a thousand parts of you belong to death. There's only one part of life that remains. Live …. Live …. Life is better …. By living you could earn merit.*

> *The path of striving through penance is hard. What will it do for you? Earn yourself merit. Lead a celibate life. Begin performing fire sacrifices.*

Dharma Dictionary

Fire sacrifices are Vedic (non-Buddhist) rituals centered on Agni, the god of fire. Brahmins have done these from ancient times through today for the sake of ancestors and worldly gain such as help with the harvest, wealth, and so on. However, religious seekers in Buddha's day turned to inner sacrifice (breathing, fasting, contemplating) to unite the self with Brahman (the supreme energy pervading the universe) and thus transcend rebirth altogether.

The unsolicited advice to get up and take it easier may have sounded good to Siddhartha. He had just resolved to stay unmoving until he awakened—even if it meant death. Now here was a contrary thought. He could save his life, gain a lot of merit, and be done with all these efforts. But something did not sit right. Siddhartha mentally stepped back to consider what lay behind the seductive plan suggested to him. He thought about why he might be inclined to follow the advice. Was he afraid of hardship? Was he afraid of death? Was he interested in earning merit that would lead to a higher rebirth? No! No! No to all! The Maha Sramana gave a reply:

Mara, you Lord of Illusion who haunts those who lose mindfulness! You came for your own sake, not mine! Confidence, discipline, perseverance, and wisdom are my spiritual practice. What makes you think you can question me about life?

I'm Not a Brahmin, I'm a Kshatriya!

Siddhartha was not going to adopt the spiritual path of the brahmins who performed fire sacrifices for well-being in this world, or for the ancestors. He was not born as a brahmin. Besides that, he was on another spiritual path with a different goal. He wanted to cut the roots of rebirth—not have a higher rebirth or a comfortable life here and now. Even many brahmins themselves were becoming wary of the ancient fire sacrifice. They were forsaking the Vedic ritual to Agni in favor of kindling an inner "fire" through fasting and meditation. They studied the Upanishads rather than the older Vedas, and sought freedom from rebirth through the union of self and Brahman. Gautama was not interested in what Mara proposed. Yes, the Vedic fire sacrifice brought merit. But it did not lead to the specific goal he'd set for himself: end suffering and rebirth.

Let us never forget that Siddhartha was a kshatriya—a warrior. He was not of the priestly caste. He did not grow up memorizing Vedic scriptures and performing rituals to the ancestors. He grew up with diplomatic and martial training. So even after he rejected political life, "Prince" Siddhartha carried himself as a kshatriya. He approached his spirituality with a warrior mind. He was out to defeat his worst enemies. They were inner enemies. And finally at the point of death he met his enemy face to face.

> ## Enlightening Extras
>
> Buddha lived in the midst of cultural tension. The pure Vedic Aryans of the Ganga-Yamuna Doab were pitted against the less-pure Vedic culture of the Middle Ganges Basin. And even among Aryans of Buddha's region, the tension between brahmins and kshatriyas was heightening. Many of the new religious seekers were kshatriyas—such as Siddhartha and Mahavira (the Jain leader). Both of them finally rejected the Aryan caste system altogether, and so rejected the supreme authority of brahmins.

The kshatriya Siddhartha announced to Mara, "I display the munja!" The munja is a crest made of munja grass worn on a warrior's head or displayed on a banner, signifying that the warrior will not retreat. So here we see the Maha Sramana saying—by metaphor—that he'll fight until either the enemy is defeated or he himself dies.

Mara's Army Attacks

At one point in the struggle to cut the root of rebirth, Siddhartha was all alone. (This means that not only had the five ascetics left his side, but various devas that were often around left this fight up to the kshatriya himself.) Now he would muster up strength from all the bodhisattva training of many eons. The Ten Perfections would be his spiritual weapons: giving, virtue, renunciation, wisdom, effort, patience, truthfulness, determination, friendliness, and even-mindedness. (See Chapter 5.)

> **Be Mindful!**
>
> Is Mara real? A modern reader may reject the historical reality of Mara and his army. But it's worth looking for the psychological reality behind various extraordinary events in Buddha's life story. For example, the regiments of Mara's army and Mara's daughters represent inner enemies, such as fear of death, desire, and delusion. The spiritual warrior must conquer these inner enemies with the weapons of virtue.

With the Bodhisattva pitted against the Lord of Illusion, a great commotion ensued. Mara attacked nine times using the power of the elements:

- **Wind:** Whirlwind
- **Water:** Torrential rain
- **Fire:** Flaming spears, hot coals, clouds of ash
- **Earth:** Rock shower, sandstorm, mudslides
- **Ether:** Boundless darkness, growing darker

Siddhartha sat through the attacks of Mara's army. The whirlwind faded away, rain didn't touch him, projectiles turned to flowers, clouds turned to incense, and darkness was dispersed by sunlight. Then Siddhartha named the regiments of Mara's army that he was confronting face to face—for example: hunger and thirst, doubt, fear, and aversion for the holy life. Siddhartha's spiritual weapons enabled him to transform this hardship into something harmless. The Perfections of patience, friendliness, determination, and others all played a role in the Bodhisattva's confrontation with Mara, whose job was to keep people living in the realm of sense desires.

Siddhartha realized that spiritual warriors need mental stability to survive the fight against their inner enemies. He realized also that such warriors require mental clarity to identify and defeat enemies encountered in the darkness of delusion. By applying the 10 virtues to counteract the force of his internal enemies—symbolized by Mara's army—Siddhartha defeated them. As a result, he overcame the fear of death.

Mara's Daughters

It might seem that a person who conquers the fear of death has mastered life. Nothing should bother people who don't fear death because they have come to terms with the ultimate fate of their bodies, right? Well … maybe not! Siddhartha's experience after he defeated Mara's army indicates that even when fear of physical death is conquered, one still maintains the desire to live on through others. This wish to prolong oneself through relatives is a core area of human longing that Mara targeted when he sent his daughters to tempt the Maha Sramana. But Siddhartha was able to identify them by name, and saved himself: Discontent, Delight, and Desire.

It is possible that Siddhartha even envisioned his own wife at this time. And thoughts of wife as mother could have morphed into concern for the happiness of his child, aunt, and aged father. After all, Siddhartha had left home for their sake—to find an end to the suffering he knew they were slated to endure. If he were to give up his search, his time away from family would have amounted to nothing. Siddhartha was backed into a corner. Did he have the stamina to sit immovable—come death or awakening? If he died right there, how would that help anyone? If he quit the search, how could he bring the help he envisioned. He must wake up. There was no choice.

The Earth Is My Witness

At the point of defeat, Mara challenged the Bodhisattva on grounds of authority. But the chief deva of the sense desire realm of samsara could stir neither fear nor desire in Siddhartha's heart. But there was still a chance that this Lord of Illusion could undermine his confidence. So Mara mounted a giant elephant and demanded that Siddhartha give him the seat. In response to Mara's bold move, the Bodhisattva challenged the Lord of Illusion with these words:

> *You've never developed virtue, renunciation, and wisdom. So this seat is not yours! Tell me, who has seen you do a good deed?*

In defense of himself, Mara rounded up some companions to justify his right to the seat. He then demanded that Siddhartha produce a witness to his own practice of virtue, renunciation, and wisdom. And at that moment, Siddhartha did something that carried deep meaning. He extended his right arm down to let his fingers touch the earth. "The earth is my witness," he said. With that, the earth quaked. Mara's elephant knelt in homage, and Mara's companions fled. And Mara himself admitted defeat.

Buddha Basics

The spiritual greatness of Earth was recognized in India 3,000 years ago. *Prithvi—* meaning Earth—is a feminine Vedic deity who provides a sacred space for all human spiritual endeavors. Buddhist texts say the earth witnessed the Bodhisattva's practice of the Perfections of giving, virtue, and so on. When Siddhartha touched the earth to call her as a witness in front of the Lord of Illusion, a terrific quake occurred as she validated his claim. The earth witnessing hand gesture has become a favorite icon in Buddhist art.

Clear Sailing

With Mara gone, the Bodhisattva was ready to move quickly toward awakening. The encounter with the Lord of Illusion and his daughters taught Siddhartha the value of mindfulness. Being mindful of Mara's daughters, Siddhartha recognized desire as a reflection of his own mind. Being mindful of Mara's army, Siddhartha recognized the fear of death as a reflection of his own mind. And so, being mindful, these powerful emotions dissolved.

Dharma Dictionary

Attention and awareness are complementary terms that refer to two branches of meditation (known as bhavana) in Buddhism: serenity and insight. Samatha (serenity) meditation results in a continuum of samadhi experiences. Vipasyana (insight) meditation results in wisdom that recognizes the Three Marks of Existence: impermanence, non-self, and suffering.

The defeat of Mara suggested a deep psychological truth to the Bodhisattva: to cut the roots of suffering, one needs both *attention and awareness.* He realized it's not enough to just see Mara and his daughters (who represent things in the sense desire realm)—one must realize their true nature. Desire and fear were none other than reflections of his mind.

The Awakening

Siddhartha awoke on the full moon night in the month of Vaisaka. In each of the three "watches" of the full moon night on which the Bodhisattva awakened, he realized something different. The decisive breakthrough to full enlightenment did not come until the third watch of the night. At that point, Siddhartha's delusions about the nature of reality dissolved.

First Watch of the Night: 6 P.M.–10 P.M.

During the first watch of the night, Siddhartha recalled his past lives in meticulous detail. Because his inner vision was unobstructed, he could focus on specific events and find out his name, family, caste, diet, pleasures and pains, and end of life.

Enlightening Extras

Both Buddhist and Hindu meditation texts speak of the ability to recall past lives. Buddhaghosa (fifth century C.E.) in the *Visuddhimagga* (XIII, 14) instructs monks to practice remembering past lives by reviewing in reverse order what they have done that day, the previous day, and on back for years up until the time of their birth and back from that. Patanjali (c. 200 B.C.E. to c. 400 C.E.) in the *Yoga-Sutras* (III, 18) explains that knowledge of past lives of oneself or others comes from the direct perception of subliminal impressions.

Second Watch of the Night: 10 P.M.–2 A.M.

During the second watch of the night, the Bodhisattva opened his wisdom eye further. The spectacle of the universe looked as though it were reflected in a spotless mirror. He turned his attention to the past lives of other beings, stretching back over eons. He saw the passing away and the coming to be of many beings and noticed the patterns of action that led to their happiness or suffering. Thus he understood the intricacies of the moral law of cause and effect of karma.

Third Watch of the Night: 2 A.M.–6 A.M.

During the third watch of the night, Siddhartha actually awakened. He became Buddha by realizing the chain of dependent arising that links delusion with rebirth. He followed this chain in the devolving direction, and thus undid his own rebirth by following it all the way back to delusion—its root. He realized the nature of suffering, its cause, its cessation, and the path leading to the cessation of suffering. (See Chapter 13.)

Now the Bodhisattva's long struggle had come to an end. He had cut the roots of rebirth and was free at last. He had attained nirvana.

The Least You Need to Know

- Siddhartha decided he should eat something after fasting to the point of starvation and decided that proper spiritual practice was a Middle Way approach.

- Mara, the Lord of Illusion, challenged Siddhartha by sending his army to frighten and his daughters to sensually captivate Siddhartha. But he failed.

- The Bodhisattva told Mara that he had practiced virtue and called upon the earth to be his witness.

- Siddhartha discovered that meditations involving both attention (samatha) and awareness (vipasyana) are needed for enlightenment.

- The Bodhisattva's awakening occurred during three watches of a full moon night in the month of Vaisaka, in which he remembered his former lives, saw the karma of many other beings in the universe, and realized how suffering comes from delusion about the nature of reality.

- Siddhartha's enlightenment is called nirvana; and the moment he attained nirvana he became Buddha, the Awakened One.

Chapter 10

To Teach or Not To Teach

In This Chapter

- ◆ Tathata is the answer
- ◆ Three realms of samsara
- ◆ Three watches of the enlightenment night
- ◆ Buddha's first 49 days after awakening
- ◆ Buddha's decision to teach

Siddhartha woke up. On a full moon night in the spring of his thirty-fifth year, the Sakyan prince-ascetic attained enlightenment, directly comprehending tathata—reality as it is. And amazingly, he was convinced that by seeing things just as they are, he would no longer be compelled to take rebirth in samsara. And perhaps more amazingly, the Maha Sramana woke up through mindfulness of his breathing. Siddhartha built upon a very natural approach to meditation that he had spontaneously discovered when he was still a prince, sitting under a rose-apple tree during a plowing festival.

Is it possible that an escape from the compulsory cycle of rebirth can be achieved by simply watching one's breath? Can freedom from the sufferings of the Wheel of Becoming be attained without any rituals? Without any priests? Without any sacred scriptures? Without severe penances? Without entering the rarified states of consciousness open only to advanced spiritual technicians? It seems that Buddha's answer to all these questions was "Yes." We may begin to see that Siddhartha's discovery under the fig tree in Urubilva might seem too easy on one hand and too radical on the other.

Gautama's awakening ends suffering—not only by stopping rebirth, but also by bringing contentment in the midst of life's trials and tribulations. This was too good to be true. This was also threatening to the status quo. Of what use were the ancient Vedic texts? Of what use were the brahmins? Of what use were the stages of life that included householding—producing sons and the sons of sons? Buddha recognized that his teaching went "against the grain." So it was not at all clear that he would be moved to teach.

Far Out!

Could the Maha Sramana teach others how to awaken? Should he? Would others psychologically survive the death of preconceptions about the world? Might a person get lost over the brink of experience? Might a person get lost just short of the brink of nonexperience? Let's look in detail at what happened to Siddhartha during the three watches of the full moon on the night of his awakening. Then we might better appreciate his dilemma: to teach or not to teach.

The Three Realms of Samsara

On the night of his awakening, Siddhartha reviewed the three realms of samsara and then broke loose. Once freed from the compulsion to return to that Wheel of Becoming, he could go through the various realms of samsara for the sake of helping others without getting caught there. He could be in samsara, but not of it. When Buddha finally decided to teach the path to enlightenment, he did in fact "travel" throughout the three realms of samsara, to guide beings caught there suffering. The realm with beings who suffer most is the sense desire realm. But even in the realms of pure form and no form, beings need enlightenment. So Buddha eventually attended to beings throughout the Wheel of Becoming.

Be Mindful!

The word *places* in Buddhism needs some explanation. Ultimately everything is mentally created, according to Buddha's philosophy. That means places can be described as states of mind or states of rebirth. With enough skill, a meditator can "visit" the different realms of samsara. But beings are born into the realms according to their karma and their state of mind when they pass away.

Sense Desire Realm

The most intense suffering in samsara occurs in the sense desire realm, where six types of beings exist. You'll recognize at least the first two of them: human, animal, hell being, hungry ghost, titan, and worldly godling (*deva*). The amount of suffering is greatest among animals, hungry ghosts, and hell beings, so these are called the three lower births. But the amount of suffering varies not only according to the type of life, but also the individual karma of each sentient being. But no matter how much or how little a being suffers in this realm, no one is stuck forever in that life form. Even hell beings get out when their karmic sentence is finished. And worldly devas can't stay longer than their good fortune lasts.

Pure Form Realm

The pure form realm encompasses four levels of subtle, boundless existence where the god Brahma dwells. The levels are experienced as absorptions called *dhyanas*. The experience of each dhyana level (climbing the ladder, we could say) is less "emotional" than the last. The first absorption starts out with the emotions of bliss and joy. By the fourth level, both emotions are thinned out and the meditator experiences equanimity.

Dharma Dictionary

Dhyanas are levels of mediation where the mind is absorbed in its object. In the Hindu Patanjali's system, the experience of these *dhyana* absorptions lead to the experience of samadhi. The difference is largely a matter of degree and depends on the amount of time one spends meditating with unwavering attention upon an object. So to say that the dhyanas are ways of *cultivating* samadhi with form fits the overall scheme of India's yoga tradition.

The four dhyanas are known as the abodes of Brahma because the god Brahma abides in them. They are associated with four boundless emotions, also known as the social virtues: love, compassion, joy, and equanimity. (Check out more on the abodes of Brahma in Chapter 16.)

Realm of No Form

The realm of no form encompasses four levels of subtle formless existence where subject and object cannot be distinguished from each other. Each level is more abstract than the last, as thinking is pared down as far as possible. But, get this. There is still *experience* in the realm of no form. There is still an *object*. But it is not a physical object.

You ask, "What's *there?*" Well … four experiences of increasing cognitive vacuity with far-out names. Each one gets more abstract than the last. The four levels are named according to the kind of samadhi a meditator experiences there:

- **Boundless space:** After coming to the fourth dhyana in the realm of pure form, meditators rise above the state of perfect even-mindedness and enter the first level of the realm of no form. There is space all around. Nothing but space. This boundless space is the first formless samadhi. Here meditators don't experience themselves as separate beings, because there are no forms at all.

- **Boundless consciousness:** After some practice abiding in boundless space, meditators see that the space is itself an object of consciousness. As their samadhi matures, they find they are abiding in boundless consciousness, the second level of the realm of no form.

- **Nothing whatsoever:** Then what happens? Nothing whatsoever. It's hard to imagine, but as meditators keep their attention fixed, samadhi matures and they realize that boundless consciousness is actually nothing whatsoever. This experience was the end of the line in Alara Kalama's teachings. Remember how Siddhartha attained this level with his first teacher after leaving his home in Kapilavastu?

- **Neither perception nor nonperception:** This was the end of the line in Rudraka Ramaputra's teachings, supposedly the last possible stop in the world of experience. As samadhi matures, at some point it dawns upon meditators at the previous level that nothing whatsoever is also an object of perception. Here, finally, there is no perception. There's no *non*perception either …. Well … you get the picture. Anyhow, Siddhartha had gotten to this level with his second teacher, but felt it was not enough to cut his ties to the Wheel of Becoming.

Buddha Basics

The concept of experience is important in the buddha-dharma. All samsara involves experience. But nirvana transcends experience itself. A meditator can scale the full spectrum of experience through samadhi, which operates along a continuum. When attention is held for longer and longer periods of time, the experience modulates and becomes more and more subtle. But samadhi alone cannot take the meditator beyond experience to nirvana.

Gautama Zooms to Awakening

In the three watches of the night of his awakening, Siddhartha scaled samsara's realms, using his concentrated attention as a tool to enter samadhi and zoom through the full spectrum of samsaric experience. He started among beings in the sense desire realm and encountered Mara, who sits at its uppermost reaches to govern it. The Lord of Illusion offered him the attractions that draw the six types of beings into this realm. The Bodhisattva overcame those attractions and left Mara powerless. Thereafter, Siddhartha began to have experiences characteristic of the more subtle realms of samsara. Finally, he transcended experience altogether and attained nirvana.

Siddhartha Sees His Past Lives

In the first watch of the night of his awakening, Siddhartha came to the higher knowledges. These include his experiences from 6 P.M. to 10 P.M.:

- The siddhis (supernormal powers)

- Recollection of former existences

- Divine ear

- Divine eye

- Reading the minds of beings

- Destruction of negative formations (evil influences)

> **Be Mindful!**
>
> You know, all this technical stuff *does* make a difference to Buddhists! It's not just a matter of theory. It's something to be practiced and realized. That's why the texts go into such fine detail. All the lists and definitions fall into the third basket of Buddha's teaching, the Abhidharma. This is basically a matter of the Buddhist psychology of meditation.

Here he did many supernormal things that sound like myth. They sound like science fiction. But these are the siddhis that are taken seriously by the Indian meditative traditions. The supernormal powers are not necessary for enlightenment—though they can be useful when a meditator wants to help others by extraordinary means such as seeing or hearing from a far distance and so forth.

Here are some supernormal feats performed by the Maha Sramana. These resulted from his excellent powers of concentration:

- He multiplied himself.

- He made himself invisible.

- He went through walls and rocks as if they were air.

- He went into and out of the earth as if it were water.

- He flew through the air, seated cross-legged.

- He recollected his former lives.

At this point, Siddhartha's steady mind was like a polished mirror where everything is reflected in true perspective. It was tranquil, pure, free from lust, pliable, and alert. From this experience, Gautama would be able to teach about rebirth—a fundamental idea in the Buddhist tradition.

Siddhartha Watches Karma at Work

In the second watch of the night of his awakening, Siddhartha continued to direct his mind to the higher knowledges. His experiences from 10 P.M. to 2 A.M. include the following:

- He heard by means of the divine ear that allowed perception of human and non-human sounds that were near and far.

- He used the divine eye through which he saw all manner of beings who were dying and coming into existence. He recognized that suffering and negative deeds were correlated—as were happiness and positive deeds.

Thus, for eight hours the Maha Sramana stayed in a high state of samadhi and gained experiences of the higher knowledges. Particularly from closely observing what he perceived through the divine eye, Gautama would be able to teach about the law of cause and effect of karma—a key to Buddhist ethics.

Enlightening Extras

The divine eye is recognized in Hinduism as well as Buddhism. Krishna (the Hindu deity) opened Arjuna the warrior's divine eye, and he saw the whole universe as one, converged into Krishna's body. The *Bhagavad Gita* (11:5–32) reports that Arjuna was terrified and his hair stood on end as he saw numberless burning divine mouths devouring worlds. Krishna explained that Arjuna was seeing Him as Time itself.

Sakyamuni Realizes the Four Great Facts

In the third watch of the night of awakening, Siddhartha actually cut the bonds to rebirth. With this act we can call him Buddha, the Awakened One, or Sakyamuni, "sage of the Sakya" people. During this four-hour stretch from 2 A.M. to 6 A.M., several things happened:

- He acquired the ability to read the minds of beings. He understood their various mental formations and knew deeply when a mind was with passion or without passion, concentrated or not, liberated or not.

- He acquired the knowledge of the destruction of negative influences. This meant that he realized the nature of suffering, the cause of suffering, the cessation of suffering, and the path to the cessation of suffering.

After discovering the path to end suffering, Gautama realized that he was finally liberated from compulsory rebirth into samsara. He'd become clear of negative mental formations! This final knowledge made clear the Four Noble Truths or Four Great Facts about suffering that would become the cornerstone of the buddha-dharma. As an Awakened One, Gautama would teach these facts for 45 years: suffering, its cause, its cessation, and the path to end suffering.

Free at Last!

Okay! Buddha tended not to talk much about nirvana. And in a moment you'll see why. It's way beyond our normal concepts. If you thought that "nothing whatsoever" or "neither perception nor nonperception" were far out, get a load of this. There's a *ninth dhyana*, which is a kind of samadhi where attention is completely still. Sensations and perceptions occur, but they arise and fall away in almost the same instant. Siddhartha moved into this ninth dhyana just as he left the brink of samsara. But he was not quite done yet. (Hold on, we're almost there!)

> **Dharma Dictionary**
>
> Gautama discovered a **ninth dhyana** (the cessation of sensation and perception) in the third watch of the night of his awakening. This was followed by the experience of experience, and finally … nirvana.

Ready for the next one? The next-to-last thing Siddhartha experienced before awakening was the experience of experience. (Technically, it's called the attainment of cessation.) This one's based on insight. This is not the experience of *existence*. And it's not a *lack* of experience. It is an experience: the experience of experience itself.

Are we there yet? Almost! Now comes nirvana. Nirvana is peace. It is free of existence in any of the three realms of samsara. But here's the good part: Siddhartha did not have to disappear from the world when he attained nirvana. He simply got a radically new perspective on life! After attaining nirvana, he could interact with beings in samsara. It's just that at the time of death, he would not be compelled to return to the Wheel of Becoming.

Hanging Out at the Bodhi Tree

How could the new Buddha talk about his experience of experience? Who might understand this? Who might be interested? It may come as no surprise that Gautama—and now we can call him Buddha or the Tathagata, needed some time to digest what had happened to him. He spent 49 days by the Nairanjana River in the neighborhood of the fig tree, which was later called the bodhi tree, or tree of enlightenment.

In the first week, the Tathagata sat unmoving under the bodhi tree experiencing the bliss of liberation. Indian tradition states that all Dharmacakrins wait a week in contemplation after being coronated. Just as the rulers of ancient Aryan times did not leave their place of coronation for seven days, so it was for buddhas. So the newly awakened Gautama followed an age-old custom as he sat in contemplation for a full week without uncrossing his legs.

On the seventh day, the Awakened One reflected on what's called the chain of dependent arising. He saw that one thing leads to another: delusion … karmic formations … dualistic consciousness … name and form … sense fields … touch … sensation … craving … grasping … gestation … birth … aging and death.

In the second week, the Tathagata stood unmoving and gazing at the bodhi tree. This is called the "unblinking look." In gratitude to the tree for sheltering him during the awakening, he said to himself: "Here I became enlightenened and put an end to the suffering of birth, old age, and death."

In the third week, the Tathagata used his psychic powers to create a staircase made of jewels and did walking meditation, pacing up and down on it.

In the fourth week, the Tathagata meditated in a jeweled chamber created by his psychic powers. In it he reflected on the interconnected nature of mind and reality. Because Buddha's mind was pure, six colors of light emanated from his body at this time.

In the fifth week, the Tathagata sat unmoving under the banyan tree where Sujata had offered him milk-rice prior to enlightenment. Rising out of contemplation, Buddha spoke with a brahmin who stopped and asked, "In what way should a brahmin live?" Buddha answered, "It's most important for a brahmin to discard moral impurities."

Buddha Basics

Some accounts have Mara's daughters—Discontent, Delight, and Desire—appear to Buddha at the end of the fifth week after his enlightenment, though others have them appear before the awakening. Otherwise, it's said that Mara (hoping Buddha would not go out and teach the path to enlightenment) approached the new Buddha and asked him to die. That ruler of samsara put his request very politely: "May the Blessed One enter nirvana now! This is the time for the Blessed One's Great Decease." Needless to say, Buddha refused.

In the sixth week, Sakyamuni sat under another tree and again enjoyed the bliss of liberation. The tree is named after Mucalinda, a serpent-king who coiled around Buddha seven times and sheltered him during a great storm that arose during this week. After the storm, Mucalinda took the form of a youth and pressed his hands together in a gesture of respect. In a moral pronouncement, Buddha said that happiness is goodwill in this world.

In the seventh week, Sakyamuni sat beneath the rajayatana tree and experienced the bliss of emancipation, closing the seven weeks the way he began them. All together, around 28 of Buddha's 49 days were spent experiencing the bliss of liberation.

"Tathagatas Are Merely Teachers"

As the Tathagata was dwelling at the foot of the banyan tree during week five of his debriefing, he had this thought:

> It's very painful to live without someone whom I can revere. Perhaps I should live near an ascetic or brahmin, and show deference to him?

This shows that some social impulse in Buddha was stirring. Some inner compass would direct him back into society. He would not remain isolated after his awakening. But now as an enlightened being he couldn't think of any brahmin or ascetic to revere! Fortunately, this thought occurred to him next: "What if I live respecting and reverencing the dharma that I have discovered?" That was the thing to do. And so Buddha—and every Buddhist after him to this day—took up the custom of revering the spiritual teachings, instead of any person.

After all the strange events of six years leading up to the enlightenment, following the enlightenment, and the seven weeks of meditation, Buddha became a teacher. He was neither a god nor a magician. He could not save people from suffering by supernormal powers. But he could offer the dharma to other living beings. And with knowledge of dharma they could seek and experience enlightenment for themselves. Thus Buddha told his disciples, "Tathagatas are merely teachers."

> ### Be Mindful!
>
> Just before reentering society after his awakening, the thought arose in Buddha's mind, "What if I live respecting and revering the *dharma?*" This thought has stuck with the Buddhist tradition ever since. Just like Buddha, all Buddhists revere the dharma above all. Buddhists do not worship Buddha. They strive to become like Buddha and take the dharma as their guide—with reverence and respect.

The Least You Need to Know

- Though many of Buddha's meditation experiences are subtle and seem hard to duplicate, waking up simply boils down to seeing things as they are: tathata.

- Samsara comprises three realms: sense desire, pure form, and no form. All experiences on the Wheel of Becoming are impermanent, subject to pain, and have no abiding self.

- During Buddha's awakening, he developed six higher knowledges that allowed him to confirm the fact of rebirth, the authenticity of karma, and the truth of nonself.

- Buddha spent seven weeks after awakening by the bodhi tree in Urubilva before he decided to go out and teach.

- Nirvana is peace. It can be experienced in the midst of samsara while one is alive, or outside the cycle of rebirth after death.

- Even though each person must transform his or her own mind, Buddha decided to teach people to help themselves. He said, "Tathagatas are merely teachers."

Chapter 11

The Community Up and Walking

In This Chapter

- The whole crew: brahmins, Sannyasins, Jains, and more
- A tour of cities in the Middle Ganges Basin
- Communities of monks and nuns
- Rules, robes, and a bowl
- Communities of laymen and laywomen
- A worldwide vision

Over his six-year period of study and penance, Gautama gradually honed his view of reality and became familiar with various lifestyles that a seeker could adopt. But when it came time to teach, he had to figure out how to live out his view of reality and find the proper way to make awakening possible for others who would follow in his footsteps.

He was familiar with life in hermitage communities as well as solitary life in the jungle. He'd become familiar with many teachers and many teachings. How would he set up his own spiritual community?

While the republics were being overrun by the emerging states of Kausala and Magadha, Buddha was establishing a new kind of spiritual community using the traditional tribal approach to community and governance—a spiritual clan in a world where urban life was making tribal life extinct. Gautama found a way to combine his distinctive view of reality with the needs of society.

No Brahmin Path for a Kshatriya

Buddha did not try to fit into the Vedic tradition. He grew up as a Sakyan, which was basically a clan of kshatriyas, and it would be against Vedic tradition to try to act like a brahmin or encourage his disciples to. Siddhartha declined to follow the Vedic path when Mara tried to tempt him on the eve of his awakening by suggesting that he give up the search for the deathless state and earn merit through doing the fire sacrifice. Siddhartha's goal was not success in this world or the next: he sought to transcend the Wheel of Becoming altogether.

Enlightening Extras

The ancient Vedic language (an early form of Sanskrit) was created for chanting. And the Vedic texts memorized for rituals are beautiful and full of deep meaning. They are believed to convey "the word beyond words" and were composed by inspired seers. The original Vedas are still chanted today by brahmins who believe that the scriptural sounds are invested with divine power.

Buddha respected brahmins, but he didn't accept the traditional claim that brahmins were spiritually superior just because they were born into that class. One day on Vulture Peak, he said:

> I don't call someone a brahmin because he was born to a brahmin mother. I call a brahmin someone who owns nothing and is attached to nothing. I call a brahmin one who wears rags covered with dust, meditates in the forest alone, and is so thin that his ribs stick out.

In effect, Buddha was rejecting the Aryan caste system by saying a person is not a brahmin just because he is born to a brahmin mother. More radically, he actually rejected his own caste standing as a kshatriya when he became part of the buddha lineage.

How About the Sannyasin Path?

Buddha spoke of ascetics, who meditated in the forest wearing only filthy rags as true brahmins. He was talking about Sannyasins—the new-style brahmins who renounced the world seeking to know Brahman by uniting their inner light with the universal energy in meditation. These Brahmacarins were moving away from the values of early Vedic culture, losing interest in a family lineage prolonged through having sons and grandsons. In the socially progressive atmosphere of Buddha's day, Aryan culture was more or less being forced to allow early drop outs (Sannyasins) to prevent more people (such as Buddha and the Jain leader Mahavira) from rejecting the caste system altogether.

> **Dharma Dictionary**
>
> **Brahmacarin** means one who seeks to know Brahman. Originally found in the Upanishads, the term came to mean all sramanas because they labored to realize the highest spiritual attainment, whether or not they called it Brahman. Unlike the Vedic Sannyasins, Buddha did not speak in terms of uniting the soul with Brahman.

The Sannyasins were brahmins who passed to the final stage of life outlined by the Aryan caste system. They had done one of two things: fulfilled their caste duties and produced a son who had a son, or taken advantage of a short cut recently opened to them within the Brahmanical tradition. These early drop-outs from society called upon the authority of the sage Yajnavalkya, who had taught (in a text called the *Jabala Upanisad*) that those who possessed an exceptional spirit of renunciation could enter homelessness even if they were still in the student or householder stage of life. They could become Sannyasins before—rather than after—the traditional householder and forest dwelling stages (which involved their wives as well).

In a sense, all the wanderers in the Middle Ganges Basin in Buddha's day were Sannyasins, who "completely cast off" worldly ties. But technically, it was only a brahmin male who did so in the context of an established life path—because brahmins were the priestly class whose vocation was the spiritual life. By contrast, when a kshatriya like Siddhartha took up the spiritual life early, he was in grave breach of his caste duty. The duty of a kshatriya was to remain in society to rule and protect. True, at the end of a long life of service and having a son who produced a son, even a kshatriya or a vaisya could pursue appropriate religious duties. But to abandon the social responsibilities of a warrior was a serious move. In fact, however, a large number of people taking up the homeless life in the Middle Ganges Basin of Buddha's day were kshatriyas.

Buddha's approach to spirituality had much in common with the new-style Sannyasins who made deep study of the internal landscape of the self. Like those Brahmacarins, Gautama sought freedom from rebirth, the deathless state. He also believed that moving from home to homelessness—abandoning householder responsibilities—was not socially or spiritually disastrous.

But even though Buddha owed much to the heritage of Sannyasins, he could not go down the road to achieving the *union of atman with Brahman*. Why? Because during the awakening he had looked for *atman*, but realized *anatman* instead. Though both he and the Sannyasins looked within to find the nature of oneself, Buddha found a new, dynamic way of looking. It's as though the Sannyasins believed in what physicists call the particle theory of light, while Buddha discovered that light was a wave with no particles. With his new discovery, method, and teaching, Gautama could not go the way of the Vedic tradition.

> **Dharma Dictionary**
>
> The brahmin Sannyasins aimed to experience the **union of atman and Brahman** as the means of getting free from rebirth. The Upanishads call the soul **atman** and the power that runs through the universe **Brahman**. By uniting the atman with Brahman, the Sannyasins erased the concept of the self as a separate, selfish entity. By contrast, Buddha taught **anatman,** or nonself, and did not speak in terms of an all-pervasive divine force.

Jains and Buddhists: Estranged Twins?

The Jain leader in Buddha's day was Vardhamana Mahavira. He claimed to be one in a long line of tirthankaras, or ford crossers, just as Gautama claimed there were many awakened ones before him. Mahavira played a big role in shaping his tradition and was much influenced by social upheavals and cultural creativity in the Middle Ganges Basin. The early Jains and Buddhists had lots in common. They may have been closer than any other two sects at the time. And of all the non-Vedic sects, these are the two that stood the test of time. Let's see their similarities:

- Both founders were from kshatriya families of Aryan tribes in the Himalayan foothills: Buddha was Sakyan, Mahavira was Licchavi.

- Both founders rejected Brahmanical rituals and the caste system.

- Both founders had been married and renounced the householding life: Buddha had a son, Mahavira had a daughter.

◆ Both Buddha and Mahavira established branches of their communities for women.

◆ Buddhist and Jain members of the order were all renunciates who wandered, except during the rains, which they spent in community.

◆ Both sects ate cooked food only before noon (and only one meal per day).

In spite of the great similarity between the outlooks of Buddha and Mahavira, they really could not be reduced to the same religious vision. As Gautama and Mahavira wandered around Vaisali, Rajagriha, and other towns, one could always tell their followers apart by their hairdos. Following Mahavira's lead, Jains pulled their hair out by the roots. Buddhists did not go to that extent, as Buddha had merely cut his hair. But their differences went more than scalp deep. Here are some:

Be Mindful!
By around 1000 C.E., Buddhism was declining in India—and was only reintroduced later. Yet it spread throughout Asia with great cultural impact. By contrast, Jainism maintained a strong presence in India from Mahavira's time until today. What's more, only recently did Jainism begin to spread.

◆ No Jain would ever eat meat, taking nonviolence as the lynchpin of their entire spiritual practice. But Buddha counseled his monks and nuns to eat whatever meat was offered as alms with three exceptions:

1. Disciples should not eat the meat of an animal if it was killed especially for them.

2. Disciples should not eat the meat of an animal they saw being killed.

3. Disciples should not eat the meat of an animal if they heard its cries as it was being killed.

◆ Mahavira's and Buddha's views on karma differed. Buddha considered a person's motivation to be the most important factor that determined whether an act was wholesome or unwholesome. Mahavira tended to emphasize the act itself. So Jains tried at all costs not to injure even the smallest animal—even by accidentally stepping on insects.

◆ Jains wished to free the jiva (living soul) from the material body and let it ascend to the top of the universe. By contrast, Buddhists did not accept the idea of an eternal soul and sought an experience beyond existence.

Enlightening Extras

Jains and Buddhists both used water filters and did not eat after noon to minimize the number of animals killed in eating. (More insects fly into cooking flames at night!) But Jains may consider Buddhists half-hearted in their practice of nonviolence, and Buddhists may consider Jains to be extreme. It comes down to how one interprets the law of karma. Is the act or the motive more important?

Three More Rejected Groups

The numerous ascetics who wandered throughout the Middle Ganges Basin held a great variety of views on the nature of reality. Three main views on life that Buddha thought were inaccurate or unhelpful for spiritual life were materialism, fatalism, and skepticism. So he did not associate his sangha with any of these groups. In the end the Sakyaputriya, or spiritual children of the Sakyan, had to create a distinct spiritual community, because they were unlike any other group in thought and practice due to Buddha's teaching on nonself.

Materialists

A fellow named Ajita Kesakambala went around wearing a hair blanket. He was a die-hard materialist. He believed that matter is all that exists, and that all deeds, positive or negative, amounted to nothing. All beings were destined to dwell in samsara for a prescribed period of time. And when a person died, the body particles dispersed into their primary elements, and that was that.

Buddha rejected the materialist doctrine of Ajita Kesakambala as incomplete and morally risky. While the die-hard materialist taught there was neither good nor evil, Buddha claimed that karma or action did carry a positive, negative, or neutral value. And Buddha clearly held that there was more to the person than its material form. From the enlightenment experience, Sakyamuni saw that beings were reborn based on the continuity of a consciousness that carried a code of one's deeds from life to life. Buddha contradicted the materialist doctrine by saying that the impact of one's deeds was not lost from life to life, so the quality of a person's actions did matter, both in the present and in the future.

Fatalists

The Ajivakas were a non-Vedic sect that believed everything in this world is prede-termined. Maskarin Gosaliputra, a strict ascetic (probably Buddha's contemporary), founded this group of fatalists. He associated with the Jain leader Mahavira for seven years, then established his own center at Sravasti in a woman potter's shop. His fol-lowers roamed through the towns of the Middle Ganges Basin and were known for using magical powers derived from meditation. Beyond mental discipline, these Aji-vakas practiced morality, even though they believed that actions of body, speech, and mind amounted to nothing.

Maskarin Gosaliputra was not a materialist, because he thought there was more to life than the body. He did believe each person had a soul that passed from birth to birth, and that living beings became increasingly pure in the course of transmigration from life to life. But all this was according to a preordained pattern. No matter what one did while living, the fate of the soul was fixed. An Ajivaka would pull out his or her hair by the roots, meditate in caves, and voluntarily fast to death over a period of six months when their time came to get off the Wheel of Becoming. But they never thought they were changing their fate by doing so.

Buddha objected to the fatalistic view of the Ajivakas. Maskarin Gosaliputra didn't think that one's karma had any impact on future lives. But Buddha, on the other hand, was certain of the impact of morality on future lives, because of what he realized in the second watch of his awakening night. At that time he saw with the divine eye that positive acts brought happiness, and negative acts brought suffering to living beings.

Skeptics

The teachings of an Indian philosopher named Sanjayin Vairattiputra were known in Buddha's day. He was a masterful skeptic. That meant he wouldn't say whether some-thing was so, was not so, was *not* not so, or was both so *and* not so. This guy used what is called the fourfold negation in his discussion of topics. So, he'd answer "no" to questions like this:

- Is the world eternal?

- Is the world not eternal?

- Is the world neither eternal nor not eternal?

- Is the world both eternal and not eternal?

The skeptics were great at knocking down positions taken by others, but would not offer any position of their own.

> **Buddha Basics**
>
> Buddhism is indebted to skepticism. Buddha did not answer "no" to a four-cornered negation as a skeptic might, but he tended in that direction by sometimes maintaining silence—as he did with the question: "Is the world eternal?" The second-century C.E. Middle Way philosopher Nagarjuna developed Buddha's silence into a masterful dialectic that transforms skepticism: he introduces opposing propositions, without positing any synthesis. And Gautama's two chief disciples, Sariputra and Maudgalyayana, switched to study of the Buddha-dharma from their studies in skeptical philosophy.

Buddha called the skeptics "eel-wrigglers" because they would not land on any position—though he himself operated from a great deal of skepticism. Buddha maintained silence on a number of questions posed according to the fourfold negation. But ultimately, Buddha thought there was a truth about reality that could be known. This was the truth of nonself or emptiness.

Hot Spots

This section tells you about places frequented by Buddha in the up and coming Middle Ganges Basin of north India—where major ethical, social, and economic changes were taking place. Here are tidbits about cities appearing on the Hot Spots map in this chapter, along with information on things Buddha did and said in the places.

Hot spots. Diagram of major places Gautama frequented in his lifetime and set up spiritual communities.

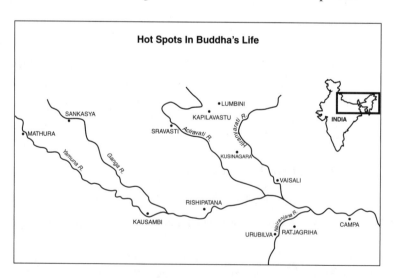

Campa

- Capital of Anga. Named for Campaka trees, which are native to India with fragrant yellow flowers.

- Buddha teaches at Gaggara Lotus Lake. Easternmost known place visited by Buddha.

- Here Buddha advises: "Morality purifies wisdom, and wisdom purifies morality: one is where the other is."

Kapilavastu

- Buddha grows up, marries, and has a son here. On his first visit home, he converts many family and clan members. In his fifth year after enlightenment, Gautama returns to see his dying father, and Maha Prajapati asks Buddha to establish a nun's order. Buddha spends his fifteenth rainy season after enlightenment here.

- Here Buddha warns his monks, "Watch out, Mara's hosts are coming." They remain alert and the hosts of the Lord of Illusion withdraw from those in whom no lust or fear can gain a foothold.

Kausambi

- Capital of Vatsa, moved from ancient Hastinapura after the Mahabharata War possibly as early as 3000 B.C.E.

- Buddha spends his sixth, ninth, and tenth rainy seasons in this area. Buddha declines an offer of marriage to Magandiya, who becomes furious and seeks revenge. Buddha retreats alone to the forest when the Kausambi monks quarrel.

- Here Buddha advises: "By quarrelling and stabbing each other with verbal daggers, you do not maintain acts of loving-kindness. Oh, misguided men your acts will bring you harm and suffering for a long time."

Kusinagara

- Questions have been raised about the actual location of this city; it might have been near Rampurva instead of near Kasia, as traditionally thought.

- Buddha attains final nirvana between two sala trees in a pleasure park of the Malla royalty on the outskirts of this city.

- Here Buddha explains that in the mythic past, King Mahasudassana lived in this very town, under the name of Kusavati, which was his capital. It was rich, prosperous, and well-populated.

Lumbini

- Both sides of Siddhartha's family—Sakyas and Koliyas— share the Lumbini Gardens, where Prince Siddhartha was born from his mother Maya Devi's side.

- Here Buddha tells Ananda of four places, the sight of which will bring a special feeling to the faithful. This is the first, because "Here the Tathagata was born."

Mathura

- Capital of Surasena. On trade routes. Birthplace of Hindu deity Krishna. Later became great center of Buddhist and Hindu art.

- Buddha visited here only once. Noted fierce dogs and lots of dust.

- Here on one occasion Maha Katyayana (Buddha's disciple who he appointed as master of dharma exposition) was living at Mathura. When King Avantiputta wanted to go for refuge with him, Katyayana said, "Don't go to me for refuge, great king. Go for refuge to that Blessed One to whom I've gone for refuge."

Rajagriha

- Prosperous capital of Magadha with 36,000 merchants' houses (half Buddhist, half Jain).

- The ascetic Siddhartha meets King Bimbisara, who asks him to return after enlightenment. Studies with second teacher, Rudraka Ramaputra.

- Buddha spends second, third, fourth, seventeenth, and twentieth rain retreats here. Teaches on Vulture Peak and in Bamboo Grove that becomes the first Buddhist monastery.

- Devadatta and 500 defecting monks stay at Gayasisa Hill nearby; Sariputra and Maudgalyayana leave their skeptic community to join Buddha's mendicant sangha.

◆ Maha Prajapati (Buddha's aunt) and Yasodhara (Buddha's former wife, Rahula's mother) are among the large gathering of disciples who listen to the Tathagata's teachings given at Rajagriha, on Vulture Peak. After Buddha finishes teaching, he sits cross-legged with his body and mind unmoving.

Rishipatana

◆ Buddha gives his first two discourses here at Deer Park (modern Sarnath, 3.7 miles/6 km from Banaras).

◆ Buddha spends his first rainy season after enlightenment here. Converts the five ascetics who had abandoned him; Yasa, the banker's son, and four friends. Around 60 new monks set out wandering—no two together.

◆ Here Buddha explains: "Monks, whoever leaves the householder's life should not become involved in either the extremes of indulgence in sense pleasures, nor devotion to self-mortification." The Tathagata realized the Middle Way by avoiding these two extremes.

Sankasya

◆ Here's where Buddha ascends to the Heaven of the Thirty-Three to teach his mother Maya Devi. Afterwards, the Tathagata descends a jeweled staircase composed of lapis lazuli, with Brahma to one side on a silver staircase and Indra to the other side on a staircase of purple gold. This became a great subject of Buddhist art.

◆ Buddha spends his seventh rainy season here.

◆ Tradition holds that all buddhas after performing the Twin Miracle spend the next Rains in the Heaven of the Thirty-Three. Buddha had performed the Twin Miracle at Sravasti before coming here to ascend to the Heaven of the Thirty-Three.

Sravasti

◆ Kausala's capital. The largest town in the Middle Ganges Basin in Buddha's day.

◆ Buddha spends his fourteenth and twenty-fifth through forty-fourth rainy seasons here in Jeta's Grove and Pubbarama.

- After King Prasenajit's son Virudhaka usurps the throne, he massacres Sakyans. Buddha tries to dissuade him here, but cannot.

- Here Buddha states: If anyone should say: "I won't lead the holy life under the Tathagata unless he answers the question, 'Is the world eternal or not eternal?'" that person will die before the question is answered. Always keep in mind what I have left undeclared, and what I have declared.

Urubilva

- Location of Buddha's enlightenment. Later known as Bodh Gaya. The bilva is a rose-apple tree whose fruit is something like a red-brown apple, which came to signify right action.

- Five renunciates join Siddhartha in the jungle here. They later abandon him, and then become his first monk disciples at Rishipatana.

- Buddha converts three Kasyapa brothers and their disciples who lived at the edge of the jungle wearing bark garments and uncut hair.

- Buddha stays in the hermitage of Urubilva Kasyapa, the ascetic with matter hair, in a woodland grove.

Vaisali

- This is the Vriji capital. It's filled with wonderful buildings, parks, singing birds, and festivities. However, plagues ravaged the city. Vimalakirti, Amrapali, and many wealthy Licchavis live here.

- Here Siddhartha studies with his first teacher, Arada Kalama.

- Buddha spends his fifth and forty-fifth (final) rainy season here. Consents to Maha Prajapati's request to start a nun's sangha. Buddha's (former) wife and other women are ordained here. Amrapali offers her Mango Grove to the mendicant sangha. Buddha encounters Mara at Capala Shrine. Buddha assembles disciples at Mahavana (Large Grove) to announce he has three months to live.

- The *Holy Teaching of Vimalakirti* (a Mahayana sutra) states: At that time, there lived in the city of Vaisali a certain Licchavi named Vimalakirti, who wore the white clothes of the layman, yet lived impeccably like a renunciate.

A Community of Four Quarters

Clearly Buddha could have chosen from several styles of asceticism, made a composite, or tried something radically new when he began to form a community based on the dharma he had discovered upon awakening. He had a clear view of what led to the end of suffering. But this view differed from each and every other teaching he'd encountered. The challenge would be to guide a new community that did two things: helped each disciple realize the Four Great Facts and reduced suffering in society.

The Tathagata seemed to envision a worldwide mission as he told disciples to go out for the good and happiness of the many. Buddha spoke of his community as a "sangha of the four quarters"—meaning that people from a wide range of social and cultural backgrounds should be included. He did not think that dharma was suited to only one group of people.

But establishing an open spiritual community was not easy, and it could not be all-inclusive. He had to deal with people seeking to join a renunciate community to avoid their social responsibilities by running from the law, avoiding debtors, rejecting their families, and others. Buddha also had to deal with personality clashes, power plays, contagious disease, and the negative temperaments of people who joined or wished to join the mendicant order. In response to the variety of demands, Buddha established a spiritual community with four assemblies: monks, nuns, laymen, and laywomen.

Monks and Nuns

Buddha formed two renunciate communities. He called these the *bhikshu-sangha* and *bhikshuni-sangha*, or the associations of monks and nuns. In creating them, Gautama stuck with what he knew best. He modeled the new spiritual orders on the political *gana-sanghas* that he saw firsthand as the son of the Sakyan raja. The gana-sanghas were tribal associations of the semiautonomous or independent tribes of the Middle Ganges Basin. They held assets communally and made collective decisions

> **Dharma Dictionary**
>
> **Sangha** can refer to either a political or spiritual association. A republic, which is a political-economic union of clan groups, is a **gana-sangha** or clan association. A **bhikshu-sangha** is an association of monks. A **bhikshuni-sangha** is an association of nuns.

pertaining to government. Learning from tribal organizations such as the Sakyans and Vrijis, Buddha held general meetings among the members and based decisions on unanimous consent in the assembly.

The Bowl and Robe of Renunciation

Bhikshus and bhikshunis were so called because they went on alms rounds once each day. The tradition of alms begging was present in India for at least a century before Siddhartha went forth into homelessness. From one group to another, sramanas were known by their begging bowls. That is why when Siddhartha first entered Rajagriha after his great renunciation, he made himself a begging bowl out of leaves—a skill perfected by some Indian tribal women. Collecting alms is a type of ceremonial begging and should not be confused with involuntary poverty or freeloading off of society. The begging bowl is an outward symbol of the person's inner spirit of renunciation.

The robe worn by the monks and nuns was symbolic … and very practical at the same time. The robe was ochre colored, as a reminder of falling leaves—hence impermanence. It was also suitable for life in the forest, because mosquitoes avoid the orange color. And to get a sense of Buddha's commitment to renunciation, let's look at the thought he put into the cloth itself. The early mendicant sangha wore robes of discarded rags, stitched together to overcome these nine defects of an ordinary cloak:

1. It is costly.

2. It is acquired by depending on others.

3. It is easily soiled by use.

4. When dirty it must be washed and dyed.

5. It must be patched and mended when it is worn a lot.

6. Obtaining a replacement is difficult.

7. It has to be guarded from enemies who would want it.

8. It might be worn for ornamentation.

9. One is tempted to burden oneself with it while traveling.

Guidelines for a Renunciate's Conduct

During the first 20 years of Buddhism, monks and nuns had only a handful of rules. As the communities expanded, more situations required guidelines. Problems were brought before the sanghas, and rules were reasoned out. There was continuous growth, and adaptation of guidelines in the years when Buddha was alive.

The guidelines for nuns tended to be stricter than the guidelines for the monks, but they also protected the women from serving the men or turning into sexual objects. And a general sense of decorum was to be observed by both men and women. They were not to run, dance, or raise their fists. They were also to remain sensitive to the environment and not break off more of a branch than needed to brush their teeth, for example.

Members of the spiritual community voluntarily were to observe 10 main rules. These prohibit the following:

1. Killing

2. Stealing

3. Sexual misconduct

4. Telling lies

5. Consuming alcohol

6. Eating after noon

7. Dancing and watching entertainment

8. Wearing perfumes, garlands, jewelry

9. Sleeping on a high or luxurious bed

10. Handling gold or silver (money)

The early guidelines and later rules for renunciates are called the pratimoksha. They belong to the vinaya basket of teaching. Rules now vary among Buddhist schools, but here's a sample:

- A member of the spiritual community is expelled from the order for purposely depriving a human being of life or encouraging someone to kill himself or herself.

- A monk must confess if he knowingly eats food gathered by a nun (unless it was intended for monks), or if he sits alone (one man one woman) with a nun.

> **Buddha Basics**
>
> After the Teacher passed away, the original guidelines established in consultation with the *bhikshu-* and *bhikshuni-sanghas* became fixed into major and minor rules. Gradually some 250 rules for monks, and generally more than 300 for nuns became standard. All the rules are supposed to help individuals in the community live in harmony and attain enlightenment as quickly as possible.

> **Be Mindful!**
>
> Far less is known about the *bhikshuni-sangha* than the *bhikshu-sangha*. Although Buddha set up men and women in parallel communities, the sect of nuns did not flourish after his death. Even the scriptures (set into writing from oral tradition) say relatively little about the Buddha's women disciples.

Laymen and Laywomen

Although first going from "home into homelessness" was common in the Middle Ganges Basin, naturally not everyone wanted to give up family life. And Buddha made provisions for those who had no wish to enter the homeless life. The Buddhist community included upasakas and upasikas: laymen and laywomen.

Services were established for laymen and laywomen to observe the first 5 of the 10 basic precepts on days of the full moon and new moon. Those who wished could wear white garments on that day and vow to abstain from killing anything, stealing, engaging in sexual activity, lying, and consuming alcohol.

Laymen and laywomen earned merit by providing alms for the renunciates. Those with wealth donated supplies or even land for the use of the orders of monks and nuns. In turn, the renunciates counseled the laypeople and modeled an alternative lifestyle for those who might wish to intensify their spiritual practice.

Two Places to Stay

The early community under Buddha's guidance would stay together in groups during three months of the rainy season. There were two kinds of gathering spots:

- The avasa was a large circumscribed area in the countryside. Buddha's renunciate disciples had to manage everything themselves when building their rain retreat housing in the countryside each year. Whatever was built was liable to be looted after it was deserted at the end of the rainy season. So, out of practicality or habit, some sangha members would come back to the same place year after year or even stay put in their local avasa.

- The arama was a tract of land that was usually in a town, city, or suburb. These tended to be permanent housing developments donated by wealthy laypeople. The aramas often began as flower gardens or fruit tree groves. The sponsor made the property suitable for sheltering a sangha during the rainy season. They also maintained the site while the monks and nuns were wandering.

> **Buddha Basics**
>
> Veluvana (Bamboo Grove) near Rajagriha was an arama donated by Bimbisara, the king of Magadha. This settlement—which was an entire village, complete with artisans—probably became the seat of the first Buddhist monastery in the world. If you go to Rajagriha today, you'll see the ruins of an arama donated by Jivaka, Buddha's physician.

Nothing is left of the country settlements because they were temporary. But some of the aramas were transformed into monasteries, and a number of them were occupied for more than a thousand years.

It's the Teaching, Not the Teacher

Buddha emphasized personal experience of the dharma and did not focus the sangha's attention upon himself as the authority. After enlightenment, he decided to respect and revere the dharma instead of any living teacher, so when the community formed, dharma was the focus of reverence, not him. Here's a story that shows this point.

One day, shortly after Buddha passed away, Ananda was standing outside the walls of Rajagriha. The king's guards saw him and informed Minister Varshakara—a brilliant statesman who was always interested in leadership, power, and group structure. (You'll read more about him in Chapter 21.) So Varshakara met with Ananda to find out how the sangha was doing without its founder.

The minister asked Ananda whether Buddha had appointed a successor, or if the sangha had elected anyone. Ananda said that the sangha had no leader. Every member of the spiritual community was on equal footing. Varshakara wondered how the sangha managed to stay together without a central figure of authority, and Ananda told him that the community took refuge in the dharma. The teachings—not a master—provided the bond among members of the sangha. They gained cohesion by assembling on the sacred days of new moon and full moon for a *dharma-rehearsal*. This famous verse chanted by members of the early sangha sums up the whole of Buddha's teaching:

> *Don't do ill.*
> *Do what's good.*
> *Make your mind pure.*

This is the teaching of all the buddhas.

Dharma Dictionary

Dharma-rehearsal is a twice-monthly gathering of the orders of monks and nuns on the days of the full and new moons to chant selected religious teachings. As the community grew, Buddha requested that the pratimoksha guidelines be recited in the fortnightly session. Later on, dharma-rehearsals served as a time for monks and nuns to confess transgressions to their assemblies.

Sakyaputriya-sramanas

Outsiders fondly called Buddha's monks and nuns by the term *Sakyaputriya-sramanas*. It means "Sramana children of the Sakyan." This label gives some idea of the closeness that members of the spiritual community—at least ideally—would have felt for each other. But Buddha encountered his share of troubles both from within and outside the community, which we'll encounter in the next chapter and beyond.

Meanwhile, it's important to keep in mind that for the Sakyaputriya-sramanas, living on alms and being homeless did not mean living without community or companions. According to Buddha, mendicants could dwell in the jungle or in a cave for periods of intensive meditation, but they could dwell also in the countryside, in a village, or in a town. Whatever was conducive to spiritual development was acceptable.

But Buddha never forgot about the lay community. He had adopted the Middle Way—and that meant contributing to society. He did not interfere with general customs of the laypersons, but he did provide guidelines for a happy and prosperous life.

The Least You Need to Know

- Buddha's view of reality was distinct from the perspectives of brahmins, Sannyasins, Jains, materialists, fatalists, and skeptics.

- Buddha modeled the mendicant sanghas on a traditional tribal style of governance used by his Sakya clan.

- Gautama conceived of his community as being of four quarters—meaning it should include people from all places and every walk of life.

- Buddha did not appoint a successor because he always kept dharma (the teachings, not the teacher) as the focal point of community reverence.

Chapter 12

Home to Kapilavastu

In This Chapter

- ◆ Buddha renews his relationship with Suddhodana
- ◆ Rahula joins his father's spiritual community
- ◆ Yasodhara becomes a Theri
- ◆ Cousin Devadatta's ambitions
- ◆ Upali the barber
- ◆ The brothers Anuruddha and Ananda

After Siddhartha attained enlightenment in Urubilva, he remained for 49 days around one tree or another, reorienting himself to the world. Then—as a new buddha—he walked to Rishipatana to find Kaundinya, Asvajit, Vashpa, Mahanama, and Bhadrika. Those five ascetics who'd abandoned him thinking he'd strayed off the path to enlightenment became the first Buddhist monks. In short order, the Tathagata next gathered more than 50 new disciples. After they all made significant spiritual progress, he sent them all out to wander for the happiness of the many. This was at the close of the first rainy season following the awakening.

When the rains stopped, Buddha returned to Urubilva and converted three entire renunciate communities led by the Kasyapa brothers. And with this impressive array of converts, the Tathagata made good on his promise to

King Bimbisara to return to Rajagriha after attaining his goal. The crowd of disciples that accompanied Buddha on his trip into Rajagriha impressed not only Bimbisara but also his people. Thus following their king, the people of Magadha's capital became sympathetic to Buddha's message.

Raja Suddhodana, from his seat in Kapilavastu, was following the early success of his son, and sent for that wayward scion of the Sakya clan. Several times, however, messengers were so captivated by Buddha's teachings that they forgot to deliver the raja's invitation. Finally, a close childhood friend was sent to ask the Tathagata to return home to the Sakyan capital. The friend was Kaludayi, and he succeeded in bringing the former Sakyan prince home.

But all was not idyllic when Gautama arrived back in Kapilavastu, and things didn't always go well with family members in the years to come. For the most part, Gautama would have a productive relationship with his family—but there were some rough spots. So let's check in on Buddha's return trip to Kapilavastu and trace his relationship with immediate family, two cousins, and a close associate from back home.

Raja Suddhodana

Raja Suddhodana had a patchy relationship with his son. He was elated when Siddhartha was born, because the infant had promising signs on his body—the marks of a great man. For a long time, he had tried to make his son follow in his footsteps, so he harbored bitter disappointment over his son's zealous renunciation. But in the end, father and son reconciled.

My Son in Rags!

A year after his awakening, the Sakyan prince returned home to Kapilavastu. Was he what people expected of a "buddha"? No … not at first. The people of Kapilavastu knew the tradition of asceticism. And Raja Suddhodana had followed his son's progress using the standard techniques of any regent—spying, or perhaps you'd call it "word of mouth"? He'd heard about the Maha Sramana nearly starving himself to death, he'd heard about the awakening, and he'd heard of the new Buddha's instant success in proselytizing. So why was the raja so shocked when his 36-year-old son came home?

When Siddhartha—now Buddha—walked barefoot into Kapilavastu dressed in a cast-off garment, Suddhodana was scandalized. Not only that—the ex-prince was begging at people's doorsteps in the Sakyan capital. We can imagine that Suddhodana was both shocked, dismayed, and angered by this spectacle. Suddhodana had tried to trick, reason, and persuade his son to maintain his life as a householder and ready himself for the post of raja. His son had run away in the dead of night seven years before, leaving his wife and newborn son.

Suddhodana had nourished high hopes over the years for his obviously gifted son. Now he thought, perhaps … just perhaps his son would be a glorious Dharmacakrin—wheel turner—after all. But apparently Suddhodana also had no real idea what a buddha was like. So the raja confronted his independent-minded son: "How could a Sakya beg in the streets like that, barefoot and wearing rags?" And Gautama's answer was consistent with a claim he'd make forevermore: "I am not of the Sakya lineage. I am of the buddha lineage. And I do what all buddhas do."

> ### Buddha Basics
> Although Buddha declared that his lineage was the long line of buddhas, certain biographers took pains to outline his earthly genealogy. This concern over status reflects India's cultural values, where pure ancestry was prized among upper-class people. A Sakyan chieftain would be legitimated normally on the basis of his birth. So when Gautama told his father that he was not a Sakyan, it was confirmation that he'd totally rejected all worldly ties.

Reconciliation and Nirvana

Raja Suddhodana was not the only one scandalized by Gautama's unseemly behavior in the Sakyan capital. The Sakyans were a proud people, and when the new buddha arrived dressed in rags, the elders didn't pay their respects. They left that to the younger Sakyans. In response, the Tathagata performed a miracle. He rose into the air and made fire flame from the upper and water from the lower part of his body—then did the reverse. Then six colors of light began intensely streaming from his body. These unusual feats indicated great accomplishment in meditation. So at the sight of his son's splendor, Suddhodana touched his head to Buddha's feet and attained the first stage of sainthood, he became a stream entrant. This means he glimpsed nonself, lost attachment to rituals, and gained faith in the Buddha, his teachings, and the spiritual community. (On the stages of sainthood, see Chapter 17.)

Raja Suddhodana made spiritual progress as a layman. He lived for four years after Buddha first returned to Kapilavastu. The old man felt fortunate that he lived to see his son become a Dharmacakrin. Raja Suddhodana passed away 40 years after hearing the astrological predictions that his son would become a great person. And what's more, he attained nirvana on his deathbed. Buddha made a point of returning to Kapilavastu when he heard his father was ill and preached dharma to his ailing father.

Thus five years after Gautama's awakening, Raja Suddhodana attained the highest level of sainthood. Perhaps father and son achieved a closeness at that moment that neither had experienced in the previous four decades. All traces of regret vanished from Suddhodana for the path of renunciation his son had taken.

Rahula, My Son

When prince Siddhartha left the Sakyan capital on the night of his Great Renunciation, he silently bid farewell to his wife and newborn son, Rahula. And now that he came back to his home as a Tathagata, how would his relationship with Rahula develop? The boy was 7 years old, for Sakyamuni had sought enlightenment for six years, and took about a year to return.

Father, Where Is My Inheritance?

When Gautama arrived in Kapilavastu, the boy's mother Yasodhara suggested that Rahula approach his father to request his inheritance—because a son is entitled to his father's wealth. And the child dutifully listened. Rahula asked Gautama, his father, "Where is my inheritance?" Now, what could Buddha say? What could little Rahula inherit, now that his father had renounced his worldly Sakya lineage with its wealth, social station, and power. Rahula's father was no longer a Sakya, he was a homeless man, and thus had no inheritance. Properly speaking, perhaps Gautama didn't even have a son.

As one in the buddha lineage, the Tathagata could give dharma. That's all he could give. Yes, knowledge of the path to enlightenment was the inheritance coming down from a long line of buddhas from the far distant past. What Gautama did next was to provide more consternation to poor Suddhodana, Rahula's grandfather. For Rahula's inheritance, Gautama arranged to have his 7-year-old admitted to the renunciate community. Rahula became a novice monk! When grandfather found out, he was at first distraught. Who from the Sakyan lineage would now take his place to rule from Kapilavastu? Even if his own son had abdicated and renounced the world, it was a crime for the ex-prince to come now and take Rahula.

Enlightening Extras

The elite kshatriyas of northern India put great stock in their family lines. And the Sakyans traced themselves back to the ancient solar lineage. But Gautama did something highly significant by cutting ties with his Sakyan clan. He shifted to a spiritual lineage of buddhas ranging back to time immemorial. The authority of a spiritual lineage far surpasses the might of any worldly lineage. The concept of spiritual lineage is found in several religions. Consider, for example, the Sikh line of 10 gurus from Nanak through Gobind Singh—culminating in the holy scripture, and the Roman Catholic line of popes stemming back to Saint Peter the apostle.

Buddha showed great care for his son. This is evident because he entrusted Rahula to Sariputra and Maudgalyayana—his two chief disciples. First the venerable Sariputra ordained Rahula. Thereafter, both he and Maudgalyayana looked after Gautama's son. Sariputra guided him in learning, and Maudgalyayana counseled him in decorum and spiritual practice. Rahula was very fortunate: Sariputra was greatest in wisdom and a skilled teacher. And Maudgalyayana was foremost in supernormal powers.

Buddha recognized his son as someone who most desired to be trained. Might this not be natural? Buddha, after all, was his father. Now he could be close to his father. In fact, this closeness was the fruit of a strong aspiration that Rahula made in a former lifetime. The Tathagata told Rahula that he had wished to be born as the son of a buddha—and that his wish had come true.

A Fatherly Lesson

Shortly after Rahula's ordination, Sakyamuni left Kapilavastu with his son and a number of other Sakyans. They made their way to Rajagriha. And one evening as the company of renunciates resided in the Squirrels' Sanctuary of the Bamboo Grove, Buddha rose from his meditation and went to find his son. He decided to give the 7-year-old a lesson on the faults of lying. We do not know what lie the young Rahula might have told, but his father wanted to correct any tendency toward dishonesty.

The Tathagata was very simple and direct in his lesson. He explained each action in terms that a 7-year-old could understand. Sakyamuni turned a bucket of water upside down, spilled water out, and turned it upright again, saying that lying even as a joke throws away virtue. Then he took a mirror and spoke of the importance of "reflection" on actions of body, speech, and mind—playing on the word that had two meanings. Finally, Buddha explained that every wrong deed of body and speech should be confessed. A person should be repelled by their mental misdeeds, although confession is not necessary.

> **Buddha Basics**
>
> Here's part of Buddha's teaching to the young Rahula, as recorded in the Pali "Middle Length Sayings" (61.2) of the Buddha. This is a father teaching his child not to lie. The Blessed One sat down on the seat Rahula had made ready and washed his feet. Rahula paid homage to his father and sat down at one side. Then the Blessed One poured out the little bit of water that was left and said to his son: "Rahula, those who are not ashamed to tell a deliberate lie throw away their spiritual striving like that water was thrown away. Therefore, Rahula, you should train like this: promise yourself, "I will not utter a falsehood even as a joke.""

The Spittin' Image

Nobody knows much about the middle years of Gautama's life because that information is not recorded in the Buddhist scriptures. So it's hard to reconstruct Buddha's relationship with Rahula or his mother Yasodhara. But Rahula was a spittin' image of his father. And it's clear that Rahula treated his father with respect, always setting him a place to sit and paying homage, as was the custom of the day.

When Rahula was around 18 years old, he realized how handsome he was—as his physique resembled his father's. Buddha noticed this and admonished Rahula, because such vain thoughts would only cause him trouble. When Rahula was 20 years old, he received full ordination. Shortly afterward, he became an arhat, destroying all mental taints and obstacles to freedom from rebirth.

Rahula would visit his mother, who became a nun. He would always visit for less than a week, due to special rules of the order. A novice monk could visit a mother or father, even if not sent for, as long as the return could be made in seven days.

Rahula died before Buddha passed away. It is doubtful whether Buddha would have passed on leadership of the sangha to his son. In any case, this was no longer even a possibility, because Buddha and Yasodhara only had one child.

Yasodhara, Rahula's Mom

There were two main women in Buddha's life as he was growing up: not his mother, for she'd died in the first week of his life, but his aunt, Maha Prajapati; and, from age 16 onward, his wife, Yasodhara. These two women did not see Gautama for seven years after he left Kapilavastu in search of enlightenment. But in time they became active in the women's movement as nuns. Let's look a bit at Yasodhara's relationship with Sakyamuni here—and take up Maha Prajapati's story in Chapter 18.

During the six years when Siddhartha was seeking the end to suffering, both Suddhodana and Yasodhara maintained an interest in him. And when the ex-prince left his second teacher, Alara Kalama, to pursue a path of severe mortification, his wife (we really should say former wife) Yasodhara followed his lead. Empathizing with Gautama, she undertook a parallel series of penances. She fasted and wore simple clothes. But Suddhodana (her father-in-law, who was also her uncle) disapproved. He forbid news of Siddhartha to reach Yasodhara so she would not harm herself. Yasodhara's relationship with Gautama went back lifetimes. Buddha

Be Mindful!

Usually the story is told that Maha Prajapati first requested Buddha—her nephew—to start a nun's order for women. But it's not out of the question that Yasodhara actually did so. I.B. Horner in *Women Under Primitive Buddhism* suggests that maybe his wife was initiated with 500 Sakyan ladies when Gautama first preached at Vaisali.

told Jataka Tales about their times together. They even had been married in former lives. And when Gautama returned to Kapilavastu after his awakening, some say she still had hopes to be reunited with him as husband and wife. But after hearing his dharma, she became a nun. Buddha called his former wife the most modest of all his female disciples. She also may have been the foremost nun in supernormal powers; as such, she's called by the name Bhadra Katyayana.

Yasodhara became a leader in the community of nuns and attained the state of a Theri, an enlightened woman arhat. And when, at the age of 78, she felt her time of death approach, she came to see her former husband. The night before passing away, Yasodhara told Buddha, "Me saranam attano" (I am my own refuge). Indeed, later that year as Gautama lay on his own deathbed, he urged all his disciples to be refuges unto themselves. Yasodhara had accomplished already what Buddha wished all his disciples could do.

Devadatta, the Rival Cousin

Devadatta was Gautama's cousin. And he was one of the Sakyan princes to join Buddha's community of monks—though it's unclear whether he was joined early or after about 15 years. Devadatta was a brilliant orator and over time he began rising to prominence in the sangha. He garnered a reputation for having psychic powers. And though he did not attain any stages of sainthood, Devadatta drew a large number of disciples who looked to him for leadership within the Buddhist sangha. Unfortunately, with all his promise, there were problems between Devadatta and Buddha.

A Childhood Rivalry Revisited

Devadatta and Gautama seem to have been at odds even as children. Remember? When they were young, Siddhartha once claimed a bird for himself that Devadatta shot down, because the Bodhisattva wanted to save the injured animal's life. (See Chapter 6.) And at Siddhartha's tribal wedding games, the Bodhisattva outdid Devadatta in the archery contest. Perhaps there were many early incidents of troubles in their relationship that haven't been recorded. But overall it appears Devadatta positioned himself as his cross-cousin's rival.

> **Enlightening Extras**
>
> Interpersonal relationships are complex. And it may be too easy to automatically see Devadatta as "the bad guy." We know of the troubles between Gautama and his cousin from Buddhist texts that place Devadatta in a bad light. But anthropological research suggests that the case of Devadatta's rivalry with Gautama makes perfect sense in the context of "cross-cousin" relationships. In some cultures, this rivalry is a built-in custom.

After the Buddhist sangha had grown considerably, Devadatta's activity attracted the attention of Prince Ajatasatru, the son of King Bimbisara of Magadha. Ajatasatru began to sponsor Devadatta and built him a monastery near Rajagriha. From his side, Devadatta emboldened the Magadhan prince to usurp his father's position, and step into his role as king without delay. In fact, Ajatasatru and Devadatta became co-conspirators in a grandiose plan of ruling Magadha from the complementary spheres of politics and religion. Both were princes whose appetite for power was great. And though Devadatta had taken vows of renunciation upon entry into homelessness, it seems that worldly ambition got the better of him.

Both Ajatasatru and Devadatta were ambitious and felt that great power was within their grasp. Ajatasatru saw the throne of Magadha within an arms-length, while Devadatta thirsted for leadership of Gautama's bhikshu-sangha. Both men's wishes were plausible: the throne was set to fall into the Magadhan prince's hands upon the death or abdication of his father, King Bimbisara. And Devadatta had developed supernormal powers through meditation and had many disciples of his own. According to plan, Ajatasatru usurped the throne and Devadatta tried to wrest authority from Buddha.

Devadatta Tries to Kill His Cousin

One day Devadatta asked Buddha to hand over leadership of the order, suggesting that the Master was too old for the position. Buddha said that he would not even hand it over to the two chief disciples, much less to Devadatta. Moreover, Buddha announced to his disciples that whatever leadership position Devadatta might take was not authorized. At this rejection and humiliation, Devadatta became vicious. He tried three times to kill his cousin. But each attempt failed:

- Ajatasatru provided Devadatta with a band of archers to assassinate Buddha. But on seeing the Tathagata, the assassins laid down their arms.

- Devadatta hurled a massive stone down the side of Vulture's Peak to hit Sakyamuni. The boulder split, but only a splinter injured Buddha's foot.

- Devadatta let loose a drunken elephant to charge Buddha, but the elephant Nalagiri was tamed by the Master's waves of loving-kindness.

After these events, Devadatta became very unpopular among the people of Magadha, and his co-conspirator Ajatasatru was forced to withdraw support.

Be Mindful!

Devadatta usually is portrayed badly because he tried to kill his cousin Buddha three times and committed the heinous crime of dividing the sangha. But his reforms must have seemed reasonable to some ascetics. For instance, he called for the renunciates to observe a vegetarian diet. In response, Sakyamuni reinforced an early guideline that meat offered as alms should generally be eaten. Here Buddha stuck to his Middle May approach to spirituality.

Devadatta the Reformer

In the early stages as Buddha's disciple, Devadatta had shown exemplary conduct. But at a certain point he began to consider his conduct more worthy than Buddha's. So he led a movement to reform the sangha of monks. He requested that Buddha purify the community by enforcing these five rules—in contradiction to the current practices:

- Monks should dwell in the forests for their whole lives—and not reside in monasteries during the rains.

- Monks should live solely on the alms they begged—and not accept invitations into people's homes.

- Monks should wear robes made from rags collected from trash and cemeteries—instead of accepting cloth from the laity.

- Monks should live at the foot of a tree—instead of in monastic parks.

◆ Monks should refuse to eat fish or meat—instead of accepting whatever is offered to them on their alms rounds.

Buddha told Devadatta that the monks were free to adopt more stringent habits, but he would not recommend that they be compulsory. In response to Buddha's refusal to enforce a stricter ascetic code, Devadatta formed his own group. This was counted as a grave offense in the early Buddhist community, and to this day, causing a schism in the order is considered among the most serious misdeeds in Buddhism. As it turned out, Sariputra and Maudgalyayana won back Devadatta's monks, and Devadatta repented. Unfortunately, he died before having a chance to see Buddha again.

Upali the Barber

Six or seven Sakyan aristocrats went forth into homelessness when Buddha came to Kapilavastu a year after his awakening. (Perhaps Devadatta was among them.) They were raised as kshatriya elites, with power, privilege, and superior training. Along with this group of converts was a man of lower caste. Upali, the barber for Suddhodana's family became a monk at the same time the handful of Sakyan princes he'd served. Buddha's policy of rejecting caste status in the sangha initially took the princes by surprise and challenged their preconceptions as to the relative worth of human beings.

> **Buddha Basics**
>
> Buddha acknowledged no caste distinctions in the renunciate sanghas that he founded, yet perhaps he made one concession to cultural values. In starting the bhikshuni-sangha, the Tathagata ruled that all monks had seniority over all nuns. Maha Prajapati, who requested the first ordination, accepted these terms. Later in life, she tried to get Buddha to eliminate the rule of seniority, but he refused.

When the initial group of Sakyan warriors came to the Tathagata for ordination, the barber Upali was with them. (Though some say Upali arrived first and was already ordained by the time the princes arrived.) Buddha encouraged Upali to join the monks. (Oddly enough, his hair fell out at the time of his ordination.) This move forced the princes to humble their strong Sakyan pride, and the kshatriyas committed themselves to revere the barber as their senior.

Dealing with Upali as an equal voice in the community and even being his junior would have been an adjustment for the Sakyan princes and others. It's curious to wonder how Upali himself felt in a position where his caste was erased, making the kshatriyas no less or no more than he was.

Upali became expert in the training rules of the sangha. At the First Buddhist Council, he was consulted and recited the precepts and circumstances out of which they developed. This became the heart of the vinaya basket of teachings. You'll read a bit more about the Buddhist councils in Chapter 23. Let's now turn to the stories of two remarkable young Sakyan brothers, Anuruddha and Ananda, whose father was Buddha's uncle. These cousins were among the Sakyan kshatriya nobles who asked Buddha for ordination when he first arrived in Kapilavastu after waking up.

Cousin Anuruddha

Anuruddha grew up not knowing the words there is none—because he lived a life of plenty. So at first it came as a shock when he was confronted with the possibility of going forth into homelessness. When his cousin Gautama came into Kapilavastu and other Sakyan youth decided to become monks, Anuruddha first hesitated. But then the privileged young man realized that the way of the householder only led to a duplication of itself for one lifetime after the next. And he felt motivated to renounce the world and escape the continual cycle of "more of the same." In the course of his spiritual practice, Anuruddha became particularly skilled at two aspects of meditation: seeing with the *divine eye* and practicing the Four Applications of Mindfulness.

> **Dharma Dictionary**
>
> The **divine eye** is known as divya chakshu in Sanskrit. It is one of the siddhis and results from the radiation of light from the mind's eye. A person cultivates this vision that can see far distances by meditating on a special circular object that is made of fire, white color, or light. After a certain preliminary level of concentration, the meditator extends the area covered by the luminous object. Whatever comes within in the extended lit area is seen with the divine eye.

Anuruddha Needs No Glasses

One of the siddhis (paranormal powers) that results from meditation is the ability to see what is not normally perceived through the human eye. This includes long distances and things in a normally invisible spectrum of light. Buddha, who attained the divine eye in the second watch of the night of his awakening, said that Anuruddha was the best at this meditation among all the disciples. At times female figures from a heavenly realm of samsara would appear to Anuruddha when he was meditating with the divine eye. He could also use this siddhi to see how people were born into a heaven or hell realm. One time some "graceful ones" from a heavenly realm

---

> **Be Mindful!**
>
> Buddha's cousin Anuruddha was accomplished at radiating light from his mind's eye to illuminate what could not normally be seen. A thought: did prehistoric people who painted the Lascaux caves in France 3,500 years ago use the divine eye to illuminate their pitch dark underground meeting place? It's currently thought that the Paleolithic artists must have had torches or lamps filled with animal fat.

appeared to Anuruddha saying they could do marvelous things. He tested them by thinking they should turn blue and they did—skin, hair, clothes, ornaments and all. Then they turned yellow, red, and white according to his thoughts. When he turned his senses away from them, they disappeared.

Anuruddha knew that his skill with the divine eye was not a measure of enlightenment. He once told Sariputra that he was not free from clinging, even though he could use the divine eye with an unperturbed body and unwavering mind. Sariputra replied that his supernormal power had become a matter of pride for him and told him to abandon pride. To gain enlightenment, Anuruddha dedicated himself to the practice of the Four Foundations of Mindfulness.

Mindfulness Matters

Anuruddha liked to spend time in solitude. He enjoyed three ascetic practices: going on alms rounds, using robes made of discarded rags, and doing the sitter's practice. In general, the monks and nuns did the first two. But the sitter's practice was not for everyone. It meant vowing not to lie down when sleeping. It seems that for many years Anuruddha may not have slept at all. He substituted meditation for sleep and relaxation … until he began to feel his age. Later in life, he'd sleep for short spells to restore his body.

Anuruddha was committed to the practice of the Four Applications of Mindfulness (satipatthana, see Chapter 16). He'd pay calm attention to his bodily movements, including breath, thoughts, feelings of pleasant or unpleasant, and so on. Anuruddha was convinced that whoever neglected such mindfulness practice was neglecting Buddha's path to nirvana. People used to remark on Anuruddha's bright, calm, and cheerful countenance—and he said it came from his mindfulness training. He said that the difference between an arhat and meditators in training was simply their level of mindfulness.

Anuruddha's mindfulness practice made him exceptional at seeing with the divine eye. So as Buddha was passing away, he was able to inform Ananda about the level of meditation their teacher was in. At one point Ananda thought Buddha had attained parinirvana. But Anuruddha, who could see into the minds of others, informed him that the Tathagata was at the highest level of meditation but was not yet finished.

Ananda Remembers

When Buddha was 55 years old, he suggested that a single person accompany him—instead of various monks trying to keep pace. Other monks thought Gautama's cousin Ananda was suited for the post. So Ananda agreed to become Buddha's attendant, but only under three conditions:

- Ananda would not wear robes or eat food given to Buddha.

- Ananda demanded the authority to introduce visitors to the Buddha and have the right to see his cousin whenever he wished.

- Buddha guaranteed that he would report any dharma teachings to Ananda if he had been unable to hear them.

These conditions were met; thus, for the final 25 years of his life, Gautama had his cousin Ananda in attendance. Many discourses given by the Tathagata make reference to Ananda, because he was almost always present, memorizing the words. He was particularly helpful to the nuns and would teach them often.

Ananda lived up to the age of 120 and provided continuity for the Buddhist sangha. After all, many key disciples passed away before Gautama himself, including Sariputra and Maudgalyayana (his two chief disciples), Rahula (his son), Devadatta (his cousin), and Maha Prajapati and Yasodhara (his aunt and wife). Besides that, Maha Kasyapa was absorbed into the rock face on Vulture Peak where he still awaits Maitreya, the future Buddha!

The Buddhist tradition is beholden to Ananda for memorizing the Tathagata's discourses. He had a photographic memory and so was able to recite what would become the sutra portion of the Buddhist canon. Ananda did this at the *First Buddhist Council*. But on the eve of the council, the great assembly of arhats gathered in Rajagriha turned Ananda away because he was not yet an arhat. (For the story of Ananda's illumination, see Chapter 23.) It may seem amazing that Ananda did not become an arhat while Buddha was alive, although he was Gautama's

> **Dharma Dictionary**
>
> The **First Buddhist Council** was a meeting of 500 (that symbolic, round number!) arhats held at the close of the first rains after Buddha's final nirvana. The council, called by King Ajatasatru, was held in Magadha's capital, Rajagriha. At the council, Ananda recited the Tathagata's discourses, and Upali recited the training precepts. These recitations became the basis for the written sutra and vinaya baskets of scripture.

attendant for 25 years. He didn't break through to the final stage of sainthood, culminating in the destruction of all delusion, revulsion, and desire—until hours before the council was to begin.

The Least You Need to Know

◆ Raja Suddhodana was scandalized by his son's begging in the streets, but Gautama told him he now belonged to the buddha—not the Sakya—lineage, and buddhas always did such things.

◆ Buddha's former wife and son both went forth into homelessness and kept in close touch with Gautama over the years.

◆ Devadatta launched three unsuccessful plots to kill his cousin Buddha and take over the sangha. He failed.

◆ Anuruddha became skilled in use of the divine eye and emphasized the practice of mindfulness as the key to end suffering.

◆ Ananda became an arhat just before the First Buddhist Council was to start and then recited the Buddha's discourses from memory. Upali recited the training precepts.

Part 4

Nobody Teaching Nothing

Buddha expressed the key points of his teaching in the Four Noble Truths. Gautama was convinced that the solution to the problem of suffering was to remove ignorance about who we really are. His idea of wisdom was couched in a radical teaching about nonself that turned India's prevailing religious paradigm on its head.

In addition to mental cultivation and wisdom, morality played a key role in Buddha's teaching on how to end suffering. He recommended paying attention to all one's acts of body, speech, and mind, because according to the law of moral causation, to be happy one must act well.

Chapter 13

What Buddha Taught

In This Chapter

- ◆ Three Marks of Existence
- ◆ The Wheel of Becoming
- ◆ The Four Noble Truths
- ◆ Eight ways to end suffering

Buddha spent 45 years teaching dharma after he attained enlightenment. But he didn't set out to teach right away, because enlightenment went "against the grain" of worldly thought. He wondered whether people could comprehend his radical discovery of nonself. Almost everyone in the Middle Ganges Basin believed in an eternal soul, and the few who didn't believed in no soul at all. So how was Buddha to convey the Middle Way truth of nonself? If people didn't reject his teaching out of hand, they were in danger of rejecting the idea of a soul altogether. How could he convey the reality of nonself, which was somewhere in between having a soul and not having a soul?

On the other hand, Buddha had many things to teach that were matters of common sense, such as "help people." So was he to just teach the easy stuff? Or was he to teach some stuff to certain people and other stuff to a different group? The problem of how to teach called for a comprehensive strategy on Buddha's part. And he settled on two basic frameworks for conveying his discoveries: he would speak in terms of Three Marks of Existence and Four Great Facts.

Three Marks of Existence

When Siddhartha woke up he noticed three qualities that describe everything in the world, and he called these the *Three Marks of Existence*. Gautama's teaching on the Three Marks of Existence gets to the heart of the Buddha-dharma. And no teaching can be considered Buddhist if any one of them is missing. Buddha thought that whoever really understands these three qualities wouldn't suffer anymore. Amazing, huh?

> **Dharma Dictionary**
>
> Impermanence, suffering, and nonself are the **Three Marks of Existence.** These three characteristics apply to all phenomena in our world. They form the basis of all Buddha's teachings. In Sanskrit these are known as **anitya, duhkha,** and **anatman, .**

- **Impermanence:** All things are subject to change.

- **Suffering:** Dissatisfaction pervades the lives of sentient beings.

- **Nonself:** We actually have no permanent self. (Yikes!)

The Three Marks of Existence are interrelated, but the realization of nonself is the real kicker: Buddha taught that whoever directly experienced nonself, wouldn't have to be reborn again ... unless by choice.

Hey! Why Don't You Stay?

The first Mark of Existence is impermanence—also called transience. The Sanskrit word for this is *anitya*. This means that things do not stay the same. Buddha noticed that big things as well as tiny little things in this world are in the midst of change. And by giving a penetrating look at anything whatsoever, a person can gain the insight that all things are subject to change.

Look at the trees: from season to season, their changes are obvious. Even from day to day, the leaves do not look the same. Look at our bodies: they change, too. From age 11 to 26, the body changes. Even from age 3 months to 4 months, we can see big changes in an infant. Look at our minds: we like to say, "I changed my mind." And we take that change for granted. But Buddha pointed out that our minds are changing as thoughts come and go—as fast as a *kshana*, which is 1/84th of a second. Through careful observation, one can see that from moment to moment, second to second, and millisecond to millisecond, things are changing … whether we want them to or not.

Can't Get No Satisfaction

Suffering is the second Mark of Existence. Buddha taught that we suffer when things change in ways we don't like. We've just seen that impermanence is the first Mark of Existence. So when things change and we don't like what they change into, we suffer. There are three kinds of suffering, which we'll talk about in a minute. In the meantime, just keep in mind that suffering is basically the experience of dissatisfaction. The Sanskrit word for this mark of existence is *duhkha*. Sometimes it's good to use the word duhkha because it contains the sense of many words in other languages to connote pain, grief, and discomfort.

Who Is Asking This Question?

To most people's ears, the third Mark of Existence is the strangest. It's called nonself, which is *anatman* in Sanskrit. What can this possibly mean, you ask? Buddha did not mean that we don't exist. Of course we exist! But … we don't exist in the way we think we exist. We are actually impermanent, according to the first Mark of Existence. But we have a mistaken sense that we are going to stay the same. And we suffer because no matter how much we may want to stay the same, we change anyway. Therefore, to end suffering, Buddha said it's important to realize that we have no *abiding* self. More about this later.

The Big Wheel Keeps on Turnin'

To understand why the Tathagata was so concerned about suffering, it helps to know that he believed in several kinds of living beings—some of whom suffer tremendously. Buddha's teaching about impermanence, suffering, and nonself—the three marks of existence—applies to beings in all three realms of *samsara:* the sense desire realm, the realm of pure form, and the realm of no form.

We are concerned with the two higher realms of samsara mostly in connection with Buddha's *samadhi* meditations (see Chapters 8 and 16). Beings in the realm of pure form have no unwholesome thoughts, and there are no "beings" as such in the realm of no form—so they suffer mainly when their lifetime in that realm ends.

The most intense suffering in samsara occurs in the sense desire realm, although the realm includes a considerable range of experience. Beings in the sense desire realm tend to suffer a lot because they are pressured by emotions and cravings as they are reborn over and over again. The Tathagata described six types of beings who live in the sense desire realm:

- **Devas:** These are godlings whose life is very pleasant. They suffer most as their lifespans come to an end, as they realize they'll be taking a less happy rebirth elsewhere in the sense desire realm.

- **Titans:** These are demi-godlings who enjoy battles. They are reminiscent of slain warriors described in Norse mythology who live in Valhalla.

- **Humans:** We are beings whose life is a mixed bag. It's said that we have just about the perfect amount of suffering—not so much that it's completely over-whelming, but enough to motivate us to seek freedom from suffering on the path to enlightenment.

- **Animals:** These are the critters whose world we share. Because they are not endowed with consciousness, they have a hard time transcending their suffering.

- **Hungry ghosts**: These are sorrowful beings who never have enough. They have huge bellies and mouths the size of pinholes, so that they never get enough to eat.

- **Hell beings.** These are tortured beings who are too hot or cold. They go through unimaginable sufferings, repeatedly and have no chance to recover peace of mind.

The greatest suffering occurs among the three types of beings who have a lower birth or are not yet enlightened: animals, hungry ghosts, and hell beings. Humans have an optimal amount of suffering—enough to stir an interest in higher values, but not so much that hope is lost.

Beyond the sense desire realm are four boundless abodes where the deity known as Brahma dwells, and the realm of no form. Beings in the realm of pure form don't exhibit desire and revulsion, but return to those negative mental states when they come down from their abodes. This is because they haven't uprooted delusion about the nature of reality. The same goes for "beings" in the realm of pure form. That's why Siddhartha was dissatisfied with all the higher states of consciousness he experienced under the guidance of his early teachers. (See Chapter 8.)

Enlightening Extras

Buddhists generally accepted the basic elements of ancient Indian cosmology. They considered this vast universe beginningless and endless. And though it has no bounds, it undergoes cycles of activity. Many worlds—even many world systems—within this vast universe emerge and dissolve again. Some images from the new physics might convey the Indian understanding of the universe. Maybe we can think of it as a Moebius strip, which is a continuous loop with a half twist in it with only one side: no beginning, and no end.

An Elephant's Footprint

Gautama presented a comprehensive version of the Buddha-dharma in terms of Four Great Facts. His entire body of teachings can be gathered into this framework, also known as the Four Noble Truths. Thus, Buddhists say that they are like an elephant's footprint. Just as every other footprint in the forest could fit inside a majestic elephant's footprint, so each teaching of a Buddha can fit into the framework of the Four Noble Truths.

In Sanskrit, the Tathagata's teachings are called the *Arya Satya*—that is, the Noble Truths or Great Facts. You'll read about them in detail through the next several chapters of this book.

Dharma Dictionary

Buddha's teachings are known in Sanskrit as the **Arya Satya**. *Arya* means "great" or "noble." *Satya* means "fact" or "truth." The Master named Four Great Facts.

1. The Great Fact of suffering

2. The Great Fact of the cause of suffering

3. The Great Fact of the end of suffering

4. The Great Fact of the path to end suffering

Buddha observed that beings suffer. But he saw that their suffering was caused by something, and noted that when the cause of something is removed, that thing exists no more. So he prescribed an Eightfold Path to remove the cause of suffering—and end it.

The Four Noble Truths approach the problem of *duhkha*, or suffering, from the perspective of the person who is suffering. This means the responsibility for ending suffering ultimately rests on the person himself or herself.

Ouch! The Nature of Reality

The Four Noble Truths begin with the topic of duhkha. Why? Because suffering is a pervasive condition that everyone can understand in some way. And—face it—the experience of suffering is what motivates most people to look for new ways of living. When circumstances in one's life appear to be going fine, it is rare to seek help. But it is common to seek help when troubles come—troubles to oneself or to one's family, friends, community, nation and so on.

So Buddha acted like a doctor and helped people who came with ills. He didn't try to convince people to listen to his teachings or become disciples. He diagnosed their ills and spoke of three main levels of duhkha: the suffering of suffering, the suffering of change, and the suffering of conditioning.

Be Mindful!

This is not Buddha's first Noble Truth: "All life is suffering." This is it: Suffering is *inherent* in existence. The word *inherent* indicates there is a strong tendency for duhkha to permeate our experience. Life necessarily involves birth and death. Aging, sickness, and death are natural. If we feel helpless in their midst, then we suffer. But Buddha taught that our suffering is eased through understanding the reality of life.

Suffering of Suffering

What does the word *suffering* bring to mind for you? Chances are that what you think of is included in this first kind of duhkha. Therefore, among the three levels of suffering, the first kind is called the "suffering of suffering." If you thought of physical and emotional pain, then you were thinking like Buddha. Pains that people get along with bodily illness, or wounds, or growing pains are included here. Pains that people go through in connection as they mentally struggle with grief, depression, anxiety, and compulsion are also included here. Mental struggles with envy, anger, and confusion also count as forms of the suffering of suffering.

But isn't it obvious that people have physical and emotional pain? Does it take an enlightened person to notice that people hurt? Why should Buddha have brought up this subject right from the start—as the *first* part of the *first* Great Fact of reality?

The declaration that people have physical and emotional pain may not sound like anything special. But might it not give comfort to people to know that duhkha is a problem for everyone? No one stands alone in this.

The suffering of suffering applies to all sentient beings, including animals and sentient beings in the other realms of samsara. Even devas, godlings in the upper reaches of the sense desire realm, suffer as their lives of luxury begin to sour. But Buddha did not dwell on the topic of suffering to make people sad or desperate. Facing the fact of suffering serves as a powerful motivating force to help oneself and others alleviate their suffering.

Suffering of Change

The second level of duhkha is the suffering of change. This kind of dissatisfaction occurs when a pleasurable physical or emotional state ends—as it inevitably will. Dismay often accompanies the natural aging process, too. The impermanence of one's strong teeth, beautiful hair, or vibrant and healthy skin becomes all too obvious as a person advances in years. This is perfectly natural. Yet it causes suffering that can be both physical and emotional.

Because all things are impermanent—thus, subject to change—it is certain that we will experience the suffering of change, unless we embrace change and see the reality of impermanence. If we can appreciate the fact of change, we will not be disappointed, shocked, or scandalized by change. We may expect change and not grieve. A great example of the suffering of change that comes naturally is the discomfort that many people experience with aging. One common response to a person's fear of getting older is to buy products that promise a youthful look. Can you think of any examples?

Suffering of Five Heap Conditioning

The third level of duhkha is the most subtle and difficult to comprehend. It is the suffering of five heap conditioning (see Chapter 14). This involves painful experiences in which we inevitably find ourselves ... just because we are sentient beings. We can become physically and mentally uncomfortable or ill as we endure the conditions that underlie our physical and mental makeup. Our conditioning includes bodily processes from cell division to functioning of the internal organs and so on. The suffering of conditioning includes all our mental processes, too.

Merely the fact that our heart beats and we breathe means we are in for an ailment. We cannot stay perfect no matter how hard we try. We must sustain ourselves with food, water, and air at the very least. We must exist within a certain temperature range and replenish our body with sleep. As sentient beings, we cannot help it. This helplessness is a form of duhkha.

Merely the fact that we can perceive things, have ideas, and generate emotions means we are in for an ailment. We cannot maintain our sanity without mental stimulation … in just the right amount. Generally, we suffer if we are deprived of love, respect, and attention. We can lose hope if we do not have enough confidence builders. As sentient beings, we cannot help it. And this helplessness is a form of duhkha.

I Scream, You Scream, We All Scream for Ice Cream

The second Great Fact of the Buddha-dharma is the truth of the cause of suffering. The first Great Fact would seem negative and pessimistic if it stood all by itself. Imagine a teaching that advised a person to contemplate suffering only! Dwelling on the pervasive suffering in our lives and in our world would be depressing. But the first Noble Truth that suffering is inherent in our existence is not the whole story. Buddha identified *Three Poisons* that are the sources of duhkha. They are delusion, revulsion, and desire. And they are the causes of suffering.

Dharma Dictionary

The **Three Poisons** are delusion, revulsion, and desire. These three mental functions ruin our lives and the lives of others. They are based in a mistaken view of who we are and what our relationship with others is. They are what make the Wheel of Becoming go 'round.

Delusion

The Tathagata observed that delusion is the most fundamental cause of suffering. When we do not see "things as they are," we suffer. This is true in an immediate sense as well as over the long term. In the short term, we can notice the results of not seeing things as they are when, for example, we fail to listen well to other people and jump to conclusions about their intentions. In the long term, we get hurt by not seeing things as they are when, for example, we allow ourselves to identify with our traumas and instigate our own failures. Overall, the term avidya is easy to misunderstand because it refers to a deep-seated condition that we may rarely think about or even notice.

The root cause of suffering is delusion or ignorance about the nature of reality. And stemming from delusion are two emotional afflictions—attraction and repulsion—that act like a magnet with a positive and a negative charge. These are called desire and revulsion.

Desire

Buddha associated desire with craving or thirst. The Sanskrit word for thirst is trishna. But what is thirst? When we need a drink we become thirsty. Thirst is very immediate. Imagine walking down the road in ancient India on one of those sweltering summer days. If you were a monk or nun, you would often have a long walk ahead of you. And you would become thirsty. Thirst and suffering go hand in hand. When you are thirsty, it's hard to think of anything else. So, at that time, you could contemplate the words of the Tathagata.

Using a simile, Buddha recited this verse about desire:

> *When desire is overcome, suffering rolls off a person like drops of water dripping from a flower.*

Buddha Basics
The Kingdom of Bhutan is a country whose leader promotes Buddhist values. When King Jigme Singye Wangchuk observed that greed has a tendency to arise in connection with materialism, he started promoting gross national happiness as an answer to the gross national product. As the 21st century opened, an international conference devoted to research on gross national happiness was held.

Revulsion

Revulsion or anger is based on a mistaken idea that others are separate from ourselves. Unfortunately, anger only breeds more anger. It is not a solution to life's frustrations. Revulsion is an intensive emotion that clouds a person's judgment and interferes with constructive action. On the other hand, when anger is reduced, the result is more happiness for oneself and others. In one of his "twin verses," Buddha said this about anger:

> *Enemies never make peace in the face of anger. Peace comes through the absence of anger. This is a basic truth.*

> *We're merely guests in this world, but most don't know this. Those who know things as they are no longer feel like quarreling.*

Nirvana, Blown Out!

The third Great Fact is that suffering can end. Buddha used the word nirvana to describe this end of suffering. Nirvana is not a place, but the lack of a place. It is a utopia … a nowhere. Think of a candle whose flame has gone out. Where did the flame go? It went nowhere. Merely the conditions that brought that flame into existence were eliminated. So when the conditions for suffering are eliminated, nirvana is attained. One who attains nirvana is like the candle flame that's been blown out.

Because suffering has a cause, it can be stopped. The way to stop suffering is to remove its cause. We have seen that the fundamental cause of suffering is not seeing "things as they are." But Buddha was confident that human beings could eliminate their ignorance about reality and attain nirvana (or peace).

The Way to Go

Buddha's fourth Great Fact is that there's a practical way to end suffering. If we only thought about all the suffering in the world, we might become hopeless or overwhelmed. But knowing there is a cause of suffering brings some hope. This is because when a cause is identified, a person can begin to address the problem by eliminating its cause. But how can we eliminate desire, revulsion, and ultimately delusion—the causes of suffering? According to Buddha, we can eliminate the causes of suffering by living according to the Eightfold Path that he prescribed. To do so is to attain nirvana.

The eight steps on the path to nirvana involve actions of insight, morality, and mental discipline. They are commonly grouped into three categories: wisdom, virtue, and mental cultivation. In the next three chapters, you will read about each step on the Eightfold Path in detail, according to these three categories. For now, just catch a glimpse of the path that Buddha recommended to attain freedom from suffering. Each step is symbolized by one of eight auspicious symbols.

Symbols of Buddha's Noble Eightfold Path

1. **Right view; wisdom:** The mustard seed reminds us of a lesson that Buddha taught his cousin Kisagotami, who was grieving over the death of her infant. He told her to go to the village and return with mustard seeds from a home where no one had died. She came back empty-handed and learned the lesson of impermanence—which is a proper insight about life.

2. **Right aim; wisdom:** The mirror reflects things as they are. By looking clearly, one can take proper aim or have the right attitude. If the mirror is dusty, one can't have a proper outward-looking sense of motivation.

3. **Right speech; morality:** The right-coiling conch symbolizes proper speech. A conch shell clearly and widely broadcasts sound, as Buddha's voice pronounces the *dharma*.

4. **Right action; morality:** Bilva fruits look like red-brown apples. They symbolize proper action because the fruits of morality are wonderful. Three in a bowl stand for the *Buddha, dharma,* and *sangha*—the Three Jewels.

5. **Right livelihood; morality:** Curd or yogurt symbolizes proper livelihood because no harm is done in making it. This reminds one of Sujata's milk-rice offering to Siddhartha as the last meal before his awakening.

6. **Right effort; mental cultivation:** Durva grass symbolizes proper effort because it is a really durable plant. Like the grass, a practitioner must persevere through thick and thin.

7. **Right recollection; mental cultivation:** Medicine symbolizes proper recollection because it works as an antidote for the disease of ignorance and directly eases suffering.

8. **Right contemplation; mental cultivation:** Cinnabar or vermillion powder symbolize proper contemplation because they are used to make a red dot on the center of the forehead like a third eye.

These steps of the noble Eightfold Path all start with the word right or proper (samyag, samyak in Sanskrit). This indicates that there are many ways of doing things in this world, but some more powerfully reduce suffering than others. These eight steps "rightly" taken together can destroy the causes of duhkha—namely delusion, revulsion, and desire.

The Least You Need to Know

- The most basic Buddhist prayer involves taking refuge in the Three Jewels: Buddha, dharma, and sangha.

- Buddha's teaching is centered on several key observations about the nature of phenomena known as the Three Marks of Existence: impermanence, suffering, and nonself.

- The Wheel of Becoming includes six types of sentient beings of the sense desire realm: godlings, titans, humans, animals, hungry ghosts, and hell beings.

- Beyond the sense desire realm—but still in samsara—is a realm of pure form where the deity Brahma dwells, and a realm of no form.

- Typically, Buddha's teachings are presented in terms of Four Noble Truths or Four Great Facts. In Sanskrit, great or noble is *arya;* truth or fact is *satya.*

- Buddha's Four Great Facts revolve around the problem of duhkha, or suffering: suffering is inherent in existence, delusion is the root cause of suffering, nirvana is the cessation of suffering, and the Eightfold Path to nirvana is the means to eliminate suffering through wisdom, virtue, and mental cultivation.

Chapter 14

No Mind! No Matter!

In This Chapter

- ◆ Buddha's radical view of the person
- ◆ Five elements that make a person
- ◆ The two wisdom steps on the Eightfold Path
- ◆ Buddha's famous silence
- ◆ What Buddha did and didn't teach

One major division of Buddha's Eightfold Path is wisdom. This includes the practice of right view and right aim. Right view involves realizing what Buddha called nonself, and right aim involves keeping the realization of nonself in mind as the grounding of one's motives. Together they establish a person in wisdom.

Right View

When you see a list of the steps on Buddha's Eightfold Path, right view is often listed first—either that or it's listed last! The Eightfold Path is more like a circle than a line from point A to point B … and on to point H. Without right view, the Eightfold Path is not specifically Buddhist. Without right view the Eightfold Path would not lead to enlightenment.

- Right view can be listed as the first step on the Eightfold Path. This is because the other steps on the Eightfold Path—such as right speech, right mindfulness, and the others—can be practiced perfectly only by a person who has right view.

- Right view can be listed as the last step on the Eightfold Path. This is because practicing the other seven steps of the Eightfold Path leads a person to fully recognize things as they are.

Dharma Dictionary

Right view is the step on the Eightfold Path that refers to the realization of nonself (*anatman* in Sanskrit). With right view a person sees things as they are, without delusion. This is the one step of the Eightfold Path that is specifically Buddhist.

Right aim is the step on the Eightfold Path that refers to the intent or motivation from which our thoughts take shape. With right aim, a person has thoughts of helping (not harming) others … because those thoughts are grounded in the understanding that we are all dependent on each other.

Suffering ends when its causes are eliminated. The root cause of suffering is delusion about things as they are. Therefore, seeing things as they are eliminates suffering. When you have right view, you see things as they are and you don't suffer. Right view describes the wisdom that comes from realizing nonself—that one's self is related to the selves of all other beings.

Right view on the Eightfold Path entails realizing nonself by seeing—fully and in detail—the interdependent nature of things from one end of existence to the other. Nonself is among the most difficult—and least understood—of Buddha's teachings. It's also among the most interesting points of the Buddha-dharma.

Buddha Basics

The Sanskrit term for right view is samyag drishti. Samyag is used to qualify each step of the Eightfold Path. It has become common to translate this as "right," but it also means "full," "thorough," and "complete." Because the word right is taken to mean "the opposite of wrong," the words full or thoroughgoing seem more appropriate, because Buddhism does not reinforce dualistic thinking. But for some reason, early commentators used the word "right," and it stuck.

The drishti is the pupil of the eye, or the mind's eye. It is a theory or way of seeing things. The word also is used for a point at which a person looks to keep from toppling over in a one-legged yoga standing pose. Most generally, drishti is used to indicate seeing, viewing, beholding.

The heart of the Tathagata's message is contained in this teaching. The claim that a person has no self does not mean that the person does not exist. It means that the person does not exist *as a totally separate and independent person.* Buddha taught that people exist in the midst of a process of life and therefore are constantly subject to the inescapable causes and conditions of life.

Right Aim

Right aim is the second step on the Eightfold Path. Through right aim we set our course of thought and action in line with right view, the first step on the Eightfold Path. Think of right view (samyag drishti) as an aid to keep us from losing balance in life. Then think of right aim (samyak samkalpa) as zeroing in on that "right *drishti*" keeping awareness of it all the time. Backed up by the right view of reality, we give right aim to everything we do.

We can begin to understand the meaning of right aim by thinking of keeping a target as a reference point. We must have an aim in life that keeps us grounded. So whatever we aim to do, it's grounded in right view (samyag drishti). To get the point, try standing in the yoga posture known as the tree pose. (First try this with one leg. Later try it on the other side.) This mini-exercise will give you a physical sense of having a correct aim. After the experience, you may have a better sense of right aim as something mental.

Yoga tree pose (using a drishti or point of regard):

1. Find a spot somewhere directly in front of you and keep your gaze on it. This is your drishti. You are using it for balance.

2. Stand on one leg … let's say your left leg. Your left leg is straight, and the left foot is well planted on the floor. The toes on your left foot are spread out to let you get more balancing power. In addition to your toes, all four corners of your foot (inner heal, outer heal, little toe side, and big toe side) are in contact with the ground. (Your arch is lifted.)

3. Bend your right knee and point it to the extreme right. This means that you are in one plane. Your bent knee is not pointing forward. It is in line with your left leg.

4. Grab your right ankle with your right hand. (You may have to lean over a bit to catch it. But try to keep looking at the drishti.) If you tend to fall over easily, stand near a wall or in a doorway where you can put out your left hand for balance.

5. Bring your right foot to lean on the straight standing leg. You can place your right foot above the left knee or below the left knee—depending on your flexibility. You can even place the ball of your right foot on the ground with just your right heel leaning on the left ankle.

6. Balancing on your left leg, press your hands together in front of your chest. Or you can extend your arms straight up in the air, fingers stretching straight up to the sky, with palms facing each other—touching, if you like. (Keep your tailbone tucked in to help with posture here.)

7. Notice how the drishti helps you balance. What is helping you balance? You are aiming your thought or mental power at the drishti.

8. To get a deep feeling for the power of right aim, try closing your eyes! Do you feel how you have to use your intention, your will, your sense of resolve to keep balance? This is your aim.

Relating Aim and View on the Eightfold Path

Standing in tree pose, you can gather something about the relationship between right aim and right view on the Eightfold Path. Right view is the perspective on reality that provides a point of reference, so to speak. Buddha's drishti or point of reference was nonself or emptiness. The view of emptiness or dependent arising allowed Buddha to perfect his aim at whatever he wished. Knowing the nature of reality grounded him, and allowed him to know what was important to do and what was not. Therefore, he'd aim at what was important.

> **Be Mindful!**
>
> Right view and right aim provide the basis for all acts of body, speech, and mind. A Buddhist aim is continually trained on the view of existence as dynamic and interdependent.

To sum up: right aim on the Eightfold Path involves thought or intention directed on the basis of a clear view of reality or right view, which is a way of looking at all objects of experience, an all-encompassing, unbiased perspective that recognizes the nonself or interdependence among things. Right aim is the complete resolve that orients all our activities in light of the view of nonself of persons and things. Every movement of body, speech, or thought springs from an intention that is grounded in a realization of the interdependence of all beings and things.

Now, let's look more deeply at this nonself or emptiness that grounds right aim as well as every other step on the Eightfold Path. In Sanskrit, the nonself of persons is called anatman; while the nonself of all things (including persons) is called shunyata or "emptiness." This is the basic content of right view.

Anatman: The "Nonself" of Persons

If there is no self, who are we? Buddha did not claim that we don't exist; he taught we are dynamic persons that come to exist on a moment-to-moment basis, dependent on and bound by causes and conditions. Buddha used the image of *Five Heaps* to explain the nonself of persons. Five heaps of what? Five heaps of body and mind stuff that intermingle to make up our everyday experience!

The Tathagata taught his disciples to carefully observe each of the Five Heaps—forms, feelings, perceptions, mental formations, and minds—to see whether there is anything beyond them that makes up their person. He pointed out that there is no separate self that exists independently of these Five Heaps that make up a person. If we can understand these, we can better relate to Buddha's teaching on nonself and realize who Buddha claimed we are.

> **Dharma Dictionary**
>
> The **Five Heaps** are components that make up the person. They work together to construct one's experience. Buddhists claim that there is no self that is independent of the Five Heaps, namely conglomerations of forms, feelings, perceptions, mental formations, and minds. The Sanskrit word for heap is skandha—sometimes translated as "aggregate."

Forms

The heap of forms is associated with our body and forms in the world that provide objects for us to sense. We sense the physical world through our eyes, ears, nose, tongue, and skin or body as a whole. As a result of contact between these body parts and colors, music, textures, and so on, we experience sight, hearing, smelling, tasting, and touching. Buddha also included a sixth sensation: thinking or cognition. The area of the body associated with thinking is the brain, or the heart, or the whole body. We might roughly associate intellectual and artistic cognition with the brain, intuition with the heart, and instinct with the body as a whole.

Knowing this about Buddha's teaching on the heap of forms we can begin to answer the question "Who am I?" in this way:

I am a body that is capable of having sensations and thoughts.

With my eyes I see shapes that appear as colors of various tones and hues.

With my ears I hear sounds that are soft, loud, melodious, harsh, and so on.

With my nose I smell odors and fragrances.

With my tongue I taste things that are sweet, sour, and so on.

With my skin I recognize through touch things that are hot, cold, rough, smooth, and so on.

With my brain, heart, body, I experience thought forms.

Feelings

The heap of feelings involves experiencing sensations as pleasant, unpleasant, or neutral. This is pretty straightforward. After we have a sensation, the first thing that occurs to us is whether what we just experienced is pleasant or unpleasant. If the sensation does not make a big impact on us, it would be considered neutral. The same three possibilities exist for everything we hear, see, smell, taste, touch, or think. But how they strike us may vary from moment to moment!

To get an idea about the heap of feelings, try for a moment to observe some of your sensations. Check to see whether you experience them as pleasant, unpleasant, or neutral. Note that I did not say "Check to see whether the sense objects are pleasant, unpleasant, or neutral." Why? Because a sense object may be pleasant for one person and unpleasant for another person. Moreover, what is pleasant at one moment for you may be neutral or unpleasant at another moment. So check how the object is striking you at this very moment.

From the Buddhist point of view, no absolute value applies to any object of the senses. A piece of music, art, or literature, for example, is not absolutely pleasant, unpleasant, or neutral. A sense object may generally strike people as beautiful if it has characteristics of balance. However, the impact of things we sense depends ultimately on our own disposition. The commonplace saying "beauty is in the eye of the beholder" fits the situation of Buddha's heap of feelings.

> **Be Mindful!**
>
> When Buddha spoke of the five skandhas (translated as heaps or aggregates), he used his words very precisely. In translation, the terms for Five Heaps may carry connotations that should not be brought along from other languages. Forms, feelings, perceptions, mental formations, and minds have very specific meanings that pertain to actual meditations that Buddha taught.

Here we go. What sense will you observe first: seeing, hearing, smelling, touching, tasting, or thinking? Begin to notice what is happening around you in light of that sense. If you chose hearing, for example, you can try this:

- Stop everything and take a moment to notice what you are hearing at this very moment.

- Try to isolate one particular sound right now.

- Try to sense whether you feel that sound is pleasant or unpleasant before you even begin to identify that sound as a piece of music, a car, the human voice on the radio, or whatever.

- If the sound you identify is neither pleasant nor unpleasant, that probably means you experience it as neutral. But are you sure it is really neutral? Listen more closely and monitor your reaction to the sound. Do you for a moment feel it is pleasant? Unpleasant? Or is it really neutral to you at this time?

Perceptions

The heap of perceptions involves categorizing one's sense experiences. After gaining a feeling of pleasant, unpleasant, or neutral, a person naturally begins to label the object of perception. Buddha used the term perception to identify this act of organization. Our experiences can be perceived (organized, labeled) in many ways. How we perceive objects through our senses depends on our past experiences and past training (even in past lifetimes!), cultural conditioning, and feelings at the moment.

After perceiving music as pleasant, unpleasant, or neutral, we have the impulse to organize our experience. We may have heard a refrain of music written by Mozart. If we are not familiar with Mozart, but know something about Western classical music, we may label the music "piano concerto." If we are familiar with that late-eighteenth-century Austrian classical composer, the label "Mozart" may occur to us, or even "piano concerto number 21 in C." If we had heard the piano concerto's second movement in a 1967 Swedish film called *Elvira Madigan*, that name might even occur to us.

Enlightening Extras

Edmund Husserl (1859–1938), German founder of the philosophical movement known as phenomenology used the term *epoche* (Greek for cessation) to mean describing an object from the first-person point of view, exactly as it is experienced. Epoche, or bracketing, is done by suspending judgment or inquiry with respect to the object. This bracketing may be an attempt to minimize the impact of what Buddha called perceptions.

Some of our perceptions may be quite refined and detailed, whereas others may be rather vague. Yet according to Buddha's theory of the Five Heaps, our mind tends to perceive things in terms of categories that have become familiar to us. Check this out with your friends: let several people touch the same object and ask them to state what word or two occurs to them as soon as they touch it. One person might say, "Cold, rough." Another may say, "Flat, big." These labels are perceptions.

Mental Formations

The heap of mental formations includes numerous emotional reactions to sense objects, experienced as the heap of forms. These mental formations include the content of our emotions and mental tools of thought. The Buddhist tradition came up with different ways of classifying the mental formations. Here we will simply emphasize two main groups of mental formations—one positive and one negative.

Positive mental formations are emotional reactions and mental developments called the Seven Factors of Enlightenment because they pave the way for enlightenment. These seven mental formations bring happiness and make the best of human potential:

1. **Recollection (mindfulness):** Careful observation of the movements of one's body, speech, and mind to notice their impermanence, lack of independent self, and suffering nature

2. **Investigation of dharma:** Exploration of Buddha's teachings in various texts and experiences

3. **Endeavor (effort):** Sincere, energetic endeavors to act with a wholesome attitude and eliminate unwholesome attitudes

4. **Joy:** A buoyant mental-physical experience derived from contemplation that is spiritual, not sensual in nature

5. **Tranquility:** A serene mental-physical experience derived from fixing one's attention in meditation without wavering

6. **Contemplation:** Advanced levels of experience in the realms of subtle form and no form

7. **Equanimity (even-mindedness):** A balanced mental attitude that is unbiased and unperturbed

Buddha Basics

The Buddhist tradition treats the Seven Factors of Enlightenment in various overlapping contexts. Endeavor, contemplation, and equanimity are among the Ten Perfections. Endeavor, recollection, and contemplation are the three aspects of the Eightfold Path in the division of mental discipline. Joy and equanimity are two of the four abodes of Brahma. And the two branches of Buddhist bhavana or meditation involve tranquility on one hand and investigation of dharma on the other.

There are five negative mental formations known as the hindrances that must be overcome in order to reach higher states of consciousness:

1. **Sensual desire:** Craving more experience of things that produce pleasant sensations

2. **Ill will:** An angry attitude that seeks harm for others.

3. **Dullness (sloth and torpor):** Lack of enthusiasm and clarity in meditation, like strings on a sitar that are too loose

4. **Agitation (restlessness and worry):** Lack of calmness and clarity in meditation, like strings on a sitar that are too tight

5. **Skeptical doubt:** Confusion arising from holding conflicting opinions about what is true or important

These Five Hindrances can become teachers about the condition of one's personality and the nature of mind in general. They can be overcome when one honestly observes them. Intent observation brings the realization that these Five Hindrances—as all mental factors—exhibit the Three Marks of Existence: impermanence, nonself, and suffering.

Minds

The heap of minds involves six different consciousnesses, which correspond to the six senses in the heap of forms. Each of the senses—sight, taste, touch, smell, hearing, and thinking—arises because a mind or consciousness enlivens it. Put yourself into this hypothetical scenario of attending a classical music concert to see how the six minds arise through contact between sense organs and objects they encounter. And though an incredible number of consciousnesses are arising all the time, let's isolate just one for each sense to see how the six consciousnesses work:

- An eye consciousness arises when the conductor appears in our line of vision, as the rays of light bouncing off his or her body strike the back of our eyeballs.

- An ear consciousness arises the moment the first violins begin tuning their instruments and the sound waves strike our eardrums.

- A tactile consciousness arises when we feel too warm in our sweater as we wait for the concert to begin.

- A consciousness of taste arises when we pop a piece of chewing gum into our mouths and sense the minty flavor.

- A consciousness of smell arises as we get a whiff of the chewing gum's strong mint.

- A mental consciousness arises as we recognize that we are feeling impatient for the concert to begin.

Enlightening Extras

Buddha and John Locke (1632–1704) seem to be kindred spirits: both were highly anti-authoritarian and committed to experience as the basis of knowledge. Locke, the father of British empiricism, argued that all knowledge derives from experience, not from innate ideas. He spoke of simple ideas that originate in each of the senses and complex ideas that combine simple ideas. Locke's epistemology and Buddha's theory of Five Heaps would be fun to compare.

So What? The Heaps Are Us!

Now that we've been through the Five Heaps, you may ask, "So what?" Well, according to Buddha, the Five Heaps are us! That's who we are: a dynamic combination of physical and mental actions in Five Heaps. The heap of forms is our body, and the other four heaps are all included in the workings of our mind. The heap of feelings, perceptions, mental formations, and minds are different ways of talking about how we experience things mentally ... dependent on having a body.

Buddha said we are made up of the Five Heaps and there is no abiding self beyond this combination of body and mind. We have a consciousness that continues from life to life like a flame being transferred on from one candle to another. But that flame-like subtle consciousness is impermanent and changing from moment to moment, according to Buddha. The subtlest consciousness "goes" from one body to another through different lifetimes, but it changes according to the kinds of contacts it makes with the heap of forms.

Buddha taught people how to meditate on the Five Heaps. The main meditation that involves our physical-mental process is called the Four Applications of Mindfulness. (See Chapter 16.)

The Least You Need to Know

- ◆ Right view and right aim are the specifically Buddhist elements of the Eightfold Path to enlightenment and fall into the category of wisdom.

- ◆ The first step on Buddha's Eightfold Path is right view, which refers to realization of the nonself of persons and things (anatman and sunyata).

- ◆ The second step on Buddha's Eightfold Path is right aim, which involves the motivation to act in a way beneficial to others based on the realization of nonself and the emptiness of all phenomena.

- ◆ A key teaching that points out the meaning of nonself is Buddha's teaching on the Five Heaps: forms, feelings, perceptions, mental formations, and minds.

Chapter 5

Do's and Don'ts of Dharma

In This Chapter

- ◆ Virtuous behavior on the Eightfold Path
- ◆ The importance of motivation
- ◆ Right speech, action, and livelihood
- ◆ Theory of karma
- ◆ Positive and negative mental formations

Buddha's Eightfold Path suggests three types of "right" behavior that fall into the category of virtue: right speech, right action, and right livelihood. These three "rights" are closely related types of conduct that produce the best results when they're based on wisdom. That is why in many accounts of the Eightfold Path, the steps of virtue are placed after the steps of wisdom. On the other hand, because virtue is so basic to happiness in the conducts of speech, action, and making a living, they often come first on the Eightfold Path. But why should a person do virtuous things, anyway? Why did the Tathagata recommend compassionate activities in his prescription for happiness and enlightenment? Well, Buddha thought that virtue would come naturally to a person who knows the nature of reality. In other words, when we see who we really are in relation to each other, we see the suffering of others as no different from our own suffering. Buddha believed that as soon as we realize nonself—the interdependence among all living beings—we spontaneously try to minimize suffering in the world. Buddha said that the root cause of suffering is delusion—ignorance about who we really are. But how does not knowing reality make us harm one another? And what are the results of harmful acts?

According to the Buddha-dharma, we harm others in a misguided attempt to gain happiness. Unfortunately, however, harming others only brings us more pain! Acts of compassion, on the other hand, actually bring us happiness. Buddha explains this causal relationship in his theory of karma, or the moral law of cause and effect.

Positive Behavior on the Eightfold Path

Positive, negative, and neutral behavior can be performed three ways by what Buddha called this "fathom-long" human body of ours. We can act by way of gesture, speech, and thought. But it's sometimes hard to figure out whether particular acts are wholesome, unwholesome, or neutral. For this reason, ethics can be a thorny subject. Which do you think might be the virtuous, nonvirtuous, or neutral acts in the following examples?

- Use our hands to play the piano, rescue someone from a fire, pick the wallet from a shopper's pocket, or knead dough for dumplings

- Use our power of language to write a declaration of independence, scandalize a competitor, sing the national anthem, or answer the telephone

- Use our mental power to plan an attack on a neighboring village or country, plan a wedding, find a cure for AIDS, or memorize multiplication tables

---

Buddha Basics

Buddha identified motivation as the key indicator of the character of an act. He thus encouraged creativity. Even if people "mess up"—the result of the work will be largely positive if their motive was clearly to help. Until people awaken, the quality of their work and its results will always be somewhat imperfect. Yet the phrase *trying one's best* meant a lot to the Tathagata.

In general, the Tathagata emphasized a person's motivation as a key factor in determining whether an action is positive, negative, or neutral. An act done with the motive of helping others would be more virtuous than the "same" act done with the motive of aggrandizing oneself. Judging the virtue of an act is complicated because the same person can do the same thing with a different motive each time. In spite of such ethical complexities, Buddha did present some guidelines for wholesome action on the Eightfold Path.

Right Speech

Buddha observed many ways that people use words. Some ways generally appear to cause suffering, whereas other ways tend to promote happiness. So, it is a no-brainer to figure that the Master suggested that people curtail speech that makes them and others unhappy.

Buddha's suggestions for disciplining one's speech are fairly universal, and pretty much based on common sense. But it doesn't hurt to review the principles of right speech with a Buddhist twist … so here goes.

Telling Lies

Prince Siddhartha made a tremendous effort to discover the actual nature of reality. So it makes sense that he encouraged people to seek the truth of any matter, small or big. Lying impacts a person's ability to discern truth. This goes for the ultimate truth of nonself as well as the truth of other matters of daily life. And realizing the truth of nonself depends on a powerful mind that is not muddled by untruth, as well as an appreciation of the close relationship among living beings.

> ### Be Mindful!
>
> Buddha's ethical teachings are not absolute rules. Keep in mind that Buddhism is a non-theistic tradition. As such, the dharma is presented as a human discovery of universal principles, rather than as divine commandments. The Tathagata specifically asked that his words not be accepted merely on the basis of his authority as an Awakened One. Rather, he encouraged people to confirm for themselves which aspects of the dharma proved useful and true in their own experience. However, when it came to living in the order, a rule of life was adopted and taken very seriously.

Lies build barriers of mistrust in society. Lies muddy communication among people and alienate them from each other. People learn not to trust a liar, and a liar feels alienated from others. A liar cannot act with comfort and ease in the presence of the person he or she wants to fool. The liar must fabricate one false statement after another to keep up the lie. The liar needs to control the flow of information and hesitates to explore situations openly. Thus communication breaks down in an untruthful society. And because virtuous acts are based on a sense of interconnectedness among people, we can see that lying inhibits virtuous action.

Slander and Abuse

Slander is speech that stands between lying and abuse. It is false speech, maliciously intended to damage someone's good reputation. Even kernels of "truth" in slanderous speech are distorted by the harmful intent of the speaker. Buddha counseled against slander not only because it harms another person but also because it breaks apart communities through internal backbiting and dissent.

Abusive speech comes in many forms—from shouting at to belittling or discouraging another person. Buddha's main guideline for action was, "If you cannot help, at least do not harm." If a person seeks to correct the behavior of another, firm guidance can be given with an attitude of loving-kindness. It is difficult to "take back" words. So the impact of harsh speech lasts far beyond the time it takes to utter unkind words.

> ### Buddha Basics
>
> Buddha recommended actions to avoid. In his ethical teachings on the Eightfold Path, he also taught people how to respond to nonvirtuous conduct done by others. For instance, he advised Ananda:
>
> *As an elephant endures arrows in battle, so I will patiently accept harsh words. In this world human beings can be cruel.*

Gossip and Idle Chatter

Gossip is a form of idle chatter. And though gossip is supposed to be the least harmful form of unwholesome speech, it is also the most prevalent. Thus what might appear to be innocuous chatter behind someone's back might become quite serious due to the negativity stirred up.

Idle chatter is speech that is not constructive and has no positive purpose. It neither helps others improve themselves nor improves those who fritter away time with vacuous talk. Therefore Buddha advised people to refrain from idle chatter and make all their speech meaningful.

Right Action

Buddha taught his disciples how to shape and delimit their actions to produce the maximum amount of true happiness for themselves and others. He taught that each action has far-reaching consequences and inspired followers to conduct themselves honorably toward peaceful ends. Right action on the Eightfold Path involves respect for the life and property of others. One's activities should be undertaken with sincere effort to avoid causing distress to living beings or the environment.

Sexual misconduct is one type of action that Buddha seriously discouraged. He insisted on celibacy for his mendicant disciples, following the ancient Indian tradition of brahmacarya (abstinence). For laypeople, the Tathagata generally reinforced culturally acceptable marital obligations and upheld the value of monogamous relationships, enjoining men not go to other men's wives. By and large, the scriptures are silent regarding conjugal relations between couples. Overall, however, Buddha emphasized the benefits of chastity and associated sexuality with rebirth and the sufferings of samsara.

Right Livelihood

The step on the Eightfold Path known as right livelihood pertains largely to laypersons who must work to support themselves. However, it also applies to members of the order who live by alms, depending on the generosity of the lay community. The same basic principles apply to earning one's living as to other virtuous acts: avoid violence, dishonesty, and communal disruption. Thus with regard to making a living, Buddha advised laypeople to avoid at least three things: destroying life, procuring goods dishonestly, and promoting ill will.

Buddha's position on food and diet sometimes causes consternation among contemporary vegetarians because many Buddhists do eat meat. In this they are unlike Jains, who have lived as uncompromising vegetarians alongside Buddhists in India since Gautama's day. Ideally no Buddhist would make a living as a butcher or fisherman. Yet Sakyamuni did not forbid monks and nuns to eat meat if it was offered as alms (and if the animal was not killed especially for them). Monks and nuns were to maintain equanimity regarding their food and humbly accept whatever was offered to them regardless of whether meat was included.

A Buddhist View of Cause and Effect

Buddha taught that a moral order was built into the universe. Just as a mango seed, under adequate climactic and environmental conditions, produces a mango tree and not an oak, so virtuous acts produce happiness and not suffering. This law of moral cause and effect is known as *karma*.

Dharma Dictionary
Karma is a Sanskrit term meaning action. It refers to the moral law of causation that operates in the universe with inevitable results: virtuous acts bring happiness, nonvirtuous acts bring pain.

The Tathagata taught virtue on the Eightfold Path to promote mental and social conditions that pave the way for enlightenment—happiness and cooperation. He knew that, according to the law of karma, virtuous acts would produce happiness, which would lead to social cooperation, which would bring closer the possibility of awakening. Buddha wished to reduce personal misery and social ills, for they both inhibit spiritual practice.

Karma—What Goes Around Comes Around

Another way of talking about karma is to say: what goes around comes around. You get back what you put out. Acting on the basis of delusion, craving, and revulsion brings suffering. To the extent that one's mind is free from these Three Poisons, happiness comes.

But how does karma work? What did Buddha say about karma? How can we create good karma? How can we avoid bad karma? The answer comes from understanding the place of karma in Buddha's Four Great Facts. Karma is produced through our mental formations, which are included among the Five Heaps. (See Chapter 14.)

The Five Heaps are part of Buddha's explanation of Great Fact 1: pain goes with the territory of being human. Suffering is inherent in our existence, and the subtlest part of our suffering is the fact that we have to constantly go through physical and mental transformations just to be alive.

Karma is created when our volition (intention or will) combines with other mental formations that are positive, negative, or neutral. Volition is one of many (some lists name 52) mental formations. It is part of our mental makeup. We have intentions all the time to do things, say things, consider things. But when we take our willpower and specifically link it to certain other mental formations (including various emotions) we create karma. That karma will bear fruit, and we'll get back experiences that are similar to the karmic actions we took.

Be Mindful!

Buddha's first Great Fact is sometimes considered pessimistic because his teaching on duhkha—pain, suffering, alienation—is misunderstood. But taken together, the Four Great Facts are optimistic and life affirming.

- The first fact exposes the tremendous amount of pain in our world.
- The second fact identifies Three Poisons—delusion, desire, and revulsion—as the basic causes of pain.
- The third fact states that we can alleviate pain by eliminating its causes.
- The fourth fact outlines eight steps—based on wisdom, virtue, and mental cultivation—to alleviate pain that comes with the territory of being human.

Oh, Those Emotions!

So what are the emotions and attitudes—known as the heap of mental formations—that combine with our will to create karma? Buddha's teachings on this subject have been organized in various ways, but here are some of the mental formations involved in our karma. They include the seven factors of enlightenment and the five hindrances that we talked about earlier in reviewing the Five Heaps that make up every person. But there are more! The mental life of human beings is complex. We have a lot going on by way of reactions to things we experience. Here are some mental formations listed in terms of the pain or happiness they produce after becoming negative or positive karma.

Wholesome Mental Formations

Many wholesome mental formations are described in terms of the lack of nonvirtuous mental formations. This shows that it is very wonderful to be able to act without being afflicted by negative emotions, such as the three poisons. Others are described directly. Combining our intention with any wholesome mental formation produces good karma and brings the karmic fruit of happiness. Here are five examples:

- **Nonharming:** Have compassion without any hatred. This means one does not think of others as enemies—so there is no wanting to harm them.

- **Carefulness:** Apply care and mindfulness to practicing virtue and abandoning harmful actions. Understand that one needs to cast off negative action and take up virtuous action.

- **Equanimity:** Do not be overpowered by emotional afflictions such as desire, revulsion, and delusion. Remain in this natural state of the mind where emotional afflictions cannot arise.

- **Propriety:** Understand that certain actions are not good in terms of one's own standards or those of the dharma. Avoid committing nonvirtuous actions not to avoid being ashamed, but to feel that one is not the kind of person who does things without thinking of the effects.

- **Diligence:** Enter into virtuous activity with delight. This allows one to accomplish virtuous work thoroughly and effectively.

Unwholesome Mental Formations

Buddha spoke a lot about emotions and attitudes that bring suffering. The major unwholesome mental formations are the three poisons. However, there are many spin-offs of delusion, craving, and revulsion. Here are five unwholesome mental formations that create negative karma when combined with intention:

- **Pride.** This is an attitude of inflated superiority in which the person feels "I'm great," "I'm a high person," "I have superior talents." This prevents a person from respecting others and causes one to be isolated and unhappy.

- **Forgetfulness:** When one cannot clearly remember virtuous objects, and the mind becomes distracted—especially during spiritual practice—one is unable to concentrate on the meaning of what one is doing.

- **Lack of conscience:** Even though one realizes the right things to do and understands why they are right, emotional afflictions get in the way of doing those things. One cannot conduct body, speech, and mind properly when the time comes to do so. This causes moral failing.

- **Deceitfulness:** One is attached to acquisitions and honor and engages in a lot of crooked dealings. This poses an obstacle to receiving instructions from a spiritual teacher. This is related to hypocrisy.

- **Fogginess:** One's body and mind feel very heavy, and one is not able to concentrate. This makes a person vulnerable to various emotional afflictions. This is the opposite of wildness, where the mind runs after things and cannot remain serene.

Buddha Basics

Buddhism speaks of many forms of internal anger, all spinning off of the poison of revulsion:

- **Wrath:** Readies one to actually harm other beings through actions such as beating.
- **Malice:** A continuous, unforgiving intention to harm someone that's hard to let go.
- **Rage:** When the causes of wrath and malice become unbearable, it comes out in rage where one's face turns red, and one speaks angry words.
- **Vindictiveness:** Outwardly one might appear gentle, but inside one seeks revenge instead of feeling love and compassion.
- **Jealousy:** Due to craving for objects or honor, one can't bear for others to have good things or qualities. It arouses anger, makes it hard to rest, and causes one to lose much merit.

What About Sleep and Remorse?

Some mental formations can be virtuous, nonvirtuous, or neutral. These are interesting. Did you ever think that you could make sleep virtuous or nonvirtuous? According to Buddhist tradition, sleep is a mental formation in which all sense fields are drawn inside. Whether sleep generates good karma or not depends on a person's state of mind as he or she is falling asleep, which can affect the dreams that follow. If sleep is virtuous, then wholesome tendencies will appear in dream state. If the sleep is nonvirtuous, then unwholesome tendencies will appear in one's dreams. Lots of times, sleep is just neutral.

Remorse is defined as unhappiness about what one has done before. This regret about past actions interferes with a person's concentration. It is very difficult to rest when one is overcome with remorse. The fascinating thing is that remorse can be virtuous, nonvirtuous, or neutral. If one uses the regret as a springboard for positive action, it is virtuous. If one wallows and uses regret as a reason to hate oneself, it becomes nonvirtuous. When not accompanied by much willpower, remorse can be neutral ... or nearly so.

Can We Escape the Fruits of Our Karma?

We've been talking about pain and happiness resulting from intentional acts. What happens after a person has done something? Is there any way to take it back or avoid its consequences?

The short answer is this: "No. After a seed of karma is created, it is impossible to destroy." However, there are ways of making the painful fruits of unwholesome karma less harsh. One is by using the four "opponent powers" to cleanse oneself of unwholesome tendencies. Another is by reacting to the karmic payback in a positive way.

Making Bad Karma Lighter

Negative karma cannot be erased, but the effects of unwholesome karma can be decreased by breaking the cycle of negativity. According to Buddha, our thoughts are habit forming. The more a person does something, the easier that thing is to do in the future. If one is angry today, it will be easier to fly off the handle tomorrow. However, if one is kind today, it will be easier for that person to be kind tomorrow.

> **Dharma Dictionary**
>
> The **Four Opponent Powers** are things a person can do to lessen the painful effects of bad karma:
>
> 1. Appeal to spiritual objects.
> 2. Confess wrongdoings.
> 3. Apply antidotes.
> 4. Resolve not to repeat.

It's no problem to keep practicing virtuous acts, such as being kind, because that results in happiness. But how can a person stop the snowball effect of doing negative acts? One has to consciously transform the negative acts into positive acts.

Buddhists have a method of transforming their negativity called the *Four Opponent Powers*. And though we'll outline these from a Buddhist point of view, you might be able to think of ways to apply them in other contexts. They have psychological value even outside a religious framework.

- **Refuge:** The first Opponent Power is to take refuge in the Three Jewels— Buddha, dharma, and spiritual community. This means that a person appeals to the spiritual objects in which he or she has trust. This has the effect of opening one's heart and mind to positive change.

- **Confession:** The second Opponent Power is to feel sincere regret for the wrongdoing and confess. Buddhists do not necessarily confess to a person. Rather, they typically sit in front of a Buddha image and think honestly about the negative act they did.

- ◆ **Antidote:** The third Opponent Power is to apply an antidote: perform virtuous deeds to replace nonvirtuous deeds, either physically doing or mentally contemplating a positive deed to compensate for the unwholesome deed.

- ◆ **Resolve:** The fourth Opponent Power is to vow to turn away from the kinds of negative acts one has done. This vow is not necessarily taken in front of a person. Rather, it can be done while imagining the object in which a person has faith. Buddhists might imagine resolving to Buddha to try to stop doing nonvirtuous deeds.

Positive Reactions to Negative Situations

A person can make the fruits of bad karma lighter by reacting positively to situations in which they are suffering. They can consider that the pain is a fruit of past negative karma. Then they can feel some sense of comfort about the fact that such pain will be over and will not arise again as long as negative karma has not been committed. To do this, it is helpful to think about the Five Heaps. Here's an example of how a person might react to pain with positivity.

Let's think again about the Five Heaps that Buddha described as an explanation of nonself. We have eyes that see, ears that hear, a nose that smells, a tongue that tastes, and skin that feels. These are the classic five senses. Plus … we have a brain, heart, and body that give us intelligence. When any of these items in the heap of forms contacts an object it can sense (including ideas!), a corresponding mind arises, such as an ear consciousness or a mental consciousness. After that, we get either a pleasant or unpleasant feeling—or we remain neutral.

Enlightening Extras

Classical Buddhist teachings on epistemology—how we come to know our world and how we become enlightened—are still meaningful today. But new scientific research surely could enhance Buddhist teachings. In his book, *The Universe in a Single Atom*, the Dalai Lama says that although they appear to have been on "the right track," certain aspects of Buddhist theory "must now be modified in light of modern physics."

But where does morality fit into this story of the Five Heaps? This gets into Buddhist ethics. After feeling a sensation or idea as pleasant, unpleasant, or neutral, our perception labels the object or situation and we construct mental formations in reaction to the experience. How we react determines the kind of karma we accumulate. We can react with virtuous, nonvirtuous, or neutral mental formations. Here are two examples:

- We taste a piece of chocolate cake and feel it is pleasant. Will we label it "mine" and construct the mental formation of craving? Or might we label it "ours" and share it with a mental formation of equanimity?

- We are shoved out of the way at the grocery store by someone in a hurry. We feel it as unpleasant. Will we label it "rude" and react with the mental formation of vindictiveness? Or might we label it "needy" and react with the mental formation of propriety and make room?

What Do We Get for Being Good?

Why should we be "good"? What is the benefit of sharing our food, being considerate of others, and doing numerous other positive acts of body, speech, and mind? According to the Buddhist theory of karma and its fruits, by being virtuous we reduce our suffering and strengthen our character. We become more courageous, peaceful, helpful, and happy. This does not mean that we lose our personalities. But we have more energy freed up because we are not conflicted by lies, cheating, killing, and other actions that contradict right speech, right action, and right livelihood.

The beneficial qualities that result from doing wholesome karma tend to reflect the specific type of deeds performed. For helping others out of their troubles and refraining from killing, we gain long life. From assisting the poor and weak, we gain health. From acts of charity we gain wealth. And the list goes on. If we do good things and still encounter problems, it means we are using up some old bad karma. Reacting with wisdom and compassion to our troubles helps us through the hard times and paves the way for a bright future.

The Least You Need to Know

- Three steps on Buddha's Eightfold Path fall into the category of virtue: right speech, right action, and right livelihood.

- Living according to the Eightfold Path leads to the accumulation of wholesome karma and freedom from suffering for oneself and in society.

- Although the seeds of negative karma cannot be destroyed, the painful effects of nonvirtue can be lightened by breaking the cycle of wrongful action using the Four Opponent Powers: refuge, confession, antidote, and resolve.

- Buddhist morality involves contemplating one's reactions to pleasant and unpleasant situations, and fostering wholesome mental formations.

Chapter 16

Mental Cultivation

In This Chapter

- ◆ Wisdom, virtue, and mental cultivation work together
- ◆ Two branches of bhavana: samatha and vipasyana
- ◆ Right effort as joyful perseverance
- ◆ Right recollection and satipatthana practice
- ◆ Right contemplation and abiding with Brahma

The three sections of Buddha's Eightfold Path—wisdom, virtue, and mental cultivation—complement each other. Virtue deals with outer conduct, whereas mental cultivation deals with inner conduct. And both are grounded in wisdom. Right speech, action, and livelihood lay the groundwork for social harmony and individual peace of mind. Right effort, recollection, and contemplation deepen that peace of mind and intensify the practice of virtue. Finally, right view and aim set the stage for all our conduct—outer and inner. This chapter explores the inner conduct Buddha recommended on the Eightfold Path.

Chapter 15 covered Buddha's wisdom teachings on nonself and emptiness. Chapter 16 covered ethics, showing how virtue prepares the way for a kind and content life. And here in this chapter we explore techniques that Buddha developed to calm the mind and gain right view. When a person has right view, he or she stops suffering and lives free of hatred and craving.

Some of the most fascinating teachings in Buddhism belong to the mental cultivation section of spiritual practice. Gautama Buddha—and the rich meditative tradition that followed in his footsteps—came up with deep insights about what the human mind can discover. And along with these observations came volumes of practical instruction on how to clear, strengthen, and awaken one's consciousness. Now we're going to look at some techniques the Tathagata prescribed to help people reach their full psychological potential.

Bhavana on the Eightfold Path

Bhavana is a Sanskrit term you'll want to remember. It means "mental cultivation"— which is meditation. To awaken as Siddhartha did, a person needs bhavana. The word *cultivation* is beautiful to use in translating bhavana because it suggests that—like land—the mind can be made ready for planting, sowing, and harvesting. As a farmer prepares the earth for planting by removing rocks, loosening soil, and fertilizing the dirt, so a meditator removes unwholesome attitudes, evens out the mind, and provides spiritual food for thought. Farmers and meditators both cultivate to improve their lots.

> **Dharma Dictionary**
>
> **Bhavana** is the Sanskrit word for mental cultivation or meditation. Right effort, right recollection, and right contemplation on Buddha's Eightfold Path all pertain to the two branches of meditation that develop serenity and insight, respectively—samatha and vipasyana.

Bhavana has two branches—one that quiets the mind and one that brings wisdom. In Sanskrit, these branches of mental cultivation are called samatha (serenity) and vipasyana (special insight). The three steps of Buddha's Eightfold Path devoted to mental cultivation are right effort, right recollection, and right contemplation. They all have to do with how we conduct ourselves psychologically. And they all involve a certain amount of calming the mind to prepare the way for insight.

Ultimately, all bhavana is for the sake of gaining wisdom—that is, realizing the emptiness of persons and things. And the three steps of mental cultivation approach the goal of right view from different angles. Right effort clears obstacles and supplies energy for meditation. Right recollection is the process of getting to "know thyself." And right contemplation allows a person to gain mental and physical pliancy (energetic flexibility) that makes realization of emptiness easier.

Right Effort

Right effort is sometimes called joyous perseverance. That's because making effort on the spiritual path involves stick-to-it-iveness. One must persevere and not give up. But making effort in virtuous endeavors is thought to be a joyous process—not drudgery.

But how should you direct your efforts? There are basically four things that Buddha recommended for right effort. They are all related:

- **Identify unwholesome thoughts you have.** Don't feed them with negativity. Notice them, but don't act on them. Meet the nonvirtuous thoughts in face-to-face combat. Expel them from the mind.

- **Identify wholesome thoughts you have.** Notice them and act on them, if appropriate. Build upon your virtues. Meet them and allow them to fully express themselves.

- **Prevent new unwholesome thoughts from arising.** Exert some control over your senses. Don't respond immediately with desire or revulsion to objects of the senses.

- **Encourage new wholesome thought to arise.** Turn negativity into positivity by considering how others need help and responding to their needs.

Buddha Basics
Soma was a lute player who was trying too hard to attain enlightenment. He could not even gain the basic stages of meditation because of it. Seeing this, the Master asked, "How do you tune your instrument?" The musician answered, "I tune it so the strings are not too tight and not too loose." Then Buddha replied, "So it is with meditation. Balance energy with calm. Be neither restless nor slack."

Tuning the Lute

Joyous perseverance is a phrase for right effort that includes the perfect balance between being too loose or too tight. It's like tuning a lute. You have to get the strings just right, so they make a beautiful sound. One main obstacle to balanced effort is distraction. Being distracted is like tuning the strings of a lute too tight. One is tense and cannot concentrate. Another obstacle is dullness, which can be mental or physical.

Having laxity or lethargy is like tuning the lute strings too loose. One is lackluster and—again—cannot concentrate. This means that in making effort, we should neither try too hard, nor give up.

You may remember the old saying "All work and no play makes Jack a dull boy." Well, we can apply that adage to right effort on Buddha's Eightfold Path. Buddha said effort should be joyous. It should not get caught up in overwhelming details, such that a person loses heart.

Enlightening Extras

Right effort when done sincerely has wondrous consequences. I once heard a young man on the radio speaking about his love for animals. One day he made a deep commitment to devote himself to helping stray animals, and after his heart was moved to compassion, all kinds of animals began to appear as he walked down the street. He had walked those streets many times before, but animals had not come out to meet him. His joyous development of compassion seemed truly powerful.

Would You Believe ... It's Just Laziness?

Chances are you'd agree, if someone said to you, "Laziness is the opposite of effort." But did you ever think of discouragement as a type of laziness? How about a sense of inferiority? How about busy-ness? Well, Buddha counted all three of these as forms of (yes) laziness. Let's see how Buddhists try to get rid of laziness in the practice of right effort.

- Discouragement saps one's enthusiasm for spiritual work, so it is considered the worst form of laziness. Actually, Buddhists feel there is no need to be discouraged, due to the Master's skillful means. With the ability to target his audience, Buddha taught the spiritual path in a variety of ways, to reach many kinds of people. Due to this wealth of teachings, there is always at least a tiny portion of dharma that a person can put into practice.

- Inferiority is feeling "How could I possibly do this?" A person who feels inferior tends to become discouraged. It may seem compassionate to feel sorry for people—including ourselves—when they feel inferior. But everyone is inferior to someone else in countless ways. However, a person can always accomplish something no matter how "bad" he or she is at it. This old adage might apply to inferiority: practice makes perfect.

◆ Busy-ness is the habit of getting caught up in activities that don't accomplish anything. Being too busy is a type of laziness, because a person is distracted from things of spiritual value. If we think about the number of useless activities the average person gets into, we can begin to understand the Buddhist point about busy-ness as laziness.

Be Mindful!

Sometimes casting new ideas in terms of an image or metaphor can help them come into focus. Let's say we want to understand better the relationship between right effort in the mental cultivation section and right aim in the wisdom section of the Eightfold Path. The metaphor of a car might well illustrate their relationship: right aim is the steering wheel, and right effort is the gasoline. Intention directs the car, and persevering endeavor carries it forward without stalling. Can you fill in more of the metaphor with other steps on Buddha's Eightfold Path?

Guarding the mind well is the essence of practicing right effort. One who guards the mind is like a shepherd who both protects the flock from predators and catches any sheep who would run away into danger. Predators of the mind are nonvirtuous mental formations that barge or creep in to destroy wholesome mental formations. If a shepherd were to sleep all day, many sheep would be hurt. Similarly, if one who pretends to guard the mind is lazy, the mental condition deteriorates. The bottom line? Avoid laziness. Cultivate joyous perseverance!

Right Recollection

Right recollection is a step on Buddha's Eightfold Path that involves careful observance of one's physical and mental processes. The Tathagata taught his disciples how to be mindful of the subtle changes in their mind-body continuum. He told them to pay close attention to these four foundations of their experience:

◆ Physical sensations

◆ Pleasant, unpleasant, and neutral feelings

◆ States of consciousness

◆ Mental contents (conceptual and emotional)

The meditation practice on these is called the Four Applications of Mindfulness or Four Foundations of Mindfulness. In the Theravada Pali scriptures this mindfulness practice is known as *satipatthana*. Here are some brief instructions on how to apply mindfulness to the four foundations. The practice often is referred to as insight training because the meditator is to gain right view by seeing things as they are—characterized by impermanence, nonself, and suffering.

Dharma Dictionary

Satipatthana is the Pali term for meditating on the four foundations of mindfulness: body, feelings, minds, and mental contents. This forms the major content of right recollection on the Eightfold Path. Nowadays, Theravada Buddhists often call the practice vipassana (vipasyana in Sanskrit) or *satipatthana vipassana*—insight meditation through mindfulness. But the original instructions for such training come from Buddha's discourse called simply (in Pali) the *Satipatthana Sutta*.

Recollection of the Body

We begin our exploration of satipatthana with recollection of the body as the first focus of attention and awareness. Start by observing your physical processes. Watch your movements … your actions. You can look at the breath, feel the sensation of heat or cold on the skin, follow the small movements of deliberate walking, note the presence of the internal organs, and so on.

Often Buddhist meditators take their breath as the object of recollection. To do this, choose a location at which to observe the incoming and outgoing breath—where air hits the tip of the nose or upper lip, or the abdomen moving in and out. Some people count their breaths from 1 to 10 over and over again; others might simply observe the flow of air.

Whatever part of the body you choose, eventually you will notice how tensions arise in the body. Tension is a physical thing that seeks release. As you become more and more aware of the alternating between tension and relaxation, you begin to approach the second foundation of mindfulness—feelings.

Recollection of Feelings

The recollection of feelings involves being alert to alternating experiences of comfort, discomfort, or neutral feelings. One begins to realize that feelings do not stay for long in precisely the same intensity or location. One also notes that physical tension is associated with discomfort, and physical relaxation is associated with comfort.

Gradually, the body tends to favor the pleasant feelings of relaxation, and you become comfortable. The body becomes calm. And with the serene lack of alternation between tension and relaxation, the feelings become predominately neutral. One begins to recognize the subtle emotional excitement of the mind, or *citta*.

Recollection of Minds

The recollection of minds has to do with becoming aware of various dispositions of consciousness. If this sounds confusing, it is because we are not used to thinking in terms of this type of awareness. To better get an inkling of the knowledge of disposition, think about when you're tired. At the moment you decide "I'm tired," how did you know? What does it actually feel like to be "tired"? How about when you are agitated? What does it feel like to be mentally agitated?

If you have a sense of what being tired or agitated feels like, you are getting close to understanding what is meant by recollection of minds. It is a kind of clear, steady awareness of one's generalized mental state. But as one observes more closely, one notes that the mental state is actually changing from moment to moment in subtle ways. It might shift from expansive to agitated, for example. Or the mind might be steady, then shift to lax. A good way to get an idea of the recollection of minds is to try it yourself! (After all, Buddha's teachings are meant to be put into practice.)

Be Mindful!

If you recognize the five heaps incorporated into the four foundations of mindfulness, you are correct. *Satipatthana* involves paying attention to momentary developments in each of the five heaps—except that the heap of perceptions (which identifies and labels experience) is included in the foundation of mental contents. It could also have included the heap of feelings, but apparently Buddha wanted his disciples to pay special attention to whether experiences were taken to be pleasant or unpleasant.

Recollection of Mental Contents

At the point of calming all the agitation, lassitude, or other dispositions of consciousness in the recollection of minds, one can begin to notice mental formations as they appear and dissolve in the vast space of awareness. The fourth focus of satipatthana is precisely this recollection of mental contents. These objects of observation include the mental formations of the Five Heaps. But they also include anything that forms as mental content.

Right Contemplation

The satipatthana practice of right recollection is sometimes called the direct way to enlightenment because serenity and insight are cultivated seamlessly. But though satipatthana thoroughly integrates serenity and insight, it does not include meditations in the realm of no form. It stays with objects that can be perceived by the senses (including ideas)—namely, the mind-body processes of the meditator in the here and now.

Right contemplation—the third step in the mental cultivation section of Buddha's Eightfold Path—stands in contrast to right recollection because it goes beyond the realm of pure form. It involves experiencing the full range of human consciousness, as opposed to remaining in the realm of pure form where right recollection stops. The Sanskrit term for right contemplation is samyak samadhi—where samadhi is a state of consciousness that can either remain unwavering with pure forms as objects, or transcend forms altogether.

Way Back When ... and *Where?*

Whew! That was a bit technical. Let's get down to brass tacks and take a peek at what goes on in the mind of someone doing right contemplation. Actually, you already got to see Siddhartha go into *samadhi* without form. Remember in Chapter 9 when the *Bodhisattva* left his home in Kapilavastu? He went to Rajagriha, met King Bimbisara, and then found two teachers. Under the guidance of each one in turn, ascetic Siddhartha reached the height of samsara through serenity meditation. But the two rarified states of formless samadhi were not altogether agreeable to him, and he declared that calm abiding by itself would not lead him to enlightenment.

Buddha Basics

Alara Kalama, the first teacher Siddhartha found after leaving his family in Kapilavastu, guided him to the contemplative state of "nothing whatsoever." This is the third of four levels in the realm of no form where only the object "nothingness" exists. Rudraka Ramaputra, the *Bodhisattva's* second teacher told him about yet a higher level called "neither perception nor nonperception," the highest level in the realm of no form, where one neither perceives nor does not perceive things. Siddhartha got there, too. What he had been practicing were serenity meditations that involved formless samadhi.

Siddhartha had been disappointed with the samadhi meditations in the realm of no form because the levels of nothing whatsoever and neither perception nor nonperception were only temporary. Even if he would be reborn into one of these psychic spaces, he'd sooner or later have to die and come out still not knowing tathata—things as they really are. But later he developed a technique of combining special insight with samadhi. Thus, when Buddha taught the Eightfold Path to enlightenment, he still included samatha (serenity meditation). He called it right contemplation because it could be combined with vipasyana (or special insight meditation).

Calmly Abiding with Brahma

Let's talk about samadhi with form. One way of cultivating samadhi with form is to practice right contemplation in the abodes of Brahma. Here meditators enter a different dhyana (absorption) by contemplating each of four social virtues in turn:

- First dhyana is boundless loving kindness.

- Second dhyana is boundless compassion.

- Third dhyana is boundless sympathetic joy.

- Fourth dhyana is boundless equanimity.

> **Dharma Dictionary**
>
> The **abodes of Brahma** are four levels of boundless consciousness known as the social virtues that a meditator can experience: loving kindness, compassion, sympathetic joy, and equanimity. These exist in a realm of pure form within samsara and are inhabited by the Indian deity Brahma.

Buddha accepted the basic Indian belief in the existence of a deity called Brahma who occupies the four levels of existence in the realm of pure form. He also thought that a person could reach the *abodes of Brahma* through contemplation. In other words, a meditator could attain four boundless emotions equivalent to Brahma's consciousness of love, compassion, sympathetic joy, and equanimity. Furthermore, Buddha taught that an accomplished meditator actually could be reborn in one of the abodes of Brahma at the time of death.

Cultivating the Social Virtues

Loving-kindness, compassion, sympathetic joy, and equanimity—experienced in the abodes of Brahma—are sometimes called the social virtues because they involve the impulse to help others. Over the years, Gautama instructed many people on the method of cultivating the four social virtues. To those interested in the Eightfold

Path to enlightenment, he put this contemplation in the context of right view. But when non-Buddhists wanted to be reborn with Brahma, he taught the social virtues in the context of samadhi training alone.

On one such occasion, two learned brahmins, Vasettha and Bharadvaja, asked Gautama to show them the way to attain rebirth in communion with the deva Brahma. The master acknowledged knowing the way to communion with Brahma from his own experience. Then he prepared them with guidelines for basic samatha and explained the method of entering the abodes of Brahma.

The Tathagata taught the brahmins to cultivate loving-kindness, compassion, sympathetic joy, and equanimity. The young men were pleased because they felt that by getting into the same state of consciousness as Brahma, they could be with Brahma both in meditation and at the time of death.

Buddha Basics

Buddha's instruction on loving-kindness goes like this:

Relate without hesitation to beings in one of the directions (such as north) with a mind full of love. Then do the same for beings in the second, third, and fourth directions (south, east, west). Do the same for beings in the upward, downward, and diagonal directions. Without interruption continue to relate to beings everywhere, equally in the entire world with a mind full of love—a mind that is untroubled, free from enmity, expansive, and without bounds.

Really Wholesome!

Loving kindness, compassion, sympathetic joy, and equanimity are listed among the wholesome mental formations in Buddhist psychology. They are antidotes to non-virtuous mental formations. So they could be used in breaking the cycle of negative thinking in applying one of the four opponent powers. But what is the experience of these altruistic states of consciousness?

- **Loving-kindness:** This is devotion to the welfare of others. It involves nonhatred and actually overcomes anger. That means there is no intention to harm others in one's mental formations. Even when frustrated by others, there is only good will. Loving-kindness has an expansive quality and embodies the selfless wish "May you be happy."

- **Compassion:** This deepens the wish to give happiness to others. Compassion is devoted to removing the pain of beings tormented by any kind of suffering. It manifests as a sympathetic vibration of the heart that responds to the call for help of all sentient beings. This mental formation is open to the sorrow of others and carries the burning wish "May I remove your sorrow."

- **Sympathetic joy:** This follows from the happiness of selflessness that springs from compassion. It is a kind of joy associated with nonattachment. It overcomes displeasure and cannot coexist with jealousy. It never resents the excellence of others and rejoices in the virtues of all beings. It says "May you always meet with success."

- **Equanimity:** This issues from the calmness that accompanies sympathetic joy. It regards all beings with an unbiased attitude, from the smallest to the greatest, the poorest to the richest, the closest to the farthest. Such even-mindedness counteracts doubt, worry, and restlessness. It says "May *every living being* be happy, free from suffering, and successful."

Enlightening Extras

Buddha was not the only spiritual leader who taught something like the four social virtues. Swami Satchidananda calls them the four keys and said they were his guiding light for maintaining a serene mind. The Hindu Patanjali speaks of them in his *Yoga Sutras* (I, 33):

The mind remains calm through cultivation of friendliness for the happy, compassion for the sad, delight for the virtuous, and patience for the nonvirtuous.

When Love Is Not Enough

In the six years of practicing intensive meditation before attaining enlightenment, the ascetic Siddhartha practiced entering the abodes of Brahma by meditating on loving-kindness, compassion, sympathetic joy, and equanimity. But after experiencing these four levels of divine consciousness, Siddhartha identified a problem. Though his experiences in the abodes of Brahma were wonderful, they were not powerful enough to cut off ties to the Wheel of Becoming.

There was a second problem with the abodes of Brahma. In spite of the refined emotions that pervade all directions on Brahma's levels, Buddha claimed that the four social virtues would eventually become corrupt unless they were enhanced by wisdom. When the meditator came out of the samadhi, unwholesome mental formations would barge back into the meditator's experience. Therefore, meditators should observe the nonself of objects in the meditation and the impermanence of the dhyana states themselves. Through such observation the insight dawns: *Even the beings encompassed in the orb of my boundless emotion have no abiding self, and my state of consciousness is itself dependently arising.*

Buddha said that if one had right view (the first step on the Eightfold Path), the anger abandoned during the experience of loving-kindness in Brahma's realm was like a baseless palm tree cut at the root. It would not grow back in the mind of one who had realized nonself. The same goes for harmfulness, jealousy, and bias, which are destructive emotions that counteract compassion, sympathetic joy, and equanimity. Right view of the nature of reality would assure that the loving-kindness, compassion, and sympathetic joy generated in the abodes of Brahma would never weaken. And the equanimity would not allow neglect of any being. Thus the meditation would be truly boundless.

The Tathagata told his disciples that to escape the cycle of rebirth, they must become completely free of the Three Poisons. Remember those nasty root causes of rebirth—delusion, craving, and repulsion? So even though one's mind gets purer by abiding with Brahma, the purity does not last. Without right view, when you come back to ordinary consciousness … zoop! Negative emotions come right back. No matter how beautiful abiding with Brahma is, the experience is not enough stop rebirth and end suffering. All beings in the abodes of Brahma—including Brahmas themselves still exist in samsara.

Coming Full Circle on the Eightfold Path

The Eightfold Path is more like a circle than a line. Its three categories of wisdom, virtue, and mental cultivation form a continuous practice. One can start or end the Eightfold Path with its wisdom steps of right view and right aim.

Many times you'll see the list of eight steps on the path ending with right view and right aim. This is because perfect wisdom is achieved when virtue and mental cultivation are practiced. Right speech, right action and right livelihood (the aspects of virtue) all contribute to a peaceful mind in which mental cultivation can be perfected. Thus, right effort, right recollection, and right contemplation (the aspects of mental cultivation) flow freely from a virtuous religious practice. In turn, these mental purifications open the way to wisdom.

On the other hand, virtue and mental cultivation cannot be perfected in the absence of wisdom. For example, there is no truly right speech without the right view that realizes nonself. One is bound to make mistakes in speech as well as action and livelihood without eliminating ignorance. The same goes for the stages of mental cultivation. Without realizing nonself, all one's aims are off the mark, so effort, recollection, and contemplation are flawed. So you'll also see Buddha's path starting with right view and right aim—as in this book.

Either way is fine because the Eightfold Path is a dynamic teaching. It's meant to be practiced over and over again. So it doesn't really matter where on the circle a person starts.

The Least You Need to Know

- Right effort is joyful perseverance that eliminates and prevents unwholesome mental formations, while enhancing and generating wholesome ones.

- Right contemplation (samadhi) allows one to experience the realm of pure form and the realm of no form through serenity meditation.

- The abodes of Brahma are associated with boundless states of consciousness in the realm of pure form known as the social virtues: loving-kindness, compassion, sympathetic joy, and equanimity.

- Buddha taught that there is no enlightenment without right view, so all mental cultivation should ultimately be directed toward realizing emptiness.

Part 5

Buddha's Disciples

Buddha's disciples came from a range of social classes: brahmins, warriors, merchants, and even servants. He tried to accommodate all kinds of people, including women and men. First Gautama started a mendicant community for monks and then set up one for nuns.

In an age of burgeoning wealth, a handful of Buddha's merchant disciples considered it an honor to support his mendicant community during the rainy seasons. The less-wealthy laypeople simply donated alms when the mendicants came to their doors with begging bowls. In return, Buddha's monks and nuns gave spiritual direction to the householders—encouraging them to lead moral lives, while maintaining the family lifestyle. As a former heir of the Sakyan rulership of a small republic, Gautama moved in and out of royal circles in the great territories of Magadha and Kausala and gave advice to their kings.

Chapter 17

The Monks

In This Chapter

- ◆ The first five arhats
- ◆ The ordination of Yasas and his friends
- ◆ Maha Katyayana becomes a disciple
- ◆ Conversion of the Kasyapa brothers
- ◆ Buddha meets his two chief disciples
- ◆ Subhuti and Gautama's last convert

Gautama awakened under a fig tree in Urubilva. After that momentous event, he spent 49 days on that sacred ground and in the surrounding area, engaged in further contemplation. Those seven weeks were a kind of debriefing period in which the new Buddha overcame the disorientation of transcending existence "in" nirvana. His awakening was a kind of death to the world. So ... coming back to the world was challenging. Mara, Lord of Illusion, was ready to give the new Buddha a way out. ("Die now," said Mara.) But the Tathagata—he who'd gone "just like that"—decided to integrate back into society. After plumbing the depths of psychological space, going just beyond the brink of experiencing experience, he was prepared to share his discovery, the dharma.

After the seven weeks—prompted by a request from the divine Brahma—the Tathagata became the Teacher. It was not long before he gathered 61 disciples who, prompted by his message, attained deep spiritual realizations. The building of Buddha's mendicant community began in Rishipatana with the ordination of the five ascetics who'd been followers of the Maha Sramana even before his awakening. It continued with the ordination of a wealthy youth named Yasas, his 4 friends, and then 50 more. This initial burst of activity was rounded out back in Urubilva, when the three Kasyapa brothers and their large following turned their minds to the Buddha-dharma.

When Buddha reached Rajagriha, he picked up two talented brahmins who became his chief disciples—to be with him through thick and thin. From there, other monks joined the bhikshu-sangha. Some of these were Sakyan kshatriyas and their associates (whose stories are found in Chapter 11). Many others were brahmins who'd been on a spiritual quest for some time. Others who joined the community of monks were of the lower castes, happy to have a new path opened up for them.

The First Rainy Season

Gautama gathered the first of his monks or bhikshus in three places: Rishipatana, the park now called Sarnath near Varanasi in ancient Kasi; Varanasi, the trading center along the Ganga River; and Urubilva, the forested area on the Nairanjana River in Magadha not far from Rajagriha.

Be Mindful!

Think about this curious encounter: as Buddha walked to Rishipatana after awakening, he encountered the mendicant Upaga—a follower of Maskarin Gosaliputra, the Ajivaka. Upaga was curious about Gautama's serene countenance, and asked, "Who preached dharma to you?" Learning that Buddha awakened by himself, Upaga said, "You are truly a conqueror!" ... *and went on his way.* Why? As a *fatalist*, did Upaga think there was nothing he could do to become awakened—so why follow anybody? But he did have an Ajivaka teacher. Buddha just admitted that he awakened without a teacher. So did Upaga think he also needed no teacher? Or was Upaga simply content as he was?

Rishipatana, a Great Place to Become an Arhat

Remember Kaundinya, Asvajit, Vashpa, Mahanama, and Bhadrika—the five ascetics who were Gautama's disciples in the old days before his enlightenment? They'd abandoned Gautama back in Urubilva when he decided to break his fast. But now, just two months later as the rainy season approached, he followed them to Rishipatana. When they first saw their old fellow sramana from a distance, the five decided not to pay any special respect. But as Gautama got closer, they were shocked by his radiance and knew something had changed. They listened carefully to his words and cut the bonds of rebirth themselves. These were Gautama's first five arhat disciples.

Soon after Kaundinya and the other four ascetics became the first members of the bhikshu-sangha, a merchant's son from Varanasi named Yasas came upon Buddha. Yasas was in an agitated mental state. He was married, but his wife could bear no children—and he'd become disappointed with worldly ambition. Gautama calmed the young man by speaking on generosity, morality, the blessings of renunciation, and so forth. Then, sensing that Yasas's mind was pliant, Buddha went into the deeper teachings. The wealthy youth got his first glimpse of nonself and gained great confidence in the dharma as a means of ending suffering (as opposed to reliance on rituals). He wanted ordination. And though his family at first did not want to lose Yasas to the mendicant life, they were deeply impressed by the Buddha and gave their blessings. Yasas's 4 close friends also joined the budding bhikshu-sangha, followed in turn by 50 of their friends.

Varanasi, a Brahmin Stronghold

Maha Katyayana was a nephew of the great seer Asita, who'd first recognized the signs of a great person on the baby Siddhartha. Katyayana's uncle, knowing he would not live to see that greatness mature, had urged his nephew to study with Gautama whenever the right time came. Katyayana prepared himself by joining a brahmin community in Varanasi. Thus, when Gautama came to speak with him within a few months after enlightenment, Katyayana penetrated the dharma right away and became an arhat. His thinking was so analytical and sharp that Gautama set up a special category of disciple for him: *master of dharma exposition.*

> **Dharma Dictionary**
>
> Buddha named Katyayana as the first **master of dharma exposition**—or (as the texts say) foremost among those who can analyze in detail the meaning of what's been stated in brief! His job was to analyze for other disciples what Buddha only stated in brief. Sometimes the Tathagata taught in detail. But other times the Teacher presented sharp declarations that needed to be unpacked through analysis.

Katyayana turned out to be a brilliant interpreter of doctrine and carried Buddha's teachings westward into the Pamir Mountains (in present-day Afghanistan). After being ordained, he lived mostly in his native territory of Avanti, to the southwest of Buddha's home turf in the Middle Ganges Basin. Although aloof from the other bhikshus, Katyayana's meticulous expositions of dharma are preserved among the sacred texts of Buddhism and were known to many disciples. In fact, Katyayana already had a longstanding reputation for his unusual skill with languages before Gautama woke up and was remembered for deciphering an old inscription found near Varanasi that had puzzled the authorities.

En Route to Rajagriha

Gautama attained enlightenment in the month of Vaisaka—which comes in April or May of the Western calendar. The monsoon in India begins around June. So basically, Buddha had gotten to Rishipatana in time for the monsoon. He'd gained disciples in Kasi and told them to go out wandering—for the good of the many, for the happiness of the many. Now he would wander back into Magadha.

It was probably September or October when the Tathagata considered making good on his promise to King Bimbisara: he would return to Rajagriha now that he was enlightened. And en route to Rajagriha, Gautama would visit again the site of his enlightenment and several hermitages that stood in the area of Urubilva.

The Urubilva Colony of Sannyasins

Urubilva was a bit off the beaten track for those who practiced a pure Vedic discipline. The Ganga-Yamuna Doab, and even Varanasi, was more their hangout. But here on the eastern edges of Aryan civilization were three colonies of Sannyasins, elite brahmins who'd adopted the renunciate life of those who strive for Brahman. The hermitages were headed by three brothers bearing the name of Kasyapa—after a great seer who founded their clan. Urubilva Kasyapa (the eldest), Nadi Kasyapa, and Gaya Kasyapa were all formally educated in the Sanskrit-Vedic scriptural language and practiced ancient Vedic rituals according to precise formulae.

The three Kasyapa brothers lived separately and had 500, 300, and 200 disciples, respectively. These traditional Vedic Sannyasins sustained themselves at the jungle's edge and lived in branch huts. They were highly respected by laypeople who knew of their renunciate colonies. The hermits were easily recognized by their bark garments and matted hair. Buddha knew of them and arrived one day at the jungle hut of Urubilva Kasyapa, the oldest of the three brothers and the most revered.

How to Impress a Sannyasin

The ascetic Gautama approached the hermit colony at Urubilva and was welcomed by the elder Kasyapa. Soon, however, there was to be a battle of wills … or of magical skills. Strange things began to happen at the hermitage, such as the holy fire not lighting or the sacrificial implements not cooperating. The hermits in residence saw this as due to the power of Gautama's asceticism. But for a while Urubilva Kasyapa thought his *tapas*, or internal fire, was still more potent. Then came a standoff in which Buddha performed miracles to gain the respect of all three Kasyapa brothers and their disciples.

Gautama asked to sleep in the sacrificial hut by the sacred fire that was kept continually burning. The Urubilva Kasyapa warned that the fearsome sacred snake inhabited the hut. Well … Buddhist texts telling this story claim that Buddha subdued the sacred snake and impressed Kasyapa and his followers. After that, it took just one more miracle to win him over: when the Nairanjana River flooded, Kasyapa went to look for Gautama (thinking the ascetic was in danger of drowning). Coming to see Gautama, the old brahmin saw his young rival walking on the water.

> **Be Mindful!**
>
> Buddhists don't consider miracles as signs of divinity. Rather, miracles indicate a meditator's level of samadhi. Buddha's finest attainment in this field was the "twin miracle" in which fire and water came from different sides of his body at the same time. This proved he could maintain two samadhis simultaneously. Common adepts concentrate on only one object at a time—producing either fire or water, not both.

After the feats performed through samadhis, the Tathagata was able to approach Urubilva Kasyapa and his followers with notice of the discoveries he'd made through insight. All three Kasyapa brothers were converted to the Buddha-dharma, and their disciples followed suit. Gautama delivered his Fire Sermon in Gaya, and they all became arhats, breaking the ties to compulsory rebirth. The band of ascetics then accompanied Gautama to Rajagriha, where King Bimbisara was at first confused as to which teacher was leading the pack. Urubilva Kasyapa—a revered brahmin elder—made it known that he'd converted to Gautama's teaching. Thus, Bimbisara and the people of Rajagriha were impressed and gained confidence in the Buddha-dharma.

Two Chief Disciples of Every Buddha

Rajagriha proved to be a fateful place for Buddha to continue his mission, for shortly after arriving, he met two brahmins who would become his chief disciples. Tradition says that every Buddha has two chief disciples. Whether or not a person takes that on faith, from the historical point of view, Buddhist scriptures speak in detail and often about Gautama's two chief disciples: Sariputra and Maudgalyayana. These two individuals have so much in common we'd be tempted to call them twins in the dharma. And what they might not have had in common in reality, they surely were given in legend and in art:

> **Buddha Basics**
>
> King Asoka laid the foundation for the great Sanchi stupa in the third century B.C.E. From that time through twelfth century C.E., temples, monasteries, and more stupas were built at Sanchi, in central India. Then from the fourteenth through the early nineteenth century, the monuments were deserted and in ruins. In 1851, Alexander Cunningham found relic caskets in stupas 2 and 3, which may contain the remains of Gautama's two chief disciples—Sariputra and Maudgalyayana.

- Buddhist art places Sariputra and Maudgalyayana standing to either side of Gautama in paintings and statues. Sariputra is always on the right hand side. Maudgalyayana is always on the left.

- Buddhist literature states that the two chief disciples were conceived on the same day and born on the same day in two villages both near Rajagriha in Magadha. Sariputra and Maudgalyayana passed away a half-month apart. (Buddha passed away six months after Sariputra.)

- In archeology, the remains of Sariputra and Maudgalyayana presumably have been found in the reliquary at the Sanchi stupa. Sariputra's urn was found on the south side; Maudgalyayana's urn was on the north side.

It's not easy to separate Sariputra and Maudgalyayana because they grew up as friends and spent their whole lives in close contact. In fact, they spent many lifetimes together. So we'll begin telling their story as a pair.

Upatissa and Kolita

In Magadha, around the capital city of Rajagriha was a village named Upatissa. A boy in that village also took the name Upatissa because he was born into one of its prominent families. Nearby was the village of Kolita. And a boy born to one of its notable brahmin families was given the name Kolita. Upatissa and Kolita were close friends, as were their families, and they shared many activities. (Later they would be known as Sariputra and Maudgalyayana.)

Upatissa and Kolita were charismatic children who won the trust of many brahmin youths in their neighborhoods. When Upatissa went on outings, a coterie of brahmin youths would follow in tow. Similarly, when Kolita went out, many young men would accompany him. So it is no surprise that when the two decided to go to Rajagriha to study with the famous skeptic Sanjayin Vairattiputra, their many brahmin friends followed suit.

"Isn't There Something Better?"

Upatissa and his best friend Kolita watched entertainments together. But one day they both had a kind of entry into a new life. It was the glimmerings of a calling to a new vocation. On the third day of the festival, Upatissa was pensive. Kolita asked him what was wrong, and Upatissa shared his thoughts: "What looks so grand here will all be over. Everyone here will die within a hundred years. We should go seek something better."

Kolita confessed that he had the same thoughts about the futility of the life of sport and entertainment. So they both decided to study under a sramana named Sanjayin Vairattiputra who was based in Rajagriha. They joined his spiritual community and mastered the skeptic's teachings. Eventually, they were anxious to seek deeper studies and practice, and traveled widely in India together to find other teachers. When they were around 40 years old, Upatissa and Kolita returned to their home territory, and were offered accommodations at Sanjayin's hermitage in Rajagriha.

> **Enlightening Extras**
>
> Upatissa and Kolita were slightly older than Gautama. A common age for a man to marry in India was between 16 and 20. But these two disciples never married. When they entered Sanjayin's hermitage, Siddhartha was 16 years old and just getting married. These two friends first encountered the Buddha-dharma when they were in their 40s, and Gautama was 35.

"Is There Nothing Better?"

Upatissa and Kolita made a pact: if one of them ever found a more profound teaching than Sanjayin's, they were to tell the other right away. So these two sramanas were open to the radical message that Gautama was prepared to give after his awakening. And it would not be long before they would encounter a teaching that would change their lives forever.

It so happened that when Upatissa and Kolita returned to Rajagriha after their travels through India, a new spiritual teacher was in town—Gautama the Awakened One. Gautama had come just after the first rainy season following his enlightenment, fulfilling a promise to King Bimbisara. (Recall that he'd met the king as a new sramana and promised to come back whenever he succeeded in waking up.) He was staying in a bamboo grove donated by King Bimbisara for the new sangha's use. From there he'd sent out his first disciples—the 61 arhats who had already taken up the Eightfold Path to enlightenment, including Asvajit.

Upatissa Meets Asvajit the Elder

Asvajit was collecting alms one day in Rajagriha when Upatissa noticed him. There was something strange about the old mendicant's bearing that Upatissa hadn't noticed before in anyone—the way he held himself. Thinking this and wishing to know what made him so steady, Upatissa respectfully followed the mendicant. Waiting until Asvajit took his meal, Upatissa offered him water as a disciple would do. Then Upatissa got to the point. He asked, "Whose dharma do you follow?"

In response, Asvajit told of a Maha Sramana from the Sakya clan who'd gone from home to homelessness. Persisting, Upatissa asked what dharma the Sakyan taught. And Asvajit replied that he was new to the teaching and couldn't profess it in detail. But this did not deter Upatissa.

A Verse That Changed the World

Upatissa asked the elder for just the essential point of the Sakyan Maha Sramana's teaching: he didn't need all the details. He wanted just a few words. Upatissa was an unusually perceptive person, who'd had excellent philosophical training under Sanjayin Vairattiputra. So he told Asvajit, "It's up to me to penetrate the meaning of the dharma you share. I can do this by means of many methods." So Asvajit uttered this verse:

> *Of things with a cause,*
> *The Tathagata told the cause,*
> *As well as the cessation.*
> *This is the Maha Sramana's teaching.*

When Upatissa heard the first two lines, he attained his first glimpse of nonself. He was convinced right then and there that the key to cutting the bonds of rebirth was in that very dharma. He went directly back to tell Kolita the verse and planned for them both to follow Asvajit to Buddha's feet. When Kolita saw Upatissa approaching, he knew something deep had happened. And when Kolita heard the verse, he, too, got his first glimpse of nonself.

Buddha Basics

Among the most important moments in Buddhist history is the instant when Sariputra (Upatissa) heard the Elder Asvajit say the following:

> *Ye dhamma hetuppabhava*
> *tesam hetum tathagato aha,*
> *tesan ca yo nirodho*
> *evamvadi mahasamano*

This verse (from the Pali scripture) contains the essence of Buddha's teaching—from which a person can become enlightened. Can you figure out the translation? You've already heard these Pali words in Sanskrit: dhamma = dharma (meaning things), tathagato = tathagata, mahasamano = Maha Sramana. Here are some more hints: hetu = cause, hetuppabhava = arising from a cause, ca = and, nirodho = cessation, vadi = word or doctrine, evam = this.

Out of respect, Upatissa went to his teacher Sanjayin. He offered to lead Sanjayin to the Buddha, too. But Sanjayin was already an established teacher and apparently didn't want to give up his position as leader of a large ascetic community to become a disciple at the feet of another. So Upatissa and Kolita went to meet Buddha. A large number of their own and Sanjayin's disciples followed suit. Half of Sanjayin's pupils returned, but in the meantime the great skeptic took the loss very hard and vomited up blood.

"An Excellent Pair"

Upatissa and Kolita met the Buddha for the first time in the Bamboo Grove, not far from Sanjayin's hermitage. And as Buddha saw these two for the first time—walking toward him from a distance—he said to the assembly: "These two who now approach shall be my chief disciples." (Indeed, it happened.) After the two arrived and paid their respects, they asked to become Buddha's disciples. And the Tathagata ordained them with the simple words:

> *Come, bhikshus!*
> *Dharma is well proclaimed.*
> *Adopt the pure life and end suffering.*

Be Mindful!

In Buddhism, relationships are thought to range back many lifetimes. So when some bhikshus thought Buddha was playing favorites in choosing Sariputra and Maudgalyayana as his two chief disciples, the Tathagata informed them: these two bhikshus had aspired in a past life together to serve as the chief disciples of a Buddha. And that aspiration finally was coming to fruition.

After their ordination, Upatissa was called Sariputra, and Kolita was called Maudgal-yayana. Let's now see what special contribution each of Gautama's two chief disciples made to the sangha. As chief disciples, they had a threefold job:

◆ Help the Teacher consolidate the dharma to make it accessible to many beings.

◆ Exemplify the pure conduct of an ideal bhikshu and supervise the renunciate training.

◆ Help administer the mendicant community, especially when the Teacher was on retreat or traveled alone.

Sariputra Destroys Ten Fetters

Once ordained, Sariputra went to meditate in a cave on the outskirts of Rajagriha and would go into the city for daily alms. He actually became an arhat one day, about two weeks later, when he was fanning Gautama from behind as the Teacher was giving a discourse. Suddenly Sariputra completed his destruction of the *Ten Fetters*. He'd already gained the first of *four stages of sainthood* upon hearing the first two lines of Asvajit's dharma verse. As a stream entrant he …

◆ Destroyed belief in an eternal self by glimpsing nonself.

◆ Destroyed the belief that enlightenment is attained by following rituals.

◆ Destroyed doubt by gaining unwavering confidence in the Three Jewels.

Dharma Dictionary

The **Ten Fetters** are negative mental formations that a person must destroy to become an arhat and leave the cycle of becoming. They are destroyed in a particular order, and progress is noted in terms of **four stages of sainthood:**

◆ A stream entrant destroys 1) Belief in an eternal self, 2) Belief that rituals lead to enlightenment, and 3) Doubt.

◆ A once-returner (who will have no more than one more human rebirth) weakens: craving and revulsion.

◆ A nonreturner (who will be reborn into the realm of pure form) destroys: 4) Craving and 5) Revulsion.

◆ An arhat (who is never reborn into any realm of samsara) destroys: 6) Attachment to the realm of pure form, 7) Attachment to the realm of no form, 8) Pride, 9) Restlessness, and 10) Delusion.

While simply fanning Buddha, Sariputra eliminated the remaining 7 of 10 fetters and became an arhat. That is, he …

♦ Destroyed craving.

♦ Destroyed revulsion.

♦ Destroyed subtle attachment to experience in the realm of pure form.

♦ Destroyed subtle attachment to experience in the realm of no form.

♦ Destroyed pride, restlessness, and delusion.

Sariputra, the Compassionate and Wise

As a chief disciple, Sariputra was to assist Buddha in managing the sangha. He was never proud in this position. (As an arhat he'd destroyed all conceit.) But he was particularly compassionate.

Sariputra would walk around the monastery grounds and sweep or straighten things up so that non-Buddhist mendicants would not speak in contempt of the bhikshus. He would counsel sick bhikshus, provide medicine, and apply oil to the sores of the old bhikshus. He accepted criticism for his faults—as when a 7-year-old novice pointed out that his robe was crooked. Sariputra fixed his robe and folded his hands saying, "Teacher, now it is proper."

Buddha called Sariputra his wisest disciple. Some 75 of Sariputra's discourses became part of the official scriptures common to both Theravada and Mahayana branches of Buddhism. In these sutras, Sariputra speaks of faith in Buddha, conduct for lay and ordained members of the sangha, stages of the path to awakening, all states of consciousness based on serenity, and realization of nirvana based on insight. Beyond that, Sariputra plays a prominent role in the Mahayana Perfection of Wisdom Sutras, which deal with sunyata or the nonself of phenomena. Even Theravadins (who tend to emphasize the nonself of persons rather than the emptiness of all phenomena) report Sariputra's meditations on the emptiness of nirvana itself.

Maudgalyayana and His Supernormal Powers

Okay! Turning to the chief disciple who always stood to Buddha's left, we have to talk about psychic powers. This guy was foremost among Buddha's disciples for his mastery of the siddhis. Many had become adept at one supernormal power or another, but no single bhikshu commanded them all with such perfection. Utpalavarna was foremost among the bhikshunis, but she, too, was no match for Maudgalyayana. Through expert practice of samatha meditation, he became a spiritual technician with skill in such things as the following:

Buddha Basics

Buddhist texts name six supernormal powers, siddhis practiced by many arhats. These are knowledge of 1) Modes of psychic power, 2) Divine ear, 3) Thought reading, 4) Past lives, 5) Divine eye, and 6) Destruction of the fetters. The first five are worldly and result from samatha; the sixth results from vipasyana and applies only to those who've cut the ties of rebirth.

- ◆ Thought reading
- ◆ Astral travel
- ◆ Clairvoyance
- ◆ Telekinesis
- ◆ Remembrance of past lives

Having these paranormal faculties did not indicate that Maudgalyayana was enlightened. But upon becoming an arhat, he gained the special knowledge of recognizing that his bonds to samsara had been cut.

Enlightening Extras

In ancient India, families were identified in terms of gotras, which were usually named after a male seer who was the clan founder. Buddha and some of his disciples carry the names of highborn gotras: Gautama, Maudgalyayana, and Katyayana. Gautami in someone's name indicates a female member of the Sakya clan, such as Maha Prajapati Gautami (Buddha's aunt) and Kisagotami or Kisa Gautami (Buddha's cousin).

Subhuti Sews His Robe in Emptiness

Subhuti was the younger brother of Anathapindaka, the merchant who donated Jeta's Grove in Sravasti to the Buddha. (You'll read about Anathapindaka in Chapter 19.) Subhuti joined the bhikshu-sangha on the day his brother offered the arama to the Tathagata. Buddha called Subhuti the bhikshu who lives without conflict. Subhuti penetrated the truth of sunyata. And that allowed him easily to give up clinging, even to Buddha. How's that?

It's said that Buddha went to a heavenly realm to preach to his mother. Various disciples wanted to be on hand to see Buddha come out of the meditation. Subhuti was sewing his robe at the time. He put down his work and was also about to go find the

Teacher when the thought struck him: "Buddha's real body can't be seen with ordinary eyes. If I go greet Buddha, it means that I am clinging to the material elements. Buddha's true nature is emptiness, which is everywhere." Thus Subhuti sat down and continued sewing his robe. To everyone's surprise, the Tathagata said Subhuti was the first to greet him … because he understood the nonself of all things. "He knows that he sees me when he contemplates dharma."

Be Mindful!

Buddha's mendicant community grew over the years. And this growth resulted in the accumulation of more precepts to follow. There was a group of six monks whose conduct was unusually troublesome. Many of the training guidelines were made in response to their behavior. In the end, most of them left the sangha. But the remaining monks were left with the rules. Thus, in speaking of Buddhist monks, it's helpful to remember that everything did not always run smoothly.

One Last Convert

Even there between the twin sala trees, as he lay dying, the Tathagata brought one last person into the bhikshu-sangha. For after he lectured to the Mallas, an ascetic named Subhadra appeared. He was known among the Mallas for his relentless curiosity—he disputed with every teacher he encountered. He wanted to grill Buddha about truth before he lost the chance.

Subhadra asked Ananda three times to allow him to speak with the Teacher. And three times Ananda refused, not wanting to disturb the Tathagata on his deathbed. But Buddha overheard Subhadra's request and invited him over. Subhadra, as usual, wanted to converse at length, but Gautama cut to the quick. He didn't have much time left.

Subhadra named six teachers and wanted Buddha to state whether any of them had realized the truth. The Tathagata said, "Enough, Subhadra! Never mind whether some or none or all those teachers realized truth. I will teach you dharma. Listen!" And Buddha began to teach—lying there in the lion's pose on the brink of his Great Decease.

Impressed by the Tathagata's clarity and insight, Subhadra requested ordination. And though normally at this point in the history of the bhikshu-sangha a person would have observed a probation period before entering the mendicant community, Buddha ordained Subhadra as he used to do in the old days—with the simple words "Ehi, Bhikshu!" ("Come, monk!")

The Least You Need to Know

◆ Gautama spent the first rainy season after enlightenment in and around Varanasi, where he ordained his first 61 bhikshus.

◆ A major boost to Buddha's reputation came with his conversion of the three revered Kasyapa brothers and their disciples, who turned from their Vedic path to the Buddha-dharma.

◆ Buddha had two chief disciples who promoted the dharma and guided disciples: Sariputra, who was foremost in wisdom; and Maudgalyayana, who was foremost in psychic powers.

◆ Buddha ordained numerous monks, and as the community grew, training guidelines were developed to maximize harmony within the mendicant community as well as in relation to society at large.

◆ Buddha continued to ordain disciples right to the very end of his life.

Chapter 18

The Nuns

In This Chapter

- ◆ Prajapati asks for a women's mendicant community
- ◆ The lifestyle of a nun
- ◆ Khema's conversion
- ◆ Patacara's perils
- ◆ Bhadra's rose-apple branch
- ◆ Amrapali's mangos

Women in ancient India wanted an alternative to being either wives or widows, and when they got the opportunity to join the Buddhist order, many did so. But the Buddhists weren't the only community who made a place for women. Mahavira, the Jain leader, also organized his community into four sections: monks, nuns, laymen, and laywomen.

In many places, the Buddhist sangha of nuns did not survive as long or as strongly as the sangha for monks. The lineage of fully ordained bhikshunis never migrated to some cultures as Buddhism moved through Asia; in others it was unable to survive the vicissitudes of history. But bhikshuni-sanghas in China, Korea, and Vietnam all claim an unbroken lineage that goes back to Buddha himself. The history of the bhiskhuni-sangha is not over.

In a way, you have to imagine the lives of Buddha's female disciples because the Buddhist scriptures don't have much detail about them. The major exception is the group of theris, Gautama's female disciples who attained enlightenment. Some of these elders' verses are preserved in the Buddhist canon. So from these poems, scriptural stories, and vinaya precepts we can piece together a picture of the lives of the early women Buddhists, the sakyadhita (daughters) of the Sakyan.

Prajapati Lobbies for a Nun's Sangha

Five years after Gautama woke up, he created a spiritual community for women renunciates. The idea was not completely new. The Jain community had women members, and female renunciates were not unknown in the Upanishads before Buddha's day. Even so, the idea of women leaving their lives as wives, mothers, or daughters was pretty radical. Buddha realized upon awakening that the dharma went against the grain of worldly society, but he decided that teaching was worthwhile anyway. But it seems even *his* radicalism had limits, and he hesitated to institute a sangha for women.

> **Buddha Basics**
>
> Buddhism speaks of a "central land" versus a remote land. From a religious point of view, a central land is a place with four categories of disciples: bhikshus, bhikshunis, sramaneras (male novices), and sramanerikas (female novices). Buddhism is not considered complete until both men and women follow the spiritual life equally.

Who better to request a women's sangha than the noblewoman who raised Siddhartha? In the scheme of things, she became a voice for women through the ages until today. Her name was Prajapati—often combined with the word Maha (Great), respectfully placed in front of her name. She was called Prajapati Gautami because she was related to Gautama the Buddha. She was his mother's sister and, as Suddhodana's second wife, raised Siddhartha from his second week of life after his mother died.

Why Leave Home?

The main reason for anyone joining a sangha for monks or nuns is to enter a life of pure moral conduct under a set of precepts or training rules, and positively change one's identity. The precepts evolved over time whenever a renunciate was doing something destructive or inappropriate. Buddha and the renunciate community experimented with ways to minimize suffering and disruptive and selfish behavior—and open the way for enlightenment.

But why wasn't Prajapati content with her life? Why did she wish for her nephew to start a spiritual community for nuns? Perhaps because the doors of her regal lifestyle had shut behind her. At the time, Prajapati was no longer in a position of political power. Her husband, Suddhodana, had just died, and leadership of the Sakya clan passed out of her sphere of influence. Descending from raja's wife to widow suddenly reduced her social status. Prajapati had little to lose by becoming a nun. After Suddhodana's death, she was free to move forward into another stage of her life. The prospect of starting a new life must have been exciting to Prajapati, if not also frightening, as she begged Gautama three times to institute a bhikshuni-sangha.

> **Enlightening Extras**
>
> In ancient India, according to Vedic custom, women were to be protected by their fathers in youth, their husbands in middle years, and their sons in old age. A widow could not remarry, no matter how young she was. An age-old custom among some groups was sati, which called for the woman to burn herself on the husband's funeral pyre. Upper-class widows would shave their heads, wear a simple garment with no ornaments, and eat a single meal per day.

But more than that, Prajapati was a leader of women and needed to find a way to help them. A large number of Sakyan widows had appealed to Prajapati for guidance—due to her charisma, talent, high status as raja's wife, and lay practice of Sakyamuni's path. These 500 widows relied on her for guidance. Not only was Suddhodana's widow free to move forward but she could take these women with her into a life of spiritual rewards.

Maha Prajapati Gautami was considered the senior among all nuns, for she was the first to be ordained, the founder of the bhikshuni-sangha. The many women she brought with her to make the request became her disciples.

"Please Don't Ask This of Me"

So was it easy to get the women's mendicant order started? No. By all accounts it took great determination on the part of Prajapati and the women who accompanied her. What was Buddha—a 40-year-old former prince and newly awakened one—to do with 500 women? He'd just barely started the monks's community after awakening five years before. And now women?

These women included Sakyan women and Koliyan widows, women who belonged to Gautama's harem before he left the palace in Kapilavastu, and his aunt who suckled him as a baby. A thousand thoughts must have crossed the Tathagata's mind as he put off Prajapati's request.

How could the men and women live together? The monks were to have left worldly life. What would the presence of women do to that resolve? The men were to be celibate. The women would have to be celibate. All mendicants must be. There was no room for promiscuity in a spiritual community whose members renounced the world. The mendicants lived off the resources of others. They contributed to the moral equation of society. If their morality failed, they would be nothing but impostors.

And would the women be safe wandering around? What if they were young and became pregnant? What about when they got old? Who would take care of them? What if the public would not support them with alms? Who would build their shelters in the rainy season? Were they used to living without male supervision? It's no wonder that, when the aging woman who raised him requested a spiritual community for women, Buddha said, over and over, "Please don't ask me this, Prajapati." … Or perhaps … "Please don't ask this of me, Mother."

Be Mindful!

In a vinaya passage, Sakyamuni predicted that dharma would decline in the world after 500 years and disappear after 1,000 years if women were given a sangha. But before thinking Buddha was putting down women, let's consider the fourteenth (and current) Dalai Lama's comment in 1987 at the First International Conference on Buddhist Nuns: "[I]n certain Buddhist texts, … bhikshus are accorded a higher position than the bhikshunis …. Many of these explanations came about in relation to the times, the place, and the social conditions, and most probably were not the original thought of the dharma itself."

A Woman's Resolve

It happened when Sakyamuni was at Kapilavastu in the banyan grove. Prajapati approached Sakyamuni and made this appeal: "Lord, it would be wonderful if women could renounce their homes and enter homelessness under the Buddha's teachings and discipline." Gautama answered: "Enough, Gautami! Don't get your heart set on women doing this."

Prajapati made the same request three times, but Buddha replied with the same words, so she departed weeping. Then Buddha set out for Vaisali without any further comment. But Prajapati was determined to ask again. She cut her hair, donned the saffron robe, and walked to Vaisali with the crowd of Sakyan women. Their feet were dusty and swollen. She wept outside the Buddha's residence. After Ananda found out what was the matter, he conveyed Prajapati's request to Buddha.

Ananda: "Lord, it would be wonderful if women had permission to enter the homeless life."

The Tathagata: "Enough, Ananda. Don't get your heart set on women doing this."

Ananda made the request three times, but was given the same answer. Then Ananda persisted through reason.

Ananda: "Lord, are women capable of attaining the four stages of sainthood?"

The Tathagata: "Yes, Ananda, they are."

Ananda: "Then if women can become perfected it would be wonderful if they got your permission to enter the homeless life under you. Think also how Prajapati helped you in the past as she raised you in place of your mother."

The Tathagata: "Fine, Ananda. If Prajapati accepts eight special precepts, she can be ordained."

Eight Special Precepts

Buddha designed eight special precepts for the first ordination of women to the mendicant sangha. He agreed to ordain Maha Prajapati and the women who followed her if they agreed to observe these precepts, which applied specifically to nuns:

1. A nun should always pay respects to any almsman no matter how recently the almsman has been ordained.

2. A nun should never spend a rainy season in a district where there is no almsman.

3. Every half-moon a nun should await notice from the monks as to the date of the Upostha ceremony and the time they will arrive to present a teaching.

4. After the rains retreat, nuns should hold the confession ritual with the bhikshu-sangha and their bhikshuni-sangha.

> **Buddha Basics**
>
> Prajapati once asked the Tathagata to retract the first of the eight special precepts for women. But he would not. Retracting it would mean that monks of lesser seniority would bow before nuns who'd been in the sangha longer—even if just by one minute. Apparently, this was unacceptable to Gautama and to the Buddhist tradition over time. Why do you think so?

5. A nun who committed a serious offense must be disciplined by both the bhikshu-sangha and their bhikshuni-sangha.

6. A novice who completed her two-year probation period observing the six precepts should seek ordination from both the bhikshu-sangha and their bhikshuni-sangha.

7. An alsmwoman must never revile or abuse a monk under any circumstances.

8. A nun is forbidden to admonish a monk, but a monk may admonish a nun.

Becoming a Bhikshuni

A nun's life was intended to be pretty much the same as that of a monk's. Entering the homeless life as Gautama's male or female homeless disciple was granted in a ceremony called *upasampada*. This was performed only after the existing community was assured that the candidate was not disqualified. Matters that would disqualify both men and women included having a contagious disease, avoiding debt or legal punishment, obligations to the ruler, and so on.

> **Dharma Dictionary**
>
> **Upasampada** is the ceremony of initiation into the sangha of monks or nuns. A person had to be very serious about leading the spiritual life to take this on. It meant spending more and more time in meditation, coupled with teaching and supervising others.

A disqualification that applied specifically to women was having abnormalities of the uterus. In other words, the community wanted assurance that a woman was not simply trying to leave the householder's life because she could not bear children. The reason for leaving the householder's life was supposed to be a commitment to the highest spiritual development.

It was not enough for a woman to sincerely wish to lead a religious life. She had to be freed from her social obligations and granted permission from the man who had authority over her. Married women were required to obtain their husbands' consent, and unmarried women needed their fathers' approval. Exceptions included orphaned and widowed women who had no one seeing to their welfare and so required no consent. No woman under the age of 20 was considered eligible to enter the order.

The Two-Year Probation

A two-year period of probation was offered for women as well as men. During the two years, the women novices had to follow 6 of the standard 10 precepts (whereas men followed all 10, adding the avoidance of entertainments, ornaments, high beds, and handling money):

1. Don't kill.

2. Don't steal.

3. Don't misuse sex.

4. Don't lie.

5. Don't drink alcohol.

6. Don't eat after noon.

This probationary period was instituted first to ensure that a woman would not be admitted to the mendicant order if she were pregnant. It also became a way for others to try out the spiritual life in a rudimentary way. Whoever observed the precepts for two-years without transgression and was not otherwise disqualified could apply to the sangha for full ordination. If they messed up on some of the precepts, they had to start counting the two years all over again!

Ordination rules were modified in Gautama's community as new situations arose. A probationary period was added to the stages of novice, designed particularly for persons under 20, and full ordination. Once, a woman over 20 (in good faith) discovered she was pregnant after receiving full ordination. So two years of probation were required for women and others to determine if mendicant life was suitable.

Full Ordination

A woman who kept the six precepts for two years without interruption could apply for full ordination if she wanted to lead a more intensive spiritual life. As a nun, she would observe around 311 precepts—as opposed to some 227 for monks. Some of these precepts prevented bhikshunis from falling into roles common to women householders. For example, bhikshunis were prohibited from sewing robes for monks, and they could not give food intended for them (gathered on alms rounds) to monks. The women renunciates were also prevented from becoming objects of sexual regard, as it was an offense for a bhikshu to sit alone with a bhikshuni.

Going through the upasampada ceremony meant making the full move from home to homelessness for a woman. But this did not mean that she became antisocial or physically isolated. Indirectly, her physical security was enhanced by the presence of monks in a society that had yet to fully appreciate the meaning of an independent woman. She was expected to grow and mature in the spiritual community. Thus 12 years after ordination, a bhikshuni could ask for permission to participate in ordination ceremonies to help new nuns find their way to enlightenment through the sangha.

Be Mindful!

The number of precepts for women is larger than for men because the bhikshuni-sangha adopted the men's rules as the foundation of their practice. On top of that, guidelines specific to women were added. But the number of precepts dealing with misbehavior of women is about half the number developed in response to improper conduct of men. The exact number of precepts came to vary slightly according to the Buddhist sect.

Fivefold Robes and Iron Bowls

When the time came for full ordination, a woman was presented with an alms bowl and three robes. That's all it was permissible to own in the early days. The bowl would be either iron or earthenware. And the earliest robes would be from discarded rags. Over time, the robes became more standardized. Nuns would own a fivefold robe, as opposed to the threefold robe of the monks.

Enlightening Extras

The Tathagata created the robe worn by nuns and monks, similar to the Roman toga. It is perhaps the oldest style of garment in the world—worn continuously for 2,500 years. The color and style changed as Buddhism spread. Theravadan monks wear a robe closest to the original style. But instead of patching discarded rags together, some cut larger pieces of cloth and patched it back together.

---

1. An outer robe used for begging alms, making visits such as to royalty, and conferring precepts. This was a 9-patch robe stitched from 9 to 25 pieces of cloth. This cloth had two layers, and was used to shelter the mendicant from the cold.

2. An upper robe worn while chanting, listening to a discourse, or practicing rites. This was stitched from seven pieces of cloth, and called a seven-patch robe. Mendicants took this on alms rounds, carrying it neatly in their hands with the alms bowl. When they approached houses, they'd put it on.

3. An inner robe that is a waistcloth. It is used as an undergarment for working, performing daily duties, and resting. It was stitched from five pieces of cloth, and called a five-patch robe. Mendicants would wear this neatly on their alms rounds.

4. A bodice worn for all occasions (for women only).

5. A cloth used for bathing (for women only).

Each morning, just like her male counterparts, a bhikshuni would go on alms rounds, and whatever went into her bowl she was to eat with equanimity. She could live in the open air and sleep under a tree, in a cave, or in a hut during the favorable months. For the monsoon, she should assemble with other nuns.

Now let's take a look at the personal experiences of some nuns—those Sakyadhitya-sramanerikas, mendicant daughters of the Sakyan sage.

Dharma Dictionary

Sakyaputriya-sramaneras is a term for Buddha's mendicant disciples. It means mendicant sons or children of the Sakyan. Putra means "son" or "child." *Putrika* or dhita means "daughter." So, **Sakyadhitya-sramanerikas** means "mendicant daughters of the Sakyan." An organization dedicated to researching the Vinaya and promoting bhikshuni-sanghas calls itself Sakyadhita (established in 1987 at the First International Conference on Buddhist Nuns in Bodhgaya, India).

Khema the Consort

Khema is known for being the highest in wisdom among the nuns. Buddha acknowledged this. He also said that she was like a scale with which the virtue of other disciples could be measured. Khema was witty, learned, and a talented conversationalist. And when Khema finally heard the Tathagata speak, she made swift progress in insight. But she seemed to avoid making his acquaintance.

Brilliance and Beauty

So who was the brilliant woman who hesitated to encounter Buddha? Khema was from a noble family of Sagala (northern Pakistan). She became the chief consort of Magadha's King Bimbisara. She loved flowers and things of beauty. She herself was beautiful, with skin of gold—and quite aware of it. In fact, some say Khema avoided meeting the Tathagata because she thought he paid no attention to beauty. Perhaps she was embarrassed, or proud.

In any case, she kept hearing about how lovely the park had become where Buddha would stay in Rajagriha. Bimbisara had donated this arama (bamboo grove) to the mendicant sangha. And it had been appointed with magnificent gardens that she was curious to see.

This, Too, Shall Pass

One day Khema decided to take a stroll through the Bamboo Grove. Some say Bimbisara practically tricked her into going, for he wanted his consort to hear the dharma. In any case, as she was enjoying her visit, she noticed from a distance a goddesslike figure, a gorgeous woman, fanning the Buddha as he sat beneath a tree. (This was an optical illusion that Sakyamuni created for her benefit, it's said.)

Khema was curious to see this lady and discover the source of her beauty. But as she approached, the ornamented figure began to age. Right before her eyes, with each step forward, the apparition became scant and decrepit. By the time Khema arrived in front of the figure, the apparition had fallen down dead.

Khema realized she was standing in front of the Tathagata as she looked at the bony corpse. She realized Buddha had created a vision to show a deep truth about beauty: its impermanence. She bowed down to the Teacher and became an arhat. Impressed with Gautama's teachings, Khema joined the bhikshuni-sangha and helped run this first community of nuns. She became known as a great teacher.

King Prasenajit was fascinated by this woman and took her as his teacher. With her brilliant speech, she delivered a discourse to the king, which he later found matched with Gautama's presentation of the same topic. Khema was brilliant indeed in practical matters, as well as subtle points of dharma.

Patacara the Madwoman

If Khema's life was one of luxurious success, Patacara's was the opposite. Yet both women wound up realizing impermanence and became arhats. Patacara was the nun whose command of the Vinaya discipline was greatest. She had a tremendous ability to withstand hardship and make sacrifices. But enduring hardship in itself is not enough to end suffering. A person needs to break through that hardship with the laser light of insight. Patacara's example shows how to transform suffering into realization.

Enlightening Extras

The theme of transformed suffering runs through many religions. Suffering without insight and forgiveness can bring bitterness, even madness. Suffering with compassion transforms oneself and the other—for at the moment of forgiveness there's no distance between them. In *The Way of Passion*, Andrew Harvey points to this alchemy of forgiving torturers and killers by quoting the Sufi poet Rumi:

From the moment you came into this world,
A ladder was placed in front of you,
That you might transcend it ....
When were you ever made less by dying?

Heaps of Disaster

Patacara started her life with promise. She was the daughter of a banker in Sravasti, the capital of Kausala. But she fell in love with a servant and ran away with him instead of marrying according to her caste. She had two children with this man, who set up house in a remote area. But he always discouraged her from returning to her family home to give birth. She would try to go anyway, but he would catch up with her and they'd turn back.

Late in the second pregnancy, Patacara took her first child and proceeded to Sravasti. Her husband followed, and they both got caught in a storm. He went off to find branches to build a small shelter but was bitten by a snake and died. Patacara went into labor. When able, she looked for her husband. Finding him dead, she still tried to make it to Sravasti with the two children. For that she needed to cross a river. She took the infant across first and left him on the farther bank. She was returning across the river for the second when a hawk attacked the baby. When Patacara screamed, her first child tried to come to her in the river and drowned. When Patacara approached Sravasti, she learned that her father's house had collapsed in the storm. Her parents and brother were dead.

"More Tears Than Water in Four Oceans"

All the death Patacara faced was too much. The poor woman lost her mind. But one day she heard about the Tathagata preaching nearby. Patacara looked so disheveled that people in the gathering didn't want such a madwoman to approach. Gautama wished to see her face to face. And when they met, he spoke kindly to her. He asked that she become mindful. Buddha listened to Patacara's story of woe and told her that over many lifetimes she had shed more tears than can be contained in four oceans. She realized that sorrow alone will not bring sorrow's end and asked to be admitted to the community of mendicants.

One day, Patacara—watching trickling water—noticed that some streams flowed a long way whereas others quickly were absorbed into the earth. This prepared her for a sudden flash of insight. She got the inkling that some lives flow long whereas others are cut short. That night in her cell Patacara pushed down the wick of her lamp. As the light went out, she realized the marks of existence: impermanence, nonself, and the suffering of ignorance. Freed from her sorrow, she attained nirvana. In the mendicant community, Patacara gained a following of women who were inspired by her austerity. After Maha Prajapati, it's Patacara who guided the most.

Bhadra "Curly Hair"

Bhadra Kundalakesa, like Patacara, was born into the up-and-coming merchant class of the Middle Ganges Basin. Her father was one of the sresthi (wealthy merchants) who used Rajagriha, the Magadhan capital, as his base of operations. To make a long story short, Bhadra was socially marginalized as a young woman because she pushed a man off of a cliff—though she did it in self-defense.

> **Buddha Basics**
>
> Names given to members of Buddha's mendicant community often reflect a significant event in their lives. Bhadra's epithet, Kundalakesa, means curly (kundala) hair (kesa). This is because she pulled out her hair by the roots upon joining the Jain mendicant sect, but it grew back thick and curly. The amba in Ambapali's name means "mango"; she was so named because she was found abandoned in a mango grove.

Bhadra's response to her misfortune was to join the women's community of Jain mendicants. She began with the most difficult program of ascetic practice and pulled out her hair by the roots. Over time Bhadra began to broaden her knowledge. She was skilled in debate and wandered through villages contesting the knowledge of anyone who would take up her challenge. Bhadra would stick the branch of a rose-apple tree upright in the ground to indicate she was up for a contest. And whoever wanted to debate would knock it down.

One day Bhadra arrived in Sravasti (Patacara's hometown). In her typical fashion, she set up the rose-apple branch to challenge anyone to debate. Sariputra, one of Buddha's chief disciples, was intrigued by the prospect of debating with Bhadra, so he asked some kids to knock down the rose-apple branch. Shortly, Sariputra and Bhadra started their debate. Buddha's disciple answered many questions to her satisfaction. And then Sariputra turned the tables asking Bhadra, "Ekam nama kim?" (What is the one?)

Bhadra was stumped. Knowing the fundamentals of Buddha-dharma she realized the answer could not be Brahman (though it would have been an acceptable answer for a brahmin Sannyasin). Obviously Bhadra was impressed with Sariputra, and asked him to be her teacher. But he sent her straight to his own teacher—Gautama Buddha. (By the way, the answer to Sariputra's question was "food," because all beings are sustained by it.)

Gautama was staying on Vulture Peak in Raja-griha, so Bhadra traveled over 200 miles across the Middle Ganges Basin to meet him. She was ripe for realization after her years as a Jain nun and perceived the meaning of what Buddha taught almost immediately, in a shock of aware-ness. Buddha's response was to admit Bhadra to his community of nuns with a simple word. He said, "*Ehi*, Bhadra." Thereafter, Bhadra was known for her sudden enlightenment.

> **Dharma Dictionary**
>
> **Ehi** means "come." This is the simple and powerful word the Tathagata used to ordain Bhadra Kundalakesa to the mendicant community. Hearing this word from Buddha's mouth was her initiation. From time to time, Gau-tama used this direct method of ordination. But normally, one had to ask for it.

Amrapali, Gorgeous Courtesan

Amrapali was a courtesan of Vaisali. She had a son by King Bimbisara, who influ-enced her late in life to join the Buddhist community of nuns. But when she was still stunning and brimming with wealth, Amrapali donated a mango grove to Buddha and the mendicant community. (An episode from her life is told in Chapter 22.)

Amrapali was one of four courtesans who became *theris*. She was not proud, but she was enormously talented. Amrapali's great aesthetic gifts prompted the oral tradition to claim that she was born miraculously at the foot of a

> **Dharma Dictionary**
>
> A **theri** is a woman elder. The nuns of the Buddhist order were called *theri*, including Buddha's (former) wife and aunt. A tradi-tional collection of poems com-posed by these Buddhist elders is called the *Therigatha*.

mango tree. Hence, her name "mango protector." Amrapali carried herself so well that even from a distance her charm could be felt. Gautama had to warn his bhikshus to be mindful as he saw her coming upon them one day. The early Buddhist monks have preserved for us a poignant poem from the lips of this once-ravishing beauty. In it, the mango woman speaks of her hair, eyebrows, earlobes, teeth, voice, neck, arms, hands, breasts, thighs, calves, and feet. They'd all succumbed to the power of aging. "Now they don't make anyone look back. Impermanence is the teaching of a truth speaker," she said.

The Theri Legacy

Woman ascetics were known since ancient times in India. But the Buddhist collection of poetry from the theris gives the first historical record of a whole group of such women anywhere in the world. Maha Prajapati, Khema, Patacara, and Amrapali are just a few of the women whose voices have come down to us through the collection of poems of the theris. Here we end with a look at two more.

A cattle girl named Sangha is among the women whose words are with us. She gave up everything she loved—house, child, and cattle—to adopt the homeless life of a nun. We don't know how old her child was, and under what circumstances she left the child. But the fact that a vaisya (the third caste beneath brahmin and kshatriya) woman could opt to become a nun indicates that Buddha's spiritual community was open to common people. Sangha became an arhat because, along with her possessions she gave up the Three Poisons—desire, revulsion, and delusion.

> **Be Mindful!**
>
> Buddha woke up. Yet a buddha can't wake up someone else. Let's say you and your twin set the clock one night. In the morning your twin wakes up, but you don't. Your twin might help you wake up by prodding you. But ultimately you have to muster yourself to wake up. No one can do that for you.

A woman named Mittakali decided to become a nun after hearing Gautama teaching the discourse on mindfulness meditation, the Satipatthana Sutta. (We should all be so lucky to hear Buddha himself give a teaching on meditation!) But for some time afterward, she had trouble mentally freeing herself from attachment to material things and praise. Finally, one day Mittakali simply saw tathata. She'd been terrified in her cell, realizing that life is short with no time to be careless. Then, through focused mindfulness she recognized the subtle impermanence of her mind and body as they fell away moment to moment. Mittakali tells us: "I saw reality as it is. I stood up. My mind was unteathered. Buddha-dharma was seen!"

The Least You Need to Know

- Overall, Buddhist texts give less coverage to female than male disciples, but the collection of poems of women arhats (theris) is the first historical record of a group of mendicant women in history.

- Maha Prajapati asked Buddha (whom she raised) to found a bhikshuni-sangha and thus opened the way for women to find a rewarding spiritual life in community.

- Women from all social stations joined Buddha's mendicant sangha, including King Bimbisara's chief consort, a courtesan, a banker's daughter, a cattle girl, an ex-Jain mendicant, and others.

- A "central land" in Buddhism is a place where both men and women follow the spiritual life equally. And though this ideal has been obscured in Buddhist history, modern women are working to make it a reality—as it was in the beginning.

- Poems of the theris are preserved in the Buddhist canon and reflect a time when—under Gautama's guidance—women in the Middle Ganges Basin could strive for high spiritual attainments and succeed.

Chapter 19

Lay Disciples

In This Chapter

- Kisa Gautami's plight
- Vimalakirti's special sickness
- Queen Vaidehi finds a new Buddha
- Queen Samavati's servant and rival
- Anathapindika, the merchant of Sravasti
- Visakha's contributions

Buddha's spiritual community was four-part: monks, nuns, laymen, and laywomen. Here we check on some of his disciples from the last two categories—women and men who stayed involved in worldly life. These lay disciples from the Middle Ganges Basin were of various social classes, including royalty, the new moneyed class, and servants. In common they had respect for the Tathagata, a keen interest in his teachings, and a degree of spiritual accomplishment. Plus they all "gave back" something to the community. What they gave depended upon their individual means and talents. (We also check in on a layperson who tried to foil Sakyamuni's work—lest you think that his success was unhampered.)

Let's now trace a large arc around the Middle Ganges Basin to look into the lives of a handful of Buddha's lay disciples. We'll make five stops:

◆ **Kapilavastu**: We start near Buddha's place of origin with Kisa Gautami. Her story is very famous and leaves us with an important lesson.

◆ **Vaisali**: We go southeastward to visit Vimalakirti—a guy who became a star in later Mahayana Buddhist circles.

◆ **Rajagriha**: We continue south, crossing the Ganges, and check on poor Queen Vaidehi, put under house arrest by her son King Ajatasatru.

◆ **Kausambi**: We proceed due west to King Udena's palace where Queen Samavati, her servant Khujjuttara, and the rival Queen Magandiya have their ups and downs.

◆ **Sravasti**: We travel northward to see the great donors Anathapindika and Visakha. To get there means dealing with five rivers … almost coming back to where we began. Starting on the banks of the Yamuna, we cross the Ganges, Gomati, and Sarayu to wind up on the banks of the Aciravati.

Are you ready?

A Snake, Mustard Seeds, and Tathata

We begin our travels not too far from Kapilavastu, where a desperate woman named Kisa Gautami sought Buddha's advice. And though she wound up renouncing the world, Kisa Gautami's insight into tathata (things as they are) came as she struggled with a universal problem afflicting laypersons—the death of a child.

Kisa Gautami grew up poor but married into a sresti banker's family. She was not well appreciated by her in-laws until she produced a son. Shock and grief came to Kisa Gautami when this child was bitten by a poisonous snake and died. Gautama was staying nearby in Sravasti, so Kisagotami paid him a visit, carrying the child. She asked for help, and Buddha told her to bring back one mustard seed from a house where no one had died. She went around, but couldn't find a single seed because every house had a tale of woe to tell. When Kisagotami returned to Gautama, she'd realized the truth of impermanence. Gautama didn't revive her son, but helped her realize the first Great Fact of duhkha. She cried: "Wretched woman, you can't even measure this pain! For thousands of lifetimes, your tears have fallen." With empathy and deep realization, she eventually became an arhat.

Enlightening Extras

Generally, names in world cultures are from family line, place of origin, occupation, or nicknames based on a particular characteristic or act of the person. Can you guess which woman named in this chapter was one of Buddha's relatives? Queen Vaidehi? Kisa Gautami? Migara-mata? You're correct if you guessed "Kisa Gautami." Her last name is simply the feminine form of Gautama, Buddha's family name.

Vimalakirti, the Licchavi Layman

Remember Amrapali, the courtesan who became a nun late in life? (See Chapter 18.) She was a remarkable Licchavi woman of Vaisali, a city renowned for its entertainments. Well, the city she beautified with her presence had another remarkable inhabitant. His name was Vimalakirti—a wealthy man who mixed with all classes of people from palaces to bars and brothels. Vimalakirti never became a monk but attained the highest wisdom as a layman, and for that very reason, Mahayana Buddhists of later times single out Vimalakirti as a model disciple. He shows us the possibility of becoming enlightened as a layperson in the midst of mundane life, which is a great theme in Northern Buddhism

Be Mindful!

Vimalakirti's name is given to a Buddhist discourse that is accepted by Mahayana (Northern)—but not Theravada (Southern)—Buddhists. The Vimalakirti-nirdesha-sutra involves Buddha and several of his most prominent monks, including Sariputra, Maudga-lyayana, and Maha Kasyapa. It presents the layman Vimalakirti's teaching on emptiness (sunyata) that even cuts through the remarkable insights of the monks typically spoken of in the Theravada Pali scriptures. The discourse illustrates a favorite Mahayana Buddhist teaching: that one needn't be a monk or nun to realize the most profound Buddha-dharma.

Once when Vimalakirti fell ill, none of Buddha's disciples wanted to visit him because on former occasions he'd challenged their wisdom. Each one had faced this unusual guy in the past and been turned around by his eloquent insights on sunyata. But finally, Buddha got Manjusri to visit him. Being the bodhisattva of wisdom, Manjusri stood a chance in a debate with the clever Vimalakirti. So the spiritual embodiment of wisdom and the ailing layman had a marvelous exchange on the emptiness of Vimalakirti's sickness—ending with the layman's advice on the way a sick person on the spiritual path should meditate. Vimalakirti performed miracles, and eventually all the monks got involved and realized the profound truth of sunyata.

Queen Vaidehi Finds Solace in the Pure Land

Vaidehi was the wife of King Bimbisara of Magadha. They were unable to conceive a child and asked a brahmin for help. The seer told them that a certain hermit would die and three years hence be reborn in the queen's womb. Bimbisara was impatient and had the ascetic killed, and sure enough the hermit was reborn to him and his wife Vaidehi. However, learning from the seer that this son would murder him in retribution, Bimbisara ordered his wife to throw the baby from the palace tower. She did so, but the baby survived with just a broken finger. Afterward, Bimbisara figured he'd better keep the child, who was called Ajatasatru (Unborn Enemy).

Prince Ajatasatru lived up to the vengeance that was predicted of him. He usurped the throne and threw both his parents into prison and began starving Bimbisara to death. (See Chapter 20.) Bimbisara's Queen Vaidehi kept her husband alive by surreptitiously bringing him food. Under suspicion, she devised clever ways to feed her husband. She smeared her body with honey and herbs, which the deposed king licked off for sustenance. When this ruse was discovered, the queen packed herbal preparations under her fingernails to feed the waning Bimbisara. Ajatasatru caught on to the trickery and nearly struck his mother down with a sword. Instead, he put her under house arrest. Before long, the old king died.

King Ajatasatru did not permit anyone to visit his mother in prison. So the desperate widow appealed to Buddha through prayer. At that time, Gautama was preaching nearby on Vulture Peak. It's said that he heard the Vaidehi's appeal and presented himself to her mind using psychic powers. Buddha showed the queen a method of prayer that centuries later spread throughout east Asia in the form of Pure Land Buddhism. Buddha taught Queen Vaidehi to pray to Amitabha (the buddha of boundless light) and meditate on his western paradise.

The queen began to recite Amitabha's sacred name and visualize the Pure Land as she'd been inspired by Sakyamuni to do. Through faithful performance of this Buddha-dharma, Queen Vaidehi attained rebirth in the Western Paradise with Amitabha.

Buddha Basics

Mahayana Buddhists accept the presence of visionary bodhisattvas such as Manjusri, as well as buddhas who abide in nonearthly places in the universe known as Pure Lands. Amitabha, the Buddha of Boundless Light, lives in a Pure Land called the Western Paradise. And Gautama Buddha used psychic powers to teach Queen Vaidehi to gain entrance to Amitabha's Western Paradise through meditation and prayer. According to Northern Buddhism, from there she could have attained enlightenment.

Ugly's Only Skin Deep

Kausambi was the capital city in the Great Country of Vamsa. There lived a ruler named Udena, who had several wives. His wife Samavati had a servant who by chance—that is, by karma—met the Tathagata. Her name was Khujjuttara, and she became famous for keeping a record of short discourses she heard from Buddha.

The collection amounted to 112 teachings that state the lessons in prose and repeat it in verse. These were put into the canon of Buddhist scriptures under the title *Itivuttaka*.

It's rare that one of Buddha's female disciples is called ugly, but that's what's said about the royal servant Khujjuttara. She was physically deformed, but a person of great mental capacity when it came to memory. Khujjuttara's job was to minister to the needs of Queen Samavati. And although she began by deceiving the queen, Khujjuttara wound up bringing the Buddha-dharma to the royal household in Kausambi.

> **Dharma Dictionary**
>
> The **Itivuttaka** is a collection of 112 sutras in the Buddhist canon. In English it's called *The Buddha's Sayings*, but literally itivuttaka means "the so was said." The collection was made by Khujjuttara, a royal servant in Kausambi who heard Buddha teach and then repeated his discourses to Samavati, the consort of King Udena, and other women of the royal palace.

Khujjuttara was charged to purchase flowers for the women's quarters every day. Entrusted with eight gold coins, she would spend half on flowers and keep the remainder for herself. This theft went unnoticed. One day the florist asked her to stay for a discourse Buddha was to deliver on the premises. At the teaching, without totally realizing what was happening to her, she was mentally transformed. Khujjuttara glimpsed the fact that the world was like a dream, and became a stream entrant. With that her inclination to be dishonest was purified. Thereafter, she brought home flowers worth the whole sum and confessed everything. The impact of Buddha's teachings made her naturally observe basic morality.

Khujjuttara developed great faith in the Buddha, dharma, and spiritual community, and went regularly to hear Buddha teach at the monastery in Kausambi. Using her stellar memory, the servant reported verbatim what she heard to Queen Samavati and her ladies in waiting.

Be Mindful!
The story is that Khujjuttara became a stream entrant after hearing just one discourse delivered by Buddha. A similar claim is made in the Buddhist texts with reference to numerous other conversions. There must have been something about the Tathagata's very presence that helped his words penetrate the hearts of people ripe for realization—although someone like Sariputra became a stream entrant merely by hearing a verse of Buddha's teachings delivered by a disciple.

Beauty's Only Skin Deep

Although this chapter is about Buddha's lay disciples, it won't hurt to hear about a lay "follower" who was Buddha's detractor. There was a woman who was physically attracted to the Tathagata and became very angry when he rebuffed her. Her name was Magandiya, and she wound up as a wife of King Udena—senior to Samavati and her servant Khujjuttara. Whereas Khujjuttara's misshapen physical form held a mind of great faith, Magandiya's beauty ran only skin deep.

Some years before her marriage to King Udena, many suitors courted the lovely Magandiya. Magandiya's father had to find the best possible husband for his daughter. And when he happened to see the Tathagata one day, he thought Magandiya should become the Maha Sramana's wife—perhaps not realizing Buddha's commitment to celibacy. So he and his wife quickly brought Magandiya—dressed to the nines—in front of the Tathagata and proposed to give her in marriage. In reply, Gautama uttered a single verse that made him an enemy for life:

> Even when I saw Mara's spectacular daughters, I had no interest in the physical pleasures of love. What's this before me now but a body filled with urine and dung? I wouldn't even touch it with my foot.

Rather than freak out, the parents actually attained a high level of spiritual development upon hearing Buddha's powerful rebuff of their daughter! They destroyed craving and revulsion by realizing that both beauty and filth are illusory from the ultimate point of view.

But the same could not be said of Magandiya. From that moment onward, she hated Buddha with a passion. So later, as King Udena's wife, Magandiya exercised her power against Buddha as well as his followers. She spread vile rumors about Buddha and his community, which turned out to be relatively harmless because public discontent settled down after one week. More horrible was the arson she commissioned, which resulted in the burning death of her rival, Queen Samavati, and palace women faithful to the Tathagata.

The Sresthi and New Money

It's impossible to talk about Buddha's lay disciples without mentioning the moneyed business class or *sresthi*. A sresthi could be a financier or banker, head of a trade guild, or merchant. These businesspeople were a natural outgrowth of urbanization. People who piled into the fast-growing cities of Buddha's day were losing their old tribal identities. The sresthi helped create a new Indian society that began to erase the prejudice of tribal loyalty as they formed communities based on occupation rather than tribal origin. With the growth of these urban communities, a market for new commodities opened, and labor was there to meet the demand. The sresthi were among the most significant players in this intensely commercial atmosphere.

> **Dharma Dictionary**
>
> **Sresthi** is the Sanskrit term for wealthy person, usually a merchant or banker. A class of such businesspersons grew up in Buddha's day. Can a person who hoards wealth be called a sresthi? Or does a sresthi voluntarily contribute to the social welfare? These questions are still discussed among people who analyze Indian society even today.

Many members of the new business class in the Ganges Basin became quite wealthy. But in the religious atmosphere of the day—with people such as Buddha, Mahavira, and other renunciates teaching ethics—prominent sresthi did not hoard their wealth. They helped spread an ethic of generosity, and were respected by rulers and the public for their contributions to social welfare. These businesspersons supported the renunciate religious groups and built houses where the poor could come to eat. In fact, a number of sresthi expressed a keen interest in religious teachings.

The Case of Sresthi Anathapindika

Anathapindaka is the most famous sresthi of Buddha's day. Spending a significant portion of his resources, he built a monastery for Buddha and the renunciate community in Sravasti. It was called Jeta's Grove or Anathapindika's monastery. And Buddha probably spent more time there than at any other single place in the 45 years of his post-enlightenment career. Here's how it happened that a wealthy merchant of Kausala's capital became one of Buddha's earliest and most dedicated lay disciples.

Anathapindika came from Sravasti to Rajagriha on business. He went to his brother-in-law's house and found everyone preparing for the arrival of the Enlightened One. Just hearing the words "Buddha, Enlightened One" ignited something in this wealthy man's heart. He experienced samvega, that deep spiritual shock. Understanding the rarity of finding a buddha in this world, Anathapindika was amazed. He could hardly sleep all night, waiting for his chance to see the Tathagata. He didn't even wait for Buddha to arrive at his brother-in-law's house. Instead, Anathapindika set out on foot before dawn to find Buddha in his monastery.

Enlightening Extras

The invisible spirit, Sivaka, is an excellent example of what folklorist Vladimir Propp called a "magical agent" or "helper" on the heroic journey. Anathapindika had the valiant wish to walk all night to arrive at Buddha's monastery by daybreak. As he set out, the obstacles of fear and uncertainty began to plague his mind. But timely advice given by the helper Sivaka encouraged him. Sivaka's remarkable verse reveals the key to success on the spiritual path:

> One hundred thousand elephants,
> One hundred thousand horses,
> One hundred thousand chariots,
> One hundred thousand maidens
> All decked out with jewels and earrings—
> Are not worth a sixteenth part
> Of a single step forward.

"Come, Sudatta!"

Anathapindika walked all night alone to find Buddha's monastery—which Anathapindika's brother had built. The merchant approached his destination at just about dawn. Through the mist, he detected someone pacing back and forth. And suddenly a penetrating voice floated to his ears, "Come, Sudatta!" At that moment Anathapindika experienced samvega, the aesthetic shock for a second time. Startled, he thought, "Who knows my name? Who recognized me?" He was surprised especially because people always called him Anathapindika because he gave alms (pinda) to the helpless (anatha). So who knew that he was actually Sudatta? Of course, you can guess it was the Tathagata who'd called out to him.

The sound of the word buddha had deeply moved Anathapindika when he first heard his brother-in-law say it. You can imagine how the man felt hearing his childhood name from the mouth of the Awakened One. The merchant fell down at Buddha's feet. In response, the Tathagata gave a penetrating discourse that prompted Anathapindika to overcome all doubts in the Three Jewels. He had a glimpse of tathata and became a stream entrant.

Prince Jeta's Grove

Anathapindika built a monastery for the Buddhist mendicants in the hills south of Sravasti's commercial center. He located a piece of prime real estate owned by Jeta, one of King Prasenajit's sons. The merchant made a generous transaction with the prince, who was at first reluctant to part with the choice land. The ritual of dedication lasted nine months, during which many people in and around Sravasti became lay disciples. Anathapindika took responsibility to maintain Jeta's Grove and provide for the resident's needs as much as possible. Later King Prasenajit himself provided means for the residents of Jeta's Grove.

Even when Anathapindika went through a personal financial crisis, he and his wife still made offerings to the best of their ability. They had two daughters who married and eventually became Buddha's lay patrons, too. In this, the merchant family demonstrated the ideal of generosity—on which the sresthi of the Middle Ganges Basin prided themselves.

> **Buddha Basics**
>
> Buddha spent the fourteenth rains (after awakening) at Jeta's Grove in Sravasti. Rahula—his son, now 20 years old—received full ordination at that time. The following year, Buddha resided at Kapilavastu. (This was the only rains that Buddha spent in his hometown.) His stay coincided with the death of Yasodhara's father, who'd remained angry at Gautama for leaving his daughter.

Anathapindika's third daughter had the keenest wisdom among the siblings but never married. She succumbed to loneliness, and its said she died from depression. But due to her spiritual attainment she was reborn in Tushita heaven. Meanwhile, Anathapindika's son seemed interested only in making money, with no concern for religious practice. Gradually, he turned toward the Buddha-dharma and became a patron. His wife also wasn't inclined at first toward religion. She was a proud, shrewish individual whose taming by Buddha became legendary. This woman had quite the opposite temperament from her own sister, Visakha, to whose story we now turn.

Visakha, a Woman of Generosity and Faith

The name of Visakha pops up right away when it comes to women disciples of the Tathagata who kept to the married life. She had deep faith in Buddha-dharma and was Sakyamuni's main benefactress. Besides that, Visakha did so much to create a close relationship between laypeople and the renunciate community. Her positive influence extends from Buddha's day all the way into our own time.

The Beginning of the Story ... If We Can Find It

By now you know that in Buddhism, a person's story begins many lifetimes back. And the first reported moment is often a virtuous wish. In Visakha's case, it's said that eons ago she knelt at the feet of a tathagata and wished the following: "May I someday become a chief benefactress of the sangha and its founder (a future buddha)." From that moment on, Visakha began doing virtuous deeds—always bearing her *samkalpa* somewhere in the recesses of her mind. And keeping her virtuous intention firm helped Visakha gain good karma faster.

Dharma Dictionary

Samkalpa is the Sanskrit term for intention. This is a mental force that stands behind all karma, whether positive or negative. This intention or will is a spiritual faculty that acts via the mind. It sets up a vow or mental form that helps shape and focus one's acts. According to the yoga psychology of Hinduism and Buddhism, making a samkalpa adds power to the karmic act and allows the wish to bear fruit more quickly. Virtuous samkalpas bring happiness.

Visakha was born fortuitously in the Middle Ganges Basin after performing acts of kindness throughout many lifetimes. (These were not random acts of kindness, by the way. They were shaped by samkalpa.) Finally, the mysterious workings of karma placed the up-and-coming benefactress in the sixth century B.C.E., in a position to meet Gautama Buddha. The fruits of all Visakha's good karma began to ripen quickly. Her wish to become a great donor was materializing.

Visakha met Sakyamuni when she was 7 years old. Their first meeting was amazing: she attained the first stage of sainthood just hearing the Tathagata speak. That is, the child became a stream entrant when three things arose in her mind: great faith in Dharma, an inkling of the truth of nonself, and loss of confidence in rituals to bring enlightenment. During the same discourse, other members of Visakha's family also entered the stream. After that remarkable day, Visakha's family gained a reputation for their great virtue.

Share the Wealth of Virtue

Visakha was from the territory of Anga, which was under the jurisdiction of the Great Country of Magadha. King Prasenajit of Kausala heard of Visakha's virtuous family and wanted his people to be inspired by their good conduct, so he asked King Bimbisara of Magadha to send some members of the family to Kausala. Bimbisara was actually Prasenajit's brother-in-law, being married to the Kausalan king's sister, so he agreed. And Visakha found herself living near—then in—Sravasti, the capital of Kausala.

By and by a wealthy merchant married Visakha. Her new father-in-law, Migara, was a lay follower of a group of naked ascetics, so he didn't invite Buddha to the wedding, although at the time he was nearby. Migara never even wanted to meet Buddha. But one thing led to another, and over time Visakha cleverly managed to bring them together. At one point she even threatened to leave the household unless Migara invited Buddha for alms. When Visakha's father-in-law finally gave in, he was deeply moved by the encounter with Buddha. Afterward, both Migara and his wife became generous supporters of Buddha's renunciate community. Migara also developed deep gratitude toward Visakha for leading him to the Dharma. Because she was so virtuous, Migara began to respect her as if she were his own mother and so gave her the nickname Migara-mata, meaning Migara's mother.

> **Buddha Basics**
>
> Sravasti was Kausala's capital—located about 100 miles (161 km) from Kapilavastu, the Sakyan capital. Although Buddha rarely stayed in his old hometown of Kapilavastu, the Tathagata spent about 19 rainy seasons in Sravasti—between Jeta's Grove and the park donated by Visakha (called the mansion of Migara's mother).

The Eight Boons

One day, Visakha asked Buddha for eight boons. Sakyamuni told her he didn't grant favors to people, but asked what she had in mind. Migara-mata then voiced her wish for eight things. She wanted to give these gifts to the Buddhist renunciates.

- Robes for the rainy season
- Food for those visiting Sravasti
- Food for those leaving on a journey
- Medicine for those who were ill

- Food for those who tended the sick

- Distribution of rice gruel on a regular basis

- Robes for nuns for bathing in the river

Buddha asked Visakha why she wanted these boons. And Visakha, who was clever as well as virtuous, gave external and internal reasons for her wishes. Visakha's external reasons were based on needs of the community. Her internal reasons were about creating positive states of mind that prepare one for awakening. Migara-mata's explanation was preserved in the history of Buddhism as an example of pure motivation for *dana* (giving) to the Buddhist order.

> ### Dharma Dictionary
>
> **Dana** means giving to the renunciate community. Dana is the main way Buddhist lay-persons earn merit for a good rebirth. They also observe upavasatha days every new moon and full moon. At that time, the laymen and laywomen remove jewelry, wear white clothes, and observe eight precepts: not to kill, not to steal, not to engage in sexual activity, not to lie, not to use drugs or alcohol, not to eat after noon, not to seek entertainment, and not to sleep on a high or luxurious bed.

The Least You Need to Know

- Laymen and laywomen are an important part of Buddha's sangha. And though they don't live in monasteries, they are encouraged to observe the eight most basic precepts each full moon and new moon day.

- The lay community supported the renunciate community by dana or giving. Their donations ranged from a handful of rice, to beautiful land and housing that eventually turned into monasteries.

- The sresthi or businesspersons of new wealth often took responsibility for sustaining Buddha's renunciate community. Many also took a keen interest in applying the Buddha-dharma to their daily lives.

- Mahayana Buddhists recognize some sutras that are not accepted by Theravadins, including one with the layman Vimalakirti's teachings on emptiness, and one with Buddha's instructions to Queen Vaidehi on gaining entrance to the Western Paradise.

Chapter 20

Royal Complexities

In This Chapter

- Siddhartha meets Bimbisara
- Bimbisara's ups and downs
- Ajatasatru's ambitions and sleepless nights
- Prasenajit's faith, failing, and flight
- Virudhaka's revenge

History shows that when there's a chance to grab wealth or power, people will take it. In the midst of the radical social movements of Buddha's day, the political landscape was changing fast. Wealth was accumulating as a merchant class grew up in the Middle Ganges Basin. A new theory of statecraft touted monarchy as the superior means of generating a new economy dependent on surplus, trade, and a breakdown of tribal exclusivity.

Two territories were fast outgrowing the old tribal models of organization and emerging as nascent states: Kausala and Magadha. Their capitals were Sravasti and Rajagriha, and their leaders were intent on expanding their influence over the smaller territories. Now we look more closely at the political advances, ambitions, and intrigues surrounding the growth of these two monarchies—for Buddha's disciples were heavily embroiled in the mix. We begin by winding back the clock to when Buddha was still

Siddhartha in search of enlightenment—for his friendship with the king of Magadha dates from that time.

Monarchs Wanted

Use of the iron plow led to accumulation of surplus grain in the Middle Ganges Basin. This generated wealth and a market for new products ... which encouraged trade and the growth of a merchant class ... which called for social mobility and communication. Traders had to move across borders. But in territories governed by tribal exclusivity and fixed trading partners, merchants could not fulfill the demand of a growing elite, and rulers could not capitalize on the new wealth within their old-fashioned tax structures.

In this atmosphere of opportunity and opportunism, a northern Indian movement arose to expand the borders of a uniform state. And on Buddha's stomping ground, the two prime contenders to establish a far-reaching central authority were the rulers of Kausala and Magadha. When opportunity knocked, Prasenajit and Bimbisara moved forward. But when they were not moving fast enough, their sons pushed for more. So when opportunity knocked again, ambition escalated into ruthless passion.

The Kausalan and Magadhan royal households became embroiled in a tale of power and intrigue. Sakyamuni was friend to the strongest rulers of the region. But his counsel and good example could not prevent people who knew him well from committing major atrocities—for the times seemed to call for flagrant aggression even in the midst of India's new philosophies of nonviolence.

A State Needs Arms

Trade was difficult in the midst of warfare. But warfare was prescribed for the establishment of a large state under a single law. The answer for anyone seriously contending to redraw the boundaries of the Ganges Basin seemed to be the formation of an army that could conquer and control territory. Members of the force should be paid to instill loyalty to the state—and not to old tribal associates. And the army should be continually at work protecting people, land, and assets, while enforcing laws year round.

These pretensions to greatness were not without warrant. In Persia, Cyrus the Great founded the Achaemenid Empire in 533 B.C.E. This is just when Prasenajit of Kausala and Bimbisara (c. 558–491 B.C.E.) of Magadha were developing their visions and

Indian political theorists were contemplating the future of statecraft. Both northern Indian rulers were in an ideal position to impose their authority over a larger theater of political operations. They had wealth and were not tied into a narrow concept of tribal affiliation.

Enlightening Extras

Cyrus the Great (558–530 B.C.E.) founded the Persian Achaemenid Empire. It survived for two centuries after his death until Alexander the Great took over in 330 B.C.E. Cyrus is known in the Bible as the great king who freed Jews from "captivity" in Babylon under Nebuchadnezzar, and allowed them to rebuild Solomon's Temple in Jerusalem. He ascended the Persian throne some 16 years after Bimbisara (c. 558–491) began to rule Magadha and swiftly built the greatest empire the world had ever seen.

Rajagriha, the Big Apple

The importance of cities was not lost on Gautama. And though he spent time in the jungle—in the manner of a certain type of ascetic—he was also interested in the cultural activity that buzzed through the growing urban centers. Gautama was drawn by the power of religious experience that was gained through solitary meditation. But the practice of meditation was based on the power of ideas: what is the nature of the person? What is the role of action? And the practice of meditation for Siddhartha was based on the motive of social transformation: where is the end of suffering?

Burning with questions, Siddhartha at the age of 29 had fled his home in Kapilavastu. He left everything behind in search of the panacea that would comfort all those he left behind. And his first destination was *Rajagriha*, which was like the Big Apple of the Middle Ganges Basin. Siddhartha headed down from the Himalayan foothills through Malla territory and made his way to the Magadhan capital, a thriving metropolis that was home to King Bimbisara.

Rajagriha was surrounded by hills and served as a mountain fortress of the Magadhans. It was a walled city with an area of about 1 square mile. Outside the city walls was land for grazing,

Buddha Basics

Rajagriha, or "king's abode," was the only site south of the Ganges settled by the ancient Aryans—due to abundant flakes of iron oxide in the surrounding hills that could be scraped off the rock and turned into tools. Seated here, the early Magadhan kings, starting with Bimbisara, started building what became India's first empire, founded by Chandragupta Maurya in 322 B.C.E.

dotted with hot and cold springs that allowed the city to withstand hostilities from either the environment or invaders. Rajagriha was further protected by 25 miles of outer walls. And with a broad-minded ruler, Rajagriha was a wonderful place to be.

A Warrior in Rags

As Gautama entered Rajagriha, King Bimbisara from his palace saw the new ascetic and noted the marks of a great man on his body. After Gautama went from house to house on alms rounds and retired to a mountain cleft, the king approached him face to face. Bimbisara went as far as his chariot would take him, then approached the recluse on foot and inquired about his lineage. The king could see from his demeanor and physique that Siddhartha was no ordinary beggar. After confirming that Gautama was a trained kshatriya, Bimbisara offered wealth and a position as head of a Magadhan squadron,

> *"Your stature is that of a noble. You would do well to head a squadron of my army, complete with elephants. I offer wealth for your enjoyment. But first inform me of your birth."*

King Bimbisara needed dedicated and capable leaders for the growing Magadhan army. Most welcome was the prospect of hiring a well-trained ksatriya whose thinking was freed from tribal pettiness. But steadfast in purpose, the Sakyan prince refused Bimbisara's offer, saying, "My ambition is only for enlightenment. My heart delights in it." Gautama was no fool. He had barely renounced the world and was not going to give in to the first occasion when worldly forces began drawing him back into the royal life. But Bimbisara was no fool either. The king recognized an exceptional warrior when he saw one, even if he was wearing cast-off rags and begging in the streets. He knew that having this clearly remarkable human being among his people would be of great benefit to himself and the Magadhans.

Thus, when Bimbisara realized that the noble ascetic was intent in his search for truth, he asked Gautama to return to Rajagriha after his aim was achieved. The Saykan prince-ascetic assented. And so it happened: after awakening, the former Sakyan prince came back to Rajagriha. After his six years of striving, the ascetic returned as a buddha—an enlightened one.

The King of Magadha Converts

Gautama kept his promise to the Magadhan king and returned to the king's capital as an awakened one after about seven years. He spent the second, third, and fourth rain retreats after enlightenment around Rajagriha. Upon returning, however, he entered the city not as a lone renunciate, but with a thousand disciples. If this number is exaggerated, it still suggests that Buddha already had more students than the number residing near Rajagriha with his second teacher, Rudraka Ramaputra.

The large group of disciples that walked into Bimbisara's walled city actually had been disciples of Urubilva Kasyapa. Kasyapa was a well-respected ascetic whose hermitage was in Urubilva near the place Siddhartha had chosen for his mortifications and enlightenment. At first it was unclear whether the thousand ascetics were taking Kasyapa or Gautama as their leader. When Kasyapa established that he himself was a disciple of the new buddha, the Magadhan people gained confidence in Gautama.

Seeing signs of the Sakyan prince-ascetic's success, King Bimbisara publicly became Gautama's lay disciple. And according to custom—as could be expected—the people of Rajagriha followed suit. This crystallized the friendship between Bimbisara and Buddha—a close relationship that was to last another 37 years.

> **Be Mindful!**
>
> King Bimbisara was a lay convert to Buddha's sangha according to Buddhist tradition. But Jains claim that their leader, Mahavira, converted Bimbisara to Jainism along with 23 of his sons and 13 of his wives. This is possible, because Mahavira was a well-known teacher in Magadha who spent 14 of his 32 rain retreats around Rajagriha—about twice as many as Buddha spent there.

The First Buddhist Monastery

King Bimbisara was a great donor to religious causes. Perhaps his generosity was a bit out of faith and a bit out of pragmatism, but he supported Jains, brahmins, and Buddhists. He donated the strategic village of Campa to a brahmin sacrificial priest. He made such offerings on more than one occasion in support of priests who performed the yajna or Vedic sacrifice designed to protect and empower the ruler and his domain. Now he donated Veluvana-arama (the bamboo grove) to Buddha and the mendicant sanghas. This royal favor is probably the first gift of an arama to the Buddhist spiritual community. It was a large arama, complete with artisans and other people who could cover all the needs of a well-appointed establishment.

Bimbisara was an important player in the life of the Buddha's spiritual community. Not only did he maintain the Bamboo Grove, he also requested that monks and nuns perform dharma recitals. These were group recitals of Buddhist legends, Tathagata's sayings, and so forth that helped the community establish a body of oral texts. The custom of fortnightly recitations continues as a monastic tradition to this day. Early on, it became customary for members of the order to review the rules of conduct and make public confession of transgressions on new moon and full moon days.

Enlightening Extras

The yajnas, Vedic sacrifices, had been a mainstay of the Aryan economy and worldview for centuries. Brahmins specialized in the performance of various rituals that became very elaborate over the generations—especially in the Ganga-Yamuna Doab where Vedic culture was strongest. In Magadha, which lay east of the pure Aryan lands, yajnas were used mainly for political ends (such as gaining advantage in warfare) and were very costly to the state. In the east, interest in yajnas was ever dwindling. And even in Aryan strongholds, Vedic ritual was changing under the impact of the new philosophy of non-violence coming from the east.

Bimbisara the Internationalist

In the sixteenth year of Bimbisara's reign, Cyrus the Great established an empire in Persia. Probably inspired by the impressive feat of a benevolent Persian peer, the Magadhan ruler sought to extend his own sphere of influence. Bimbisara was a resolute man and a good organizer. He built roads, took tours of inspection through Magadha, and called in the village leaders for counsel. Beyond that, he was an internationalist.

The raja worked through a combination of diplomacy, conquest, and marriage bonds to enrich his growing state:

Buddha Basics

Takshasila (also called Taxila) was a city just northwest of the Indus River in present-day Pakistan. Located at the northwestern end of the *uttarapatha* (northern trade route), it had been a major center of Aryan culture. Brahmins and kshatriyas from the Ganges Basin were sent to Takshasila and further west for a higher education (for example, medicine, proper Sanskrit, and Vedic rituals).

◆ Bimbisara had an open line of communication that reached westward beyond the Indus River. He made contact with King Puskarasarin, ruler of Gandhara, and sent young Magadhan men to Takshasila, a significant center of education and trade.

◆ Bimbisara conquered Anga on the border of modern-day Bengal to facilitate his plans for trade. He made use of Campa, an eastern river port, to import spices and gold that came from southern India up the coast and along the Ganges.

◆ Bimbisara's chief queen was the sister of King Presenajit of Kausala. As part of her dowry he gained control of a piece of the Kasi region that included Varanasi on the Ganges.

A Case of Twisted Karma

Perhaps Bimbisara was too successful, for his son became an impatient prince and wanted to rule Magadha without delay. Ajatasatru befriended Buddha's cousin Devadatta, and the two envisioned themselves dominating the political and spiritual spheres in the Middle Ganges Basin. Between the two, they would have command of state and religious affairs of Magadha, which was swiftly becoming the greatest state of the region.

To incite Prince Ajatasatru to passionate revenge, Devadatta passed on the rumor about his crooked finger: as a baby his parents tried to kill him. Ajatasatru became enraged and in the year 490 B.C.E. he imprisoned his mother Queen Vaidehi and his father King Bimbisara.

Bimbisara willingly ceded the throne to his son, but that didn't slake Ajatasatru's thirst for revenge. He had his father's feet cut with razors and starved the old man to death.

Enlightening Extras

If there is an Indian counterpart of King Oedipus, it has to be King Ajatasatru. Sophocles (c. 497–406 B.C.E.) wrote several Greek plays about Oedipus, who killed his father and slept with his mother due to unfortunate twists of fate. India's version of "fate" is called karma—and it stretches beyond a single lifetime. Ajatasatru's murder of his father fulfilled the negative karma that Bimbisara created by killing his son in a former life.

Ajatasatru's evil acts would come back to bite him. Ajatasatru had ascended the throne of Magadha and was assuring his father's impotence by starving the old king to death. But it so happened that *his* wife gave birth to a son while Bimbisara was in prison. Only in having a son of his own did Ajatasatru realize the value of a father's love. In the moment of his heartfelt realization, Ajatasatru was seized with terror and commanded that his father be fed. But—alas—Bibmisara had already died. A remorseful Ajatasatru named his son Udayibhadra, "Happily Good."

Ajatasatru became an insomniac and got boils all over his body. Jivaka, the royal doctor, advised him to see Buddha. The patricidal king repented in front of the Master, who prescribed for him a special purification ritual. Although generally Buddha

Dharma Dictionary

Acccording to Buddhist ethics there are five **heinous crimes** that prevent a person from reaching enlightenment in their lifetime: matricide, patricide, murdering an arhat, wounding a buddha, or causing schism in the sangha. Ajatasatru would have attained his first glimpse of nirvana and thus become a stream enterer if he had not killed his father.

underplayed ritual, he obviously thought it was something that could help Ajatasatru. Listening to Buddha, he might have become an arhat and ended his round of rebirths, but this was spiritually impossible because he had committed one of the most *heinous crimes*—killing his father.

Buddhists still count Ajatasatru as an able and just ruler. He ruled Magadha for 32 years and increased its territory to include part of Kasi and the north banks of the Ganges in Licchavi territory. Because the city of Rajagriha was unsuited to the needs of the larger state, Ajatasatru's son Udayibhadra moved Magadha's capital to Patali. Not much is heard of King Happily Good after that, although he ruled for 16 years.

Prasenajit, King of Kausala

Magadha was one hub of political power in the Middle Ganges Basin and Kausala was the other. King Prasenajit was the ruler of Kausala, the contemporary and counterpart of kings Bimbisara and Ajatasatru of Magadha. His capital, Sravasti, was a mere 90 miles (145 km) from Kapilavastu, the Sakyan capital. And though neighboring Sakyans were autonomous in most matters, ultimately the Kausalan ruler was overlord of the Sakya clan. That meant he could exercise the power of life and death over them. Prasenajit was not heavy-handed with his Sakyan neighbors—but the same cannot be said of his son, Virudhaka.

Be Mindful!

In northern India many clans (extended families) that held territories were Aryan tribes, including the Sakyas, Mallas, and Licchavis. And though the political circumstances differ, one can think of the Kurds in Iraq to get a mental picture of an extended Aryan tribe in our own day. Kurds live in a territory settled by their ancestors and have a strong desire to be independent.

Prasenajit, like Bimbisara, seems to have been a close friend of the Tathagata's. In fact, Buddha lived in Sravasti longer than anywhere else—as most of the final 25 rainy seasons of his life were spent in Prasenajit's capital. Over the years, the king noticed the positive results of monks living together in the sangha and paid a great compliment: "The monks were neither skinny, nor selfish." He had much faith in Buddha's teachings.

The Kausalan king, like Bimbisara, donated whole villages to Brahmins in repayment for ritual performances. He was enthusiastic in his patronage of ascetics—although he had many wives himself—and earned a reputation for devoting excessive wealth to the cause of the sramanas. At the same time, he appears to have been rather inefficient in his rule of Kausala. Perhaps he was not interested, but Prasenajit never managed to extend his influence eastward over the Mallas or the Licchavis, who were completely independent. These two tribes governed by tribal assembly and continually honed their ksatriya skills in the martial arts.

Family Matters in Kausala

Prasenajit, out of admiration for Sakyamuni, asked the Sakyas to give him a wife. He may have been a rather low-born kshatriya, though he claimed otherwise. And the Sakyans were proud people. Well, for whatever reason, the Sakya officials gave Prasenajit a lovely Sakyan bride, or so he thought. She was indeed born of a Sakya tribesman, but her mother was a slave.

The Kausalan king was unaware of the compromised social status of his new wife. If he had known her mother was not a Sakyan, he probably would have been bothered more by the trickery than by the woman. In fact, Prasenajit's chief wife was the daughter of a flower gardener. In any case, the king and his "Sakyan" wife had a son named Virudhaka. We'll hear more of him shortly.

Speaking of wives—Prasenajit gave his sister Vaidehi in marriage to Bimbisara. And the union of that marriage was Ajatasatru, whom we met already. From this it is evident that the elder kings of Kausala and Magadha were coexisting in fair harmony. But things got complicated when the sons of Prasenajit and Bimbisara came to maturity.

Family Doesn't Matter

When Prasenajit presented Bimbisara with Vaidehi, he gave a portion of the territory of Kasi as a dowry. This gave the Magadhan ruler strategic access to the Ganges River, so important for trade. But when Ajatasatru nearly cut down his mother by sword, the horrified Kausalan king reclaimed the territory he'd given to Bimbisara as a dowry with his sister. Prasenajit's retraction of Kasi was to no effect, as Ajatasatru went to war and retrieved it. What's more, although Bimbisara had received part of Kasi through his wife's dowry, Ajatasatru now waged a campaign and captured all of Kasi, including the notable trading city of Varanasi, already famous for its *kashaya*.

Prasenajit was the first Indian ruler to create the office of senapati (lord of the army). He raised Virudhaka to that high post of commander-in-chief and then assigned to him a general named Dirgha Carayana who was a masterful theoretician of statecraft. But the king's well-intentioned move proved to be a double error. First, Virudhaka wished to compete with Ajatasatru and overthrow his father too. Second, Prasenajit had just murdered Dirgha Carayana's uncle under suspicion of treason. So it's not surprising that in a disgraceful coup, Virudhaka-senapati and his general stole the throne from their aged king.

A Coup de Disgrace

One day Prasenajit went to visit Buddha, who was also a man of 80 years. (Presumably they had the same birthday.) On this occasion, as so often, Sakyamuni was staying in a place inaccessible by chariot. So Prasenajit entrusted his royal insignia to General Digha Carayana and instructed him to wait. The king then humbly approached the Tathagata on foot.

Prasenajit's visit to Buddha would be his last. The day would be his last as king and nearly his last in the world. Upon returning from his visit with Buddha, Prasenajit found that Dirgha Carayana had absconded with the royal insignia. The general had left the elderly Prasenajit with Buddha and organized a coup to put the king's heir, Prince Virudhaka, on the throne.

Fearing for his life, Prasenajit would not return to Sravasti. Instead, he made his way to Rajagriha in Magadha to seek protection from his nephew Ajatasatru. Unfortunately, the old man arrived at the walls of Rajagriha after nightfall when the gates were locked. There, the poor deposed king, Buddha's old friend, perished—perhaps of dysentery, certainly of exhaustion, and perhaps of heartbreak. When Prasenajit was discovered dead by the city gate, Ajatasatru arranged for an elaborate burial that befit a king. Prasenajit predeceased Buddha—but just barely.

Kausala and Sakya ... Nevermore

We know that Virudhaka was the son of King Prasenajit and a woman presented to his father from the Sakya tribe. We also know that the woman's mother was a dasi (slave), unbeknownst to him. When Virudhaka discovered the truth of his heritage, he was furious.

After Virudhaka deposed his father, the new king was obsessed with a desire to destroy the Sakya clan as revenge for the humiliating trick they'd played on his father—resulting in his mixed blood. Buddha managed to dissuade Virudhaka from acting on this vengeful impulse. However, shortly before Sakyamuni himself passed away, King Virudhaka annihilated the entire Sakya clan. Whereas the Sakyas had been vassals of Kausala before, now the territory simply fell to Kausala.

> ### Enlightening Extras
>
> Kausala was a more powerful state than Magadha at the start of the sixth century B.C.E. due to its control of major trade routes. By contrast, Magadha was not well situated on these routes being beyond the river and bordering uncivilized jungle areas. But its longtime wealth (based on rich deposits of iron ore) gave Magadha an advantage that multiplied exponentially when the long stretch of Ganges from Varanasi to the Bay of Bengal came under its control.

King Virudhaka actually had more than revenge in mind. He'd hoped to gain control of the trade routes by eliminating extra tariffs put on by the Licchavis. But King Virudhaka would never benefit from the Sakyan conquest, nor move eastward to Vaisali. It is said that, by some coincidence of karma, he and his army were drowned in a sudden rush of the river where they were camped on their way back from the massacre. Alas, Virudhaka-senapati was the last Kausalan king in history.

A few Sakyas may have survived. The Burmese people trace their ancestry to a fugitive Sakyan prince and the daughter of a chieftain of the city of Taguang in Upper Myanmar. Other stories tell of a family here and there who claimed to be descended from the Sakya clan. Beyond that, a number of Buddha's disciples were Sakyas. But because they gave up their worldly ties and maintained celibacy, they apparently did not leave any offspring. Thus the whole of Buddha's clan in India was to perish with the younger generation.

It was not long before King Ajatasatru of Magadha overtook the "Great Country" of Kausala. He also waged a campaign against the Vriji confederacy, which was the most powerful nonmonarchical state in the Middle Ganges Basin. Among the eight clans in the confederacy, the Licchavi alone managed to resist Ajatasatru's advances. Thus shortly after Buddha's parinirvana, Magadha had no rivals to stand in the way of its increasing power over the Middle Ganges Basin.

The Least You Need to Know

- In the first millennium B.C.E., northern India was branching out by land and sea—exploring the Deccan and trading with Iran and Mesopotamia.

- In Buddha's northern India (entering an era of monarchy), Magadha was becoming a most successful state as Bimbisara and his son Ajatasatru were the first to conceive of an overarching Indian empire.

- The most progressive development in Buddha's day included the creation of a paid army headed by able leaders who stood unaffected by tribal loyalties.

- Bimbisara, king of Magadha, was imprisoned and starved to death by his son, Ajatasatru, who repented and appealed to Buddha for counsel—but never let up on his political ambitions.

- Prasenajit, king of Kausala, had his Kausala throne usurped by his son, Virudhaka, who then vengefully massacred the Sakya clan, sparing those who had joined the Buddhist sangha.

Part 6

Buddha's Great Decease and Legacy

Buddha passed away at the age of 80 of food poisoning—barely a year after his Sakya clan was massacred under the strain of political ambition. In the last months of his life, Gautama took a long journey on foot. He seemed to be walking—in reverse—the path he first took after leaving home 50 years earlier.

After the Tathagata passed into final nirvana, his Buddha-dharma spread throughout Asia. Popular cults grew up around Buddha's relics which were enshrined in stupas. To enhance the teachings, and fill in for a missing teacher, a tradition of Buddhist art grew up.

The Buddha-dharma died in India pretty much after 1200 C.E. But before perishing in the homeland, Buddha's teachings were committed to writing. Buddhism made its way across Asia. Nowadays, Buddhism seems to be finding a place in Europe and the Americas. The 2,500-year-old tradition still has much to offer, from nonviolent ethics to environmentalism.

Chapter 21

Buddha's Farewell Year

In This Chapter

- ◆ Buddha leaves the king's capital
- ◆ Sakyamuni and his disciples walk from town to town
- ◆ Three months to live
- ◆ The Tathagata's final gesture

Gautama Buddha died as a result of digestion problems. After a meal offered by a metal worker, he was debilitated by dysentery. It was a tough year all around. Already the Tathagata's clan had been massacred, his two chief disciples had passed away, and the old kings of Magadha and Kausala—his royal friends—had died miserably. You might say Buddha's death closed an era.

In the last year of his life, Buddha virtually traced backward the original journey he made upon first adopting the homeless life. At the age of 80, he passed through towns and villages of the Middle Ganges Basin for the last time, starting in Rajagriha and ending in Kusinagara—not far from where he was born as a Sakya prince in the Himalayan foothills.

On the outskirts of Rajagriha was a bamboo grove where Gautama and his disciples used to practice long hours of meditation and then enter the city to gather alms before noon each day. Buddha regularly taught on nearby

Vulture Peak in the tradition of many ancient buddhas before him, but after one conversation on the mountain Buddha determined to leave the place forever. This was a talk with King Ajatasatru's minister, the Brahmin Varshakara.

A Visit from the King's Minister

King Ajatasatru was plotting to overtake the Vriji republic. The Magadhan ruler was clever as well as ambitious, so he sent his chief minister, Brahmin Varshakara, to learn from Buddha the secret of Vriji prosperity and determine a means of undermining their strength. Thus the brahmin minister ascended Vulture Peak, riding as far as possible and walking the rest of the way up the rocky precipice. Varshakara approached Gautama, inquired after his well being, and delivered the news: Magadha and the Vrijis were at odds, and King Ajatasatru intended to subdue the Vrijis. Gautama informed the brahmin that he personally had taught the Vrijis the conditions of success. As long as they maintained those conditions, he advised, they could not be defeated.

Varshakara wanted more detail. The Buddha answered indirectly, putting a series of questions to Ananda, who stood behind fanning him: "Have you heard that the Vriji chiefs meet regularly, carry out their business in harmony, and so on?" Ananda said in every case that he'd heard it. Then Buddha said, "As long as the Vrijis continue thus, they will prosper."

This oblique manner of responding to Varshakara was one of several tactics Buddha used to deal with questions. Depending on the occasion, he would answer directly, indirectly, with another question, or with silence.

Enlightening Extras

Shortly after Buddha's death, Magadha's King Ajatasatru went to war with the Vrijis. He sent minister Varshakara to live in the Licchavi capital of Vaisali for three years to sow dissent among various chiefs of the Vriji confederacy. When Ajatasatru finally declared war, the Vrijis failed to present a united front. Vriji leaders argued among themselves and were defeated. Some Licchavi nobles apparently migrated northward from Vaisali to form a dynasty that emerged to rule Nepal's Katmandu Valley from the second to ninth centuries C.E.

Hearing the exchange between Buddha and his attendant, Varshakara realized that the Vrijis could be weakened by propaganda and decided he must sow discord among them. With this insight the minister took his leave, saying he was a busy man. In response, Buddha ended their audience with the simple statement: "Go. Do as you see fit." At this point, Gautama did not seek to deter the Magadhans from their plan; after all, he had tried—in vain—to prevent Kausala's ruler from decimating the Sakya clan.

Nalanda, a Place of Ideas

Buddha came down from Vulture Peak. He decided to leave Magadha, never to return. On this final journey, Ananda and a large company of monks traveled with him. It is not clear whether nuns accompanied the Tathagata at this time. In any case, their first stop after leaving Rajagriha was a mango grove at King Ajatasatru's summer residence in Venuyastika. There Sakyamuni again taught something basic to his 45 years of preaching: morality, mental discipline, and wisdom. One wonders whether, in visiting the royal compound, Gautama attempted to dissuade Magadha's ruler from his path of war.

A few miles from Ajatasatru's summer residence was Nalanda, a well-populated center for trading goods as well as religious ideas. Centuries later, the place would garner an international reputation as the site of *Nalanda University.* Imagine this great Indian university where 100 lectures per day were delivered in 10 monastic colleges! But for now, lone spiritual masters and their disciples were busy planting the seeds of Nalanda's debate tradition. The accomplished religious men of the day frequented this town to give teachings, including the Jain leader Mahavira and his Ajivaka friend Maskarin Gosaliputra. (On these teachers see Chapter 11.) After leaving Venuyastika, Buddha went to Nalanda and gave teachings there, too.

> **Buddha Basics**
>
> **Nalanda University** was established in the fifth century C.E. A couple centuries later, Hiuan Tsang reported that 10,000 monks and students resided at the university. In the twelfth century, invading Turks badly damaged Nalanda. It is said that everyone fled except one old monk and his student. Today you can ride a bus 56 miles (90 km) from Patna to the Nalanda ruins.

Patali Predictions

After the stop at Nalanda, Gautama made his way northward to a village port on the Ganges River called Patali. There Buddha and his party received the kind of hospitable welcome that villagers in India offer even today. The faithful brought out seats, oil lamps, and a container with water for hand washing and for drinking. People here were used to hosting itinerants—be they merchants or wandering ascetics—because Patali was a fast-growing commercial center. Town residents were pressed into diversity. They would have seen Buddha and others, such as the Jain Mahavira, as venerable pillars of an emerging caste-free cultural alternative.

Buddha's final journey is shown here. In the last months of his life, Buddha seemed to be retracing the steps he took some 50 years earlier when he first renounced his worldly station as prince.

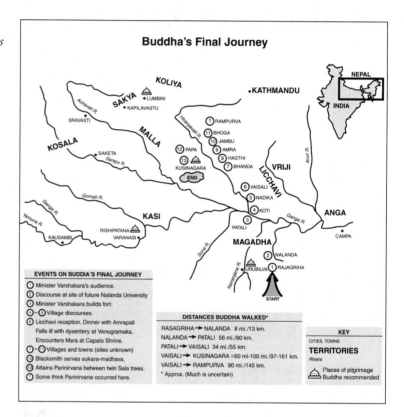

Buddha's Final Journey

EVENTS ON BUDDHA'S FINAL JOURNEY
① Minister Varshakara's audience.
② Discourse at site of future Nalanda University
③ Minister Varshakara builds fort.
④–⑤ Village discourses.
⑥ Licchavi reception. Dinner with Amrapali
   Falls ill with dysentery at Venugramaka.
   Encounters Mara at Capala Shrine.
⑦–⑪ Villages and towns (sites unknown)
⑫ Blacksmith serves sukara-madhava.
⑬ Attains Parinirvana between twin Sala trees.
⑨ Some think Parinirvana occurred here.

DISTANCES BUDDHA WALKED*
RASAGRIHA ➤ NALANDA 8 mi./13 km.
NALANDA ➤ PATALI 56 mi./90 km.
PATALI ➤ VAISALI 34 mi./55 km.
VAISALI ➤ KUSINAGARA ≈60 mi-100 mi./97-161 km.
VAISALI ➤ RAMPURVA 90 mi./145 km.
* Approx. (Much is uncertain)

KEY
CITIES, TOWNS
TERRITORIES
Rivers
🛕 Places of pilgrimage
Buddha recommended

Buddha Basics

The fortunes of **Patali** on the Ganges River rose ... and later fell. The town grew into a magnificent commercial city known as Pataliputra. It served as the capital of virtually all India during the Mauryan dynasty (323–185 B.C.E.). Today it is called Patna, capital of the state of Bihar.

After having refreshment, Gautama began speaking at length to the crowd that had gathered. Well into the night he counseled them on various results of virtuous and nonvirtuous action. After the ethical discourse, Buddha predicted to Ananda the impending greatness and doom of Patali: it would become a thriving metropolis. But it also would be ravaged by flood, fire, and internal dissent. Gautama was fascinated by the impermanence of all things and regularly contemplated the transformation of towns along with everything else.

Minister Varshakara Turns Up Again

A familiar face turned up in Patali: Varshakara, Magadha's chief minister last seen by Buddha in the king's capital. Back at Vulture Peak during his audience with Gautama, Varshakara had figured out a way to undermine Vriji prosperity. Now he was furthering Ajatasatru's plan to overtake the Vrijis. Varshakara was building a fortress at Patali to serve as the staging area for a Magadhan conflict. You see, Patali was on the south bank of the Ganges River in Magadha. Vriji territory was on the north side of the Ganges, held fast by eight tribes including the Licchavis. And to the west of the river fork was Kausala, Virudhaka's kingdom. Before long, all of this would belong to Magadha.

Learning of Gautama's presence in Patali, Varshakara invited Gautama for an alms meal. After preaching to Varshakara on ministerial duties, Buddha left town and crossed the Ganges, heading straight into Licchavi territory with his company of disciples. Is it not strange that Buddha and his party crossed the Ganges River into enemy territory right after meeting with the Magadhan minister, whose task was to help Ajatasatru plot an attack on the Vrijis? How did Buddha and his disciples feel crossing into the land that Magadha's king wanted to consume?

As Sakyamuni crossed into territory at odds with Magadha, so Varshakara later crossed the Ganges. The minister was sent with other Magadhan spies to mingle among the Vrijis to stir up discord. Spying was an ancient Indian political institution. And certainly marginal members of society—such as beggars, merchants, smiths, and courtesans—were in an ideal position to gather intelligence. Would the people think that every monk was immune to politics?

Onward to Vaisali by Leaps and Bounds

The season was spring. They say the river was so swollen that a crow could drink from it. Thus travelers were waiting for a boat or raft to ferry them across. But rather than pay for passage, Buddha and his monks mysteriously appeared on the far shore of the Ganges—as swiftly, it was said, as a strong man could stretch out his arm and flex it again. Then off they went to the villages of Koti and Nadika. At Koti, Buddha discoursed on the Noble Eightfold Path. And at Nadika he told villagers about where many deceased followers had been reborn.

Finally, Sakyamuni and the monks arrived at Vaisali—a busy commercial center where Buddha had come to spend a year fairly soon after his enlightenment. Vaisali was the capital of Vriji territory, controlled by the Licchavi tribe. The Licchavis always gave Buddha a warm welcome, feeling that he protected them from ills. So when Sakyamuni and his party arrived in town, they were comfortable lodging in a mango grove that belonged to the courtesan Amrapali.

Dinner from Two?

The rich and cultivated Amrapali was one of Buddha's long-time disciples, and very faithful. When she heard of Gautama's arrival in Vaisali, the courtesan rode by carriage as far as the path allowed and walked the rest of the way to the place where Buddha was teaching. Seeing the beautiful Amrapali approaching with a group of bright young women, the Tathagata uttered a word of advice to his monks: "Be mindful!" In the typical Indian manner, Amrapali greeted Sakyamuni by bowing with hands pressed together before sitting down to one side. After hearing the dharma, she invited Sakyamuni and his disciples to have dinner at her home the next day. For his part, observing custom, Buddha accepted the invitation by remaining silent.

Soon after the courtesan had secured her dinner guest, the Licchavi nobles came to meet Gautama. Loving brilliance and excitement, they arrived in procession garbed in vibrant hues. Buddha noted their spectacular appearance and told his monks to have a good look at these fantastic Licchavis for an idea of how "gods" appear in the Heaven of the Thirty-Three. Some of the young Licchavis were decked out entirely in blue—with blue makeup, blue clothing, and blue jewelry. Others appeared all in yellow—with yellow makeup, yellow clothing, and yellow jewelry. Others were decked out thoroughly in red. Still others were made up completely in white.

Enlightening Extras

One of the oldest festivals of Hindus and Buddhists in Nepal is Gai Jatra, celebrated the day after the August full moon. Participants in high spirits march in a long procession garbed in stunning clothes—sometimes with men dressed as women. Yellows, whites, and other bright hues give the participants a cheerful, attractive look. Gai Jatra may be traced back to the Licchavis, whose ancient costumes even struck Buddha as heavenly.

The Licchavis met Buddha after Amrapali the courtesan already had invited him to dinner. And though the Licchavi nobles of Vaisali wanted the Tathagata to eat a meal with them, Buddha stuck by his plan to dine with Amrapali. In this, he observed the traditional courtesy of abiding by one's commitments and keeping the appointment made first. After partaking of Amrapali's dinner, Buddha gave a discourse on the merit of generosity. This inspired the courtesan to donate her mango grove to the order. Later on, Amrapali became an arhat.

The First Illness

The monsoon rains were now pummeling Vaisali. And the area was experiencing famine. Because it was a problem to walk about and find food, Buddha advised his monks to disperse and spend the rains around the capital where they had friends and supporters. Meanwhile, he and Ananda stopped for the inclement season in a nearby village named Venugramaka.

The Indian monsoon was a time for dysentery. And this was the year Gautama would succumb. In Venugramaka, during the rains, Buddha's health sharply declined. Through most of his life Buddha was robust and healthy. Now he became gravely ill. Because he was a great meditator, Gautama was able to check the illness. He withdrew attention from body sensation as a turtle draws in its limbs and managed to appease his pain.

The symptoms of Buddha's dysentery subsided. And one day he rose early, got dressed, and went on foot to Vaisali with alms bowl in hand. Then he and Ananda, who carried a mat for him to rest upon, walked to the Capala Shrine. This beautiful old shrine was just one of many in the area, including the Shrine of Many Sons where an age-old banyan tree granted male offspring. Generations of villagers had revered such places for their spiritual vitality. So it is not surprising that Mara, Lord of Illusion, appeared to Buddha at the Capala Shrine, but only after seeing a chance to bring the Tathagata into his realm.

To Live or Not to Live?

Ananda sat with Buddha under the trees of the Capala Shrine soaking in the lovely atmosphere of the place. The Tathagata turned from speaking of its beauty to a subject that was not entirely new to Ananda—the means by which any tathagata could live for a century. Gautama was now 80 and stated three times to Ananda that, in spite of his illness, he had the meditative skill to live out a full life span of 100 years.

Buddha's intimations about the possibility of living a long time did not move Ananda. Ananda did not think to ask Sakyamuni to extend his life. Thus when Ananda responded to this glaring hint with silence, the Tathagata suggested, "Go now. Do as you see fit." What seemed fitting to Ananda at that moment was to go meditate.

Buddha was seated alone under a tree at the Capala Shrine, with Ananda some distance off under another tree. The Tathagata went into a deep meditation. Suddenly he became aware that Mara, Lord of Illusion, had appeared to his mind. Perhaps Mara personified Buddha's realization that his death was impending. In the past, Mara tended to appear when questions of death were in the air. And since Ananda failed to request that Buddha extend his life, the Lord of Illusion now seized the opportunity to have Buddha end his life. Mara wanted Buddha to make this his last day, but Buddha put him off. The Tathagata resolved to wait three months before his *Great Decease*.

> **Dharma Dictionary**
>
> The **Great Decease** is Buddha's parinirvana (final nirvana). It is the culminating moment of Buddha's life, because after this passing away there was no more rebirth for him.

Supernatural Earthquakes

We left Ananda meditating beneath a tree somewhere near the Awakened One. Sitting some distance from Buddha at the Capala Shrine, Ananda suddenly felt a dreadful, hair-raising earthquake. He went to his revered cousin to ask what caused it, and Gautama answered with a traditional explanation: the earth always quakes when a tathagata renounces the life principle. He explained that Mara, Lord of Illusion, had come to cash in on an old promise, and that he, Buddha, would pass away in three months.

Learning that Gautama had renounced the life principle, Ananda panicked. He now begged three times for his teacher to live longer. But Buddha replied, "Enough, Ananda! Do not beg. The time is not right." He reminded Ananda of 15 former times when, at places of great beauty, he had given the same hint by speaking of a tathagata's power to extend life. He explained further that if Ananda had requested him to stay, on any of those occasions, he would have twice refused and the third time consented to live on. Now it was too late.

The fact that Buddha would only try to extend his life if requested to do so reflects a more general custom that he observed. Typically, a person with a request needed to persist through two refusals and make a third attempt. Such was the case with Prajapati, who requested that Buddha institute a mendicant sangha for nuns. She was twice refused. But her proposal was accepted on the third try.

The Elephant Look

Soon after Mara's appearance at the Capala Shrine, Buddha and his party of monks left Vaisali. Standing on the road, early in the day, the Tathagata turned around to gaze at the lovely city with his *elephant look.* Buddha was aware that this was his last look at the beautiful city, for the Great Decease would occur in three months. As he moved on, rain fell from a clear sky. These large water drops were the tears of local spirits, who also knew that Buddha would never return.

Buddha journeyed on foot anywhere from 60 to 100 miles north and west from the Vriji capital of Vaisali to Papa. (The distance is approximate because no one is sure exactly where Buddha stopped.) On the way he visited the villages of Bhanda, Hasthi, Amra, and Jambu. The Tathagata preached at each place, skillfully adjusting both his speech and appearance to meet the needs of the villagers. Finally Gautama and his party settled down north of the city of Bhoga in a grove of sinsapa trees with their clusters of small gold flowers.

Whether they realized it or not, Ananda and other monks were nearing their final destination with the Tathagata. Two more towns and that would be it—with a number of halting stops in between. But for the moment they thought simply that their visit to Papa would be like so many visits before: they stopped at a mango grove. But in Papa, a metal worker named Cunda would host a meal that was a bit too elaborate.

> ### Dharma Dictionary
>
> The poignant moment when Buddha looked at Vaisali is called the **elephant look** because he turned his body completely around—full faced to the right—to gaze upon Vaisali. Elephants likewise turn their whole body around when they want to look at something.

A Meal to Remember

Cunda was the son of a metal worker. According to tradition, he had taken up the profession of his father. And like many people with commercial interests in the Middle Ganges Basin, Cunda had an interest in Buddha's teachings—which abrogated caste distinctions. Thus Cunda was in the crowd, listening to the Tathagata's discourse. Afterward Cunda remained seated. And when he got a chance, the smith asked Buddha to accept a meal from him. In the customary manner Buddha consented by keeping silent. Likewise, according to custom, Cunda kept Buddha to his right side as he departed.

Cunda went home to prepare the typical Indian fare of cakes and sweet rice to serve Sakyamuni's party the next day. He also made a special dish for the Tathagata, and served it in a metal bowl, with his own hands. In an interesting twist, a Tibetan version of the story mentions that this bowl changed hands. Whatever the case, the dish served to Buddha was destined to become among the most famous in world history. It was called sukara-madhava, and it became the material cause of Buddha's

Be Mindful!

No one knows what virtually indigestible food Cunda served to Buddha at Papa. It is called sukara-madhava (sukara = pig, boar; madhava = mild, withered, soft). Traditional commentators thought sukara-madhava might have been flesh of wild pig, soft-boiled rice, or a special elixir. Nowadays people think the dish may have been truffles, a delicate underground fungus sniffed out by boars.

death. When Buddha tasted some of this delicacy, he instructed Cunda to bury the rest, declaring that no one but a tathagata could digest such food.

Shortly after eating the meal presented by Cunda, the metal worker, Buddha began to feel physically ill. The dysentery that he had subdued at Venugramaka now recurred in full force. The Tathagata began to bleed internally. He somewhat controlled the bloody diarrhea and violent back pain through meditation and mustered enough strength to continue the journey to Kusinagara. But he needed to rest many times along the way. In spite of this debility, the Tathagata wanted Cunda to know that his act was virtuous— for there is great merit in offering a tathagata his last meal.

Between Two Sala Trees

Gautama, Ananda, and the disciples pressed onward. Sakyamuni bathed in the Kakudha River, a small branch of the Hiranyavati, and they continued on. Buddha was now close to his final resting place near Kusinagara. This area was then as it is today, a sprawling plain where farmers cultivate rice and sweet potatoes. Coming into a grove, Buddha located a pair of sala trees and lay down between them on a low bed that Ananda had prepared for him. The Tathagata reclined on his right side with crown facing north in the lion's pose. Buddha typically slept in this posture, with his head supported upright and one leg resting on top of the other. And now for his final nirvana, Buddha assumed the lion's pose for the last time.

Seeing that his revered cousin was about to expire, Ananda suggested that the Tathagata not pass away in Kusinagara, but in an illustrious city. They could go west to Sravasti, back to Vaisali or Rajagriha, or even to Kausambi, Varanasi, or Campa. Any one of those northern Indian cities was more suitable for the Great Decease, he thought. But Buddha put geography, economics, and politics into a longer perspective, going back many lifetimes. Although Kusinagara appeared to be an insignificant town, he told Ananda that it once had been a great capital called Kusavati. Nobles, royal elephants, and horse-drawn chariots had paraded through the streets long ago. From Kusavati ruled a certain King Sudarshana, who was none other than Gautama himself in a past life.

Appealing to an age-old tradition, the Tathagata explained that he would be the seventh Buddha to attain final nirvana on that very spot between the twin sala trees. Yes, near the village of Kusinagara where he lay in the lion's pose, six former buddhas had taken their Great Decease. He would be the seventh tathagata to do so. And so he did.

The Tathagata Bares His Chest

In response to the momentous seventh repetition of the Great Decease, the buds of the sala trees bloomed out of season, and fragrant flower petals fell upon the Tathagata's body. In spite of this glorious embellishment of nature, however, Buddha declared that living according to the dharma was even more wondrous.

As a parting gesture, Sakyamuni bared his chest. He told the fortunate to take a good look at this, a tathagata's body: such a body is as difficult to find as a flower on a fig tree. Sakyamuni then counseled those in his presence with the final words: "Decay is inherent in all composed things." Then Buddha entered the state of great equanimity and attained his final nirvana. Nature marked this event with an earthquake.

Ananda went into Kusinagara to conveyed the news that the Tathagata had passed away. The Mallas came to pay their respects, and Ananda ushered them in groups to see his beloved cousin. He invited the women first so that they might return home safely before dark. Later Ananda was blamed for this courtesy—because as the women wept, their tears fell onto the Buddha's chest.

> **Be Mindful!**
>
> Not all versions of Buddha's story have Gautama bare his chest as a parting gesture. And not everyone finds the same meaning in this gesture. Did Buddha expose the bare chest of an old man to demonstrate that all compound things are subject to decay? Or did Buddha bare his chest to demonstrate a tathagata's radiance unobstructed by the robe? What do you think?

The Least You Need to Know

- In Buddha's old age, political ambitions mounted, and Magadha's king had designs on Vriji territory.

- In his last year of life, Buddha traveled from the Magadhan capital or Rajagriha to Kusinagara, a small town in Malla territory—with a number of stops in between.

- ◆ Buddha contracted dysentery and, though he controlled it through meditation, passed away shortly after eating an indigestible meal.

- ◆ The Great Decease is the ultimate marvel of Buddha's life story because he attained final nirvana and transcended rebirth.

- ◆ Impermanence is a key theme of the Buddha-dharma; and in his final hours, the Tathagata taught it both by words and through the gesture of baring his chest.

Chapter 22

The Art of Awakening

In This Chapter

- Buddha's advice on lay worship
- About Buddhist stupas
- Early Buddhist art
- Symbolism of the Buddha image
- The art of awakening leaves India

Art related to Buddha's life and teachings is basically an art of awakening. It attempts to convey Buddha's enlightenment—which is the heart of dharma. But monks and nuns in the early days of Buddhist tradition were not particularly concerned with this art—for they were uninvolved in worship of any sort. During Buddha's life and in the centuries immediately following his Great Decease, Buddhist art was geared to benefit lay followers.

Gradually, Buddhist artists took up the challenge of capturing the Buddha and dharma in material form. Over the centuries, the art of awakening became a huge feature of Buddhist tradition. Here we check out the symbolic components of that art in several cultural situations.

Buddha's Artistic Gifts

From time to time, Sakyamuni gave specific instructions on how to handle matters of art and ritual to help his lay disciples. Though people don't usually think of Buddha as involved in material culture, he seems to have had appreciated the spiritual value of art. Here's some of Buddha's advice on the subject of symbolic ritual and representation.

Buddha Commissions His Portrait

The first artistic likeness of Buddha was commissioned by the Tathagata himself— even though generally he was not represented until the first century C.E. According to Tibetan scriptures, Sakyamuni wanted to present something to please the daughter of the king of Sri Lanka, Princess Ratnavali. He said that, in his very lifetime, she'd been a maidservant who died of heartbreak because she was deprived of seeing him.

Here's what happened: the girl (Princess Ratnavali in her last life) was the hand-maid of the wife of Buddha's elder cousin Mahanama. Got that? Okay ... so one day Mahanama's beautiful wife and her handmaid went with many other Sakyan women to the banyan grove near Kapilavastu to hear Buddha teach. But as they approached, one of Buddha's disciples advised Mahanama's wife to remove her jewelry for the teaching, so she gave her jewelry to her handmaid to take home. The girl had set her heart on seeing Buddha, and suddenly being told to return home with the jewelry hurt her deeply. Sadly, the poor young woman was so distressed that she died on the way back to Kapilavastu. She was soon reborn to the ruling family on the island of Sri Lanka.

> **Be Mindful!**
>
> Usually Buddha told stories about people's former lives that happened many years back in the past. But the story of Ratnavali presents a situation in which a young woman lived twice in the span of Gautama's own lifetime— first as his cousin's servant, then as a ruler's daughter in Sri Lanka.

Now for the second part of the story: some merchants from Sravasti happened to be in Sri Lanka. There they met the young Princess Ratnavali and told her about Buddha, events of his life, and something of his teachings. Ratnavali was fascinated— from her former life's connection. She wrote a letter to Buddha asking for some favor. When Buddha got her request, he arranged for the merchants to present Princess Ratnavali with a likeness of himself. Apparently, the artists were unable to paint his portrait. So Buddha had them trace his shadow on a piece of cotton cloth and color in the outlines. He then instructed them to inscribe some dharma teachings below the portrait, such as the refuge prayer, the Five Precepts, the 12-Fold Chain of Dependent Arising, and the Eightfold Path. And on the back they wrote two inspirational verses for Princess Ratnavali.

A Shrine for Anathapindika

The great donor Anathapindika felt sort of lonely when Buddha was not around Sravasti. When the Tathagata was in town, he used to visit the monastery twice a day if he could. But when Buddha was away, the merchant felt the place was empty. So Anathapindika told Ananda he wanted to build a shrine. To oblige, the Tathagata described three types of shrines—the corporeal, the memorial, and the representational. He decided which was most suitable for Anathapindika:

- ◆ A shrine with a corporeal relic. This type of monument contains the remains of a deceased Buddha or arhat. Obviously, Buddha did not select this type for Anathapindika at Sravasti. (Constructing one of these would come later.)

- ◆ A shrine with a biographical relic, a sacred space that contains something used by a Tathagata or arhat, such as an alms bowl. Because such a relic was available, Buddha decided this type of shrine would make the most satisfying gift to Anathapindika. Buddha chose a sapling from the tree under which he attained enlightenment. He said it should be planted in Sravasti.

> **Buddha Basics**
>
> Had Sri Lankan Princess Ratnavali lived a couple hundred years later, she would have had the same type of shrine that Anathapindika built in Sravasti—a shrine that used a cutting from the bodhi tree as a relic. When King Asoka's daughter Theri Sanghamitta went to Sri Lanka to establish a nun's order, she brought a sapling from the tree under which Buddha awakened.

- ◆ A shrine with a visible symbol or picture. Buddha had a portrait of himself made for Princess Ratnavali. But generally, it seems that the earliest shrines of this representational type used an empty throne, or a footprint to symbolize Buddha's absence from samsara, and a wheel to symbolize the Buddha-dharma.

Prasenajit, as ruler of Kausala, would have been the person to plant the bodhi tree sapling for the new shrine in his capital city of Sravasti, but in recognition of Anathapindika's great faith, he asked the merchant to do the honors. Thus Anathapindika planted the young tree outside the gate of Jeta's Grove, which he'd donated to Buddha. When the tree grew, the Tathagata actually meditated beneath it when he stayed in Sravasti. Needless to say, this wonderful relic shrine provided much solace for Anathapindika and others who visited the site.

Places That Give Happiness

Buddha recognized that after his death the faithful would want to maintain some kind of closeness to him, so as he was dying, he recommended that people who wanted to draw inspiration from enlightened beings should visit the spots where four events of his life took place:

- Birth

- Enlightenment

- First teaching

- Parinirvana

Over the years the sites connected with the four key events in Buddha's life became places of pilgrimage. Buddha wanted people to be happy when they visited these places. And it seems they were. King Asoka built monuments at the sites Buddha recommended—and at many, many more. He commemorated the Awakened One's birth, enlightenment, first teaching, and parinirvana, and made travel to them user friendly. In time, pilgrims came from far and wide to visit the sacred places named by the Tathagata. Noteworthy are two Chinese pilgrims who left fascinating accounts of their pilgrimages.

Enlightening Extras

Two Chinese pilgrims traveled to India in the days when Buddhist tradition was still vibrant in its homeland. Historians and archeologists still use their accounts today to reconstruct the fragments of a tradition that was dead in its homeland for almost a thousand years (from about 1200 C.E. until modern times). Fa-hien left China in 399 C.E. and returned in 414 C.E. It took him six difficult years to reach India, where he traveled widely, including a stop in Sri Lanka. Hiuen-tsang left China in 629 C.E. and returned in 648 C.E. He left a detailed record of his harrowing travels along the Silk Road, through Central Asia and India, complete with distances.

A Wheel Turner's Funeral

As the Tathagata lay dying, he told Ananda how his remains should be treated. He said the monks should not worry about his funeral, however. It was proper for laypersons to take care of it. And because he was dying in territory governed by the Malla tribe, the Mallas should dispose of his remains. So, Ananda went to inform the Malla leaders of the imminent death of the Teacher. They were to do the following to his body, treating a Buddha as a monarch would be treated:

- The body should be wrapped in three layers of cloth in the following order: a new linen cloth, a teased cotton wool, and a new cloth.

- The cloth wrapping process should be done 500 times, all together. That makes 1,500 layers of cloth, if the number 500 is taken literally. In any case, the body is wrapped in three layers of cloth numerous times.

- This cloth-covered body should be placed in an iron vat (or perhaps gold). The vat is then covered with another iron vessel.

- The vessel is placed on a funeral pyre made with many scented substances. Thus the body is cremated.

It's interesting to think that Gautama's final state would have been the same no matter which of the two options for his life he'd chosen. At birth it was predicted he'd turn the Wheel of the Law. So whether he'd stayed in political life instead of taking up a spiritual vocation, the outcome would have been the same: he'd get a Dharmacakrin's funeral.

Sunwise 'Round the Stupa

The cremated remains of the Tathagata were to be placed in a funerary monument known as a *stupa*. The stupa was to be placed at a crossroads. Buddha said that this was the proper burial for monarchs, buddhas, and arhats. Why? Buddha explained as he was dying that people's hearts become peaceful when they come to such a stupa. And this peaceful feeling helps them gain a peaceful rebirth. Such a destiny is helpful for laypersons who have not yet come close to enlightenment.

> **Dharma Dictionary**
>
> A **stupa** is a funerary monument. Normally they contain relics of a buddha or an arhat. They symbolize the body of an enlightened being and sometimes even have eyes painted on them.

The Mallas arrived at Buddha's resting place between to sala trees with perfume, wreaths, and musicians. They honored the Tathagata with six days of song, dance, and music. On the seventh day, they removed his body for cremation. And typical of the holiest persons, no ashes remained. Only small particles of a hard substance known as sarira remained. This sarira is thought to be other than simple bone, and becomes the sacred relic of an enlightened person.

The Tathagata's relics were honored for one week. Then a distribution process began. Hearing of the Buddha's Great Decease, leaders from the region of the Middle Ganges Basin came to pay their respects. Each wanted to receive a portion of the relics to install in their territory. And though the Mallas at first hesitated to part with any, a brahmin named Dona proposed dividing up the remains into eight portions. He further stated that eight stupas should be built all over the region to house the relics. Dona kept the urn and erected a stupa for it, too. One more representative was given the embers from the cremation site to be placed into a stupa. So an initial 10 stupas were built on the occasion of Buddha's Great Decease. These served as pilgrimage sites for the faithful.

After that, stupas became a key focus of lay Buddhist ritual. Even today you'll find the faithful circling stupas sunwise—that is, always going around clockwise keeping the monument to their right side. The stupa is a "stand in" for the Tathagata and is accorded the same type of respect: the faithful always kept Buddha to their right side.

Where Buddha Wasn't

Recall that shrines could be made with relics from a Buddha's body, sacred objects from his life, or symbolic representations. With a limited number of corporeal and biographical relics, people set to work on making representations of the Tathagata. Artists working during the first 500 years after the Tathagata passed away tended to symbolically represent the Teacher in these forms:

- An empty throne

- A footprint

- A wheel

> **Be Mindful!**
>
> Just because the oldest surviving Buddhist art is aniconic—not containing a likeness of Buddha—does not mean that no likenesses of the Master existed before the first century of the Common Era. Who's to say that among perishable items kept by early Buddhists there were no objects containing a likeness of the Tathagata?

People revered the Tathagata because he woke up, not because he was a Sakyan prince. So early representations of Buddha didn't show a human figure. Nirvana was the key to Gautama's message, not his hairstyle! (At least, not at first.) A footprint—hinting at where Buddha was-but-wasn't—became a favorite symbol of awakening. Also an empty throne presented a trace of Buddha, showing where a world emperor no longer sat.

The footprint and empty throne were paradoxical symbols of Buddha's silence. Recall, Gautama taught his disciples to see tathata for themselves. And sometimes he was positively silent, to give others an opportunity for self-discovery. After the Tathagata attained final nirvana, his disciples were to realize Buddha-dharma themselves. They shouldn't cling to their Teacher.

Why Buddha Looks Greek ... or Not

The earliest statues of Buddha from the northwestern corner of Greater India have him looking Greek! That's because the Gandhara sculptures were straight out of Afghanistan—the farthest outpost of Hellenistic culture. By the time anybody got around to sculpting Gautama's human likeness, Alexander the Great had come all the way to the Indus Valley—taking over the Persian Empire, created in Buddha's day by Cyrus the Great, and more!

Alexander decided to return home when his men refused to go into the jungles of India, but died on the way. And though his personal reign was short-lived, Alexander left plenty of Greek culture behind. Greek artistry percolated through Hellenistic culture from the Mediterranean to the northwest edge of Greater India. Thus, thanks to Alexander, it became natural for the artists of Gandhara to sculpt likenesses of interesting people like Buddha.

Enlightening Extras

Alexander the Great (356–323 B.C.E.) conquered territory from Greece to India over a period of 10 years. After coming to the Indus River in 326 B.C.E., his men gave up. So he turned around and died on the way home. Rumor has it that the young Chandragupta Maurya met Alexander and was inspired to start his own empire in 322 B.C.E., centered in the Magadhan capital of Pataliputra. Within two generations the Mauryan Empire included Afghanistan, Kashmir, Bengal, the Deccan Plateau, and everything in between. It fell in 186 B.C.E., some 50 years after Asoka Maurya adopted a policy of nonviolence.

As world communication developed, Gandhara was crossed by trade routes linking China with the Roman Empire. In this fertile environment, King Kaniska (second-century ruler of the Kushan Empire) sponsored a Northern Buddhist council in Kashmir and supported the sculpting of Buddha images. And in fifth-century

Gandhara, two huge Buddha statues were carved into the mountainside in the Bamiyan Valley along a great east-west trade route. The larger statue was 165 feet tall. And here's a fun fact: dharma was preached from the Buddha's nostrils to amplify the sound to pilgrims coming from India and far-off China.

But no more! In March 2001, these treasures were dynamited to rubble under the direction of Taliban leaders in Afghanistan who for religious reasons objected to what they perceived as expressions of "idolatry." (From the Buddhist point of view, these are not idols: they're not worshipped.) In response, the then director-general of the United Nations Education Social Cultural Organization described the destruction as a "crime against humanity," and UNESCO took interest in restoration of the monuments as a way to preserve the ancient culture of Gandhara and attract tourists. Researchers at the Swiss Federal Institute of Technology have reconstructed a 3D digital image of the statues. Their reconstruction is something to watch for in the future.

While Gandharan sculptors were chipping their way into art history, sculptors in Mathura were busy producing figures in a distinctive Indian style. And both took Sakyamuni as a favorite subject. No matter whether Buddha was a Greek-looking mustachioed character or wore a robe with refined Indian folds, artists of each school took advantage of the ancient Indian concept of the great person.

The Marks of a Great Person

India had a ready-made iconography that was easily applied to representations of Gautama when the time was ripe. Remember at Siddhartha's birth, when brahmins detected the marks of a great person on his body? Well, the traditional catalog of 32 major and 80 minor marks gave artists lots of material to use. Here's a sample of the major marks on the bodies of great persons:

1. **A thousand-spoked wheel on the foot:** Buddha's feet were very flexible. This wheel symbolizes the law.

2. **Level feet:** Buddha would walk evenly, not leaving a lopsided footprint. If he wore our shoes, they'd not have one heel worn out more than the other, or be bent to one side.

3. **Sensitive taste buds:** Buddha could extract nutrition from poor foods, and so endure conditions of famine if need be.

4. **Finely webbed fingers and toes:** This allows for flexible movement.

5. **Crystal canine teeth:** Ananda could tell when Buddha was smiling—even when walking behind the Teacher—because these teeth sparkled.

6. **Radiant 10-foot aura:** This indicates the intensity of Buddha's subtle energy, which is very great.

7. **Forty teeth:** These teeth were a single set that did not fall out. In other words, Buddha didn't have a set of baby teeth.

8. **A resonant, deep voice:** The shape of Buddha's tongue, neck, and jaw helped project his voice. Also a pure heart projects words of truth.

9. **A white curled tuft of hair between eyebrows:** This right-curling wisp of hair is prized in Indian culture.

10. **A protuberance on the crown of his head:** This is shown as a royal topknot. It's a sign of wisdom.

> **Be Mindful!**
>
> The tradition of the marks on the body of a great person was part of Indian tradition relating to royalty. It's not clear how many marks were detected on Siddhartha's infant body or whether later tradition simply wanted to symbolically emphasize Gautama's greatness. In any case, the royal marks of a great person inspired the artistic representations of Buddha's body in painting and sculpture.

Indian art is full of symbolic meaning. Take hair, for example. Traditionally in India the topknot (ushnisha) was linked to royalty. The topknot was a favored hairstyle for Buddha and took on the connotation of wisdom. Developing the hair symbolism, artists gave monks and arhats shaved heads to indicate renunciation of the world. Later, Mahayana Buddhists became fascinated with bodhisattvas—those saints who teetered on the brink of nirvana to serve others. Bodhisattvas would have long, bound hair as a sign of being in the world, but not of it.

Now, Put Your Hands Together for ...

Indian culture had a repertoire of *mudras* in store for the artists of awakening. With simple hand gestures, the Tathagata's body could convey deeper meanings and add a layer of symbolic meaning to the artwork. Here are some key mudras in Buddhist iconography:

- **Turn the dharma wheel.** Thumb and index finger of each hand touch at heart level, while remaining three fingers face upward. Right palm faces out. Left palm faces in.

- **Touch the earth.** Right hand drapes over knee and reaches down to touch the earth, while left hand rests palm up in lap.

- **Fear not.** Right hand is raised to shoulder level, while left hand rests palm up in lap. Right palm faces out in friendship, showing that no weapon is kept.

Dharma Dictionary

A **mudra** is a sacred hand gesture with symbolic meaning. Mudras were widely used in Indian dance, yoga meditation, and iconography. Several mudras traveled throughout the world as Buddhist artists represented the Tathagata and various bodhisattvas.

- **Meditate.** Both hands on lap, right upon left, palms up with thumbs touching. Amitabha, the Pure Land Buddha of Boundless Light, bends index fingers at middle knuckle, contacting thumbs.

- **Give compassion.** Left hand hangs gently at side facing forward, palm open. The feeling of compassion is unassuming and reaches down to help. Can be combined with raised right hand gesturing fear not.

Three Postures

Buddha's posture was full of grace. Sometimes the Awakened One's radiance is tacked onto a sculpted or drawn figure in the form of a halo. But here's where a statue or picture could never match the living, breathing form of one who has penetrated the depths of reality. Even the most beneficent smiles on the most wonderfully rendered Buddha images can't come close to the meeting of one's own mind with the Tathagata. Ultimately, the light of wisdom and compassion must shine through one's own consciousness. Nevertheless, Buddhist art has shown Gautama with beauty in various positions, including the following:

- **Standing.** Standing Buddha statues are sometimes extremely tall, with height symbolizing the great extent of virtue.

- **Seated in meditation.** This can be a peaceful looking figure or a skeletonlike starving Siddhartha. The seated figures show lots of variation in hand gestures.

- **Lying in lion's pose.** Sakyamuni lies on his right side, with right arm bent to hold up his head—as he did on passing to final nirvana.

Traces of Buddha Seep Out of India

While Buddhism was extending roots far beyond India, curious developments took place in the homeland itself. A kind of Indian yoga known as tantra filtered into Mahayana practice. And from it, a wonderful art of awakening developed in Tibet, after Buddhist yogi scholars carried tantric ritual over the Himalayas. Some tantric influence was felt in East Asia, too. But China, Korea, and Japan had their own ritual and artistic contributions to make.

> **Buddha Basics**
>
> Tantra yoga works on the body's subtle nervous system through visualization of prana (breath) running through energy centers, channels situated along the spinal column. Mandalas and mudras are used frequently in tantric ritual.

Tantra in Tibet

The art of awakening in Tibet is connected with ritual visualizations. A sacred iconography developed among sculptors and painters of colorful thangkas. Proper mathematical proportions are of key importance in the creations. And the artist should be able to visualize the form of the figure clearly before bringing it into material being. The eyes are always done last—painted on both statues and thangka images with special prayers of consecration.

Meditators are also involved in the art of awakening. The human body as well as the whole universe are regarded as works of art—and are made sacred through tantric Buddhist visualizations. As Mahayana practitioners, both artists and meditators include numerous bodhisattvas, or beings of enlightenment, among the figures visualized. Beyond that, specially trained monks perform tantric rituals for world peace and other compassionate objectives. They create sacred representations of the cosmos in the form of elaborate sand mandalas (cosmic diagrams) around 5 square feet big—which they sweep up at the ritual's end.

The Big Zero in Japan

Zen Buddhists of East Asia appreciate the symbol of Buddha's silence. Maha Kasyapa had realized Buddha's mind when Sakyamuni simply held up a flower and spoke no words. He thus became the first Zen patriarch. In that spirit of silence, those who practiced in Maha Kasyapa's lineage became minimalist in their art of awakening.

Dharma Dictionary

Enso is the term in Zen calligraphy for a great empty circle, mostly drawn with a single brushstroke. It shows the simplicity of enlightenment and the interconnectedness of all things. The skill with which it's drawn reflects the degree of enlightenment—or beginner's mind—of the artist.

With the *enso*, Zen Buddhists captured what they loved best: emptiness. They captured the heart of Buddha-dharma with the great empty circle. With one stroke of the brush, a circle of ink appears on paper. With one breath, the calligrapher presents a trace of awakening and captures the Buddha's mind in silence. Painting the enso became a key ritual in Zen art, symbolizing Buddha and dharma—which are not-two. The simple, ritual painting expresses tathata. That's it!

The Least You Need to Know

- ◆ Buddha taught that shrines could have bodily relics, sacred objects from his life, or visual representations as an aid to spiritual practice.

- ◆ The earliest surviving representations of Buddha were symbolic—including footprints, empty thrones, wheels, and stupas.

- ◆ In the first century of the Common Era, Buddhists began sculpting likenesses of the Master, both in Gandhara (Afghanistan) and in Mathura (India).

- ◆ Buddhist iconography is based on traditions of ancient India, including the royal marks of a great person, symbolic hand gestures, and postures.

- ◆ The Buddhist art of awakening changed to fit different cultural practices—including tantric visualizations in Tibet and calligraphy in Japan.

All's Well That Ends Well

In This Chapter

- ◆ Overview of Buddhist history
- ◆ The First Buddhist Council
- ◆ Buddhism splits into Theravada and Mahayana
- ◆ Buddha-dharma in the Middle East
- ◆ Modern spread of Buddhism

The 2,500-year history of Buddhism resembles the passing of an Olympic torch from one geographic region to another. As if a torch really had been passed, Buddhism seemed to pick up new life in one place as it lost light in the other. And as in a marathon, the torch was passed regularly—just about every 500 years. The Tathagata's tradition had a lasting impact throughout Asia, stimulating individuals and societies for 2,000 years. During the past five centuries, however, it began to be questionable whether the torch would pass.

In this final chapter of your book on Buddha's life, we begin with a historic overview of Buddhism. It's impossible to detail the entire development of Buddhism here, but that's okay. You can read plenty of books later to fill out 2,500 years of history! We'll just linger a while in the early days of Buddhism to see how Gautama's tradition got off the ground in India. Then we'll see how Buddhism made its way to the West. Finally, we'll ask what Buddha-dharma can offer us in the here-and-now, as the sixth 500-year period of Buddhism on the planet begins.

Peeling Off Pages of History

It's not easy to chart the development of Buddhism in a few words. But here's a quick list that shows the path traversed by the dharma torch every 500 years. Take a look at the map in this chapter to follow along. And don't hesitate to peruse Appendix C to follow up on what interests you.

- **500 B.C.E.–1 B.C.E.** The torch is lit in the Middle Ganges Basin. Buddhism is established there and spreads to the edges of Greater India (Sri Lanka and Afghanistan). A string of official councils clarify and preserve Buddha's teachings. Finally somebody writes them down in Pali.

- **1 C.E.–500 C.E.** Foreign influences fertilize Greater India at the edges. Buddhism splits into two branches: Sri Lanka takes Theravada, and Afghanistan takes Mahayana. From there Buddha-dharma rides a powerful wave into South, Central, and East Asia. Through trade, Buddhism gets exposure in Persia. The Buddha image is born, and Buddha-dharma gets put into foreign languages.

- **500 C.E.–1000 C.E.** Streams of Buddhism flow back and forth through Asia. A meditation tradition trickles from India into China. Tibet gets exposed from India. And Buddhism flows from China into Japan (through Korea). Islam replaces Buddhism in western areas, during the final century of this period. The Chinese Buddhist canon is fully printed.

- **1000 C.E. –1500 C.E.** Second waves of Buddhism enter Tibet from India, and into Japan from China. These enliven Buddhist arts—thangka painting in Tibet and the ways of Zen in Japan. By 1200, Buddhism transforms itself, blends into Hinduism, and fades away in India!

- **1500 C.E.–2000 C.E.** The Buddha-dharma settles and suffers in Asia. Tibet sees the age of Dalai Lamas come and go. And Buddhism faces serious political challenges from communism in parts of Russia, Mongolia, China/Tibet, Vietnam, Laos, and Cambodia. Finally Buddhism shows new signs of life. It trickles back to India and begins streaming into Europe and the Americas.

- **2000 C.E.–The future.** The Buddhist torch passes to Europe and the Americas. Age of Socially Engaged Buddhism begins. Buddhism converses with science. Where does Buddha-dharma go from here?

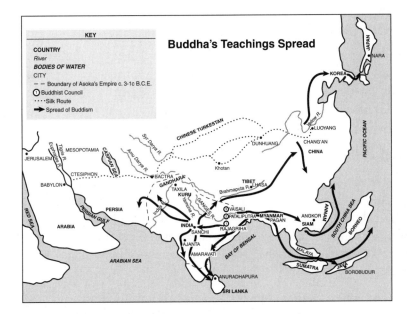

The 2,500-year spread of Buddha's teachings. During 500-year periods, the tradition settles in Greater India, including Afghanistan and Sri Lanka; spreads in all directions; crisscrosses Asia, but is muted by Islam west of India; dies in India, but is revitalized in Tibet and Japan; maintains itself or else perishes under communism, reenters India, and finds new ground in Europe and the Americas; holds promise for the future—who knows where.

Who's Who at the First Buddhist Council

Whenever a genius introduces a radical new viewpoint to a culture, there's bound to be some confusion after that person leaves. What was meant? What should we do now? How do we continue? Should we change anything? To help resolve such questions, several general councils of high-ranking Buddhists took place in this first 500 years after the Tathagata passed away. By the time of a fourth council, the decision was made to capture Buddha's teachings in writing.

Ananda and Upali Come Through

During the first rains after Buddha passed away, 500 arhats—that wonderful symbolic number meaning "a lot"—assembled to hold a council in Rajagriha. Maha Kasyapa called the council, and King Ajatasatru sponsored it. The assembly's task was to decide what should be handed down as Buddha's teachings. So in 483 B.C.E., the arhats grouped all the teachings into two main divisions: dharma and vinaya. And two arhats in the assembly took responsibility to present these baskets of teaching orally from memory.

Ananda, Buddha's cousin, recited Gautama's dharma discourses, as he remembered them from more than two uninterrupted decades at the Tathagata's side. Ananda's presentation served as the foundation for the Buddhist sutras.

Upali, the former Sakyan barber, recalled many stories to remind the group of situations that had caused new rules to be made for their community. Upali's presentation served as the foundation for the Buddhist vinaya—including the pratimoksha, which contained more than 200 monastic precepts.

Who Didn't Recite ... and Why

Ananda and Upali weren't the only arhats who had knowledge of Buddha's teaching. But they were the stars of the show at the First Buddhist Council—because others either had passed away or didn't speak up. The Tathagata's two chief disciples, Sariputra and Maudgalyayana, had already died—so they didn't speak. Gavampati, Purana, or Maha Kasyapa himself might have enriched the council's store of knowledge, but they didn't take on the task.

The assembly of arhats initially wanted Gavampati to come to Rajagriha to recite Buddha's teachings. He'd been close to Sariputra, the wisest of Gautama's disciples and was thoroughly familiar with both the dharma and vinaya. But Gavampati declined the invitation to attend the council. After the messenger confirmed that both Sariputra and Buddha had passed away, Gavampati entered nirvana from his mountain retreat instead of coming to Rajagriha.

The arhat Purana might have recited some teachings not covered by Ananda, but he apparently chose not to. He arrived at the council late, and after the content of Ananda's recitation was repeated for him, Purana simply said he preferred to keep what he'd personally heard from Buddha's mouth. Beyond that, nothing is recorded from him.

Maha Kasyapa, leader of the council, had special insight into the Buddha-dharma from a silent *Flower Sermon* Buddha had delivered to him. But this teaching he passed on silently to Ananda. In turn, Ananda passed on this piece of Buddha-dharma silently … and so it went on through a wordless lineage. Unlike Ananda's oral recitation in the midst of the whole council, the insight passed during Buddha's Flower Sermon to Maha Kasyapa, and Ananda remains a silent and unwritten transmission to this day.

Dharma Dictionary

The **Flower Sermon** is a teaching Buddha gave on Vulture Peak, in which he held up an Udambara flower and spoke no words. Only Maha Kasyapa smiled, indicating that he'd received the Dharma transmission and was enlightened. This silent transmission began the tradition known as Dhyana (Meditation), which is pronounced Ch'an in China and Zen in Japan.

Second Council Schism

One hundred years after the first council—in 383 B.C.E.—the Buddhist arhats held a follow-up meeting in a city about 100 miles from Rajagriha. Can you guess where? It was in Licchavi territory, north of the Magadhan capital, across the Ganges—in a city famous for its celebrations: Vaisali. But, by that time of the Second Buddhist Council, our friends Amrapali the courtesan-turned-nun, and Vimalakirti, the wise and wealthy Licchavi layman, would have passed away. Yes, every one of the folks you've befriended in this book would have passed away—except Maha Kasyapa, who was stuck in the mountain crag at Vulture Peak.

Buddha Basics

Soon after the First Buddhist Council, Maha Kasyapa decided to pass away. In meditation, he entered the cliff face at the summit of Vulture Peak. He took the robe given by Sakyamuni, to keep it for Maitreya, the future Buddha. Meanwhile, Maitreya is waiting in Tushita Heaven until earthlings forget Gautama's teachings. Then he'll reintroduce the Buddha-dharma and get the robe. In turn, Maha Kasyapa will pass to nirvana.

Is it any wonder that by this time people were disagreeing about what Buddha taught and what he intended? Issues came up about the holiness of arhats, the role of laypersons, and the nature of nirvana. What shook out were the beginnings of a split into two main branches of tradition that we see today: Theravada and Mahayana.

A majority of monks actually broke away and held an alternate council. And 18 schools (sometimes called the Hinayana schools) came out of this schism. Today's Theravadins, or Southern Buddhists, are the only survivors among all these.

One party disagreed with all the Hinayana schools. They called themselves the Great Assembly (Mahasanghikas) because they thought the spiritual path—and council participation—should be open to laypersons as well as monks and nuns. These Buddhists became today's Mahayanists.

Third Council, Third Basket

A third Buddhist council was held just more than a hundred years after the second. In 250 B.C.E., the famous King Asoka (274–236 B.C.E.) wanted to clarify and preserve Buddha's teachings—so he called the assembly. At this time, the oral texts of the Buddhist canon known as the *Tripitaka* (the Three Baskets of Teaching) were basically completed. Arhats had felt the need to comment on the sutra material and make it more systematic. So a new basket of literature called abhidharma was added to the sutra and vinaya baskets.

Get It in Writing!

As time passed, the oral transmission of dharma was endangered. So in the first century B.C.E., a fourth council was held for Theravadins. It happened in Sri Lanka, where Asoka's son and daughter set up orders for monks and nuns. Finally, the Tripitaka was put into writing. These writings formed the basis of the oldest Buddhist canon, the Pali Theravada, or Southern Buddhist scriptures. Gradually new works were composed in Pali, as well as in Sanskrit. Then the Mahayana or Northern Buddhist scriptures were compiled. In turn those spread and were translated from Sanskrit to Chinese, Tibetan, and onward. Now, in our own day, translations of both canons are available in Western languages.

After the Southern Buddhist council, Buddhists occasionally held assemblies. For example, King Kaniska in the second century C.E. called a fourth council for Mahayanists in Kashmir. But due to differing viewpoints, universal councils had become a thing of the past. Only nowadays, some people are hoping for a return to widespread cooperation between Theravada and Mahayana Buddhists. One big project on the table is reviving a Theravada nuns' sangha (which had been lost) and developing a full-fledged Tibetan Mahayana nuns' sangha (which never completely formed).

Buddha Basics

King Asoka's daughter and son (third c. B.C.E.) started sanghas for nuns and monks in Sri Lanka. Political turmoil (eleventh or twelfth c. C.E.) wiped them out. But just the male sangha was reinstated—through ordinations by Thai monks. Nowadays, the only surviving women's lineages tracing back to Buddha are in China, Taiwan, Korea, and Vietnam. But these are Mahayana lineages. So many Theravadins say they're not legitimate. Even so, since the 1980s, Western and Asian women of both Theravada and Mahayana branches began spinning off of them.

What's Up with the West?

Isn't it curious that the movement of Buddhism seems to have flowed basically from India to the east and not the west? Well … the impact of Buddhism in South, Central, and East Asia is easy to see. But there's a lot that remains to be researched about the impact of Buddhism in Afghanistan and Persia. King Asoka sent missions in the third century B.C.E. to Afghanistan. Then Kaniska, the second ruler of the Kushan Empire (1–3 c. C.E.) took up the cause of Buddhism, seeing himself as a second Asoka, who'd been the only Buddhist ruler up to that time. From Afghanistan, it flowed into Persia. Buddhism faded with the fall of the Kushan Empire, and lost its cultural impact with the advent of Islam in the seventh century.

In the early thirteenth century, the Mongols conquered Persia and reintroduced some Buddhism. But, by and large, a great monotheistic Islamic buffer had been established, fanning out from Arabia between India and Europe. On land from the western edge of Greater India across the Middle East and the Mahgreb into Spain, Muslims left the footprint of monotheism. In that atmosphere, a nontheistic tradition such as Buddhism fell out of favor, and remains so to this day.

Folk Tales Go Where Religion Cannot

Trade along the Silk Road was a key reason Buddhism could spread from India to China as well as to Persia. And what went along the trade routes? Books and art objects, among other things. In this way the Pancatantra, a collection of Indian fables related to the Buddhist Jataka Tales, made its way to the western and eastern endpoints of the Silk Road. It was translated into Persian in the sixth century C.E.

Enlightening Extras

The Pancatantra is a set of moral observations (with political undertones) put into the mouths of animals. It's among the most influential Sanskrit works of world literature, forming the basis of Aesop's Fables—and even impacting The Arabian Nights and the stories of Sinbad. The original text dates from the second century B.C.E. But starting in the sixth century, the text was translated first into Persian, then later into Arabic, Hebrew, Greek, Latin, and other European languages.

Folk tales percolate through a culture with much less difficulty than religious texts. Even when religious ideas are rejected due to differences in belief, folk tales are easily modified to suit changing cultural circumstances. So although Indian religion didn't survive in countries of the Middle East and points west, some threads remain. And a lot more research on Buddhism in Persia (Iran) is yet to be done!

A version of Buddha's life story flowed from India to Europe through Persian and Arabic sources, and a Greek translation was made in the eleventh century (although it's also said that Saint John of Damascus in the eighth century translated it). From there the tale was translated into Latin, Old Slavonic, Ethiopian, and other languages. The story is known as Barlaam and Josaphat—where the name Josaphat is based on the Persian word Budasif, for Bodhisattva, and refers to Siddhartha. In the Christian version of the story, a character from India named Josaphat comes to enlightenment through love of Jesus Christ.

Buddha Basics

The first Buddhist peoples in Europe were the Kalmyk Mongols. In the seventeenth century, they established Kalmykia along the Volga River, east of the Black Sea in Russia. These Mongols practiced Mahayana Buddhism as developed by the Tibetans.

Jacopo de Voragine included a short version of the Barlaam and Josaphat story in his thirteenth-century medieval sourcebook known as The Golden Legend. And generally the story was hugely popular among Europeans of the Middle Ages. On the Greek Orthodox calendar, August 26 is dedicated to Josaphat; November 27 is the date he commands according to a traditional Roman list of heroes. Indeed, a saint or two in Roman Catholic circles even carry the name of Josaphat. So there he was—India's Bodhisattva—lodged in the nooks and crannies of European culture.

Enlightenment Times Two

In the European Middle Ages Josaphat (that is, Buddha) was regarded as a Roman Catholic holy man. But people didn't even realize that the story of Josaphat was a

Christianized version of Buddha's story! It would take almost 500 more years for Europeans to begin a study of Buddha's teachings. Europeans had to go through a process of freeing themselves from the strict bonds of religious authority that came with the Holy Roman Empire.

The *Enlightenment* or *European Enlightenment* was an intellectual movement within what historians call the Age of Reason in European culture. The Enlightenment (typically dated from the 1700s) was marked by challenges to religious and political authority in the name of human reason and rights. The work of Baruch Spinoza, Voltaire, David Hume, and other philosophers in the seventeenth and eighteenth centuries pushed the envelope of free thought. And only after the climate of authoritarianism in Europe lightened up could people begin to speak of things such as Buddha's enlightenment.

> **Dharma Dictionary**
>
> The **Enlightenment** or **European Enlightenment** was an intellectual movement dating from the seventeenth century that stressed reason over blind faith and obedience. It opened the way for challenges to religious and political authority, scientific thinking, and the field of biblical criticism.

Arthur Schopenhauer (1788–1860), a famous German thinker born in what's now Poland, was probably the first European philosopher to be influenced by Buddhism. Schopenhauer really thought Buddhism would be valuable for the West. What did he like about Buddhism? Buddha's ethics, because he considered animals as sentient beings, rejected discrimination based on social class, and was concerned with human suffering. He also appreciated Gautama's ideas on overcoming illusion.

After Schopenhauer, gradually more interest in Buddhism developed among Europeans. In the 1870s, Edwin Arnold wrote a biography of Buddha called The Light of Asia. It jumped the ocean and became the first popular Buddhist book in the United States. Following that was Herman Hesse's novel based on Buddha's life, called Siddhartha, which was first published in German in 1922 and subsequently became a hit in America.

> **Buddha Basics**
>
> The first Buddhist temple in America was built in 1853 in San Francisco for the immigrant Chinese community. By 1900, there were around 400 Chinese temples, containing elements of Confucianism, Taoism, and Buddhism.

Crossing the Oceans Blue

But who brought the Buddha-dharma across the oceans into America? The spirit of the European Enlightenment had already hit what became the United States of

America in the form of the American Revolution and skipped back over the Atlantic Ocean for the French Revolution (1789–1799). In the wake of this transplanted European Enlightenment activity, Buddhism entered the intellectual life of Americans in the mid-1800s when Ralph Waldo Emerson (1803–1882) and Henry David Thoreau (1817–1862) founded the philosophical/literary movement known as transcendentalism. They both had a deep appreciation for Buddhism and the philosophies of India.

The first American to convert publicly to Buddhism was Henry Steel Olcott, a co-founder of the Theosophical Society, established in 1875. And while New England intellectuals were seeking Buddhist ideas from across the Atlantic Ocean, Chinese immigrants seeking employment sailed the Pacific Ocean to the New World, bringing with them a Buddhist cultural heritage that first took root in California. So Buddhism trickled into America across oceans on both its east and west coasts. The Americas represent a new front for the Buddha-dharma in the sixth 500-year period of its history on the planet.

Coming Full Circle

But how about Buddha-dharma in the land of its birth? Buddhism had been missing in India since around 1200 C.E.! And it's still only back in bits and pieces. Three main sources now water the withered vines of Buddha-dharma on Indian soil: the commitment among lower caste Indians perpetually seeking release from mental and social suffering; the devotion of Tibetan Buddhists in exile; and the dedication of the Tathagata's spiritual children worldwide.

Bhimrao Ramji Ambedkar (1891–1956) was a leader of India's dalit (untouchable) community who reintroduced Buddhism to the lowest strata of Indian society. The movement, known as Neo Buddhism, is contained mainly in two of India's provinces, and is followed primarily by people who traditionally have been kept out of the Hindu varna system. The Neo Buddhists have modified their social customs to conform to Buddhist precepts when practical, and they are devoted to social transformation.

Tenzin Gyatso (1935–), better known as the fourteenth Dalai Lama has reintroduced the Buddha-dharma to India and to many parts of the world including the West. In 1959, he felt compelled to escape to India from Tibet because the Chinese communist takeover of his country meant devastation for Buddhism. As a Dalai Lama, Tenzin Gyatso's responsibility to the Tibetan people was (and is) to preserve the Buddha-dharma. As head of the Tibetan government-in-exile (seated in Dharmsala, India), the Dalai Lama works tirelessly to make the Buddha-dharma available to anyone interested.

Thanks to the efforts of the Dalai Lama and other exiled Tibetans, Buddhist renunciate sanghas have grown up in India, and worldwide. A generous Indian government provided land to exiled Tibetan monks in southern India. And though it was jungle, they cleared it and built some Tibetan Buddhist monasteries (and still had ample land to cultivate for sustenance).

Beyond the Indian community of Tibetans in exile, there is a growing community of Sakyaputriya sramanas concentrated in Bodh Gaya, the site of Gautama's awakening. From every country in which Buddhism has life, "children of the Sakyan" have come to India to practice their renunciate life in Buddhist temples. This activity has made Bodhgaya once again a great place of pilgrimage. Buddhism has come full circle, back to India.

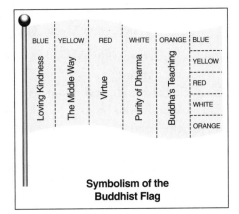

Symbolism of the
Buddhist Flag

Buddhist flag. Six colors of light radiated from Buddha's body: blue, yellow, red, white, orange, and a combination of the five. They are depicted on the Buddhist flag, adopted in 1952 by the World Buddhist Congress.

Buddhism, Here-and-Now

Buddhism has taken on a new vitality in recent years. Here's a sample of what Buddha-dharma brings into the sixth 500-year period of its history, which began in the year 2000:

- Buddhist classics have been translated into Western languages, and the establishment of several Buddhist presses is spawning new translations and original commentaries on the Buddha-dharma.

- The revival of the Theravada, and enhancement of Mahayana Buddhist nuns' orders, is ongoing. Buddhist nuns are communicating in international conferences and have hopes for a great future.

- Interest in Buddhist philosophy is strengthening among scholars at universities in Japan, the United States, and elsewhere.

Be Mindful!

A sign of Buddhism's spread to the west is the Buddha image turning up in popular culture. Buddha appears in cartoons, on T-shirts, and as a lawn ornament throughout the Western world. Is this a sign of the degeneration of Buddhism or an indication of people's wish to acquaint themselves with the Man Who Woke Up in India so many years ago?

- Buddhist leaders—such as the Tibetan Dalai Lama (1989 Nobel Peace laureate), the Vietnamese Thich Nhat Hanh, and others are traveling around the world inspiring new and seasoned practitioners.

- Grassroots, socially engaged Buddhists are working in South Asia to better the lives of the poor in Thailand under the leadership of Sulak Sivaraksa, and the Dalits in India inspired by B. R. Ambedkar, for example.

- A new ethics of Buddhist environmentalism is being developed and implemented by people such as Joanna Macy, Kenneth Kraft, and others.

- The growth of Buddhist centers worldwide is bringing Buddha-dharma into mainstream western society. As of the year 2000, a modest 6 percent of the world population identified as Buddhist (or approximately 376 million adherents), but many others are taking an interest in how the Buddha-dharma can further the needs of personal and social transformation.

All's well that ends well. In the 1500s, William Shakespeare wrote a play by that title, and it applies to the coming 500 years of Buddhism on the world stage. Shakespeare described a series of misadventures that culminated in a happy ending. And when it seemed that the torch wouldn't be passed in the most recent 500-year period of Buddhism's life, both a new and an old front opened up: Buddhism began growing roots in the West and reviving on the withered vine in India. This appears to be a happy outcome. The tradition stoked its embers after a considerable period of merely flickering in some Asian countries and after being all but snuffed out by communism in others.

The Least You Need to Know

- Buddhist history can be described in terms of five 500-year periods in which different geographic areas were influenced. The sixth period is just starting, with the West as a vital new arena.

- Three important Buddhist councils were held about a century apart, starting in the first rainy season after Buddha passed away. Afterward, the tradition was too large and varied to call such meetings.

- The long-term creative activity of Buddhism historically has been concentrated in Asia rather than the Middle East, although some early influence in Afghanistan and Persia was felt.

- Europe became receptive to Buddhism during the European Enlightenment (eighteenth century), in which thinkers emphasized reason and challenged religious and political authoritarianism.

- In modern times, Buddhism reentered India after about 700 years and made its way west to Europe and the Americas.

Glossary

abhidharma   The systematic presentation of major concepts set forth in the sutras. The last basket of the Buddhist Tripitaka to be written. Differs among various schools of Buddhism.

abodes of Brahma   Four levels of boundless consciousness known as the social virtues that a meditator can experience: loving-kindness, compassion, sympathetic joy, and equanimity. These exist in a realm of pure form within samsara and are inhabited by the Indian deity Brahma. Brahmavihara in Sanskrit.

anatman   Sanskrit term for nonself. Buddha's key insight about the nature of who we are. We are composed of a dynamic combination of mind and matter. We exist—but not as static entities. A stream of consciousness, not an atman or soul goes from life to life. *See also* sunyata.

anger   Mental formation with many variants, all of which create negative karma, and cause suffering. Also called revulsion, ill will, and hatred. Spin-offs include wrath, malice, rage, and vindictiveness. *See also* Three Poisons.

Arya Satya   Sanskrit term for Buddha's teachings, translated as Noble Truths or Great Facts. Arya = great or noble. Satya = fact or truth. Buddha named four Great Facts.

attachment   Synonym of clinging, thirst, greed, or craving. It signifies being mentally entrapped by things and ideas—most fundamentally to the idea of an independent self. Buddha taught that attachment leads to suffering. *See also* Three Poisons.

attention and awareness   Complementary terms that refer to two branches of meditation (bhavana) in Buddhism: serenity and insight. Samatha or serenity meditation results in a continuum of samadhi experiences. Vipasyana or insight meditation results in wisdom that recognizes the Three Marks of Existence: impermanence, nonself, and suffering.

Axial Age   Period between 800 and 200 B.C.E. in which thinkers from the Mediterranean to Yellow seas played a pivotal role in the shift of thinking toward individual responsibility. A sample of figures with their B.C.E. dates: Zoroaster (626–551), Jeremiah (627–586), Ezekiel (620–570), Thales (625–547), Pythagoras (581–507), Heraclitus (540–480), Parmenides (515–450), Socrates (470–399), Mahavira (599–527), Confucius (551–479).

bhavana   Sanskrit word for mental cultivation or meditation. Buddhist meditation has two branches of meditation that develop serenity and insight respectively—samatha and vipasyana. Right effort, right recollection, and right contemplation on Buddha's Eightfold Path all pertain to bhavana. *See also* attention and awareness.

bodhicitta   Mind (citta) of awakening (bodhi) in Sanskrit. When a person generates this wish and determination to free sentient beings from suffering he or she becomes a bodhisattva. *See also* bodhisattva (in Appendix B).

Brahmacarya   Striving for Brahman. More generally, it means a spiritual path. It implies a celibate life due to the move from home to homelessness.

Brahmanic   Describes the second phase of Aryan culture, embedded in the Ganga-Yamuna Doab between 900 and 500 B.C.E. Sacrifice became the key ritual in this period, so both priests and their handbooks were called Brahamanas—meaning possessors of Brahman or spiritual energy.

Buddha-dharma   Term for Buddha's teachings, sometimes simply called dharma.

compassion   One of the social virtues of Buddhism in which a person continually relates to all sentient beings with a mind of boundless compassion that wishes them to be free from suffering. This is not to be confused with pity. Bodhisattvas develop this to its greatest extent.

dana   Giving to the renunciate community. Dana is the main way Buddhist laypersons earn merit for a good rebirth.

delusion   Mental formation with many variants, all of which create negative karma and cause suffering. Often called ignorance or stupidity. Spin-offs include lack of conscience, concealment of one's own faults, and mental fogginess. *See also* Three Poisons.

desire Mental formation with many variants, all of which create negative karma and cause suffering. Also called greed, attachment, lust. Spin-offs include jealousy, hypocrisy, and so on. *See also* Three Poisons.

dharma Sanskrit term meaning law or duty. Buddha's teachings are called the dharma. In broad terms it refers to the underlying law of the universe discovered by Buddha.

dharma-rehearsal A gathering of the renunciate sanghas of monks and nuns on full moon and new moon days to chant religious teachings. As the orders grew, their members recited the pratimoksha, and confessed their transgressions.

dhyana Sanskrit term for the level of consciousness achieved through concentrating one's attention. In Patanjali's Hindu system, the experience of dhyana precedes the experience of samadhi. *See also* ninth dhyana.

divine eye A siddhi acquired through meditation on a luminous circular object that allows a person to see things that come within the range of light radiated from the mind's eye, including distant objects in this world or in other realms of time and space. During Buddha's morning meditation, the virtuous and nonvirtuous who needed his help appeared to him vividly, even if they lived far away when he opened the divine eye. Called divya-cakshu in Sanskrit.

drishti Sanskrit term for view in right view (samyag drishti) on the Eightfold Path. The pupil of the eye or the mind's eye. It is a theory or way of seeing things. The word also is used for a point at which a person looks to keep from toppling over in a one-legged yoga standing pose. Most generally, drishti is used to indicate seeing, viewing, beholding.

Ehi! Means "Come!"—Buddha used this simple and powerful expression, or "Ehi passika!" (Come and see!) in the earliest days to ordain people into the mendicant community. He ordained Bhadra Kundalakesa saying simply, "Ehi!"

Eightfold Path The path to nirvana (freedom from suffering) prescribed by Buddha. The fourth of the Four Noble Truths. *See also* right action, right aim, right contemplation, right effort, right livelihood, right recollection, right speech, right view.

elenchus Greek term for cross-examination. Through cross-examination, Socrates exposed contradictions in a person's assumptions, leading to self-knowledge.

elephant look The poignant moment when Buddha looked at Vaisali for the last time is called the elephant look because he turned his body completely around—full-faced to the right—to gaze upon the city. Elephants likewise turn their whole body around when they want to look at something.

enlightenment   Term for awakening to the actual nature of reality as it is. After Gautama attained enlightenment, he was called Buddha or the Awakened One. *See also* European Enlightenment; tathata.

enso   Japanese term in Zen calligraphy for a great empty circle, mostly drawn with a single brushstroke. It shows the simplicity of enlightenment, and the interconnectedness of all things. The skill with which it's drawn reflects the degree of enlightenment of the artist.

European Enlightenment   An intellectual movement dating from the eighteenth century that stressed reason over blind faith and obedience. It opened the way for challenges to religious and political authority, scientific thinking, and the field of biblical criticism.

fire sacrifice   The Vedic (non-Buddhist) ritual centered on Agni, the deva of fire. Brahmins have performed these from ancient times through today for the sake of ancestors and worldly benefits. However, newer-style religious seekers in Buddha's day turned to inner sacrifice (breathing, fasting, contemplating) to unite the self with Brahman and thus transcend rebirth altogether.

First Buddhist Council   A meeting in Rajagriha of 500 (i.e., many) arhats during the first rainy season after Buddha's final nirvana. Sponsored by King Ajatasatru. Ananda recited Buddha's discourses, and Upali recited the training precepts. These recitations became the basis for the written sutra and vinaya literature later on.

Five Heaps   Five aggregates (components) that make up the person. They work together to construct one's experience. Buddhists claim that there is no self that is independent of these Five Heaps, which are conglomerations of forms, feelings, perceptions, mental formations, and minds. Skandha is heap in Sanskrit.

Five Heinous Crimes   Five acts that prevent a person from reaching enlightenment in his or her lifetime: matricide, patricide, murdering an arhat, wounding a Buddha, causing schism in the sangha. Ajatasatru would have attained his first glimpse of nirvana and thus become a stream entrant if he had not starved his father to death.

Flower Sermon   A teaching Buddha gave on Vulture Peak, in which he held up an Udambara flower and spoke no words. Only Maha Kasyapa smiled, indicating that he'd received the dharma transmission and was enlightened. This silent transmission began the lineage of practice known as Dhyana (Meditation), pronounced Ch'an in China, Son in Korea, and Zen in Japan.

Four Applications of Mindfulness Meditation with mindfulness on the body, feelings, mental formations, and minds. These provide the basic content of right recollection on the Eightfold Path. Mindfulness or recollection is smriti in Sanskrit and sati in Pali. *See also* satipatthana.

Four Great Facts, Four Noble Truths Formulation of Buddha's key teachings on suffering, its cause, its cessation, and the Eightfold Path leading to cessation of suffering.

Four Opponent Powers Four things a person can do to lessen the painful effects of bad karma: take refuge in the Three Jewels, if Buddhist; confess wrongdoings; apply antidotes; and resolve not to repeat.

Great Decease Buddha's act of attaining parinirvana or final nirvana. The culminating moment of Buddha's life, because after this passing away there was no more rebirth for him.

Great Renunciation Buddha's act of leaving worldly life as a Sakyan prince. The turning point in Siddhartha's life when he set out from Kapilavastu, cut his hair, and became a sramana.

investment and savings Policy Buddha recommended to householders at a time when the merchant class was growing rapidly in the Middle Ganges Basin.

Iron Age Copper and bronze were going out of style during the Iron Age. At the start, primitive metallurgists developed iron mainly for weapons, such as arrowheads, spearheads, and knives—and to a lesser extent for tools used to clear land. In India, iron was used in agricultural technology from about the mid-first millennium B.C.E., though it first appeared much earlier. It is interesting that Buddha received his last (indigestible) meal from man who may have been an "iron" worker and was cremated in an iron vessel.

Itivuttaka A collection of 112 sutras in the Buddhist canon. In English it's called The Buddha's Sayings, but literally itivuttaka means "the so was said." The collection was made by Khujjuttara, a royal servant in Kausambi who heard Buddha teach, and then repeated his discourses to Samavati, the consort of King Udena, and other women of the royal palace.

Jataka Tales Birth Stories or tales Buddha told that referred to his past lives. They were written down in the fourth century B.C.E. during the Mauryan period of Indian history, but contain verses that may date back to Buddha himself. These became part of the Buddhist canon.

karma Sanskrit word for action. It refers to the moral law of causation that operates in the universe with inevitable results: virtuous acts bring happiness, nonvirtuous acts bring pain.

kasaya The famous orange-brown dye produced in Varanasi from ancient times until today. Buddhists first used it to color their robes. The name comes from Kasi, the territory in which Varanasi was located. Now it's called Banaras katthai.

kshatriya A member of the warrior, ruling class of ancient India. In the Middle Ganges Basin of Buddha's day, to be a kshatriya meant to be a landed nobleman and not a simple warrior or rajanya. The kshatriyas of the most powerful territories became the monarchs. Over time, not all Indian monarchs were kshatriyas; but as a rule they were expected to come from a strong kshatriya line.

lineage An unbroken chain of relatives that spans generations. A political group of kin that extends back through one parent to an historic or mythic founding ancestor. A spiritual chain of people through whom a certain insight is gained, such as the Meditation lineage extending from Gautama to Maha Kasyapa to Ananda, and so forth.

loving-kindness One of the social virtues of Buddhism in which a person continually relates to all sentient beings with a mind of boundless love that wishes them to be happy.

Middle Way A way to describe Buddha's teachings. It refers to the practical course of moderation between harsh asceticism and lush indulgence and the philosophical rejection of the extreme views of idealism (which posits the independent existence of a self) and nihilism (which radically denies any existent self).

monism The theological doctrine positing a single entity that pervades the entire universe. From the Greek word *monos*, meaning one. Many thinkers of ancient Greece and India were monists. Buddha countered the view of the brahmanical monists who posited an atman or soul that merged with brahman the impersonal spiritual force pervading the universe. *See also* Upanishads.

motivation Buddha identified this as the key indicator of the character of karma one creates. The outcome of an act depends largely on what motivation prompted it.

mudra A sacred hand gesture with symbolic meaning. Mudras were widely used in Indian dance, yoga meditation, and iconography. Several mudras traveled throughout the world as Buddhist artists represented the Tathagata and various bodhisattvas.

ninth dhyana In the third watch of the night of his awakening, Buddha discovered this level of concentration beyond the realm of no form. This ninth dhyana is called the cessation of sensation and perception, which was followed by the experience of experience, and finally, nirvana.

nirvana Sanskrit word that literally means blown out. Highest spiritual attainment that transcends experience itself. Contrasted with samsara or the cycle of existence in which the unenlightened beings must take rebirth. To attain nirvana means to be free from suffering and compulsory rebirth in samsara.

nirvana with remainder The experience of nirvana or peace beyond the ninth dhyana while the meditator is still alive. It can be sustained for a maximum of seven days.

nontheism Religious perspective that does not involve worship of a deity or deities on its spiritual path. Buddha's teachings can be called nontheistic, rather than atheistic because they have a spiritual component.

Northern Buddhism A way of describing the Mahayana branch based on geographical distribution. Includes a variety of Buddhist sects of Central and East Asia, such as Pure Land, Zen, Tibetan Buddhism, Shingon, and so on.

parinirvana Sanskrit term for Buddha's final nirvana, attained at the time of his Great Decease in Kusinagara on a full-moon day in the month of Vaisakha.

pratimoksha Part of the vinaya basket of the Buddhist canon, containing major and minor training precepts or rules some 227 for monks, and 311 for nuns. The rules are supposed to help individuals in the community live in harmony and attain enlightenment as quickly as possible. *See also* vinaya.

raja A member of the ancient Indian ruling class. Initially it meant leader in battle. It changes meaning to signify a protector of settlements, or tribal chieftain (such as Buddha's father). The term *maharaja*, great king came into use during the Gupta Empire (c. 320–550 C.E.), along with *rajatiraga*, king of kings, which imitated Persian royalty.

religious symbols Objects representing extraordinary things that cannot be expressed literally.

right action A step on the Eightfold Path in the category of virtue. Involves doing things that help others and minimize suffering. Samyak karmanta in Sanskrit.

right aim Step on the Eightfold Path in the category of wisdom. It refers to the motivation from which our thoughts take shape. With right aim, a person has thoughts of helping (not harming) others … because those thoughts are grounded in the understanding that we are all dependent upon each other. Samyag drishti in Sanskrit.

right contemplation   A step on the Eightfold Path in the category of mental cultivation. Involves samatha, which leads to experiences in the realm of pure form and then in the realm of no form. Samyak samadhi in Sanskrit.

right effort   A step on the Eightfold Path in the category of mental cultivation. Sometimes translated as right endeavor. Vyayama carries the sense of struggle, exertion, striving. Involves work to generate and maintain wholesome states of mind, while avoiding and getting rid of those that are not wholesome. Samyag vyayama in Sanskrit.

right livelihood   A step on the Eightfold Path in the category of virtue. Involves earning one's living in a way that avoids killing sentient beings or unnecessarily harming the environment. Samyag avija in Sanskrit.

right recollection   A step on the Eightfold Path in the category of mental cultivation. Often translated as right mindfulness. To perfect right recollection, Theravada Buddhists practice satipatthana, or the four applications of mindfulness on body, feelings, mental formations, and minds. Samyak smriti in Sanskrit.

right speech   A step on the Eightfold Path in the category of virtue. Involves using one's words to promote happiness and conflict resolution. Speaking Buddha-dharma is one example. Samyag vac in Sanskrit.

right view   Step on the Eightfold Path in the category of wisdom. It refers to the realization of nonself. With right view a person sees things as they are without delusion. This is the one step of the Eightfold Path that is specifically Buddhist. Samyag drishti in Sanskrit.

sacred biography   An account of a person's spiritual journey with three dimensions: literal, mental, and symbolic. These involve historical, psychological, and mystical events.

samadhi   Sanskrit word for subtle states of consciousness attained by keeping one's attention unwavering for long periods of time.

samatha   Sanskrit word for the branch of meditation that brings serenity or calm abiding. It leads initially to samadhi with form and then to samadhi without form, corresponding to experience of the realm of pure form and the realm of no form. *See also* Abodes of Brahma; satipatthana.

samsara   Sanskrit for the cycle of becoming, which is characterized by suffering and rebirth. There are three realms of samsara: (1) the sense desire realm that has devas, titans, humans, animals, hungry ghosts, and hell beings; (2) the realm of pure form that has brahmas; (3) the realm of no form that has four levels of abstract consciousness. Whoever becomes enlightened transcends the compulsion to be reborn into samsara—though for them nirvana paradoxically can exist within samsara.

samvega An inspirational encounter that shocks a person into a new perspective on life and reality. Both art and religion in ancient India deal with these sudden, radical psychological encounters.

samyag, samyak Sanskrit adjective describing every step on the Eightfold Path. Also used to describe the kind of buddha who comes into the world to teach the entire path to enlightenment. It has become usual to translate this as right. It also carries the sense of full, thorough, complete, and supreme.

sangha The Buddhist community. Buddha set up four sanghas: one for monks, nuns, laymen, and laywomen. The Sanskrit term refers generally to either a political or spiritual association. A republic, which is a political-economic union of clan groups, is a gana-sangha or clan association. A bhikshu-sangha is an association of monks. A bhikshuni-sangha is an association of nuns.

satipatthana Pali term for meditating on the Four Applications of Mindfulness: body, feelings, mental formations, and minds. Nowadays, Theravada Buddhists often call the practice vipassana (Pali for vipasyana) or satipatthana vipassana—which is to say, insight meditation through mindfulness. The original instructions for such training come from Buddha's discourse called the *Satipatthana Sutta. See also* Four Applications of Mindfulness.

sentient being Living beings who have sense consciousnesses. All sentient beings abide in samsara and are capable of attaining enlightenment.

seven factors of enlightenment Seven of the most important positive mental formations. The Buddhist tradition treats these in various overlapping contexts. Endeavor, contemplation, and equanimity are among the ten perfections. Endeavor, recollection, and contemplation are the three elements on the Eightfold Path. Joy and equanimity experienced in the Abodes of Brahma. And the two branches of Buddhist meditation involve tranquility on one hand and investigation of dharma on the other.

siddhi A supernormal power. Buddhist texts name six, involving knowledge of (1) Modes of psychic power, (2) Divine ear, (3) Thought reading, (4) Past lives, (5) Divine eye, and (6) Destruction of the fetters. The first five are worldly and result from samatha; the sixth results from vipasyana and applies only to those who've cut the ties of rebirth.

silence   Buddha is famous for his silence on certain metaphysical questions, such as these: Is the world eternal? Or not eternal? Or neither eternal nor not eternal? Or both eternal and not eternal? Does the saint exist after death?

Southern Buddhism   A way of describing the Theravada branch of Buddhism based on geographical distribution. Includes Buddhist countries in South and portions of Southeast Asia, such as Sri Lanka, Myanmar, and Kampuchea. In contrast to Mahayana Buddhists, the Southern Buddhists are fairly homogenous.

stupa   A funerary monument. Normally they contain relics of Buddha or an arhat. They symbolize the body of an enlightened being, and sometimes even have eyes painted on them.

sunyata   Emptiness. Mahayana Buddhists use this term to indicate that all phenomena are nonself. Whereas anatman normally applies to persons, sunyata applies to everything in the cosmos. It's all interdependent or empty.

sutras   Buddha's discourses. First "basket" of the Buddhist canon. *See also* Tripitaka.

tantra   Type of yoga that works with the body's subtle nervous system through visualization of subtle breath running through subtle energy channels, and centers situated along the spinal column. Mandalas and mudras are used frequently in tantric ritual. Sophisticated tantric visualizations impacted the art of awakening in Tibet.

tathata   Sanskrit term for thusness. Reality as it is with no preconceptions. It's the "just so" perspective on existence that enlightened people have when they perceive reality as no more and no less than it is in the moment. Realizing thusness means penetrating the surface appearance of things to notice that everything is sunyata. Buddha liked to call himself the Tathagata, or one who goes (gata) the way of tathata.

Ten Fetters   Ten negative mental formations a person must destroy to become an arhat and leave samsara. They are destroyed in a particular order, and progress is noted in terms of four stages of sainthood. *See also* saints (in Appendix B).

Ten Perfections   Ten virtues that bodhisattvas cultivate to pave their way to enlightenment: generosity, virtue, renunciation, wisdom, effort, patience, truthfulness, determination, friendliness, and even-mindedness. These frame the Jataka Tales, which relate Gautama's experience through many lifetimes as a bodhisattva before being reborn as Prince Siddhartha. Some Buddhists prefer a list of six perfections: generosity, virtue, patience, effort, meditation, and wisdom.

Three Marks of Existence   Three characteristics that apply to all phenomena in our world: impermanence, nonself, and suffering. Along with nirvana, these form the basis of all Buddha's teachings. A teaching is not "Buddhist" without these four ideas.

Three Poisons   Three mental poisons that ruin our lives, and the lives of others: delusion, revulsion, and desire. (There are many English translations, including ignorance, hatred, greed.) Based in a mistaken view of who we are, they negatively impact our relationship with the environment as well as the beings who inhabit it.

transmigration   Continuation of the spiritual force from one lifetime to the next. Buddhist theory says a transient stream of consciousness transmigrates; Hindus say it's the soul (atman) that goes from life to life.

Tripitaka—Three baskets. It refers to the three sections of the Buddhist canon. *See also* sutras, vinaya, abhidharma.

Upanishads   Texts composed as the "end of the Vedas." Discusses subject of atman and Brahman. The Sannyasins of Buddha's day were carrying on the tradition of composing them.

upasampada   Ceremony of initiation into the sangha of monks or nuns. A person had to be very serious about leading the spiritual life to take this on. It meant spending more and more time in meditation, coupled with teaching and supervising others.

upavasatha   Sanskrit term for the new-moon and full-moon days that Buddhist laypersons use for religious observations. They remove jewelry, wear white clothes, and observe eight precepts: (1) Not to kill, (2) Not to steal, (3) Not to engage in sexual activity, (4) Not to lie, (5) Not to use drugs or alcohol, (6) Not to eat after noon, (7) Not to seek entertainment, and (8) Not to sleep on a high or luxurious bed.

varna   Sanskrit word for caste. There are four varnas, three of which derive from Aryan lineages: brahmins, kshatriyas, and vaisyas. Below these came a caste of sudras. Eventually pancammas (untouchables) were added to the scheme below the sudras.

Vedic   Describes the Aryan culture of western India from about 1200 to 900 B.C.E. So called because worship centered on the gods of the Rig Veda, the oldest of the sacred texts known as the Vedas.

vinaya   Collection of writings on the Buddhist lifestyle, including training precepts. Upali, the arhat who was a former barber recalled this material for members of the First Buddhist Council. *See also* pratimoksha.

Wheel of Becoming   Refers to samsara, where beings cycle around from rebirth to rebirth until they attain nirvana.

Wheel of Dharma   Refers to Buddha's teaching. As a Dharmacakrin he turned this Wheel of the Law.

yojana   A measure of distance used in ancient India. Opinions differ as to the length, generally ranging from 5 to 12.5 miles (8 to 20 km). The *Mahavamsa*, a Sri Lankan chronicle (sixth century C.E.) states that Buddhist viharas (temples) were built at a distance of 1 yojana from each other.

People and Places

Ajatasatru King of Magadha during the last years of Buddha's life. Imprisoned and starved his father, King Bimbisara.

Amitabha The Buddha of Boundless Light who lives in a Pure Land called the Western Paradise. Gautama Buddha used psychic powers to teach Magadha's Queen Vaidehi to gain entrance to Amitabha's Western Paradise through meditation and prayer.

Amrapali Courtesan from Vaisali. Donated mango grove to Buddha. Later joined the nun's order and became a Theri. The amba in her name means "mango" because at birth she was found abandoned in a mango grove.

Ananda Buddha's cousin. Attended Buddha for the last two decades or so of his life. Became an arhat just prior to the First Buddhist Council, where he recited from memory the body of Buddha's discourses that became the core of the Buddhist canon.

Anathapindika Most famous of Buddha's male lay disciples. A sresthi (wealthy merchant) who donated Jeta's Grove in Sravasti.

Anuruddha Buddha's cousin. Monk who was most accomplished in use of the divine eye siddhi. Saw into other realms of samsara, and knew the state of mind of Buddha at the time of his death.

Arada Kalama Siddhartha's first spiritual teacher after he renounced the world at age 29. Under his direction, Siddhartha attained the state of nothing whatsoever—the third of four levels in the realm of no form.

arhat Sanskrit term for a person who attains nirvana and will not be born again into samsara. To become an arhat is the goal of Theravada Buddhists.

Aryan Sanskrit term meaning noble, used with reference to an Indo-European people who overcame the settlements along the Indus Valley and later moved to the Ganga-Yamuna Doab region. Scholars still dispute their place of origin.

Asoka Third monarch of Indian Mauryan dynasty. First Buddhist monarch. Grandson of Candragupta Maurya, founder of the Mauryan Empire. Stopped extending the span of his empire after becoming Buddhist. His daughter and son started sanghas for nuns and monks in Sri Lanka.

Awakened One A literal translation of the word Buddha.

Bhadra Kundalakesa A female disciple of Buddha's. Kundalakesa means curly (kundala) hair (kesa). She was so called because she pulled out her hair by the roots upon joining the Jain mendicant sect, but it grew back thick and curly.

bhikshu/bhikshuni A person who "lives on alms" or begs (mentioned in some older Upanishads). A Buddhist monk (almsman) nun (alsmwoman).

Bhutan A modern-day country whose leader promotes Buddhist values. Its Buddhist king, Jigme Singye Wangchuk, promotes gross national happiness as an answer to gross national product.

Bimbisara Ruler of Magadha. Ousted from power by his son Ajatasatru. Buddha's good friend who donated a bamboo grove to the renunciate community outside of Rajagriha.

Blessed One Term for Buddha, used out of respect.

Bodhgaya Place where Siddhartha attained enlightenment. It was called Urubilva at that time.

bodhisattva A Sanskrit term meaning a being (sattva) of enlightenment (bodhi). The word bodhi (as in buddha) comes from the Sanskrit root budh, to wake up. Buddha was called a bodhisattva before enlightenment. Mahayana Buddhists emphasize the goal of becoming a bodhisattva, vowing to take voluntary rebirth for the sake of others. They are in the world, but not of it. The term Bodhisattva is used as as Gautama's title before he became a buddha. *See also* Buddha's names and arhat.

Brahma   World creator in Indian cosmology. Brahma has four abodes in the realm of pure form. The role of Brahma is always filled, but not with the same being, because brahmas (like all beings in samsara) must eventually die. They live up to 84,000 world cycles and tend to be reborn as humans or devas. *See also* Mara, Abodes of Brahma (in Appendix A).

Brahmacarin   One who seeks to know Brahman, which is the Vedic term for universal energy . Originally from the Upanishads, the term is later applied to all sramanas because they labored to realize the highest spiritual attainment, whether or not they called it Brahman. *See also* sramana; Upanishads (in Appendix A).

buddha   A title used for an awakened person—that is, someone who woke up to *tathata* or reality as it is. The word *buddha* is based on the Sanskrit root budh, which means to awaken. *See also* Buddha's names.

Buddha's names   Many names are used for Buddha. Some are titles, whereas others have historical connections, such as family associations. Certain names are used only before the enlightenment, some only after, some always, and some from the point of the Great Renunciation onward. *See also* Awakened One; bodhisattva; Enlightened One; Maha Sramana; Sakyamuni; Siddhartha; supreme buddha; Tathagata.

Campa   Easternmost place known to be visited by Buddha. Capital of Anga in Buddha's day. Has beautiful Campa flowers. Modern Campanagar.

Candaka   Siddhartha's chariot driver. Explained the Four Sights to Siddhartha and accompanied him when he left the palace of Kapilavastu.

Central Land   A place with four categories of disciples: (1) bhikshus, (2) bhikshunis, (3) sramaneras, and (4) sramanerikas. Alternatively, (1) bhikshus, (2) bhikshunis, (3) upasakas, and (4) upasikas. Contrasted with a Remote Land, which doesn't have these sanghas. *See also* bhikshu/bhikshuni and upasaka/upasika.

deva/devi   A male/female godling. The cosmology of India includes numerous Vedic godlings. Buddhists say they are not enlightened and therefore don't appeal to them for help on the spiritual path. Thirty-two devas plus their leader Indra abide in the Heaven of the Thirty-Three, which is still part of samsara or cycle of rebirth.

Devadatta   Buddha's cross-cousin who joined the order of monks. He tried to kill Gautama three times. They had disagreements in childhood.

Dharmacakrin   Sanskrit term for a great person who turns the wheel (cakra) of law (dharma). Such a person can turn the wheel of political law as a universal monarch or spiritual law as a world savior. *See also* great person.

Dipankara   The supreme buddha who preceded Gautama Buddha. Gautama, eons back in a former life as the ascetic Sumedha, first generated bodhicitta upon meeting Dipankara.

Enlightened One   A literal translation of the word Buddha. A name used for Gautama.

Gandhara   Region in present-day Afghanistan from where early Buddha statues come. The custom of representing Buddha in human form arose here about the same time as in Mathura.

Ganga   River running across northern India. Buddha lived in the Middle Ganges Basin. Great commercial activity developed along this river. Patali and Varanasi are both on it. Also known as Ganges.

Gautama (623–543 or 563–483 B.C.E.)   Family name of the Buddha whose story we follow in this book. This family was part of the Sakya clan.

great person   A fortunate person destined to become a Dharmacakrin. Recognized by 32 major and 80 minor physical traits. Diviners saw these marks on Siddhartha's body, and they were later used in Buddhist iconography.

Himalayan Mountains   The mountain range to the north of India. Buddha was born in the Nepali Terai, the marshy area situated in the foothills of this range at the northern edge of the Middle Ganges Basin.

Kalmyk Mongols   The first Buddhist peoples in Europe. Established Kalmykia along the Volga River, east of the Black Sea in Russia in the seventeenth century. Practiced Mahayana Buddhism as developed by the Tibetans.

Kapilavastu   Capital of the Sakya clan where Siddhartha grew up. Site of the ruins of a stupa that probably housed some Buddha relics. Now a Nepalese village called Piprawa.

Kausambi   Capital of Vamsa one of the four Great Countries in the Ganges Valley. Located west of Varanasi, on the Yamuna River.

Kusinagara   Town where Buddha generally is said to have attained final nirvana. Modern Kasia.

Licchavi   Powerful tribe centered around Vaisali. Part of the Vriji confederacy.

Lord   Respectful term referring to Buddha. This does not connote divinity. Buddha is always seen as a human being.

Lumbini Garden   Pleasure grove in which Siddhartha was born, generally thought to be Rummindei in present-day Nepal.

Magadha   One of four main Great Countries in the northern India of Buddha's day. Capital city was Rajagriha (modern Rajgir). This became the core of the Mauryan Empire under Candragupta and his grandson Asoka Maurya.

Maha Kasyapa   One of Buddha's great disciples. Woke up during Buddha's flower sermon and thus was the first to receive the silent transmission so prized by the Dhyana (Ch'an/Zen) school of Buddhism. Mystically entered the cliff face at the summit of Vulture Peak after the first Buddhist council, where he keeps the robe given by Sakyamuni for Maitreya, the future Buddha.

Maha Prajapati   Siddhartha's mother's sister and foster parent. Requested Buddha to start a bhikshuni sangha.

Maha Sramana   Great Sramana. Appelation given to Siddhartha Buddha. Soon after he left Kapilavastu, the ascetics in Rajagriha called Siddhartha Maha Sramana because he showed unusually "great" (maha) zeal in his spiritual exertions.

Mahavira (599–527 B.C.E.)   Jain leader who lived at the same time as Buddha in the Middle Ganges Basin. Buddha sometimes encountered his disciples. Bhadra Kundalakesa had been a Jain nun before joining Buddha's mendicant sangha.

Maitreya   Name of the future Buddha. Means friendliness in Sanskrit. Waits in Tushita Heaven until Buddha-dharma vanishes from humanity, at which point he'll descend to show the way to enlightenment. The next supreme buddha. *See also* supreme buddha, Maha Kasyapa.

Mara   Lord of Illusion who confronted Gautama on various occasions. Highest deva in the sense desire realm of samsara, who uses illusion to keep people ensnared in the senses.

Mara's daughters   Three daughters of the Lord of Illusion, named Discontent, Delight, Desire. They appear to Buddha before his awakening … though some biographers say they appeared at the end of the fifth week after the awakening.

Master   Term of respect used for Buddha because he had many disciples.

master of dharma exposition   One whose job is to analyze for other disciples what Buddha's stated succinctly. Buddha appointed Katyayana as the first one because he could brilliantly analyze in detail the meaning of what Buddha stated in brief.

Mathura Region in India from where early Buddhist statues come. The custom of representing Buddha in human form arose here about the same time as in Gandhara.

Maudgalyayana One of Buddha's two chief disciples. Foremost in supernormal powers.

Maya Devi Siddhartha's mother. Died when Siddhartha was seven days old. Younger sister of Maya Prajapati.

Nalanda University Illustrious Buddhist university, established in the fifth century C.E. Buddha used to pass through Nalanda centuries before the university was built.

Papa Where Buddha had his last meal, which made him sick and aggravated his dysentery. Modern Padarauna.

Patali Town on the Ganges River with a long history. From a trading town, it grew into a magnificent commercial city known as Pataliputra, which served as the capital of virtually all India during the Mauryan dynasty (323–185 B.C.E.). Modern Patna, capital of the state of Bihar.

Prasenajit Ruler of Kausala, very devoted to Buddha. Ousted from power by his son Virudhaka. He governed from Sravasti but died in front of the gates of Rajagriha after being ousted from power by his son.

Prithvi Earth. A feminine Vedic deity who provides a sacred space for all human spiritual endeavors. Buddhist texts say the earth witnessed the Bodhisattva's practice of the perfections of giving, virtue, and so on. When Siddhartha touched the earth to call her as a witness in front of Mara, a terrific earthquake occurred as Prithvi validated his claim.

Private Buddha A buddha who becomes enlightened without a teacher, in a time when the Buddha-dharma has been lost. They don't teach.

Rahula Buddha's son, who became a sramanera as a 7-year-old. Foremost among disciples in motivation to learn. He passed away before his father did. Name means "fetter," or makes reference to Rahu, the mythical dragon responsible for eclipses.

Rajagriha Capital of Magadha. The "king's abode." An early eastern outpost the ancient Aryans settled due to abundant flakes of iron oxide in the surrounding hills that could be scraped off the rock and turned into tools. The early Magadhan kings began building what became India's first empire, founded by Candragupta Maurya in 322 B.C.E. Vulture Peak is outside the town. Modern Rajgir.

Ratnavali   Sri Lankan princess for whom Buddha had a portrait of himself made.

Rudraka Ramaputra   Siddhartha's second teacher under whom he reached the state of neither perception nor nonperception through samatha meditation.

saints   Theravada Buddhists outline four stages of spiritual progress leading to nirvana: stream entrant, once returner, nonreturner, and arhat.

Sakyamuni   After enlightenment, others called Gautama by this name meaning Sage of the Sakyas, because Sakya was the name of his tribe. *See also* Buddha's names.

Sakyaputriya-sramanas   Term used by outsiders for Buddha's mendicant disciples, meaning mendicant sons or children of the Sakyan.

San Francisco   Place where the first Buddhist temple in America was built in 1853 for the immigrant Chinese community.

Sankisa   Town where Buddha descended after teaching his mother in Tushita Heaven.

Sannyasin   A renunciate brahmin. Traditionally, a sramana is in the last stage of the traditional brahmin life cycle, having left the world after fulfilling duties as a householder. In Buddha's day, these new-style brahmins would skip the householding stage and renounce the world, seeking to know Brahman.

Sariputra   One of Buddha's two chief disciples. A Brahmin named Upatissa who'd studied skeptical philosophy prior to joining the bhikshu sangha. Foremost in wisdom. Rahula's teacher.

Sarnath   The newly realized Buddha gave his first teaching to five ascetics in its Deer Park. It was called Rishipatana. Now a town in northern India near Varanasi.

Siddhartha   A name that some early biographers used with reference to Gautama until he was 36 years old and attained enlightenment. It means One Whose Aim Is Accomplished.

skeptic   A person subscribing to the philosophy of skepticism, which claims one can not know anything for certain. Buddha called skeptics "eel wrigglers" because they wouldn't settle on an answer to questions. Buddha's two chief disciples were students of a leading northern Indian skeptic before joining the bhikshu sangha. Buddha's debt to skepticism shows in his refusal to answer questions such as "Is the world eternal?"

sramana   A laborer in the spiritual life. The word is related to terms meaning to exert, make effort, and strive. Related terms from ancient India include parivrajaka, monk, nun, muni, yati. *See also* Brahmacarin, Sannyasin.

sramanera/sramanerika   A novice monk/nun.

Sravasti   Kausala's capital. Buddha spent about 19 rainy seasons here in Jeta's Grove, and in the park donated by Visakha called the Mansion of Migara's Mother. Modern Saheth-Maheth.

sresthi   Sanskrit word for wealthy person, usually a merchant or banker. A class of such businesspersons grew up in Buddha's day.

Suddhodana   Buddha's father. Head chief of Sakya tribe. Was a raja, but not a monarch.

Sujata   A village girl who offered Siddhartha milk-rice as he sat starving under a tree at Urubilva. It was his last meal before awakening.

Sumedha   Name of "Buddha" in the early incarnation eons ago when he first resolved to become a supreme buddha after an encounter with Buddha Dipankara. *See also* Dipankara.

supreme buddha   The most traditional definition of a Buddha, as one who exhibits all the marks of a great person and descends from a subtle realm called Tushita Heaven, attains enlightenment, turns the Wheel of Dharma, and attains final nirvana. Gautama is said to have been one in a long line of these—perhaps the fourth, seventh, or twenty-eighth. Samyak sambuddha in Sanskrit. *See also* Private Buddha.

Takshasila   A city just northwest of the Indus River that was a major center of Aryan culture in Buddha's day. Located at the northwestern end of the *uttarapatha*, the northern trade route. Brahmins and ksatriyas from the Ganges Basin were sent to Takshasila and further west for a higher education, including medicine, proper Sanskrit, and Vedic rituals.

Tathagata   After waking up, Gautama called himself a Tathagata, or Thus Gone One, because he had gone the way of nirvana (away from the normal condition of suffering in the cycle of existence or samsara).

Teacher   Term used for Buddha because he taught the universal law (dharma) that he discovered.

theri   A woman elder. Accomplished nuns of the Buddhist order were addressed as theri, including Buddha's (former) wife and aunt. A traditional collection of poems composed by these Buddhist elders is called the *Therigatha*. A male elder is a thera.

Tushita Heaven   Heaven of the "contented" devas. The fourth heaven in Indian cosmology above the Heaven of the Thirty-Three (devas), but below the Abodes of Brahma. It's called "contented" because devas there are not plagued with desire though it is within the desire realm of samsara. The Bodhisattva was there before he was conceived in Maya Devi's womb, and the future Buddha Maitreya is there now. Humans (Maya Devi, for example) sometimes are reborn as devas in Tushita Heaven due to their own virtue.

Upali   Barber of the Sakyan nobles who joined Buddha's bhikshu sangha when they did. Recited the vinaya at the First Buddhist Council after Buddha passed away.

upasaka/upasika   A layman/laywoman who temporarily observes Buddhist precepts on new-moon and full-moon days.

Urubilva   Area where Siddhartha attained enlightenment. One of the Kasyapa brothers had a hermitage in this area. *See also* Bodhgaya.

Vaisali   Capital of Vriji confederacy where the Licchavi tribe was settled. Asokan pillar there commemorates Buddha's last sermon. Mahavira's birthplace, Kunpur, is 2.5 miles (4 km) away. Modern Basarh.

Varanasi   Ancient city on Ganges River in the region of Kasi. Holiest city for contemporary Hindus known as Banaras.

Veluvana   Means bamboo grove. An arama donated by Bimbisara, which was an entire village, complete with artisans. This probably became the seat of the first Buddhist monastery in the world. Near Rajagriha.

Vimalakirti   A wise and wealthy layman from Vaisali, famous among Mahayana Buddhists for his realization of emptiness. Those teachings are recorded in a discourse bearing his name.

Virudhaka   Ruler of Kausala who stole the reigns of power from his father, the aged Prasenajit. Led campaign to massacre the Sakya tribe and drowned on the way home.

Visakha   Famous female lay disciple from Sravasti who helped shape the custom of dana (giving to Buddha's renunciate community).

Vriji   Confederacy in Middle Ganges Basin, including a tribe called Vriji. Some say the confederacy was the first republic in world.

Yamuna   River in northern India. Area between Ganges and Yamuna is known as the Doab. This is where the Vedic Aryans settled after migrating east from the area of the Indus River Valley. Known also as Jamuna.

Yasodhara   Siddhartha's wife. Also called Rahulamata, meaning Rahula's mother. Other names that possibly refer to this woman include Gopa, Bhadra Katyayana, and Bimba or Bimbasundari (beautiful Bimba).

Further Reading

Here's an annotated list of 50 books and 30 websites for further reading on Buddha's life, teachings, and times—with an emphasis on the life and times. (Many of these works were among those used as background for this *Complete Idiot's Guide*.) The book list is a mix of general and specialized materials, so you can choose the level of detail you want. To give variety, some titles are by writers from Buddhist countries; others are by Western authors.

For a 400-page annotated listing of books on Buddhism, see Frank E. Reynolds, *Guide to the Buddhist Religion* (Boston: G. K. Hall, 1981). Also see the end of the website list for a partial list of Buddhist presses and publications.

This list is divided into six parts:

- ◆ Biographies of Buddha and his disciples
- ◆ Ancient Indian history and Buddhist culture
- ◆ Buddhist scriptures, commentaries, and teachings
- ◆ Buddhism in the present and future
- ◆ Websites on Buddhism
- ◆ Websites of presses and magazines

Biographies of Buddha and His Disciples

These 20 books are either simple biographies, biographies with commentary, or books with lots of biographical material. It's good to read several to get a broader feel for Buddha's life.

Arnold, Edwin. *Light of Asia*. First published in 1879. Trailblazing book that introduced Buddha's life to an English-speaking audience. Free download at www.gutenberg.org.

Asvaghosa. *Buddhacarita or Acts of the Buddha*. E. H. Johnston (ed. and trans.). Publications of the University of the Punjab, Vol. 32. Calcutta: Baptist Mission Press, 1936. Tibetan version of this translated by Johnston is in the *Acta Orientalia*, Vol. XV. Leyden, 1936. Translation of one of the first Buddha biographies ever written.

Barrett, William E. *Lady of the Lotus*. New York: Doubleday, 1975. Historical novel written from the perspective of Gautama's wife, Yasodhara.

Burlingame, Eugene Watson (trans. and ed.). *The Grateful Elephant and Other Stories*. New Haven: Yale University Press, 1923. A children's book of 23 tales of Buddha's former lives.

Jataka Tales: Stories of Courage. Mumbai: India book House Pvt Ltd, 2004. This is one of many kid's comic books of India's folklore and religion published in India (available on the web through Amar Chitra Katha www.amarchitrakatha.com).

Carrithers, Michael. *The Buddha*. Oxford: Oxford University Press, 1983. Weaves Buddha's life and teachings together in a contemporary style.

Foucher, A. *The Life of the Buddha: According to the Ancient Texts and Monuments of India*. Abridged translation by Simone Brangier Boas. Westport, CT: Greenwood Press, 1972. Thorough, readable, biography based on archeology, scripture, and classical biographies of Buddha, with author's commentary interspersed.

Herold, A. Ferdinand. *The Life of Buddha According to the Legends of Ancient India*. Translated from French by Paul C. Blum. Tokyo: Tuttle, 1954. This biography based on Mahayana sources puts a lot of conversation into the narrative.

Horner, I. B. *Women Under Primitive Buddhism: Laywomen and Almswomen*. London: Routledge, 1930. Groundbreaking work on women in early Buddhism. Many biographical sketches of Buddha's women disciples.

Landaw, Jonathan and Brooke, Janet. *Prince Siddhartha: The Story of Buddha*. London: Wisdom, 1984. Children's version of Buddha's life, richly illustrated.

Marshall, Georg N. *Buddha, The Quest for Serenity: A Biography*. Introduction by Huston Smith. Boston: Beacon Press, 1978. This biography has the feel of an historical novel. Author wanted to write the biography of "a dynamic personality."

Murcott, Susan. *The First Buddhist Women: Translations and Commentary on the* Therigatha. Berkeley, CA: Parallax Press, 1991. Provides enhancement to Horner's classic on early Buddhist women. Includes fresh translations of poems of Buddha's female disciples, biographical sketches, and cultural commentary.

Nakamura, Hajime. *Gotama Buddha*. Tokyo: Buddhist Books International, 1987. Life of Buddha by a Japanese scholar. Combines scriptural excerpts with cultural and historical commentary.

Paul, Diana Y. *Women in Buddhism: Images of the Feminine in Mahayana Tradition*. Berkeley, CA: Asian Humanities Press, 1979. Foreword by I. B. Horner. Answer to Horner's classic. Treats women in the Mahayana branch of Buddhism.

Pye, Michael. *The Buddha*. London: Duckworth, 1979. Biography of Buddha divided into three parts, giving the bare bones of history, a biographical account from scriptures, and a section on mythical embellishments of the biography.

Rockhill, W. Woodville. *The Life of the Buddha and The Early History of His Order*. London: Trubner & Co, 1884. Yes, first published in 1884! A work on Buddha's life and the early history of his order based on Tibetan sources. Later authors relied heavily on this work, with its many footnotes that document discrepancies among versions of the story from other scriptural sources.

Saddhatissa, Hammalawa. *Before He Was Buddha: The Life of Siddhartha*. Berkeley, CA: Seastone, Ulysses Press, 2000. Narrative of the full sweep of Buddha's life based on the Pali sources.

Thera, Nyanaponika and Hecker, Hellmuth. *Great Disciples of the Buddha: Their Lives, Their Works, Their Legacy*. Boston: Wisdom Publications, 1997. Brings together what's known about many of Buddha's disciples from the Pali sources, considering their stories one at a time. Provides ample discussion on Buddha's teachings.

Thomas, Edward J. *The Life of Buddha as Legend and History*. London: Routledge & Kegan Paul, (1927) 1976. A classic compilation of Buddhist biographical materials, presenting lengthy primary source quotations in the midst of a continuous life story. Additional chapters on Buddhism in relation to Christianity.

Wickremesinghe, K. D. P. *The Biography of the Buddha.* Colombo: Gunaratana Press, 1972. A thorough rendering of Buddha's life with notes on sources and alternative renditions.

Ancient Indian History and Buddhist Culture

Here are 10 books on Buddha's culture—past to present. Those marked with an asterisk (*) are more general. If you are in the mood for more details, try some of the others.

Armstrong, Karen.* *A Short History of Myth.* New York: Canongate, 2005. 159 pages. Brief chapter on the Axial Age that helps put Buddha into worldwide context (pages 79–103).

Basham, A. L.* *The Wonder that was India.* New York: Grove Press, first published 1954. Treats ancient India's culture in terms of history, society, art and literature, politics, religion, and everyday life. A classic.

Bechert, Heinz and Gombrich, Richard (eds.).* *The World of Buddhism.* London: Thames and Hudson, 1984. A series of articles that range from Buddha's day to our own. Get an idea of what it meant and means to be Buddhist in different cultures.

Bryant, Edwin. *The Quest for the Origins of Vedic Culture: The Indo-Aryan Migration Debate.* New York: Oxford University Press, 2001. Reviews in detail the state of the prickly question of Aryan origins. Linguistic and archeological discussions.

Dutt, Sukumar. *Buddhist Monks and Monasteries of India: Their History and Their Contribution to Indian Culture.* London: Allen & Unwin, 1962. New edition from South Asia Books, 2004. Makes use of archeological research to reconstruct the life of the monks of ancient India from the origins of Buddhism through the disappearance of Buddhism from India in 1200 C.E.

Grousset, Rene.* *In the Footsteps of the Buddha.* Translated from French by J. A. Underwood. New York: Grossman Publishers, 1971. (Originally published 1929.) An account of the seventh-century C.E. travels of two Chinese Buddhist pilgrims (Hiuan Tsang and Yi Tsing) to India.

Kosambi, D. D. *Ancient India: A History of Its Culture and Civilization.* New York: Meridian Books, 1965. Includes lots of archeological material in addition to literary works and anthropological observations.

Lamotte, Etienne. *History of Indian Buddhism: From the Origins to the Saka Era.* Translated from French by Sara Webb-Boin under supervision of Jean Dantinne. Louvain-Paris: Peeters Press, 1976. (First published 1958.) 870+ pages. A meticulous study that uses lots of primary and secondary sources. A classic.

Tsomo, Karma Lekshe (ed).* *Buddhist Women Across Cultures: Realizations.* Albany, NY: State University of New York Press, 1999. Collection of articles about Buddhist nuns throughout Asia and the direction the nun's movement is headed today.

Vidal, Gore.* *Creation: A Novel.* New York: Random House, 1981. Historical novel that explores the interaction between peoples in the Axial Age (around the fifth century B.C.E.) from Athens through Persia and India to Cathay. Includes such characters as King Darius, Buddha, King Ajatasatru, and Confucius.

Buddhist Scriptures, Commentaries, and Teachings

Sample of 10 Buddhist scriptures, with classical or modern commentaries:

Bercholz, Samuel and Kohn, Sherab Chodzin (eds.). *Entering the Stream.* Boston: Shambhala, 1993. Anthology of readings on Buddhist practice from contemporary Buddhists and classic texts, including review of Buddha's life.

Bodhi, Bhikkhu. *The Middle Length Discourses of the Buddha: A New Translation of the Majjhima Nikaya.* Edited and revised from the original Pali translation by Bhikkhu Nanamoli. Boston: Wisdom, 1995. Collection of discourses from the Pali Buddhist canon, including 152 suttas, with 40-page introduction.

Buddhaghosa, Bhadantacariya. *The Path of Purification: A Classic Textbook of Buddhist Psychology.* (2 vols.) Bhikkhu Nyanamoli (trans.). Berkeley: Shambhala, (1956) 1976. "A classic textbook" is right! Used by Theravada Buddhists since it was written in the fifth century C.E. One volume on each branch of Buddhist meditation (serenity and insight) weaving stories into technical explanations.

Dhammapada. Translated from Pali by John Ross Carter and Mahinda Palihawadana. Oxford: Oxford University Press, 1987. One of many translations of Buddha's popular verses on various subjects. This one has commentary from Pali sources.

Gunaratana, Bhante Henepola. *Mindfulness in Plain English.* Boston: Wisdom Publications, 2002. Contemporary "how to" presentation of classic Buddhist meditation by a Theravada monk.

Lalitavistara Sutra: The Voice of the Buddha (2 vols.) Translated from French into English by Gwendolyn Bays. Berkeley, CA: Dharma Publishing, 1983. A Mahayana Buddhist biography of Buddha. One of the oldest, with verse embedded in the narrative.

Rahula, Walpola. *What the Buddha Taught.* New York: Grove Press, 1974. Here's a book people often read first, to get an idea of Buddha's Four Noble Truths. Has a few scriptural texts in the appendix.

Salzberg, Sharon. *Lovingkindness: The Revolutionary Art of Happiness.* Boston: Shambhala, 1995. Practical, do-it-yourself presentation of the Buddhist social virtue known as loving-kindness, from a Western Theravada practitioner.

Tsong-kha-pa. *Great Treatise on the Stages of the Path to Enlightenment.* (3 vols.) Joshua W. C. Cutler, editor-in-chief. Ithaca, NY: Snow Lion Publications, 2000–2004. A classic textbook on Buddha's teachings from a classic Tibetan commentator.

Walshe, Maurice (trans.). *The Long Discourses of the Buddha: A Translation of the* Digha Nikaya. Boston: Wisdom Publications, 1987, 1995. Updated translation of the 34 "long" discourses that comprise the first of 5 collections of discourses in the Pali canon of Theravada Buddhism. Has a concise, great introduction covering Buddha's life, times, and teachings.

Buddhism in the Present and Future

Here are 10 titles that relate Buddha-dharma to non-Buddhist perspectives, or look to the future of Buddhism.

Badiner, Allan Hunt (ed.). *Dharma Gaia: A Harvest of Essays in Buddhism and Ecology.* Berkeley, CA: Parallax Press, 1990. Essays devoted to eco-Buddhism, including "The Greening of the Self" by Joanna Macy.

Fields, Rick. *How the Swans Came to the Lake: A Narrative History of Buddhism in America.* Boulder, CO: Shambhala, 1981. Starting with an overview of Buddha's life and the early spread of Buddhism, this book traces all steps of the transfer of Buddhism to America.

Gyatso, Tenzin. (Dalai Lama) (Bstan-'dzin-rgya-mtsho). *The Universe in a Single Atom: The Convergence of Science and Spirituality.* New York: Morgan Road Books, 2005. Reflections on the interface between the scientific method and the Buddhist introspective method by a Nobel Peace Prize recipient and founder of the Mind and Life Institute.

Harvey, Andrew. *The Way of Passion: A Celebration of Rumi*. Berkeley, CA: North Atlantic Books, 1994. Adapted from his lectures on the Sufi poems of Jalal-ud-Din Rumi, Harvey draws upon India's religious heritage (including Buddhism) to bring the poetry to contemporary Western life.

Jones, Ken. *The New Social Face of Buddhism: A Call to Action*. Somerville, MA: Wisdom Publications, 2003. This is a handbook for Buddhist social activism, which makes an appeal for peace and justice based on social awareness.

Kotler, Arnold (ed.). *Engaged Buddhist Reader*. Berkeley, CA: Parallax Press, 1996. Anthology of articles on engaged Buddhism, ranging from meditation to ecology.

Moon, Susan (ed.). *The Practice of Engaged Buddhism: An Anthology from 25 Years of Turning Wheel (The Journal of the Buddhist Peace Fellowship)*. Boston: Shambhala, 2004. Collection of articles on engaged Buddhism, giving a history of the movement.

Sivaraksa, Sulak. *Seeds of Peace: A Buddhist Vision for Renewing Society*. Berkeley, CA: Parallax Press, 1992. By a Thai Buddhist social activist, deals with Buddhist ethics in the modern world.

Thurman, Robert A. F. *Inner Revolution: Life, Liberty, and the Pursuit of Real Happiness*. New York: Penguin Putnam, 1998. Part autobiography, a look at the course of our civilization and the potential contribution of "enlightenment scientists" from the Buddhist tradition through the ages.

Tsomo, Karma Lekshe (ed.). *Sakyadhita: Daughters of the Buddha*. Ithaca, NY: Snow Lion Publications, 1988. Abridgement of proceedings from the International Conference on Buddhist Nuns in Bodhgaya, India. Informative perspectives on the Buddhist nuns' movement in Asia and the Western world.

Websites on Buddhism

Here's a list of 15 Buddhist websites. They show you Buddhism from many sides with links to neat art, Buddhist texts, language study, live chat, asynchronous chat, links to other Buddhist links, and more.

Access to Insight: Readings in Theravada Buddhism
www.accesstoinsight.org

Buddha Dharma Education Association, Inc.
www.buddhanet.net

Buddhist Information of North America
www.buddhistinformation.com

Buddhism Portal E-Sangha
www.e-sangha.com

Buddhist Studies WWW Virtual Library
www.ciolek.com/WWWVL-Buddhism.html

Huntington Archive of Buddhist and Related Art
kaladarshan.arts.ohio-state.edu/database.htm

Internet Sacred Text Archive
www.sacred-texts.com

Mettanet-Lanka
www.metta.lk

Order of Buddhist Contemplatives
www.obcon.org

Osel Shen Phen Ling Tibetan Buddhist Center
www.fpmt-osel.org

Sanskrit Documents and Dictionary
sanskrit.gde.to/home.html

The Living Dharma
www.livingdharma.org

Vipassana Meditation Website
www.dhamma.org

Washington Buddhist Vihara
www.buddhistvihara.com

Zen Guide
www.zenguide.com

Websites of Presses and Magazines

Here's a list of 5 presses, and 10 magazines. Most of them are dedicated to Buddhism:

Dharma Publishing (publishing house)
www.dharmapublishing.com

Parallax Press (publishing house)
www.parallax.org

Shambhala Publications (publishing house)
www.shambhala.com

Snow Lion Publications (publishing house)
www.snowlionpub.com

Wisdom Publications (publishing house)
www.wisdompubs.org

Buddhadharma: The Practitioners Quarterly (magazine)
www.thebuddhadharma.com

Buddhism Today (magazine)
www.buddhism-today.org

Gateway Journal (Newsletter of The Engaged Zen Foundation)
www.engaged-zen.org

Journal of Global Buddhism (online journal)
www.globalbuddhism.org

Journal of Buddhist Ethics (online materials)
jbe.gold.ac.uk

Shambhala Sun (magazine)
www.shambhalasun.com

Tricycle (magazine)
www.tricycle.com

Turning Wheel (magazine of Buddhist Peace Fellowship)
www.bpf.org

Western Buddhist Review
www.westernbuddhistreview.com

What is Enlightenment? (magazine)
www.wie.org

Index

A

abhidharma, 6
abodes of Brahma, 125, 211-214
abuse, right speech concept (Eightfold Path), 194
actions
    good karma actions, 197-198
    negative karma actions, 198-199
    right action concept (Eightfold Path), 195
Aesop's Fables versus Jataka Tales, 48
aesthetics, samvega (aesthetic shock), 86
afternoon routine, 12-13
agricultural prosperity, 75
Ahura Mazda, 26
Ajatasatru, King
    campaign against King Prasenajit, 269-270
    overtaking of Kausala, 271
    plot to overthrow the Vriji republic, 276-277
    revenge against father, 267-268
Alara Kalamas hermitage, joining of Siddhartha (Buddha), 102-103
Alexander the Great, 293
alms begging tradition, 146
Ambedkar, Bhimrao Ramji, 308

Amrapali (nun), 245, 280-281
Ananda (Buddha's cousin)
    as Buddha's disciple, 163-164
    First Buddhist Council, 163, 302
    supernatural earthquakes, 282
Anathapindaka (lay disciple), 255-257, 289-290
anatman (nonself), 136, 168-169
    Five Heaps principle, 189
    heap of feelings, 184-185
    heap of forms, 183-184
    heap of perceptions, 185-186
    mental formations, 186-187
    minds, 187-188
anger, forms of internal anger, 199
Angra Mainyu (hostile spirit), 26
animals
    sacrifices, Tale of Virtue (Jataka Tales), 51-52
    sense desire realm, 170
anitya (impermanence), 168
antidote (Opponent Power), 201
Anuruddha (cousin of Buddha), 161-162
argumentation (Parmenides), 27
Arnold, Edwin, *Light of Asia, The*, 307

art of awakening, 287
    empty throne, 292-293
    footprints, 292-293
    funeral customs, 290-291
    Japans enso, 297-298
    marks of a great person, 294-295
    mudras, 295-296
    places of pilgrimage, 290
    portraits, 288-289
    postures, 296
    shrines, 289-290
    statues, 293-294
    stupas, 291-292
    tantric rituals, 297
    wheel, 292-293
Aryans
    Brahmanic culture, 33-34
    migration from Punjab to Ganga-Yamuna Doab, 32-33
    orthodox versus heterodox groups, 40
    Rig Veda, 32
    varna system, 36-37
    Vedic culture, 33-34
Arya Satya. *See* Four Great Facts
ascetics
    ancient India, 40-42
    Tale of Even-Mindedness (Jataka Tales), 59
Asita (sage), 70, 104
Asoka, King, 304-305
Asvajit (disciple of Buddha), 113, 220-221, 226
atman, 136

G

Z

Check Out These
Best-Sellers

Read by millions!

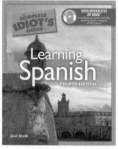

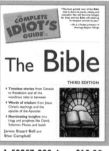
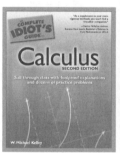

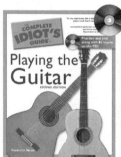